OUR UNINVITED GUESTS

Also by Julie Summers

Fearless on Everest: The Quest for Sandy Irvine

*The Colonel of Tamarkan: Philip Toosey and the Bridge
on the River Kwai*

*Remembered: A History of the Commonwealth
War Graves Commission*

*Stranger in the House: Women's Stories of Men
Returning from the Second World War*

British and Commonwealth War Cemeteries

When the Children Came Home: Stories of Wartime Evacuees

Rowing in Britain

*Jambusters: The Story of the Women's Institute
in the Second World War*

Fashion on the Ration: Style in the Second World War

OUR UNINVITED GUESTS

The Secret Lives of Britain's Country Houses
1939–1945

JULIE SUMMERS

**SIMON &
SCHUSTER**

London · New York · Sydney · Toronto · New Delhi

A CBS COMPANY

First published in Great Britain by Simon & Schuster UK Ltd, 2018
A CBS COMPANY

Copyright © Julie Summers, 2018

The right of Julie Summers to be identified as the author
of this work has been asserted in accordance with
the Copyright, Designs and Patents Act, 1988.

1 3 5 7 9 10 8 6 4 2

Simon & Schuster UK Ltd
1st Floor
222 Gray's Inn Road
London WC1X 8HB

www.simonandschuster.co.uk
www.simonandschuster.com.au
www.simonandschuster.co.in

Simon & Schuster Australia, Sydney
Simon & Schuster India, New Delhi

The author and publishers have made all reasonable efforts to contact
copyright-holders for permission, and apologise for any omissions or errors in
the form of credits given. Corrections may be made to future printings.

A CIP catalogue record for this book
is available from the British Library

Hardback ISBN: 978-1-4711-5253-5
eBook ISBN: 978-1-4711-5256-6

Typeset in the UK by M Rules
Printed and bound by CPI Group (UK) Ltd, Croydon, CR0 4YY

MIX
Paper from
responsible sources
FSC® C020471

Simon & Schuster UK Ltd are committed to sourcing paper that is made
from wood grown in sustainable forests and support the Forest Stewardship
Council, the leading international forest certification organisation. Our
books displaying the FSC logo are printed on FSC certified paper.

To Helena Pozniak,
Mrs P, the bravest Polish lady I have ever known

CONTENTS

Glossary of Abbreviations   ix
Introduction: An Invasion of Privacy   1

 1 Brocket's Babies   13
 2 Waddesdon at War   37
 3 Girls, Ghosts and Godliness   65
 4 Twice Removed   101
 5 Lady Grey's Guests   137
 6 Dear 'K'   159
 7 Secret Saboteurs on the Home Front   183
 8 Guerrillas in the Mist   219
 9 Three Lime Trees   255
10 Birds of Passage   287
11 Station 43: Audley End   321
12 The Army at Home   353

Conclusion: Restoration and Reintegration   371
Bibliography   399
Acknowledgements   409
Notes   415
Index   435

GLOSSARY OF ABBREVIATIONS

ADC – aide-de-camp

AI – Air Intelligence

ARP – Air Raid Precaution

ATS – Auxiliary Territorial Service

CIGS – Chief of the Imperial General Staff

DMO – Director of Military Operations

EH – Electra House

FANY – First Aid Nursing Yeomanry

GHQ – General Headquarters

GSO – general staff officer

GS(R) – General Staff (Research)

IO – intelligence officer

MI(R) – Military Intelligence (Research)

MI5 – Military Intelligence (Security)

MI6 – Military Intelligence (Intelligence)

MOI(SP) – Military Operations (Special Projects) [cover name for SOE]

MTI – Military Training Instruction

NAAFI – Navy, Army and Air Force Institutes

NID(Q) [cover name for SOE]

NORCAP – National Organisation for Counselling Adoptees and Parents

OB – Observational Base

OSS – Office of Strategic Services [USA]

RASC – Royal Army Service Corps

SAS – Special Air Service

SDS – Special Duties Section

SIS – Secret Intelligence Service, alternative name for MI6

SOE – Special Operations Executive

STS – special training school

TRE – Telecommunications Research Establishment

VAD – Voluntary Aid Detachment

WVS – Women's Voluntary Services

An Invasion of Privacy

On 30 April 1940, Mrs Frances Cameron-Head received the unwelcome news that her home in north-west Scotland was needed for use by the military. She was in London at the time but hotfooted her way north as fast as wartime travel would allow. 'When I arrived at Lochailort station there were only two officers who said the castle was half emptied and that they had no accommodation for me and I could not go to it. They have taken my three garages and planted tents everywhere, even in the middle of the farmyard without any permission from me or anyone representing me.'[1]

When she wrote those anguished words to her friend, Donald Cameron of Lochiel, she could not have known that she would never again set foot in her ancestral home, Inverailort Castle in the west Highlands. Her property had been requisitioned under the Defence (General) Regulations 1939 made under the Emergency Powers (Defence) Act 1939, passed in Parliament on 24 August, the day after the Nazi–Soviet Pact was announced. It gave the government sweeping powers to make regulations as appear 'to be necessary or expedient for securing the public safety, the defence of the realm, the maintenance of public order and the efficient prosecution of any war in which His Majesty may be engaged, and for maintaining supplies and services essential to the life of the community.'[2]

The details of the act were of no interest to the eighty-one-year-old widow. All she knew was that she urgently needed somewhere to stay and that her home was no longer available. It must have been a very bitter situation for her. She was not alone. Many thousands of people, from dukes in castles to families in four-bedroom houses in the countryside, in coastal towns or Highland glens were ousted from their dwellings – some temporarily, others for the duration. A few, like Mrs Cameron-Head, never lived in their homes again. That the vast majority of people gave up their properties without formal complaint shows just how powerful the government's powers were but also that people realised they had to pull together in a time of national emergency.

I first became interested in the subject of what happened to houses that were requisitioned, to the people who were evicted and to their wartime guests when I was on a visit to Harrogate with my nineteen-year-old son, Richard. I had always believed that my paternal great-grandfather, Harry Summers, had spent his twilight years living in the Majestic Hotel, dying there in January 1945. So I decided to visit and see if there were any traces of the long-term guest arrangements. The hotel lives up to its grand name, dominating the town from its site halfway up the hill and looking as much like a French château as an English hotel. It was opened in 1900 and boasted a lounge that ran the full length of the ground floor and a magnificent winter garden. It earned the nickname the 'Yorkshire Crystal Palace'. I can remember thinking it was very grand for my Victorian great-grandfather.

At the outbreak of the Second World War the hotel was requisitioned by the government and the intention was to move the Air Ministry into the building. All long-term residents, many of them retired army officers, were required to vacate the Majestic and find lodgings elsewhere. However, this turned out to be a temporary measure as the expected national emergency did not happen and no bombs fell on London that autumn. The hotel received permission to reopen and by Christmas some of the long-term residents had returned. It later became an RAF Personnel Reception Centre for 850 sergeant pilots.

As it happened, Harry Summers had not lived in the Majestic

Hotel but in the Prince of Wales, at the junction of York Place and Parliament Street opposite The Stray – such is the inaccuracy of family memories. The building is no longer a hotel but a block of luxury flats called Prince of Wales Mansions. It does not appear to have been taken over during requisitioning and my grandfather died at the hotel in January 1945 aged 80.

Nevertheless, my visit to the Majestic Hotel kindled questions in my mind about the extent of house requisitioning during the war. How were they selected? Did the owners have any choice but to hand them over? Where did they go? Who were the uninvited guests who came in such numbers? And what happened to the houses after the war? As I began to research the answers, I saw a complex and fascinating picture developing – far more colourful and fast-changing than I had imagined. It is a story that involves some startling, interesting, funny and dangerous characters and that, for people who know me and my work, is really what piqued my interest.

This book is not a charting of thousands of houses that were requisitioned during the war, although there will be some statistics that will give the broad-brush picture, but rather a series of individual, secret histories of houses that saw 'action' between 1939 and 1945 that ran counter to anything that had been experienced in their long and often colourful pasts. And because walls cannot talk, the heart of this book beats with the stories of people who occupied the houses during the war and the owners who shared their properties with these guests, and who were to live through years of dislocation, uncertainty and, for some, great loss.

Over the course of the Second World War, over 3.5 million evacuees fled to the countryside at one time or another in search of safety from the threat of German bombing. There were three significant waves of evacuation: one in September 1939, a second in June 1940 as a result of the fall of France and fear of a German invasion and a third in 1944 as those in London and the south-east fled the V-bombs. By 1945, over 2 million servicemen and women had arrived from abroad to help the Allies win the war. They came from all over Europe, from the Commonwealth and from the United States of

America, who sent over 1.5 million GIs. The Post Office recorded 38 million changes of address over the course of the war, and that for a population of 38.5 million people. The impact of air attack on the capital and other cities meant that only 12 per cent of married couples could expect to be living in a home of their own by the end of the war. To put it mildly, this represented a monumental upheaval and reshaping of the status quo and makes for untidy history.

For the government, much bureaucratic cartwheeling and quick changes of direction were needed in order to keep abreast of the war on every front. From petrol, food and clothes rationing to health care, education and hospital provision; from munitions, equipment and uniforms to the secret services and the cloak-and-dagger operations necessary to prosecute a modern war – the government gradually assumed such minute control over the lives of its citizens that it could take over a person's house at less than two hours' notice. And then there was the army, the navy and the air force, all of whom needed to practise, train and practise more. A new kind of normality had to be established at a time of uncertainty and upheaval when no one really knew the rules, not even the government. And in planning for this uncertain future, the government realised that the civilian population would need to be taken into consideration in a way it had not in previous wars.

Much of the story of the war on the home front concerns the sheer chaos of numbers of lives coming together and contains multitudes of perspectives. We have a natural desire to tidy up historical incidents in order to make sense of them. But the fact is that two people standing feet apart and witnessing the exact same event could easily form divergent impressions. Two children separated by evacuation; a husband and wife working as scientists in two different laboratories; an elderly widow and her daughters – one working as a volunteer for the Red Cross, the other in the ATS might all have had completely different experiences. The examples are manifold. And because the Second World War was Total War it affected every single person – man, woman or child – in some way or another over a period of five and a half years. For children born shortly before, or during the war, it was all they had ever known. On the whole, it is the job of the historian to make sense out of the disorder – and yet sometimes it is interesting to look at history from the other end of the kaleidoscope and examine the messy.

Pared down to the barest minimum, the government had two roles: to protect the country and to protect its citizens. The two are almost mutually exclusive: 'Because war means the organisation of killing and wounding it must also mean the organisation of services to heal and repair'.[3] In his survey *Problems of Social Policy*, Richard Titmuss neatly summed up the paradox of war: in order to protect the country, every possible means of keeping ahead of the enemy militarily, tactically and with intelligence has to be explored and pushed forward with energy and focus. At the same time, the civilian population might be subject to brutal attack from that same enemy and needs, where possible, to be put out of harm's way. This dilemma is at the centre of this book.

On 15 April 1937, the Committee of Imperial Defence – a body set up in 1924 to assess the potential risk to civilians of aerial bombardment in the event of another major war – decided to conduct a survey of buildings in all parts of the country to see what use they might be put to in the event of the war that was almost certain to come. The survey would also help avoid overlapping demands and conflicts between different government departments on the one hand and local authorities on the other who would have requisitioning powers for civil defence purposes under the Air Raid Precautions (ARP) Act. Such was the bureaucracy and the civil servants' love of secrecy that the existence of this register was not made public until 1972.

The Office of Works took the decision that it was better not to tell owners that their houses had been earmarked, although some owners of very large properties were aware of the likelihood of their houses being requisitioned because of the experience of the First World War when many large country properties were used as hospitals. A number decided to offer their homes rather than wait for requisitioning, as it often meant they could influence to some extent who would occupy them. Owners of properties that were forcefully requisitioned had no say in how they were used. All that civil servants were allowed to say when asked was that compensation would be paid 'on a basis which will be determined hereafter by Parliament', hoping that invoking such high authority would reassure homeowners.

When war finally came, the owner was generally given no explanation as to why his or her house had been chosen and some did not know for what purpose it had been requisitioned until the order to move came. The owner had almost no power to resist the forced takeover of his or her property. 'They found themselves with very little time to pack up valuable collections of works of art, or to carry out protection work to fragile decorations and architectural features.'4

Ralph Dutton, later Lord Sherborne, had to leave his house, Hinton Ampner in Hampshire, at short notice. He had just finished refurbishing it and was understandably unhappy that everything had to be stored away. He received a telegram on 29 August 1939 informing him that the Portsmouth Day School for Girls would be arriving in forty-eight hours:

> It was a moment of intense bitterness: just as many months of work and effort had reached their culmination, all was snatched from me. Nowadays one is more accustomed to the buffets of fortune, but in 1939 I found it difficult to comprehend that I was being turned out of my own house. However, the situation had to be accepted, and picking up my suitcase, I left.5

Later he realised how fortunate he had been to have a girls' school at the house and not the army. In a list of preferred occupants, a girls' school would come close to the top and the army at the bottom.

Conscription was introduced in the spring of 1939, with units required to double their numbers so the need to accommodate large numbers of troops for training was ever-expanding. Certain areas of the country were favoured by different arms of the military: the British Expeditionary Force was largely stationed in Wiltshire, Somerset and Dorset before going out to France, while anti-tank training concentrated in the south-west where they would be out of the way of the Luftwaffe. Northern Scotland would become a training ground for the Commandos and Special Operations Executive, after their formation in 1940. By 1941 there were 2 million troops living in Britain; by 1944 that number had risen to 3 million. They all needed to be accommodated and, although many men lived under canvas or in camps, houses were needed as officers' messes, headquarters for key figures, such as General Patton who lived at Peover Hall in the build-up to D-Day, and for training establishments.

The Dunkirk evacuation caused the first pinch point in the war, when there was a sudden need for large amounts of accommodation. Over 350,000 Allied troops were evacuated over the course of eight days; houses had to be found as quickly as possible. Some people were very cooperative but others, like a lady owner of a property in Sussex, were determined not to give up their homes. In this case the only way to deal with her was to take the house forcibly, locking the lady in the kitchen.

Some people tried to resist requisitioning, but by and large their pleas or protests were ignored. Lord and Lady Desborough received a letter in 1942 announcing that part of the park at their home Panshanger in Hertfordshire, would be taken over to construct a hospital for American wounded. Having tried approaches to various ministers, Lady Desborough tackled the prime minister himself: 'Dearest Winston, would you be such an angel as to glance at the enclosed letter. We have simply longed, all through, to consult you on the subject, but could not bear to add one featherweight to your burdens.'[6] The main reason she gave was that the hospital would be just 130 yards from the edge of an aerodrome, clearly a target for the Luftwaffe, and just 800 yards away from a secret RAF installation. She ended the letter: 'I wrote this letter last night, and now the glorious news from the Middle East has arrived and we send you our dearest congratulations – for no people can rejoice more truly, or be more aware of what you have done for this country.'[7] She signed the letter 'Yours affectionately, Ettie'. The prime minister responded with a telegram to Lady Desborough saying, 'Have received your letter and am looking into it. Winston'[8]. In this case it did the trick, but in most cases appeals to the government or to Churchill failed.

Very occasionally a case reached the press but there seems to have been little public sympathy with people who owned large houses complaining of unfair treatment. In the main, people in Britain accepted that the war would require great sacrifice and that everyone would have to shoulder a portion of the burden if the war was to be won.

An unexpected result of my research was to discover how much property was required by foreign governments-in-exile in Britain. The houses were mostly around London and in the south-east for obvious reasons of proximity to the capital and the British government. These eventually numbered eight: Czechoslovakia was the first to arrive in 1938, though it was not officially recognised until 1941. Poland followed after the fall of France, where they had been based at Angers. Next came Norway, including members of their royal family, then Belgium and Luxembourg. The Netherlands were represented by the Dutch government, Queen Wilhelmina and the Dutch Resistance, who would meet and plan missions in Soho. Lynne Olson, the author of *Last Hope Island* wrote:

> Of the seven occupied countries that found refuge in London in the spring and summer of 1940, six presented their British hosts with invaluable dowries of men, money, ships, natural resources and intelligence information. The lone representative of the seventh nation, France, brought only himself.[9]

By the end of the year some 100,000 foreign exiles had taken up residence in London. By autumn 1941, the Greek government and the royal family arrived, the latter moving into Claridges, which became the wartime home of many other European royals. It is hardly surprising that the charity worker and diarist Vere Hodgson, wrote of London in 1943: 'Piccadilly is such a thrilling place these days. All the uniforms of all the nations jostle you on the pavement...'[10]

One of the great delights of writing social history is researching and getting to know men and women whose lives had a major impact on the people they worked alongside. In the normal course of my life I would never meet such people, and if I had, I would almost certainly never get to know them well – just a fleeting handshake or a conversation with an elderly person reliving the past. Many of them had already died long ago. Yet in the course of researching this book I have had the privilege and joy of becoming familiar with the lives, through books and archives, of some of the most extraordinary men and women whose stories breathe life into the secret histories of these houses.

There is a broad cross-section of characters, including a sprinkling of literati, such as the author of *Ring of Bright Water*, Gavin Maxwell, who you will encounter in northern Scotland, not far from the island that became the fictional Camusfeàrna. He was described by a friend as 'mad, bad and dangerous to know', quoting Lady Caroline Lamb about Byron, and indeed during the war he would often be found sitting under a tree reading poetry. He was a man used to living on the edge of society, with aristocratic connections and personal flaws, but in 1941 he found himself surrounded by similar misfits destined to become special agents to be dropped into occupied Europe. He was in his element. To me he was both frightening and fascinating, but his understanding of the natural world was alluring and the stories of how he inspired his students compelling.

Then there is the Roman Catholic scholar, Monsignor Ronald Knox, who translated both the Old and New Testaments of the Bible from Latin over the six years of the war while chaplain to girls and their nuns evacuated from a convent school. He is known by few today outside the Catholic community, but he was a remarkable scholar, a great wit and an infinitely fascinating human being. If I had ever met him I should no doubt have been tongue-tied, and he too, for he was very shy, especially in the company of women. However, through his writing and biographies, as well as stories from the girls I met and the Acton family, whose house they all shared, I hope I have been able to bring him to life for you.

Two prominent Jewish families offered up their homes to help the war effort. Their generosity and determination to stand up for everything they believed in is impressive and moving. It is good to be able to celebrate the impact of Jewish families who, only too aware of and touched by the atrocities against the Jews on the continent, were able to change lives and fortunes in a positive way. And both families left their magnificent country houses and art collections with large endowments to the nation, giving us Waddesdon Manor and Upton House.

The country house of a colourful peer, whose friendship with Joachim von Ribbentrop was so close that he named a bedroom in his house after the German foreign minister, became a nursing home where almost 9,000 babies were born. This appealed to me as a clarion call for the future in a present that seemed anything but optimistic.

Several houses were occupied by multiple bodies, as the need for properties ebbed and waned, while others were fortunate to have a single group for the whole war. Two were burned down – both accidentally but through carelessness. It is a fact that the uninvited guests suggested in the book's title did have, in many cases, a lasting impact on the future of a number of Britain's country houses. Over the course of a little less than six years the fate of some houses changed more dramatically than in the hundreds of years of their previous existence.

In all cases I have tried to explore how the houses were used, or abused, and what happened within their walls, and what that tells us about the way the war was conducted on home soil. In selecting the twelve properties I have chosen as studies for each chapter, I was mindful to try and pick houses that were less well known than, for example, Bletchley Park and would give as vibrant a picture as possible of behind-the-scenes wartime Britain. I preferred to focus on houses whose histories had been documented at the time or very soon after the war.

I was fortunate to meet people who had first-hand experience of requisitioning and their memories bring colour to the stories of the houses they lived in. One of the most productive and thrilling introductions came by accident. I had taken a morning off from editing the final draft of this book to visit a remarkable school for badly damaged children in Standlake. There was a war connection – the Mulberry Bush School was founded in 1948 by Barbara Dockar-Drysdale, who started it by scooping up hard-to-place evacuee children who had been deserted by their parents. The conversation turned briefly to what I was writing and one of the hosts, Jane Smiley, said tentatively, 'I don't suppose you have heard of a house in Shropshire that was taken over to house nuns and girls from London . . . ?' I burst out with an exclamation of delight: 'Yes, of course I have. It's in the book!' Aldenham Park was owned by her family, the Actons, and she was able to introduce me to her older sister, Pelline, who lived there during the war and who could give me a first-hand account of life among the convent school. It was a glorious moment and gave rise to a fascinating interview.

Our Uninvited Guests is a book of two halves and moods. Two sides of the same coin: from bouncing babies at Brocket Hall to assassins at Arisaig. In the first six chapters, we see how the population was kept safe from the enemy by housing people away from the dangerous cities and coastal towns. The stories are of individuals and groups coming together and working out how best to adjust to their new homes. We see a mixture of optimism and humour combined with a good dose of making-do and mending. From newborn babies to crusty scholars, the impact of war for these evacuees was felt more in the adjustment to a new way of life than in the frightening news coming out of Europe.

The second half of the book has an altogether darker feel to it. In protecting the country, the military, paramilitary and intelligence organisations had to plan for violence. Behind the closed doors of houses tucked away in the countryside secret and at times explosive goings-on occurred cheek by jowl with everyday life and no questions asked. Special Operations Executive, nicknamed Stately 'Omes of England, used scores of properties to train foreign agents to become resistance fighters, radio operators, saboteurs and silent killers before sending them back into Nazi-occupied Europe to harass, interrupt, sabotage and even murder the enemy. This is not a military history, although I have done my best to make sure the military detail is correct. My real interest is in the stories of the individuals who were involved in the training and carried out the missions.

Our Uninvited Guests starts with birth because war does not halt everyday life, it just changes it.

Brocket Hall was requisitioned in 1939 as a nursing home for expectant mothers from the East End of London.

CHAPTER I

Brocket's Babies

*I took the risk of bringing a baby into the world while
a war was on ... as I wanted to have something if my
husband did not come back.*

Quoted in *How We Lived Then* by Norman Longmate

There can have been fewer more unusual juxtapositions during the
Second World War than a Cockney mother giving birth in Lord
Melbourne's bedroom suite in a grand house in Hertfordshire. The
leap from a small council flat in Mile End to one of the most sumptuous country houses in Britain might seem improbable but it happened
over 8,000 times. The first baby was born there on the day war broke
out and his mother, Lily Lowe, wrote after the birth:

> I was taken (with one or two others) to Brocket Hall in a small car
> by someone who of course didn't know the way and we hoped our
> babies would not be arriving before due date! Having arrived and
> gone into the grounds, we had a lady come out of a small house at
> the right side, bob to us and then open the gate which was right
> across. We continued for a while and eventually came to Brocket
> Hall itself where they found deckchairs for us to sit on. (What a
> sight, with our bellies sticking out in front).[1]

Lily had been dropped off by her husband Leslie at the City of London Maternity Hospital in the East End to have her pre-planned Caesarean section. Her first baby had been stillborn two years earlier and the doctors didn't want to risk a repeat of the tragedy. Leslie was already thirty-five, so too old to be conscripted, but he was not able to be near his wife as he was acting as an escort for trainloads of families to the south-west. Communication being limited, he did not know when he would be able to find out what had happened to his wife and was surprised when he returned to London to find she was not at the hospital where he had left her.

No sooner had Lily arrived at the hospital than she was told she and other expectant mothers were to be sent to 'someone's large home'. The large home was Brocket Hall, a magnificent Regency house near Welwyn. The hall was still in a state of transformation when this first contingent of mothers arrived. The original beds, furniture, paintings and precious works of art had been removed from the bedrooms to safe storage. These were in the process of being replaced by metal-framed hospital beds and the preparations for the delivery suite were not yet quite complete. Norah Hern, a midwife from the City of London Hospital, was in the advance party ready to set up the hall: 'Nurses, midwifes, mums to be (with at least five days to go), plus lots of medical equipment were loaded onto eight charabanc type buses and half went to Brocket Hall. On arrival, all the rooms were empty shells. There was a delivery of beds in one room that needed carrying upstairs and putting together. This took most of the day.'[2]

Everywhere was bustling. Storerooms downstairs in the cellars had to be cleared to accommodate hospital equipment, rather than game and beer. The kitchens, scullery, drying room and servants' hall became hives of activity as the maternity home got into its stride. The babies' bathroom was downstairs in a white-tiled room near the wine cellar. None of the mothers ever ventured below stairs. They had dormitories on the first and second floors and they were encouraged to go into the beautiful gardens whenever the weather was fine and they were allowed out of bed. For the nurses and midwives, the accommodation at Brocket Hall was inadequate in the first four weeks. None of the nursing staff had beds of their own and slept two to a mattress on the top floor in the servants' area.

Lily Lowe was fascinated by the luxury that surrounded her and above all by the size of the rooms. She told her son years later that just before he was born, 'We nosey ones went about the house – no one to stop us and found the bathrooms (<u>huge</u> rooms) – talk about how the other half lives!'[3]

Her son was born by Caesarean section on 3 September 1939 and Lily wrote to her mother:

> I don't know whether you will have heard from Leslie as I have not seen or heard from him since he saw me in London on Friday. I hope he is all right – only it is so difficult to get any news. They brought me here and operated on Sunday – a bonny boy of 8 lbs 13 ozs – I knew it would be heavier than the other. They haven't let me have the baby to feed yet so I hardly know I have it yet – except for what I've been through, by Jove. I've had loads of injections and can still only just see enough to write this or would have done so before. The words keep swimming.[4]

The next letter was written on 12 September when her baby son was nine days old. Lily had received two visits from Leslie by then and she told her mother how shocked she was by his appearance on the first occasion. 'He nearly cried when he told me of the hundreds of mothers and babies he had to herd into the trains for Somerset and go with them there.'[5] She went on to tell her mother that he had refused to get rid of the cat even though Lily had thought it best for the animal to be put down given the uncertainty of the war. It is a sad fact that over 600,000 family pets were destroyed in September 1939, most of them healthy, as frantic owners could not face an indeterminate future for their animals among the upheaval of evacuation and the uncertainty of what would happen if the Luftwaffe dropped the feared tonnage of bombs on London. In the event, it turned out to be a premature act and many families regretted their haste, while vets all over the country were saddened by having to destroy healthy animals.

Lily's main concern was her bonny baby. She told her mother: 'We are calling the new baby Alan Brocket Lowe, the "Brocket" after this Hall in which we have found such a blessed haven in this time of stress. Lady Brocket came in yesterday and I was introduced to her – she was very pleased and interested to hear that it was a son. We had quite a little conflab on the history of the house.'[6]

Brocket Hall's history is colourful, even by the standards of the aristocratic goings-on of the eighteenth and nineteenth centuries. Two Victorian prime ministers, one of Byron's many lovers and the Prince Regent's mistress were all at one time occupants of this magnificent house but at the outbreak of the war the hall was in the hands of the second Lord Brocket who had a link to the extreme right.

Lord Brocket inherited the title and the hall from his father, Sir Charles Nall-Cain, who had bought the house in 1923. His fortune came from a brewing dynasty in Liverpool established by his own father in the late nineteenth century, which later became Allied Breweries. Sir Charles inherited vast wealth and was determined to establish himself as part of the English aristocracy. Inevitably there was resentment and snobbery against 'new money' but he put his fortune to good use by establishing retrospectively that there was blue blood in his family history, tracing the Cains' ancestry back to a king of Ulster. The Cain family crest includes three salmon 'which denotes the fishing rights of three Irish rivers (the Bann, the Boyle and the Roe) and the "bloody hand" of Ulster. The Nall-Cains attached the crest to gate posts at the side of the house and placed it above the front door.'[7] His ancestral credentials established, Sir Charles set out to prove himself in high society.

He used his wealth to woo royalty. In 1925 the Duke of York was invited to Brocket Hall and Sir Charles regularly took shooting parties to Scotland. He also spent a large amount of money on philanthropic activities, some of which benefitted the local community in Hertfordshire. This made it easier for people to accept him, and in

1933 his wish came true and he was at last accepted into the aristocracy when he was created a peer. He chose the title of Lord Brocket.
He died less than two years later and his son, Arthur Ronald, took
over the title and his father's estates in Hertfordshire and Hampshire
as well as properties in north-west Scotland.

The second Lord Brocket was thirty-one when he inherited
the title. He was a committed member of the Anglo–German
Fellowship, an organisation that existed between 1935 and 1939
to build a closer understanding between the United Kingdom and
Germany. It was largely non-political and it folded at the outbreak
of the war. However, there were some who used the fellowship as
a cover for covert activities. 'Both the Cambridge spies Philby and
Burgess, on instruction from Moscow, joined the group to cover the
tracks of their Communist connections, while Hitler sent Charles
Edward, Duke of Saxe-Coburg and Gotha, to Britain to lead the
Fellowship, while he conducted negotiations with Edward VIII to try
to engineer an Anglo-German pact. Philby was, for a while, editor of
the organisation's newsletter.'[8]

The fellowship was widely perceived as being closely allied to
Nazism, as members of the fellowship had close friends among
the senior Nazi party members. This is borne out by the fact that
National Socialist members of the earlier Anglo–German Club
'resigned en masse in protest at Jewish club members'.[9] Lord
Brocket, who held extreme right-wing views, was close personal
friends with Joachim von Ribbentrop, then German ambassador to
Britain, who was a regular visitor to Brocket Hall. In fact, he was
so closely associated with Lord Brocket that one of the bedrooms
was christened the Ribbentrop Bedroom. In April 1939, Brocket
travelled with Major General John Fuller, a well-known supporter of
Hitler, to Germany to celebrate the Führer's fiftieth birthday. Neville
Chamberlain claimed that the foreign secretary, the Earl of Halifax,
used Lord Brocket as a conduit to convey the views of the British
government to leading Nazis. At his two great houses, Brocket Hall
and Bramshill Park in Hampshire, Lord Brocket hosted several meetings for the supporters of Nazi Germany.

When Brocket Hall was requisitioned it was immediately handed over to the Red Cross for use as a maternity home. For the next ten years the hall became the home of the London Maternity Hospital from the East End. Though it was set up by the Red Cross, it was fully staffed with doctors, midwives, nurses and orderlies from the hospital to run as a nursing home for evacuated mothers who were prepared to leave London for the birth of their babies. It was a sound decision. The East End hospital was hit by German bombs in September 1940 and again in April and May 1941, sustaining considerable damage.

Brocket Hall, just twenty-five miles from London, but deep in the Hertfordshire countryside, was believed to be an ideal location: close enough for transport for the expectant mothers to be arranged and for husbands to visit by public transport, yet far enough from the capital to be out of the bombing range of the Luftwaffe, or so the local authorities calculated.

Many of the children who were born at Brocket Hall are exceptionally proud to have an association with a stately home. Today the 'Brocket Babies' are scattered all over the world but some meet annually to celebrate their birth heritage. Mothers, now in their nineties, have been back to the hall to rekindle memories of a life-changing event and their link with British aristocracy. It is this human story, set against the backdrop of Brocket Hall's opulence, that is intriguing.

A week before Alan Brocket Lowe was safely delivered in the birthing suite at Brocket Hall in September 1939, London hospitals were instructed to cease admitting patients except in the most urgent cases. Those already in hospital who could be sent home were. Outpatients departments and special clinics closed down. The government needed 140,000 beds cleared for air-raid casualties in the event that the Luftwaffe launched their much-feared *Kolossal* raid on London. This created a significant problem for all hospital services, including maternity.

Of all the services, maternity was the most predictable in terms of numbers so it made sense to move these services pre-emptively out of London and other big cities. The government planned to move pregnant women into billets in the countryside where they could await their confinement in safety. Dorothy Beasley was moved from Walthamstow to Hitchin in Hertfordshire and later to Brocket Hall. She said of her arrival in Hitchin: 'The Red Cross unloaded us from the coach and instructed us to walk in twos, which we did although we had to pass all these workmen who wolf whistled at us all the way. It was most embarrassing for all of us as we had big bumps.'[10] A few days later she went into labour and the Red Cross picked her up and drove her to Brocket Hall for the delivery. She was just twenty years old and giving birth to her first baby many miles from her family home. 'I cried all the way as I was frightened with no Mum or Dad at hand and my husband had been shifted with his Unit to another district and we were losing contact. At night it was quite frightening for a young girl in those days having her first child on her own. As I laid in my bed I could see all these white statues up the corridors and it was quite creepy.'[11]

There has been a dwelling on the site of Brocket Hall since the thirteenth century, but the house one sees today was built by the architect James Paine in 1760. It is believed to be the only complete house Paine built. He was essentially a Palladian and his hallmarks were villas with a central building, usually with a fine staircase, and two symmetrical wings. Sir Matthew Lamb had acquired Brocket Hall in 1746 and asked Paine to design a new house that would 'use all the technology and style of the age to bestow glory on the newly emergent Lamb dynasty.'[12] Money was no object. When Sir Matthew died in 1768 his estate was worth the equivalent of about 13 billion pounds in today's money.

The result was a handsome brick mansion with gabled roofs standing above a lake, fashioned out of the river Lea, which was widened when the gardens were laid out in the style of Capability Brown. The interiors are more striking than the exterior. Architecturally the rooms are restrained and elegant but sumptuously decorated. There are mirrors designed by Thomas Chippendale and Robert Adam's hand can be seen in the marble chimney pieces. The ceilings were decorated by the Florentine artist Giovanni Battista Cipriani, who created motifs for the various downstairs rooms including hunting and banqueting reliefs, classical medallions and a series of geometrical patterns in pinks, blues and turquoises.

The grand central staircase rises out of the hall, below a great glass cupola and splits to lead to eight first-floor bedrooms. All the rooms have their own individual design and are named after some of the most famous individuals who slept in them. Lord Melbourne's bedroom, dressing room and bathroom became the birthing suite where the majority of the Brocket babies were born. It was named for Sir Peniston Lamb, who became the first Lord Melbourne after his wife, Lady Elizabeth Lamb, who was charming, ambitious, single-minded and determined to further the position of her husband and her family in society, procured for him the role of master of the bedchamber for the future George IV. Her charms so captured the prince that he made her his lover, despite the difference in their ages – she was eleven years his senior. The affair lasted for four years – although they remained on friendly terms for the rest of her life – and Elizabeth's son George, born in 1784, was widely held to be the son of the Prince of Wales, not Lord Melbourne. In fact only the first of Lady Melbourne's children was believed to be the legitimate son of her husband. It was said that she was so disillusioned by her husband's limited intellect, and his constant and blatant infidelity that she chose fathers for her other children who showed greater promise and talent.

Two years after their affair began, the Prince Regent specified a particularly colourful décor for his bedroom suite at Brocket Hall: hand-painted Chinese wallpaper, which was highly fashionable at the time. Peacocks and other birds with colourful plumage perch delicately on boughs of cherry blossom, roses and tulip trees. A red-legged wren pecks at a stylised rock formation while parrots, swallows and butterflies flit and wheel around the exotic three-tiered red and gold lacquered pagoda bed-head, complete with golden bells. Lady Melbourne requested a special 'diplomatic door' to be cut through the wall from her bedroom into the stairwell so that she did not have to bypass Lord Melbourne's suite during night-time visits to the prince.

This beautiful room, so full of history, passion and intrigue, was used during the war as the recovery room. Mothers who had been given anaesthetics or painkillers would come round in their hospital beds to glimpse the wallpaper and see the great red pagoda against the wall where the prince's bed had once stood. Some women told the present Lord Brocket that they thought they had died and gone to heaven as they found themselves surrounded by what appeared to be paradise.

A third bedroom is today named after Queen Victoria. When she came to the throne in 1837, the second Viscount Melbourne, William Lamb, was sixty-one years old and prime minister. During the first three years of Queen Victoria's reign, he became her confidant, political instructor and most trusted advisor. His biographers claim that he was happier then than at any other time in his life.

> As her subject (and a sixty-year-old one, at that), flirtation with Victoria was not in question. But he could expose all of his foibles—his loose talk, his cynicism, his odd mannerisms, indeed his occasional outbursts of naked emotion—without fear of reproof or ridicule from a devoted young woman, while simultaneously doing his duty as man and statesman by tutoring her in society and politics. For her part, she could depend on him totally without impropriety, and yet by virtue of her status and her own strong will never quite appear dependent or lose the power to command. Melbourne liked both her dependence and her authority: she was Caroline [his wife] within safe bounds.[13]

He acted as her private secretary with his own bedroom at Windsor, spending more time with the new queen than he did on his prime ministerial work. In her journals for May 1838, she mentions his name on every page, writing about requesting his advice on her choice of young women to hold her train at her coronation, what pictures she should hang in the sitting room and wanting to know what was happening at Brocket Hall. Such was Melbourne's devotion to Victoria that he sent her flowers every week from the Brocket gardens and greenhouses. Queen Victoria stayed at Brocket on more than one occasion, preferring a modest bedroom at the back of the house rather than one of the more opulent suites at the front. The bedroom in which she slept is today called the Queen Victoria Room, but it was this room that was known in the 1930s and during the war as the von Ribbentrop Bedroom, after the German ambassador. Mothers gave birth to babies in the Ribbentrop Bedroom as well as Lord Melbourne's suite and more than one Brocket baby has told me that their start in life was marked by the association with an unpleasant historical figure.

The routine at Brocket soon settled down as the hall was properly equipped with baby baths, early designs of washing machines in the basement and indoor and outdoor beds for mothers and cots for the babies to take in fresh air. The hospital had a strict regime, as did all nursing homes and maternity units throughout the country, but it was also clean and hygienic. Childbirth in hospital was intended to be structured, clinical, regimented and as far from the chaos and risk of home births as it could be. Childbirth had been something to fear in the last century, but now, with more medical intervention, women had less to be worried about. At the beginning of the war, nurses, mothers and auxiliaries wore masks at all times when handling the babies in order to keep them germ-free for as long as possible. Nurses, midwives and Matron wore white uniforms and headdresses or caps, black stockings and sensible shoes.

Once the baby was born – gas and air was permitted at Brocket Hall but not available for women giving birth at home – the mothers would be taken into the recovery room where they would repose in the plush surroundings enjoyed by the Prince Regent 130 years earlier. When ready to move to a ward, the mothers were pushed on their trolleys into one of the various rooms where they were kept in bed for a week. Bedbaths and bedpans were part of the routine for the first few days. The babies were taken away from the mothers at birth. There were weighed, swaddled and settled in the nursery where they were immediately subjected to a fixed routine of feeding, sleeping, changing, bathing and contact with their mothers for a few hours a day.

Over the course of the next months and years, Brocket Hall developed into a highly efficient maternity home. In 1942, the Ministry of Information sent a photographer to record details of life there for inclusion in an official album. There is a strange contrast between the luxurious décor in the wards and the austere hospital beds; mothers are neatly tucked in and knitting white woollen garments for their babies, who are absent, either in the nursery or being bathed by student midwives. The bathroom in the basement caught the photographer's eye. One picture shows a nervous young student nurse, masked up and anxiously holding a screaming baby above an enamel-coated tin bathtub set up on a trolley with all the equipment to hand – towels, nappies, soap and talcum powder. It is hardly a reassuring image for a modern parent but the caption emphasises that the nurse 'is wearing a surgical mask to prevent the spread of germs'.[14]

Miss E. F. Stock, formerly a sister at City Road Maternity Hospital, who had swapped handling babies for tending the plants in the kitchen garden, is shown on her knees by a flowerbed. Miss Stock's job was to keep the hall supplied with vegetables so that they could be as self-sufficient as possible and supplement the diet available on wartime hospital rations. The photograph shows her next to her wheelbarrow, on the rim of which are perched her Jack Russell and dachshund looking as if they owned the hall. In the background, a nurse is tending a new mother who is lying outside on a day bed 'taking the air' while her baby is sleeping peacefully in a pram under a tree. It is a bucolic and heartwarming scene until you look closer and see the windows above the door show signs of blast damage from a bomb that landed nearby during the Blitz. Despite being twenty-five miles outside London, it seems Brocket Hall was not entirely safe from enemy attack.

Janice Hawker was born at Brocket Hall on 29 January 1943 and was delighted in later years to find letters from her mother to her father during her stay, giving some insight into the daily routine of the hospital. Just after Janice was born, her mother wrote to her father: 'It is 6 o'clock in the morning. It was gone 11 o'clock last night before the lights were put out, and we were up again at 4.30. We have washed and fed the babies and have had breakfast already. Tomorrow Mrs Ives and I go down to the nursery and dining room and I shall be able to have a look round this place.'[15]

The next letter must have been sent after she and Mrs Ives had been allowed to move from the first-floor ward to the more relaxed ground-floor bedrooms set up in the morning room, library or billiard room, in preparation for leaving hospital:

> This ward is a lot more jolly than the other, I think. It seems more free and easy down here and not so strict. The girls are able to walk from ward to ward and have a 'jaw' with each other ... This morning we have had the windows right up and have been able to see across the park. It's a really lovely view to look out on. They say that the trees are alive with squirrels. The ward is full now, we had two more boys in, so that makes us three girls and three boys.[16]

Doreen Glover explained how she was treated after having given birth at Brocket Hall:

> I spent about two weeks in a room with a couple of other mums. It was quite a busy time for the nurses and tiring for the mums. We were confined to bed for eight days in those times before we were allowed to put a foot out of bed. We had blanket baths daily, bed pans when wanted, and were sponged down with Dettol water. We read, knitted, and slept daily between feeding babies. I was very lucky as my bed was close to a window where I could look out on the cold frosty mornings across the vast grounds and see birds and rabbits.[17]

At the end of her stay, Doreen was invited to go and see the other rooms in the Hall. She was particularly struck by the Prince Regent's room and the grand entrance with Paine's magnificent decorative staircase rising from the hall and dividing at the first-floor landing. She told her son, Brian, she had walked up it helped by two ambulance men as she was already in labour and 'for the first couple of days I thought I had dreamed of my grand entrance, but the nurse assured me I wasn't dreaming.'[18] When she left she saw for herself that is was as splendid as she had recalled in her semi-delirious state two weeks earlier.

Barbara Perry's mother told her she sat on a lavatory seat in one of the first-floor bathrooms and looked up to see coronets mounted on the canopies above to acknowledge the royalty who had occupied the bedroom suites in the past. It tickled her to think she had enjoyed the same luxury as the aristocracy. Her baby was born on 23 August 1941, a chilly damp day with little to remember it by but for the next two weeks the sun shone, the temperature rose to the mid-twenties and Barbara's mother enjoyed a happy fortnight in comfortable surroundings before being collected and taken back to London to resume life again at home. For many of these women the few days in bed after the birth of their babies was a brief period of calm and tranquillity during the war. They were taken care of and had none of the worries of coping with rations and other children.

Marjorie Brisland spent Christmas in confinement at Brocket Hall and remembered the nurses putting on a show for the mothers while the only doctor at the hall dressed up as Father Christmas. The nurses made presents for the babies and she was given a toy duck with a felt beak. June Godby was born in the hall and returned with her father to collect her newborn sister, Stella, who was also born at Brocket in January 1947. June remembers her mother telling her she saw the stars through the window on her way to the delivery room and decided to name the baby Stella if it was a girl. June's memory is of sitting on a bench seat at the bottom of the grand staircase which struck her as very decorative, even at the age of five.

There was a dark side to maternity care in the 1930s and 1940s.

June was born at 9am on 15 February 1942, the day of the fall of Singapore and the greatest British military defeat in history. June's mother was listening to the wireless and heard the news just after she had given birth. She told June how much she loved being at Brocket but was disturbed by the fact that 'unmarried mothers had to wait on the married mothers and clean and scrub the floors. She thought this was very wrong.'[19]

Women who were carrying illegitimate babies were considered a disgrace by society and usually by their families as well. Their babies were removed from them at or soon after birth and put up for adoption unless there was some very powerful force at hand to stop this. The situation at Brocket Hall was no different and yet it seems ironic given the colourful history of the house, when illegitimacy was accepted as part and parcel of life for the upper classes at least, that young women were treated so punitively during the war. A mother who gave birth to an illegitimate baby at Brocket during the war, but who wished to remain anonymous, told her story in 2009. I shall call her Elsie for the purpose of making her story seem as human as possible, for at the time she was not accorded that dignity.

'The year was 1944 and I was leaving my home of twenty years, the last time I would be calling it 'my home'. On my journey I was joined by my 'partner in crime', the father of my unborn, illegitimate child. The small case I carried contained most of what I was to wear for nearly two years.'[20]

The next paragraph of her tale is entitled: Welcome to the Brownies. 'At Brocket Hall I joined a group of girls called Brownies because we all had to wear a very unattractive brown dress. We were all carrying illegitimate babies and for different reasons were separated from our families to become the 'downstairs' maids, kitchen staff, laundry maids and other jobs required to run the City of London Hospital, now relocated to Brocket Hall.'[21]

The Brownies were used as skivvies: they worked as cleaners, maids, bottle and nappy washers or helpers in the kitchens from the time they arrived at Brocket until they went into the second stage of labour. Sometimes this was just weeks, but for Elsie, who had found herself leaving home for good at an early stage in her pregnancy, it was months. When she arrived at Brocket Hall she was told her duties would not start until the next day so she was directed to the attic by 'a rather stern-faced Sister Albertella', where she was to share a room with eight other Brownies.

The seven small attic rooms are off a corridor on two sides of the round glass atrium that lights the ground-floor staircase. The corridor is joined to the basement via a servants' staircase. This meant the young women could go up and down the back stairs without being seen by the mothers who were lying in the state rooms, sheltered from the stigma that accompanied illegitimacy.

The morning after her arrival, Elsie was shown to the extensive basement where she was told she would become a laundry maid. Over the course of the next five months she washed hundreds of nappies, towels and baby clothes. She said she had never worked so hard in her life. Matron was a stickler and she would return stained nappies with a stern rebuke for the wash-girls who had not scrubbed them clean. When the weather was poor Elsie had to carry tubs of clean, wrung-out nappies into the drying room: 'The heat was tremendous. Some nurses said it was like the black hole of Calcutta which didn't mean much to me – all I knew was that it was hot!'[22] The nappies were rough and caused the babies to develop sore, red bottoms. Elsie remembers feeling so sorry for the little tots with aggressive nappy rash.

The routine was the same, day in day out, regardless of how advanced their pregnancies were. 'We rose at 6am and began work, stopping for breakfast at 7am. We had another break at 11am where our big treat was a slice of bread and home-made dripping.' They had lunch after the patients had been fed, and tea which comprised one slice of bread, one portion of butter and one cup of tea. 'Kath, the cook, ran the kitchen like a sergeant major, no-one ever crossed her or questioned what she did or said.'[23] Elsie knew full well that she heartily disapproved of the Brownies. The girls, for most of them were just that, were not allowed to go to bed until all of them had finished their work, 'which often meant that at the end of the

day we would all be standing in the kitchen peeling spuds.'[24] There
was half a day off a week and a pay of ten shillings, but for all that
Elsie enjoyed the camaraderie and the fact she was with like-minded
women.

> So the days, weeks and months passed. I remember some of the
> girls well. Florrie, who was the upstairs maid, had been 'pro-
> moted' after her baby was born to collecting dirty dishes and
> bringing them down in the lift to wash them in the kitchen.
> Wearing her blue uniform and without the tell-tale bump, which
> as a Brownie she had to hide from the 'innocent' mothers to be
> upstairs and with whom she was now allowed to mix.

At last it was time for Elsie to give birth to the baby she knew would
be taken away from her for adoption just a few days after the birth.

> Sister Albertella saw I was in the first stages of labour and advised
> me to go to the labour ward, first changing my dress so as to look
> as though I had just arrived! 'Too soon' they said. 'Go back, you
> are not due for three weeks, you cannot be in labour'. So back I
> went downstairs to continue the routine, with sympathetic sounds
> from fellow Brownies. The pain continued until we were all in
> bed then the ward sister came in with a phial of liquid and said
> 'Drink, it will give you a good night's sleep'. It did, but only for
> me to wake up the next morning definitely in labour. My daughter
> was born that morning, three weeks premature. Well, any mother
> will tell you how they feel absolutely ecstatic, no one could pos-
> sibly be as clever as you. What a feeling! She was without doubt
> the best-looking baby in the nursery. Rosemary, who was second
> in charge to Matron and had seen hundreds of babies whilst work-
> ing for City of London Hospital in London and at Brocket agreed
> she was absolutely beautiful. Her father came to see her very soon
> but when he went to leave was told never to come again by the
> matron.[25]

Elsie's partner was banned by Matron because both of them were married to other people and that was utterly unacceptable at the time. Matron regarded it as a crime. Having a man of 'that sort' at the nursing home, even though he felt he had a perfect right to visit his baby daughter, was thought to bring a whiff of scandal into the pure and innocent wards of the legitimate birth mothers. Elsie, as an 'irregular' mother, was only allowed to visit her baby to feed her and she was discouraged from forming any kind of bond with the little girl. The babies were in the nursery, which had previously been the butler's pantry, with a line of bells just inside the door with the names of the rooms they referred to painted above them. It was agony for her not to be able to see the baby more often. Sister Albertella, who had taken a shine to Elsie, promised she would pick up the baby and cuddle her whenever she had a spare moment. She told Elsie that the little girl like to hold onto her nose which made Elsie laugh.

After just a few days Elsie was told that her baby would be taken away and she could go back to her work below stairs. It must have been bitter and heartbreaking. She did not tell the story of how she felt when her beautiful daughter was taken from her but she did write of the experience of seeing other babies being given up:

Most of the girls knew it would be impossible to keep their babies and all they had to look forward to was leaving Brocket heart-broken. Sometimes we got to hear when one of the Brownie babies was going to be collected for adoption. We all congregated at the window which overlooked the back entrance to watch the baby being carried out by the nurse and handed to the adopting parents. How can you hope to ease the pain after the mother had witnessed that? She had loved the baby so much for just a few days and may never have the chance to have another. It was sheer torture for her and we all went to bed very sad and subdued on those nights.

The time came for Elsie to leave Brocket Hall, but she had nowhere to go. One of the ward maids was leaving so she asked whether she could take her place until things became more stable in her life. 'I was interviewed by Matron who started by giving me a thoroughly good telling off.' [26] She was given a job sewing patches onto old Brownie uniforms and made sure she did an excellent job. Her sewing companion was a prim and proper spinster with whom she had little in common but at least for now she had been given a uniform of a different colour, which meant 'I was now allowed to be viewed by the "public" i.e. the married parents.'[27]

After doing two weeks of sewing she was deemed fit enough for more heavy work and was sent back to the kitchens to collect the dirty dishes. For the next few months she lived in the twilight world between the orderly maternity hospital upstairs, full of light and flowers, crisp white sheets and the domineering matron, and the downstairs world of the brown jobs where the kitchen, laundry and drying rooms were hot and very busy. Yet she looked back on that time, especially before the baby was born, and found that despite the disgrace and disapproval, she had been happy. She wrote:

> I loved ... the people, the work, the bonding with similar situated folks. It wasn't a holiday camp but it was war-time and everyone was used to hard times – we were very fortunate, looked after by professionals. Our babies had the very best care, safe from bombs and no queuing for rations.

After Elsie finally left Brocket she married her daughter's father and went on to have three more children. What happened to her baby girl born during the war is not known. The first legitimate child she had was a son who was also born at Brocket Hall, in 1948. This time she was well above stairs in every sense. What a contrast that must have been for her but she made no comment about it in her memoir. Elsie was lucky that she had a supportive husband-to-be who she knew would be there for her even though the circumstances were far from ideal. Others were not so fortunate.

Norah Hern, a midwife at Brocket Hall in the 1940s, described to a friend the situation for other girls and women bearing illegitimate children:

> There were two tiers of unmarried mothers, those with money and those without. Those without were asked to work at Brocket and associated lodgings to earn their stay. The babies either kept or adopted. Those with money, either well to do folk (or girls made pregnant by well to do folk) went to Lemsford House before giving birth and for rest after birth. They went to Brocket Hall to give birth as the facilities were there for any complications. If the babies were in good health and were to be kept they would return to Lemsford with their mother but if they were up for adoption they would stay at Brocket Hall and be looked after by nurses, they would be kept away from the other babies as most were secret babies.[28]

Lemsford House was built in the mid-nineteenth century as a vicarage but it was thought too large by the incumbent in the early twentieth century so he moved to Church End, further down Brocket Road. The Brocket estate rented Lemsford House out to wealthy tenants until the Second World War when it became part of the package run by the maternity hospital.

One nurse described how 'most didn't want to keep their babies as it would make them unsuitable for marriage so they never got to see their child, they weren't even told if it was a boy or girl or if it was healthy, etc. This was private and very expensive, around £500. If you think you could buy a house for that sort of money [in those days].'[29] Lemsford House was run by the church and the unwanted babies were sent to the Church of England Children's Home in Muswell Hill for adoption. Records in the parish register show that 133 babies were baptised between October 1940 and February 1948. The mothers gave their address as Lemsford House and the father's name was not recorded on the birth certificates. This is evidence only of the babies who were baptised, so it is probable that more than that number were born to mothers at Lemsford House.

There are stories of illegitimate babies who found out, some quickly, some much later in life, that they had been born at Brocket Hall. Julie Bloomfield was adopted by a couple called Maryon and William Gray when she was three, though she had no idea that she was not their birth child until she applied for a passport at the age of eighteen. She had had a very happy childhood and wrote: 'This didn't distress me at all because I had always loved them both very much and would never have considered trying to find out who my natural mother was as I considered it would have been too traumatic for her and my adopted parents. Of course, I always wondered what my mother was like and why I had been adopted.'[30] She decided against trying to trace her birth mother as she felt it might be too upsetting. All she knew about her was her name: Iolanthe Whitburn, and that she had been named at birth Valerie Rosalind Whitburn.

It was not until 2004 that an Australian who was tracing his family tree got in contact with Julie to say he thought they might be related. She then obtained a copy of her birth certificate showing that she had been born at Brocket Hall Maternity Hospital on 28 July 1941 and that her mother had been a hotel receptionist in Wiltshire. There was no mention of a father. Eventually, after a lot more digging, she discovered that her mother had died but she had a half-sister. Julie plucked up the courage to get in touch with her and learned that there was another half-sister. The three of them got together and Julie was overwhelmed to see a photograph of herself in her mother's old blue wallet, aged about three. It was the end of a puzzling journey for Julie's two half-sisters, who had never known who the little girl in the photograph might be.

Mo Neate was also born to an unmarried mother. She arrived on 15 April 1944, born to Constance 'Connie' Kennedy who originally came from Aspatria in Cumberland. Connie was initially meant to give birth at the London Hospital but was moved to Brocket Hall after the hospital had been damaged by a bomb. Shortly after the birth, Connie returned to Aspatria and Christine, as she was then known, was sent to the Church of England's Home in Muswell Hill for adoption. She remained at the home for three months until she was taken in by Mabel and Cecil Crouch who came from East Dulwich. They renamed the baby as they did not like names that could be shortened: 'They called me Maureen – and I have been called Mo for many years!'[31]

After her adoptive parents died, Mo set out to trace her birth mother and eventually discovered that Connie had married a year after Mo's birth and went on to have two more children. 'When I first heard that I was born in Brocket Hall I thought perhaps (erroneously) I had connections with the landed gentry and maybe the proverbial bike sheds!'[32] She discovered her mother was living in Burnley and made efforts through an intermediary at the National Organisation for Counselling Adoptees and Parents (NORCAP) to visit Connie. Tragically, three days before the meeting was due to take place, Connie died. However, there was a crumb of comfort: 'NORCAP had written to Connie asking if she could help one of their clients with information about a child who had been born in the spring of 1944 in Hertfordshire – Connie knew immediately it was me and was apparently overjoyed.'[33] This sad story ended at her mother's funeral, where Mo met her nine uncles and aunts for the first time. Her sister had died at six months and her brother died in 2001 but she remained in touch with her sister-in-law.

Such was the stigma of a pregnancy out of wedlock that it sometimes even affected married couples. Les Cook, who now lives in Spain, was born at Brocket Hall on 21 April 1945. His mother, Evelyn, had had a difficult pregnancy and she was sent to Brocket Hall in March. Her husband was in the RAF in Ceylon and Les believes that his conception was the result of a 'final fling' on his father's last home visit. When his father returned to Britain he became convinced the baby could not possibly be his. As Les was born ten months after the last opportunity the parents would have had for intimacy he forced through the divorce. It was a family tragedy that was seldom discussed. Les lived in Enfield with his mother, his aunt and his grandparents, and he never had contact with his father again. Years later he discovered that his father had remarried weeks after the divorce had gone through and had moved back to the family home where he lived for sixteen years, just three miles away from the legitimate son he refused to accept as his own. Les's father and his new wife had a son in 1955 and a daughter in 1963. Les wrote: 'My father died in 1990 but I was able to visit his grave and finally say hello and goodbye. I have a wonderful wife and family but so wish that I had asked questions earlier and been able to share a much broader based family.'[34]

Inevitably there were personal tragedies for mothers whose babies died at birth or within a few days. The register in St John's Church records sixty-two babies who died during the war soon after birth, all of them bar one from Brocket Hall, and some of those were buried in the churchyard. There is, however, no reference to babies who were stillborn. In the 1940s these babies would be passed to the undertaker with half a crown. They were then put in a coffin with another body and buried with no record as to their whereabouts in the graveyard. Andy Chapman, a local historian at the Lemsford Local History Group, has been researching this subject for some time, trying to help to bring closure to women whose stillborn babies were classed as clinical waste, and to get recognition of this sad footnote to the history of Brocket Hall as a maternity home. He was inspired by a woman called Pauline, who contacted him and explained that her mother's baby boy had been stillborn and was taken away from her at birth without explanation. She never knew what had happened to her son. She described her mother's grief and sadness as part of her own DNA. Another woman, called June, who had a similar experience, was a little more fortunate in that her husband was able to visit and see his dead child before it was taken away. In April 2016 there was a church service in St John's to commemorate these children and there will be a memorial to them in due course.

We know that a total of 8,388 babies were born over the ten years of Brocket Hall's existence as a maternity hospital, including several pairs of twins, although the birth records from the war years no longer exist and are said to have been destroyed by fire when they were returned to London. Among the famous Brocket Babies are the distinguished novelist Jim Crace, who was born in the von Ribbentrop Bedroom; Colin Berry, the BBC Radio 2 presenter and the film director Mike Leigh.

In 1946, the City of London Maternity Hospital took over financial responsibility for Brocket Hall from Hertfordshire County Council, who had administered it on behalf of the Red Cross during the war years. Their own buildings in London had been damaged during the Blitz and the City of London had to make up its mind whether to replace the existing buildings or start again from scratch. The decision to rebuild the maternity hospital in London was taken at the end of the war but it took three years to complete the new hospital in a different site away from the noisy City Road. Meantime Brocket Hall continued to function as a maternity home until 1949. Lord Brocket, like many other home owners, had to wait until long after the end of hostilities to reclaim his property.

Waddesdon Manor built by Ferdinand de Rothschild to entertain house parties at weekends was used during the war as a children's home.

CHAPTER 2

Waddesdon at War

*If humanity means anything it is impossible to shut our
eyes. It is equally impossible to refuse to take action.*

G. K. A. Bell, Bishop of Chichester [1]

In January 1939, Mr and Mrs James de Rothschild received a letter
from Aylesbury Borough Council containing advice from the min-
ster of health, Walter Elliot, about the transfer of population in time
of war entitled 'What the Householder is Asked to Do'. The minister wrote that it was necessary to prepare in good time and that
'Children must come first. That, I am sure, will be agreed by all, and
I feel sure too that we can rely on willing help from all.'[2] The note
concluded: 'In every case as much notice as possible will be given to
householders.'[3] When the moment arrived the Rothschilds had four
days' warning.

Dorothy de Rothschild's first thought had been to offer their
home, Waddesdon Manor, to the Ministry of Health as a possible convalescent home or hospital. This had been the fate of
many houses in Britain during the First World War as hundreds of
thousands of beds were needed for sick, injured and recovering servicemen. It was assumed that the same would be required in the new
war, but the nature of the fighting did not follow the same pattern

and, as the government foresaw, houses for evacuees and government departments, as well as the armed forces, would be the most pressing need. Nevertheless, some houses would be needed for civilian hospitals and an official from the Ministry of Health came to Waddesdon to make a preliminary inspection. He gave the manor a damning report which rather surprised the Rothschilds. Dorothy wrote later: 'His verdict was disappointing: "the most unsuitable house for a hospital which could be imagined". We came to understand that *boiserie* [sculpted French-style panelling] even if covered up, would be a first-class harbourer of germs, and so we had to give up that idea.'[4]

Waddesdon Manor is one of the most striking and unusual of Britain's stately homes. It was built by Baron Ferdinand de Rothschild as a country retreat in which to surprise and entertain his friends. He wanted a house built in the grand style of the Renaissance châteaux of the Loire Valley and he could afford to realise his dream. The baron stemmed from the Austrian branch of the Rothschild dynasty that had started in Frankfurt's Jewish ghetto in the sixteenth century. In the eighteenth century, the five sons of Mayer Amschel settled in Frankfurt, Vienna, Naples, Paris and London, the financial capitals of Europe at the time. Ferdinand was of the line that had settled in Vienna but he moved to London in 1859 when his mother, who was the daughter of the founder of N. M. Rothschild & Sons, passed away. In 1865 he married his cousin, Evelina, who died two years later giving birth to a stillborn son. He grieved for her for the best part of a decade and built the Evelina Hospital for Sick Children in London's Southwark as a memorial to her. It is now part of the Guy's and St Thomas' NHS Trust and is the second-largest provider of children's services in London. Ferdinand never remarried but instead spent the rest of his life living next door to his younger sister, Alice, who was also unmarried. She is purported to have said: 'No man will wed me for my looks, and I will make certain no man will wed me for my money!'[5]

Ferdinand's passion, apart from hunting, was collecting art and furniture. He had a house in Piccadilly but he wanted somewhere in the country to house his growing collection. When his father died in 1874 he came into a substantial inheritance. Farming land at Waddesdon belonging to the Marlborough estate came up for auction in 1873 but was not sold. Ferdinand bought it and the site where the manor now stands, commanding stunning views of Buckinghamshire and the Vale of Aylesbury, for £200,000. He commissioned the French architect, Gabriel-Hippolyte Destailleur, to design and build his vision, while Elie Lainé formalised the gardens. Ferdinand had been greatly impressed by the ancient châteaux of Valois during his stay in Touraine, and wrote: 'I determined to build my house in the same style, and considered it safer to get the design made by a French architect who was familiar with the work.'[6] The foundation stone was laid in 1877 and the bachelor's wing completed three years later. To turn a bare wilderness on the crest of a hill into a house and park was a remarkable achievement, but to do it in just three years with little mechanised aid, requiring hundreds of men labouring with wheelbarrows, ponies and traps and shovels seems from our modern point of view almost inconceivable. To the inhabitants of Waddesdon village it must have looked like a fairy-tale castle rising out of the air. The eclectic style incorporated towers based on the Château de Maintenon and the twin staircase towers on the north side which were inspired by the staircase tower at the Château de Chambord.

By 1880, the main part of the manor was finished and Ferdinand held house parties for twenty guests. After a few years, he realised that his architect had been right when he said that 'one always builds too small'. Ferdinand wrote later: 'he prophesied truly. After I had lived in the house for a while I was compelled to add first one wing and then another.'[7] The large morning room on the ground floor and two bedroom suites above it were completed in 1891. The manor was constructed to the most modern standards and included structural steel, which impressed engineers working on repairs a century later. The interior was luxurious with all the comforts of up-to-date plumbing, central heating and electricity, which were usually missing in country houses belonging to people in his social circle. For the next seven years, Ferdinand de Rothschild entertained the high aristocracy of Britain at his famous 'Saturday to Monday' social gatherings. It became the site of some of the great political house parties of the era as Rothschild was both a Liberal MP and a leading member of the Prince of Wales' set and visits from royalty were not uncommon. Queen Victoria paid a private visit on 14 May 1890, which required endless preparation and planning. Fortunately it played out well and she was so impressed by the set-up and above all the catering that she sent her chef, head gardener and furniture keeper to learn from the Waddesdon methods. Victoria was said to have been so fascinated by the electricity, with which she was unfamiliar, that she spent ten minutes turning the newly electrified eighteenth-century chandelier on and off.

Ferdinand de Rothschild died in 1898 before reaching his sixtieth birthday and the house passed to his sister Alice who saw it as her duty to act as the protector of his creation. She is best remembered for her strict housekeeping rules that ensured the preservation of the collection. Visitors to the house in the mid-twentieth century would often comment to Dorothy de Rothschild on the exquisite, undamaged porcelain. This, she would reply, was down to Alice who believed 'when touching china, *always* use two hands and maintain complete silence.'[8] She ensured the longevity of the silk wallpapers by insisting on low light levels, especially when the sun was high, and had cotton covers designed for the silk upholstery. Alice was also a passionate gardener but during the First World War she gave over the formal gardens to vegetables to feed people in need. After the war she restored the layout of the beds, some of which can still be seen in the summer planting today.

When Alice died in 1922, the house, estate and all its contents passed to her great-nephew, James de Rothschild, but not the family papers. Ferdinand ordered that all his personal papers be destroyed upon his death. Alice did the same. The more intimate history of Waddesdon, therefore, comes from the next incumbents, James and Dorothy, the last members of the family to live in the house. Fortunately for posterity, Dorothy did not dispose of James's letters and writing, nor, after a change of heart, did she request her own fascinating diaries, menu books and letters be destroyed. Thus the history of this great house in the twentieth century is impressively preserved in one of the best-kept archives which contains, among other documents, over 20,000 letters written to James and Dorothy over the years.

James had been brought up in Paris, the grandson of the French branch of the Rothschild family, and educated at Trinity College, Cambridge. In 1913, when he was already in his mid-thirties, he met and married Dorothy Pinto, seventeen years his junior, and the couple enjoyed what Dorothy described as a 'whirlwind existence' between London and Paris, getting married just six weeks after their engagement was announced. Within eighteen months their lives, like those of the rest of the world, were disrupted by the First World War. After the war, during the latter half of which he had fought for the British Army, James went to Paris to be part of the Zionist delegation at the Paris Peace Conference. In 1920 he came back to Britain and applied for British naturalisation. This enabled his aunt, whom they had visited regularly since their marriage, to leave him her estate, something neither of them was expecting. 'Waddesdon is not an inheritance, it is a career,' Lord d'Abernon told Dorothy and James when hearing of their good fortune. Catherine Taylor, Waddesdon's archivist explained: 'Alice and Ferdinand used Waddesdon for entertaining, whereas Dorothy and James used it as a permanent home. The estate was no longer run as it had been in its Victorian heyday when it employed around 200 men.'[9] For the next seventeen years, the Rothschilds lived at Waddesdon, becoming an integral part of the village as well as using the great house to entertain political and personal friends, royalty and family. By the Second World War Dorothy was used to running the house like a well-oiled machine.

While discussions continued about Waddesdon's potential use in wartime the Rothschilds became increasingly aware of the desperate plight of the Jews in Germany. James gave a speech in Glasgow in March 1939 appealing to his audience to consider especially the children. He described how 600,000 men, women and children were being sacrificed to the cause of the monstrous Nazi experiment. 'What is the influence of this situation upon the character and out-look of the Jewish child in Germany today? To be kept in a state of constant fear, I do not necessarily mean fear of physical violence, but mental and moral fear, must eventually produce a cowardly dis-position. Fear is the most soul-destroying element in the world . . .'[10] He knew that thousands of families were desperate to get their children out of Germany, even in the knowledge that it might mean they would never see them again. It was a passionate speech by a man not given to expressing his emotions in public and it reflected a deep anger and frustration at the horrific mental impact of the Nazi regime on the Jewish people.

The Rothschilds received a letter in early 1939 from the daughter of a Jewish school teacher in Frankfurt. Her father had been arrested after Kristallnacht in November 1938 and she was anxious to find out whether his students could be removed from Germany to safety. The letter, which arrived at Waddesdon, was addressed simply: 'Lord Rothschild, London'. James de Rothschild asked a friend, Julian Layton (born Loewenstein), to go to Frankfurt to arrange the safe exit of the school from Germany and to bring the boys to the Waddesdon estate. The Loewenstein and Rothschild families had known each other in Frankfurt in the nineteenth century and the friendship had continued when both families moved to London.

The Flersheim-Sichel Institute in Frankfurt was run by Hugo and Lilly Steinhardt as a residential school for boys. The rise of the Nazis had meant that Jewish children could not be educated in the main-stream German school system because of their race, so desperate parents sent them to Frankfurt for their school years. Over a period of several weeks, Layton dealt with the German government and with the parents of the boys, not all of whom were prepared to give permission for their sons to leave the country.

Twenty-one boys between the ages of six and thirteen arrived at Waddesdon from Frankfurt on 16 March 1939 and were accommo-dated in a house on the estate called The Cedars. They were lucky to escape. A second group of children from the school was stopped from leaving for South America. No one knows about the fate of that later group, but one of the boys who came to Britain said after the war that he could not believe it would have been a good outcome for those who remained in Germany.

The Cedars, formerly a nursing home, had been built by Miss Alice, and had room for the boys and their guardians, the Steinhardts. Hugo Steinhardt had spent several months in Buchenwald following his arrest. Thanks to James's agreement to sponsor the children in Britain indefinitely and to Layton's intervention, he was released and allowed to travel to Britain, though he died in October 1942 after a long illness exacerbated by the treatment he had received in the concentration camp. The Steinhardts' two daughters, aged fifteen and eleven, came with them and eventually helped their mother to run the home. They were joined a month later by Miss Bertha Butzbach, who took over the kitchens and by eight other boys who managed to escape from Germany in June. As it was critical for the children to integrate as quickly as possible, they were forbidden to speak German in the house and were sent to local schools in Waddesdon and Aylesbury. The Cedars was too small to accommodate all the boys so five of them were billeted with village families. This was a thrilling thing for the boys, who missed their homes and parents. Now they had the chance to live with a family and to be immersed in the English way of life. They were invited to take it in turns to 'live out' for six-week periods. As a result they learned English quickly and assimilated into the community successfully, most forming lifelong friendships. They became universally known as the Cedar Boys. Dorothy wrote of her pride that Waddesdon received these bright young children with such kindness:

It says much for the understanding of the village, and for the tact of the newcomers, that this little orphanage was welcomed with open arms. The children were all educated either in the village school or in the grammar school in Aylesbury ... They were not only quick to learn but also proved their worth on the playing

field: football came naturally to them and one boy even represented Aylesbury in a boxing contest . . . During the war they were
unfailingly helpful: the Waddesdon village Salvage Collection
record reached dizzy heights thanks to the regularity of their assistance and their persuasiveness.[11]

Henry Black, the oldest Cedar Boy, said: 'It was my responsibility
to line the boys up and see that they arrived smartly at school. But
soon word came back saying "Let boys be boys. We prefer a little
unruliness to unnatural regimentation. Just keep the boys safe on
the road." That is the good sense and kindness we remember about
Waddesdon.'[12]

The Cedar Boys seldom came to the manor during the war but
James and Dorothy were regular visitors to the Cedars and both
took a personal interest in their education, arranging scholarships
for those boys who showed academic promise. During the school
holidays the boys took summer jobs on the estate to keep them occupied, though a small number were able to visit relatives in other parts
of Britain.

In the summer of 1940, when everyone in Britain was on tenter-
hooks awaiting the probable invasion by the Nazis, some of the boys
from the Cedars were arrested and interned as enemy aliens on the
Isle of Man. At this time two boys left for the United States and one
for Israel. Fortunately all those who were interned were released
by September but it must have been a very unwelcome interlude for
them and the Steinhardts. At the end of the war the older boys began
to leave Waddesdon to start their careers. Guenter Gruenebaum
went to Manchester to work in a garage and wrote to Dorothy and
James to thank them for their kindness over the years he spent at
the Cedars. 'Also I would like to thank you for bringing me over to
England; if you would not have had pity on me, the same fate might
have been my lot as was the fate of practically all my dear ones.'[13]
His mother had died in a concentration camp and his father was
missing.

James de Rothschild followed the fate of Europe's Jews with

increasing concern throughout the war. He was the Liberal MP for
the Isle of Ely from 1929 until he lost his seat in the 1945 election
and was a member of the coalition government as undersecretary to
the Ministry of Supply in 1944. In December 1942, a statement was
read out in the House of Commons about the 'extermination camps'.
That night, Conservative MP Sir Henry 'Chips' Channon wrote in
his diary how 'Jimmy de Rothschild rose, and with immense dignity, and his voice vibrating with emotion, spoke for five minutes in
moving tones on the plight of these peoples.'

> There were tears in his eyes, and I feared that he might break
> down; the House caught his spirit and was deeply moved.
> Somebody suggested that we stand in silence to pay our respects
> to these suffering peoples, and the House as a whole rose and
> stood for a few frozen seconds. It was a fine moment and my back
> tingled.[14]

Two and a half years before this speech, but after the arrival of the
Jewish boys from Frankfurt to the Cedars, the government evacuation plans began to take shape. A visit to Waddesdon village in June
1939 led civil servants to conclude that the village could take 175
evacuees, although when canvassed earlier in the year the inhabitants, numbering approximately 1,300, had offered to take 475
children, while the manor could accommodate over a hundred from
a single or multiple organisations. In mid-August Dorothy met an
emissary from the London County Council, who, with her housekeeper, Mrs Green, measured up the manor. Ten days later, on 25
August, she returned from London to find the house 'in an advanced
stage of packing up'[15]. She and James moved into the bachelor wing
on 29 August and her diary brims with details of meetings on behalf
of the evacuees not to the manor but to the village, for which she
evidently felt some responsibility. In the end and after many con-
sultations, the Ministry of Health concluded that the only suitable
function for Waddesdon Manor was as a safe harbour for nursery-
aged children from London who would otherwise be at risk from

air attack. It was for this reason that four separate schools and an orphanage from Croydon ended up in the magnificent surroundings of Waddesdon Manor during the Second World War.

The evacuation of unaccompanied schoolchildren to billets in the countryside has so dominated the wartime story of the mass movement of people that it is easy to forget the picture was more varied. Children's homes, orphanages, nurseries and schools for the disabled all had to be considered in the evacuation scheme and their needs catered for. It was far more difficult to evacuate entire institutions than it was to find willing householders to offer a child or two a room in their homes, though some owners of large properties did take larger groups, as John Colville noticed when he went to spend the weekend at Stansted Park outside Portsmouth. He wrote in his diary: 'They were just *en famille*, Lord and Lady Bessborough and Moyra [Ponsonby], Eric [Duncannon] having joined his regiment. There were also sixty or more orphans, who played cricket happily on the lawn in front of the house but were carefully excluded from the main part of the house itself, which remains as cheerful and comfortable as ever.'[16] Those evacuees remained for only a matter of weeks before returning to their home in Portsmouth. Others needed to be evacuated from London for the long term.

By the 1930s, counties and county boroughs were responsible for homes and for fostering schemes, with London County Council overseeing dozens of different services for orphans and vulnerable children who were at that time described as 'waifs and strays'. Once war was imminent the need for large houses to accommodate the children from these homes became critical and the council spread its net wide in order to find suitable properties. Richard Titmuss, in his survey *Social Policy during the Second World War*, estimated that a residential home for forty young children would need over 4,000 articles of equipment including beds, bottles and baths, as well as cooking equipment, outdoor clothing and a very large number of clean clothes. 'Until central buying departments and regional stores were properly functioning, equipment had to be scraped together in bits and pieces.'[17]

The Ministry of Health finally informed the Rothschilds on 2 September that children and staff from an orphanage and nursery schools from Croydon would be evacuated en masse to Waddesdon and they would be arriving that week. Dorothy wrote: 'We had been given four days' notice to prepare for them ... this went much more smoothly than could have been hoped. With the exception of three rooms on the ground floor, all the others were stripped and emptied, as were all the bedrooms on the first floor. We ourselves were evacuated to the Bachelor's wing. There we and our household occupied the first and second floors and we shared the kitchen with the children.'[18]

At eleven o'clock on Sunday 3 September, Audrey Baker was listening to the radio with her family in Croydon. They heard Chamberlain's announcement that England was at war with Germany. It was something they had been prepared for and it was not unexpected. Her father immediately picked up his packed suitcase and set off for Whitehall, where he worked. Shortly after lunch the Bank of England called and asked her sister to report to Finsbury Circus the following morning with a packed suitcase. As a secretary at the bank she was to be evacuated away from the capital. Later that evening there was a knock at the door. A school friend of Audrey's was there with her mother, the chairman of the Croydon Education Committee. 'Could I help with the evacuation of the Nursery School and be at the centre of the town, 9am tomorrow, with packed suitcases?'[19] Audrey agreed on the spot and spent the evening frantically packing for an unknown destination and for an unspecified length of time. All that she knew was that she would be acting as a helping hand to the nursery-school teachers and that she should be prepared to do anything asked of her. She had no previous experience of working with children but she was willing and eager to learn as she went along.

When she arrived in Croydon the following morning she found double-decker buses waiting. The lower decks were packed with the nursery-school furniture and the upper deck crowded with anxious and excited children, teachers and helpers. In addition to the nursery school there were children who came from the Mayday Road care home that had hitherto been housed in three pairs of cottages. There the orphaned children had lived with 'house mothers' in small groups and there was a lively atmosphere of rivalry between the six units or 'houses' in the three cottages. Although the administrators in charge of the home knew of the plans to evacuate the children, to the house mothers it appears to have come almost completely as a surprise and to the children of both homes it was a great adventure in a bus.

Only the drivers knew where they were heading: Waddesdon Manor. Within two hours they turned into the drive on the outskirts of the village, through a great set of black and gold gates between pillars of stone topped with glass lanterns, and up the drive towards the manor on the hill. Audrey said later: 'The scale of the whole place was overwhelming. Versailles came to mind immediately. We were received by the chief steward who conducted us into the state apartments stripped of all furniture. I recall the great gilt picture frames and the paintings removed. Just the highly polished floor remained, upon which the four-year-olds slid and skidded.'[20]

The children came from the Croydon Toddlers' Home and Fox Hill Home, from Croydon Nursery, the May Day Nursery and Croydon Queen's Road Nursery. In all, there were 104 children ranging from one month to five years in age and twenty-nine helpers, including Audrey Baker. James and Dorothy were childless and James was already in his early sixties, so the prospect of their home being overrun by a hundred children under five and their attendant nurses, teachers and matrons must have been quite alarming. However, they appeared to take this invasion in their stride which was, one imagines, led by Dorothy. While James was somewhat austere, Dorothy was warm, generous and infinitely approachable. She was as deeply loved and admired in the village as she was by her wide circle of friends drawn from all over the world. 'She maintained the Rothschild tradition in Waddesdon of unfussy support and interest in all that was good in village life.'[21]

James had inherited Ferdinand de Rothschild's outstanding collection of fine art, furniture and tapestries and added works from his parents' estate in Paris. All this had to be moved to safety in the shortest possible time. The great Reynolds, Gainsborough and Romney portraits were stored in the cellar in specially fitted wooden cases made by the house carpenter, Mr Chapman. 'Fortunately, after a fortnight, he thought he would open one or two of the cases just to see that the pictures inside were all right. To his horror, in case after case, he found a blue haze creeping over the surface of each canvas or panel. Expert consultants told us that the only hope was to remove all the pictures from their damp confinement in the cellar and expose them to fresh air.'[22] The Grey Drawing Room was not in use by the children so Mr Chapman made racks for the pictures and they were stored there, in safe and dry conditions, for the rest of the war, except for four paintings that were sent to the National Gallery of Ottawa who offered to house them for the duration. They were returned postwar in excellent condition. Only three paintings by the eighteenth-century French artist, Watteau, suffered lasting damage as a result of being stored in the cellars at Waddesdon for those brief weeks. Dorothy wrote: 'We comforted ourselves with the thought that the danger of Hitler's bombs falling on Waddesdon was less than the known peril of Waddesdon damp.'[23]

Although the rooms had been stripped of priceless works of art, the decorative plasterwork, wood panelling and silk-lined walls remained. Ornate fireplaces and immense gilt mirrors became the opulent backdrop to the day nursery. The carpets had been rolled up and removed and the handsome marble and wooden floors revealed. While the children simply accepted the new surroundings, the staff from Croydon had never seen such grandeur. Grace Bartlett, who had been a social worker sent to Waddesdon wrote in 1989: 'Although when I was first at Waddesdon the treasures were necessarily hidden securely for the duration of the Second World War, the sense of rare and beautiful things seemed to pervade the house and grounds and I wondered if one day I might enjoy a peacetime visit.'[24]

She did return almost fifty years later and was delighted to find the house as exquisite and elegant as she had remembered, but now filled with the real treasures that had been but a ghostly presence during the war.

Some of the children who had been under five during the war shared their recollections with Waddesdon staff in more recent times and a few had vivid memories. Alan Frampton was sent to Waddesdon aged three. His mother had died and his older brother went to live with relatives. He clearly remembered the rocking horse and children's slide that was set up in the corridor once a week, when a member of the local fire brigade came to play with the children. He also recalled the wooden floors which were very noisy when the children were racing around on them playing games.

When Audrey Baker was shown to her bedroom in the attic at the end of the first tiring day at Waddesdon she found it rather a come-down after the first-floor bedrooms with their commanding views of the countryside that had been allocated as dormitories for the children. She found a small, bare room with an iron bedstead and a straw palliasse, which became her bed for the next few weeks. 'I did not know at the time that you had to run at it with army boots on and jump up and down to make it usable! Rolling off was inevitable. However, the days were so busy and tiring I crashed out.'[25] She was in awe at the way the Rothschilds and the staff looked after the house and the new inhabitants, attending to every detail. She described how two huge kennels were wheeled onto the front terrace each evening and the watchman would bring two large hounds who would sleep in the kennels and keep watch over the front entrance. 'We were well guarded,'[26] she wrote.

On their arrival, the evacuees met the Waddesdon 'family' who would be part of their lives for the next few years. According to Dorothy, the housekeeper, Mrs Green was 'red-haired, formidable and an unmistakable member of the old school, but with a heart of gold.' The linen maid, Mabel, was kind and generous. Dorothy described her as angelic. She was Mrs Green's closest friend and ally at Waddesdon. Dorothy wrote: 'Whenever Mrs Green and I, in our household perplexities, had a divergence of opinion and she wished to be assured that her own view would prevail, her final and nearly always winning argument was to restate her opinion and add "And Mabel thinks so too".[27] Another member of the household who the children soon grew to know and like was Mr Tissot, the chef, who, Dorothy wrote, 'cooked every one of the meals eaten by the children'. Other records say that Mr Tissot only cooked at Christmas and that otherwise the food was disgusting. The truth is probably somewhere in between. Certainly he cooked for the children, teachers and the Rothschilds at the beginning of the war but he always travelled with Dorothy when she left Waddesdon. For the remainder of the time the children's food was prepared by the cook, Mrs Kate Skinner, with the assistance of the nursery staff. Dorothy wrote: 'The first few days were naturally somewhat chaotic, as the children came from three separate establishments in Croydon. Their staffs were unknown to each other and unaccustomed to co-operation, being used to their own routines. It took a little time to persuade them to combine their hours for food.'[28]

The children from the nursery schools and children's homes were kept separate from one another. One group ate in the breakfast room, the other in the dining room. The Red and Grey Drawing Rooms were used as playrooms with day cots, so that the children only went up to the first floor at night. There were eight cots to a bedroom and Dorothy later recalled how tiny the furniture at first appeared to her. The tables, chairs and cots were children-sized and looked very small in the drawing rooms and bedrooms, normally full of large, lavishly decorated furniture.

The staff of the children's home wore uniforms whereas the nursery staff did not. This differentiated the women immediately and there was a great deal of friction between two of the nursery-school teachers and the matron of the home, who was a brusque middle-aged woman from Yorkshire. Three days into the 'invasion' Dorothy de Rothschild wrote to Miss Mabel Hill, matron of the Homes for the County Borough of Croydon Children's Home, complaining that there was a woeful shortage of staff to cope with such a huge number of children. Miss Hill immediately arranged for a further six helpers to arrive over the next two days. She came up to Waddesdon herself on 10 September to meet local tradesmen in the village and make arrangements for supplying rations for the children at the manor. This was to be paid for by the Croydon Committee.

The first week the staff struggled to cope with the varying needs of their charges and the wholly unfamiliar surroundings. The peace of Waddesdon had been shattered and Christine Bride, who was one of the two nursery-school teachers in charge of the May Day School, wrote to Dorothy in August 1941: 'I think the trouble [...] has been caused by the fact that nobody wanted the plan to succeed. The May Day School committee did not help much ever – in fact they hindered always and were rather unkind. They were pretty hopeless before the days of evacuation and anyhow never had the children at heart so were bound to fail.'[29]

The main issue was that the staff had set out on the first Monday of the war full of enthusiasm and energy but with woefully little experience to cope with the impact of being completely uprooted from their previous lives in every possible sense. Miss Bride wrote: 'I could never have believed that life could change so drastically – the awful homesickness of the first weeks – those ghastly nights when we were to sit limply on the side of our beds having been up a million times and not having the energy to get up again.'[30]

Audrey Baker was one of those inexperienced girls. She wrote in 2011:

The first morning after our arrival there was an air raid warning (which must have been alerted privately as the whole estate was too remote to hear any sirens). We were directed down to the cellars (I noted they had already been well shored up). Little children just accept what happens and calmly sat on the benches. Two tall figures also appeared and calmly walked along – Mr and Mrs de Rothschild – he in trousers and pyjama jacket, she fully dressed. Then somehow the chef produced porridge.[31]

Two days later, Dorothy made an inspection of the children's area of the manor with a representative from the London County Council and Helen Crosfield of Croydon nurseries, with whom she was to correspond regularly for the entire length of the children's stay at Waddesdon. Mabel Hill of the LCC described the set-up for the infants and children at Waddesdon: 'The mansion has proved to be ideal for the purpose to which it has been given. At the present time, six separate units are being run including two units for sick children. It is hoped that at some later date to re-organise and have the children in small groups of twelve to fifteen children. In this way the child becomes more of an individual and receives some recompense for the love of their parents that is lost to them for the time being.'[32]

Helen Crosfield seemed more concerned that the whole place worked well, including for the staff who she knew were finding it a wrench to be out of London and away from home. Her own daughter was one of the nursery staff working alongside Christine Bride. She wrote: 'It is marvellous for the children to be in such lovely surroundings and I am sure they will gain in lots of ways.'[33] Dorothy was convinced that the children would thrive once they got over their homesickness and although she never interfered with the arrangements put in place for the children, she became a confidante for the young nursery teachers who found themselves out of their depth in unfamiliar surroundings. On 7 October, she wrote in her diary that she had had an interview with Matron and one can only assume that this was an unusual but necessary intervention.

The main cause of the friction was that the matron from the children's home had a different attitude towards discipline and routine than the nursery nurses who were younger, more relaxed and from a different social background. By and large the nursery staff had more in common with their hosts than they did with Matron and Christine Bride confided in Dorothy several times when she was at Waddesdon after she had come in for a tongue-lashing from Matron. The experience stayed with her for months afterwards:

It <u>was</u> my fault but possibly, it was only inexperience and youth-fulness. Life had been so sheltered and happy at home and I just couldn't understand the conflicts that arose so suddenly. Matron made me so angry though – I used to weep from sheer anger! I still meet her in dreams and can hear yet her grating Yorkshire accent beating me down because I could never find words to keep pace with her. I can always see her advancing across the Red Drawing Room towards Miss Butterworth while we were all at break-fast – claws out and tongue loosed – and me springing to defend Butterworth with a whole volley of abuse I had had saved up for days – and all this only 12 hours after we had declared one of our weekly truces! It's terribly laughable now but then it was so deadly serious. Haven't you ever got up against anyone like that? You <u>did</u> understand, didn't you?[34]

Helen Crosfield tried to intervene in the row between the nursery teachers and Matron. She came to the conclusion that it was ter-ritorial warfare. 'We do want to cooperate as far as we can without losing our own nursery school identity and freedom of action for our own children.'[35] She said she would be sending another volunteer helper and apologised to Dorothy, saying: 'It must be worrying for you to have disharmony in the household and it seems a poor return for your open-hearted hospitality.'[36]

In addition to the staff, there was a matron and a night nurse who was responsible for the 6am feed. The other daytime staff started work at 7am helping the children to wash, dress and make their beds before breakfast at 8:30am. Every morning the children went out for their morning walk from 10am until 12:15 accompanied by members of staff. Lunch was served at 12:30 and all the children had an hour's rest at 1:30pm. A further one-and-three-quarter-hour walk was pen-cilled in for the afternoons followed by tea, play time and bath and bed. 'It is most essential that each child should have at least twelve hours' sleep in addition to their midday nap.'[37] It was undoubtedly the intention to tire the children out by making them spend over four hours out of doors but it was also lovely for the nursery staff who did not have to worry about traffic or roads as they had done in the past. There are photographs of the children wearing wellington boots and rain jackets so even on days when the weather was wet they went out if possible. A nursery nurse who came later to Waddesdon described the children's boots lined up in the conservatory like a miniature army.

At first, the teachers, matrons and children were able to make use of the 165-acre grounds and gardens surrounding the house. The children were taken to the aviary to see the birds and to feed the deer who were in a large pen not far from the house, but later an army petrol depot opened in the grounds and the children were confined to within 100 yards of the manor for their own safety. The flower beds in the front garden were dug up and planted with grass, while other parts of the garden were used to grow vegetables. The four-and-a-half acres of glass houses, that once used to be used to nurture tender exotic plants, were given over to food production as well. Dorothy sent the Churchills a basket of Comice pears grown in the orchard and Clementine wrote to her in delight that they were Winston's favourite and a taste they had not enjoyed since the war began.

Dorothy made a point of visiting the dormitories on Friday evenings. She would wish each child goodnight and give them a sweet, which naturally they loved her for. Sweets were rationed during the war and were a glorious treat. Many adults today who were children during those years still remember the excitement of their sweet ration. The only other time the children got sweets was when they walked down to the shop at the end of the main driveway and spent their penny pocket money.

A few mothers of the nursery-school children were able to get to Waddesdon to visit their infants though these visits were infrequent enough to be mentioned individually. Mrs Fillingham from West Croydon wrote to Christine Bride after her visit to Waddesdon of her gratitude towards Dorothy for giving her two little children sanctuary at the manor. She had met Dorothy but, '... I never know who she was till I got back to Standon a cabman told me who she was. If

I had know [sic] then I would have felt out of place, but I think she is the nicest and kindness [sic] Lady in England. Miss Bride I have lived over 50 years and that is the first time I have had a good turn done for me and that made me want to thank her and yourself ...'[38]

By the end of the year, Dorothy had received a steady stream of letters from grateful parents thanking her for looking after their sons and daughters. Some were short and polite, others long and meandering. One young mother of four children lived in Crystal Palace and was distraught that she had forgotten to send her little boy a card for his fourth birthday. She had been ill and working long hours, she explained. In a two-page letter, written without a single full stop, she gave Dorothy a potted version of her life story with a ne'er-do-well husband 'who isn't worth such lovely children', having left her with three girls and one little boy, Henry. She explained that he was meant to be evacuated with his sisters but they had been separated, while her three-year-old daughter was still at home. 'I am out in the morning from 7am til nine at night so it is no very much life for her.'[39] She wrote: 'I suppose I should be very grateful and appreciate whats [sic] being done for them but I am more than that, it is a good job we have some kind folks about like the homes to take care of our little ones and see they are well and healthy.'[40] Yet her greatest fear was that the children would become strangers to one another if they were apart for too long. This fear was well founded. Children evacuated for extended periods to different families or homes during the war had often such completely unrelated experiences that they could not get along together when they were reunited at the end of the hostilities. Mr Hook from California observed that his wife, Glenys, who was born in July 1940 and who spent her early years at Waddesdon, had not only had a wonderful start in life living in style and surrounded by opulent décor but also had a different speech pattern from that of her siblings. He had always found this strange until he visited Waddesdon and realised the background against which she had spent her early childhood. Glenys showed him the dining room where she had been sitting when the breakfast doors were flung open to reveal a huge

Christmas tree and a real-life Father Christmas and the fountains on the parterre where she had played with other children from what she called 'The Waddesdon One Hundred'.

Audrey Baker had unbounded admiration for the nursery-school teachers who not only looked after the children all day but were responsible for them at night as well. Unlike the orphans from the children's homes who had never known family life, many of the nursery-school children were homesick and the nights for the first few weeks were very disturbed. It was a strange juxtaposition for Audrey, who had come from a sheltered, middle-class home in Croydon: 'This was my introduction to one of the grandest country mansions in England; it was also my first experience of nits and impetigo.'[41]

She was surprised and distressed when the children started crying when they heard the noise of the gardeners mowing the lawns one morning soon after they arrived. Many ran to the windows to look out. 'It probably reminded them of Dad or Granddad. It was such a traumatic time for such young children – it must have deeply affected their lives. No one knows how much.'[42] Soon the children got used to the noises around the house and the gardeners allowed them to run alongside the lawnmower. In later life, some of the older children recalled with real pleasure the freedom of the outdoors at Waddesdon. Their daily walks took them into the woods, down to the farm, across the fields to stand on the five-barred gates and stare at the world beyond their boundaries. On occasion they even went down to the airfield at Westcott behind the manor and one little girl remembered being shown how to get into an aeroplane while carrying her gasmask.

Every child who spoke of their memories of Waddesdon recalled the magic of Christmas there. It was all carefully stage-managed by Dorothy. The children and the staff were to be guests of her and James for the day. She supervised her own staff decorating a magnificent Christmas tree in a secretly guarded room. Matron's assistant, Caroline Crelling, was the foster mother of the home. She told the story for the first Waddesdon Christmas of the war, describing the day with the kind of Victorian formality that would have grated on Christine Bride and the other nursery-school teachers:

> At 7:30am on that day, Father Christmas and Matron visited the children and distributed to them gifts which had been supplied for that occasion. After breakfast, the morning being favourable, the children were taken for the usual walk in the grounds. But about 11 o'clock a very pleasing yet quite informal little ceremony took place. As Mrs de Rothschild was walking towards the Dining Room, three children, who had been kept behind to do so, presented her with a lovely spray of pink carnations; and a spray of chrysanths was also handed to Mrs Green, the housekeeper, who accompanied Mrs de Rothschild. The occasion was sweet in its simplicity and informality, whilst Mrs de Rothschild was charming. The flowers had been generously provided by the Staff connected with the children.[43]

The children were given minced chicken and vegetables for lunch followed by Christmas pudding and custard. After their rest they were all brought down to the Long Gallery in their party-best to have a tea party. Miss Crelling continued in her report:

> Some of the tinies looked bewildered at the gaily decorated tables and room; the older children who understood the occasion, look radiant and happy, and so were the staff ... After tea Mr and Mrs de Rothschild and party arrived whilst receiving cheers. The doors of the secret room were opened and the Xmas tree was in full view. Father Xmas was standing by it, and with helpers, quickly disposed of the presents which were hanging on it. Nor were the staff forgotten. Each of us received a handkerchief which was daintily tucked into a seasonal envelope.[44]

Dorothy had arranged a treat for the staff as well. Once the children were tucked up in bed, they were invited to a festive dinner in the dining room, waited upon by the Rothschilds' staff. It made a huge impression on them all and, Miss Shelling commented in awe that the chef and the valet carved the turkey for them. The Rothschilds supplied sherry, wine and port for the dinner and this was followed by a dance in the servants' hall. The staff were so touched that they planned to hold a party for the Rothschilds in return, but it was cancelled because James had a serious car accident shortly after Christmas and spent some time in a nursing home near Oxford.

In 1942 there was a changing of the guard. Now that the threat of the Blitz had receded, at least for the moment, the schools and orphans' home at Waddesdon returned to Croydon where the council had found suitable buildings for them. Waddesdon, however, was still needed as the requirements of the War Office and other departments for accommodation changed. The Rothschilds took in the Columbia Market Nursery which had come not from London but from Alwalton Hall near Peterborough where they had been since the outbreak of the war.

Beatrice Whitehouse was a newly qualified nursery-school teacher and this was her first job. She was in charge of twenty children and their downstairs base was the Red Drawing Room. By the time Beatrice and her children arrived at Waddesdon all the early teething problems had been resolved and her recollection of Waddesdon was as bucolic and relaxed. She described the children shelling peas into bowls on top of the portico and blowing bubbles on the gravel outside the conservatory.

Beatrice had a boyfriend called Jack who she married in 1943. All their courting was done in the silk-walled Blue Dining Room, she told the archivist at Waddesdon, Catherine Taylor, in July 2012. It was the only private space they could find. The children got very excited when he came to visit and would queue up 'to hold Uncle Jack's hand'. She realised that they had very little male company. 'It was one of the things that convinced me to marry him – the fact that he was so good with children.'[45]

Barbara Schweiger, a nursery-school teacher from Columbia Market Nursery, was a refugee from Germany, who arrived in

Britain just before the war broke out. She remained at Waddesdon until 1945 and put together a photograph album of the children's activities. The album charts the delights of the life led by the children in the latter half of the war. There are photographs of their walks around the estate and down to the dairy farm run by Mr Caderer and washing one of the dogs in a mass of bubbles. By 1943 the children had their own vegetable patch and were encouraged to grow lettuces, cabbages and leeks. In 1944 the Princess Royal came to visit Dorothy and the children were asked to line up along the drive with flags and wave a welcome to Her Royal Highness.

Dorothy continued to receive visitors and to entertain throughout the war, though on a much smaller scale than in the pre-war years. She kept a visitors' book and a menu diary, so that it is possible to see what she asked M. Tissot to prepare for Princess Mary or Lady Reading, the director of the Women's Voluntary Services (WVS) who stayed at Waddesdon on no fewer than thirty-four occasions over six years. At the beginning of the war there were few shortages and there is frequent mention of lobster, always in French: *homard froid printanier* or *croquettes de homard*, but this would be replaced over the course of the war by rabbit curry, boiled tongue and Woolton pie, a pastry dish with vegetables created by the master chef of the Savoy and named for the minister of food, Lord Woolton. It was generally held to be tasteless as it was wholly lacking in meat and the shortage of onions did not help the bland flavour. Dorothy served Lady Reading Woolton pie at lunch on 12 December 1942, followed by risotto and sardines for supper. Princess Mary fared somewhat better, getting *poulet à l'espagnole* and *framboises à la suedoise*, presumably possible because of the fresh raspberries grown in the fruit cages at Waddesdon.

In 1944, Stella Reading rang Dorothy in a state of great anxiety. The WVS stores were housed at the headquarters in Tothill Street, which was in a doodlebug target area close to Downing Street, Buckingham Palace and Westminster. Could Dorothy find a 'cranny' for the miscellany that had accrued in London? She immediately suggested the stables, which since the departure of the racehorses were available and in fact had become what she described as a general dumping ground. James had at first kept the horses in Britain but in September 1940 there was a tragedy at his stables at Lambourn. 'Three mares were in a paddock by themselves, and three bombs were dropped, all of which fell in the paddock, one of them about twenty yards from where the mares were, so that death in each case was absolutely instantaneous.'[46] It was the payload of a German bomber that had been damaged over Southampton and dropped its bombs to gain altitude. The plane was later believed to have been brought down near Eastbourne. One of the mares, Char Lady, was in foal and the estate manager found the perfectly formed foal, about the size of a rabbit, lying some fifteen feet from the mare. It was a dreadful blow to James and he decided to send the rest of his precious string of horses to Ireland for the remaining years of the war.

A WVS volunteer who was in charge of all the stores, Maria Brassey, was delegated to drive a very noisy three-ton lorry 'brimming with its load' up and down between London and Waddesdon several times a week 'until even the Waddesdon accommodation could take no more'.[47] Maria Brassey became an invaluable friend and constant companion to Dorothy from that time onwards, ready with her wit, sense of humour and indefatigable patience.

Earlier in the war, the main drives and the parkland had been requisitioned by the War Office and Italian prisoners of war helped to construct an open-air fuel storage dump for the army. Violet Griffiths, an ATS driver who worked with the RASC at Waddesdon, described 'huge quantities of petrol and oil in cans and drums ferried from Quainton station into the dump by a stream of lorries, and there were stacked ready for rapid use.'[48] Dorothy wrote of how envious they all felt of this petrol stored on their land but absolutely unavailable for their personal use. Like everyone else, she and James were entitled to civilian petrol rationing only, although she could claim extra petrol in relation to her WVS work. Violet remembered cycling around the estate on her bicycle, catching a lift up the hills by holding on to the tail of a lorry. She also recalled being taking once a week to Westcott, just a few miles from Waddesdon, to RAF dances.

Beyond the house to the north and below a large stand of trees lay a large flat area of land which was commandeered by the Royal Air Force. Westcott airfield was completed in September 1942 and was commissioned as No. 11 Operational Training Unit (OTU), along with Oakley, its satellite airfield. Over the next three years, No. 11 OTU trained almost all the New Zealand aircrews that flew with Bomber Command. The course lasted ten weeks and after that the crews moved on from Wellington Bombers at Westcott to be trained in four-engine Stirlings or Lancasters. Locally it was said that the airfield was used operationally for bombing raids but that was not so, however crews from Westcott took part in 'Nickel' operations when leaflets were dropped onto enemy-occupied cities. The airfield was occasionally used for emergency landings when aircraft were diverted from their home fields. Sometimes they landed while still 'bombed up' and that could lead to fatal accidents. Ivor Gurney and Norman Carr in their book *Waddesdon Through the Ages*, wrote: 'Crashes of aircraft from nearby training and operational air fields were occurring with dreadful frequency. One crashed into the trees on Lodge Hill, and as a result obstruction lights were installed on and around the Manor for use when appropriate.'[49]

An immediate problem was Westcott Hill Wood, south of Lodge Hill, which restricted the pilots' view of the airfield on the approach from the south or south-east and was particularly dangerous for low flying. It was a twenty-acre wood with some 18,000 fir trees and 2,000 mixed hardwoods. The RAF requested the wood be demolished, which caused a great deal of excitement for the children and a big headache for Dorothy's cousin, the Waddesdon land agent, Philip Woolf. The children were particularly fascinated by the two-handed saw used by the wood cutters to slice through the enormous trunks. These were dragged away by the estate tractor and sold as timber, but the thinner branches were given to the villagers in Waddesdon. Philip Woolf negotiated compensation in 1944 of £100 for the felling and removal of the trees at Westcott Hill Wood two years earlier. This in no way compensated the estate for the cost of the ornamental wood, nor did it cover the postwar replanting.

The Waddesdon estate cost around £54,000 a year to run, including all expenditure on wages and services. The income from sales of farm and garden produce and billeting came to some £51,000 per year, so the estate made a loss year on year during the war. The accounts show the cost of the evacuees to Waddesdon was £1,481 per year and included eleven gallons of milk per day and 21,000 gallons of water per week for cooking and bathing. The county council was responsible for the costs of running the homes at Waddesdon but the Rothschilds gave the nurseries a great deal of help in kind, from M. Tissot's kitchen to the use of the laundry.

The nursery schools remained at Waddesdon for the rest of the war and the house was the centre of additional activity. James de Rothschild ran his parliamentary office from there and continued to support Zionist causes, donating 6,000,000 Israeli pounds towards the construction of the Knesset building in Jerusalem, worth about £240 million in 2016. Dorothy was involved with the WVS and continued to take a great interest in the Cedar Boys, some of whom needed her help and support for further education or medical issues.

The memory of Waddesdon in the Second World War for those who lived and worked there is one of a wonderful safe haven at a time of great uncertainty and dislocation. The beauty of the house and its grounds, the kindness of the Rothschilds and their staff and above all Dorothy, whose warm efficiency had solved so many problems in the early days, remained a remarkable legacy. The women and girls who ran the nursery at Waddesdon in the second half of the war were genuinely sad to be leaving and Dorothy, too, was sorry to see them go. 'There are two images of the children's stay with us which will always remain in my mind,' she wrote. 'The first, seeing them being carried down the winding staircase to their prepared beds in the basement during an air-raid warning ... and then the Christmases the children spent at Waddesdon. The house never looked so attractive as when they all assembled in the East Gallery, and the door of the Breakfast Room was suddenly flung open revealing a huge lit-up Christmas Tree with a live Father Christmas to greet them and hand out gifts.'[50]

Dorothy continued to be closely involved with Waddesdon until her death at the age of ninety-three in 1988. She spoke of the war years at Waddesdon in a guided tour in the late 1950s with great affection: 'I can hear their songs now – I must say these are very happy recollections. These were the first – and last – children to live in the house.'

Aldenham Park was the ancestral home of Lord and Lady Acton. The house and grounds were used as a school during the war.

CHAPTER 3

Girls, Ghosts and Godliness

A good sermon should be like a woman's skirt: short enough to arouse interest but long enough to cover the essentials.

Monsignor Ronald Knox

It is hard to imagine that the idea of isolating fifty-four teenage girls, fifteen nuns, a nursing mother with an expanding family and an agonisingly shy, middle-aged male scholar in a large, draughty house with a leaking roof and several ghosts in a remote corner of Shropshire was a good one. However, this pot pourri co-existed happily – with few hiccoughs – at Aldenham Park, near Bridgnorth, for the whole of the Second World War. The tangible by-products included a new translation of the New and Old Testaments. The intangible were a lifetime's memories of a remarkable time and of the holiest and wittiest man any of the girls would ever meet.

While the government was keen to ensure that children were moved from vulnerable areas to safe zones with all possible speed, it did not interfere with organisations it felt should be able to take care of themselves. Private schools fell into that category and their fates over the next six years were varied with a small number of them closing permanently. Convent schools, with their connections in the world of the Roman Catholic country families, seemed to fare better than others. The Convent School of Our Lady of the Assumption in Kensington Square was one example of this, although giving up city life for a rural idyll at Aldenham Park did not always live up to expectations.

The house's owners, the Acton family, were prominent Catholics, whose ancestors included a nineteenth-century cardinal, Charles Januarius Edward Acton. The family had received a baronetcy in 1643 for loyalty to Charles I and had been settled at Aldenham for centuries. Thomas Acton first acquired the Manor of Aldenham in 1465. At that stage the house was a fortified manor, but it was rebuilt in the early seventeenth century and underwent modifications over the next two hundred years.

Aldenham Park stands proud on a ridge of high ground with an avenue falling gently away through some twelve hectares of gardens and grounds, leading down to a magnificent gate screen and railings that form the entrance to the grounds. The drive, which is half a mile long, is set in an avenue of trees, the design of which dates back to the seventeenth century. The house as it stood in 1939 was substantially the design constructed by William Smith for Sir Whitmore Acton between 1716 and 1720, and was made up of two storeys and extensive attics, with a stable block built in the eighteenth century, a chapel, a cottage for the gardener and a gate house.

In 1869, Sir John Acton, historian and liberal commentator, was created a peer on Gladstone's recommendation, becoming Baron Acton of Aldenham. After building a great library at the house which contained 60,000 volumes, he went on to become a professor of modern history at Cambridge. It was he who coined the dictum that 'power tends to corrupt, and absolute power corrupts absolutely'. He died in 1902 and the park was inherited by his son, Richard, who died in 1924, when it passed to John, third Baron Acton and owner of the estate at the outbreak of the Second World War. The first baron's fortune had derived from the Dalberg family estates in Germany, which had to be forfeited in 1914, so by the Second World War things were financially tight. Lord Acton worked for a firm of stockbrokers in Birmingham to supplement the rents he received from the tenants of the farms which made up the estate. On the outbreak of war he took up his commission with the Shropshire Yeomanry, a regiment he had been affiliated to since the 1930s. His salary ceased and in order to make ends meet he needed to find a solution for the house.

Lord Acton, whose full name was John Emerich Henry Lyon-Dalberg-Acton, was born in 1907 and educated at Trinity College, Cambridge and the Royal Military College, Sandhurst. In 1931 he married Daphne Strutt, daughter of the fourth Baron Rayleigh, and it is her story and that of one shy scholar which shaped the war years at Aldenham. Daphne Acton was a great beauty who, though her only education was from a private governess, was a woman of great intellect. Both her grandfather, who won the Nobel Prize in Physics after discovering the gas argon, and her father were eminent scientists and outstanding scholars. Her home at Terling Place in Essex had been full of intellectual debate and curiosity. Brought up a Protestant, Daphne dismayed her family by her choice of fiancé and her father only consented to her marriage on the condition that Lord Acton agreed to forego a Catholic wedding and 'refrained from raising any children according to his faith'.[1] The Actons' oldest daughter Pelline explained that it was Daphne's aunts, who were evangelical Christians, who made most fuss about the fact that their niece was marrying a Catholic. In those days it was considered a disgrace on the Catholic side to marry 'outside the Church' and those who did so could not expect other Catholics to attend their wedding. She believes her father was sacked from his job for the same reason. The couple married at Chelsea Registry Office in November and the society press was outraged that Daphne had not worn a hat to her own wedding. They had quite expected the marriage to take place in Westminster Cathedral.

Pelline was born on Christmas Eve 1932 and a second daughter, Charlotte, arrived two years later. Daphne had already begun to have qualms about the conditions under which Lord Acton had agreed to marry her and when Charlotte developed influenza at three months, Lord Acton baptised the dying baby in line with his Catholic faith. The tragedy proved to be a catalyst for a sequence of events that led to Daphne's conversion to Catholicism in 1938.

Two years after Charlotte's death, Daphne Acton was introduced to Father Ronald Knox who had agreed to instruct her. He was dreading the prospect. Shy, retiring and at times conspicuously uncomfortable in female company, he had been frightened into believing Lady Acton to be a formidable bluestocking. As it was, he was captivated by her and thus began a long intellectual and entirely platonic love affair which resulted in him moving to Aldenham after he had retired from the chaplaincy of Oxford University. Lady Acton provided him with the peace and quiet of rooms at the Park where he could enter into his life's work.

Ronald Knox is little known today outside Catholic circles but in his time he was considered to be one of the most outstanding scholars of the twentieth century. He was known and celebrated for his wit, his brilliant sermons and speeches and his ability to do *The Times* crossword by doing the down clues and then guessing the answers to the across clues without reading them. As he had such a profound impact on the Acton family and on the school that was soon to invade the peace and quiet of the Shropshire countryside, I would like to look at him in a little more detail.

Born Ronald Arbuthnott Knox in 1888, he was the youngest of four sons and two daughters of a distinguished Church of England family. His mother died when he was four and he went to live with his uncle and grandmother until he went to school. It was a blissfully happy childhood and he entered Summerfield School in Oxford at the age of eight full of quiet confidence. There he met three boys who would become intimate friends for the rest of their lives: Julian and Billy Grenfell and Edward Horner.

Ronnie, as he was known to his friends, was not sporty but he had exquisite poise: 'He had an acrobatic gift of balance which later made him an expert at the delicate arts of punting a canoe, walking on a garden roller, going upstairs on a pogo stick and holding the attention of a class of seminarists while he tilted his chair, raised his feet from the ground, and, gravely addressing them, remained poised for minutes at a time on its back legs.'[2]

In 1900 he went up to Eton where he excelled academically and found the school just challenging enough to entertain his enquiring mind. He made friends easily and they were intensely loyal to him. The masters appreciated his outstanding, effortless intelligence and enjoyed, most of the time, his quick wit. He wrote for the school magazine and his contributions, though anonymous, were easily recognisable for their satire and brilliant use of language. His ability to support any view in the debating society meant that he acquired an unenviable reputation for defending the indefensible. He wrote, 'I have once, owing to a shortage of speakers, opened and opposed the same motion.'[3] In 1906 he was spoken of as the cleverest Etonian in living memory.

Ronald's father was a Church of England clergyman who remained resolutely firm in his faith for the whole of his life, eventually becoming Bishop of Manchester. To his dismay he discovered that his youngest son had come to consider joining the Roman Catholic Church. It caused a rift between the two of them which was never fully healed. Ronnie designated Christmas Day 1903 as the birth of his Catholicism. In one of his early and finest works *A Spiritual Aeneid* he wrote:

> I think I could still point to the precise place on 'Chamber Stairs' where I knelt down at the age of seventeen one evening and bound myself to a vow of celibacy. The uppermost thought in my mind was not that of virginity. I was not fleeing from the wickedness of the world I saw round me ... I thought it my obvious duty to deny myself that tenderest sympathy and support which a happy marriage would bring. I must have 'power to attend upon the Lord without impediment'.[4]

In 1907 Ronald left Eton and went up to Oxford, which in the pre-First World War era was a little world of its own. It was a place where 'the sun rose over Wadham and set over Worcester'.[5] Balliol

welcomed him as one of the most promising scholars in the memory
of the college and he did not disappoint them. A friend described the
man he got to know at Oxford: '... his face was always seen alight
with humour, affection and flashing intelligence.' Evelyn Waugh,
who wrote a biography of Knox in 1959, said: 'Ronald had no desire
to grow up. Adolescence, for him, was not a process of liberation
or of adventure. Manhood threatened him with tedious duties and
grave decisions. His mind had flourished and matured while his
heart was still a child's. He grew up slowly. Each stage of his growth
imposed a burden; each enlargement of spirit, the loss of something
fond.'[6]

In 1912 Ronald, by now a devout Anglo-Catholic, was ordained
a priest in the Church of England. Two years later his world
changed forever with the outbreak of the First World War. His
health, which had been poor since he nearly died of peritonitis in
1906, precluded him from being called up and he was painfully
aware that he could be regarded as a coward, so he wore a cassock
rather than civilian dress throughout the war. He was so haunted
by the futility of wartime Oxford that he took a teaching post at
Shrewsbury School where he was a popular, if somewhat bewil-
dering, teacher for the younger boys, and seen as a breath of fresh
air with his entirely self-constructed lessons in Greek and Latin.
He set the boys tests and puzzles, teased them with his own witty
sentence constructions and gave them something to look forward
to. He concluded that the younger boys needed to be entertained
whereas the older ones were probably destined for the trenches and
would not survive the war.

In 1917 Ronald Knox converted to Catholicism. After leaving
Shrewsbury he worked in the War Office in a civilian capacity until
the end of hostilities and then went to St Edmund's, a new school
set up by Cardinal Bourne. He was there for seven and a half years.

Of his seven friends who had gone up to Oxford together, only
two survived the slaughter of the Great War. The Grenfell brothers,
sons of Lord and Lady Desborough, died two months apart in 1915.
However, it was the death of Guy Lawrence, a man he had guided

into the Catholic faith and whom he loved deeply, killed in August 1918 that affected him the most.

It was during his time at St Edmund's that he began to write detective stories to supplement his income: 'he was not seeking to write novels. He had no concern with the passions of the murderer, the terror of the victim, or the moral enormity of the crime. He eschewed psychology, violence, the occult and the macabre.'[7] Rather these stories were games between the reader and writer, like his crosswords and the puzzles that he set for his students. His first book, *The Viaduct Murder*, was described as a classic golden age 'whodunit' and was published in 1926. While they never brought him worldwide acclaim, his seven detective stories gave him a healthy income and the opportunity to satirise institutions or habits that the modern world seemed to him to accept without critical thought. He particularly wanted to lampoon pretentious behaviour. The books are delightfully irreverent and full of parodies, with characters like Mordaunt Reeves, a retired spy and keen golfer who does not like to give up his sport to solve a murder, and the Hon. Vernon Lethaby, a flamboyant headline-seeking exhibitionist with serious gambling debts. Ronald was a founder of the Detection Club alongside Agatha Christie and G. K. Chesterton, and wrote ten 'rules' for detective fiction, which prohibit the inclusion of more than one secret room or passage, as well as the use of undiscovered poisons, doubles or twins (unless the reader has been suitably prepared).

In 1926, Ronald caused a sensation by broadcasting a hoax on the wireless. He presented a short programme from Edinburgh on 16 January, which interrupted an academic lecture from Oxford, to announce that rioters were gathering in Trafalgar Square and had been seen on the steps of the National Gallery; the transport minister had been hanged from a lamppost; the Savoy hotel had been destroyed; and Big Ben blown up. The report was accompanied by sound effects and, as this was still in the very early days of broadcasting, it was taken seriously by the public. 'Women fainted, mayors dusted off their emergency plans and one angry listener called the Admiralty and demanded that the Navy be dispatched up the Thames to quell the riot.'[8] 'Terror caused in villages and towns!' screamed one headline of the day and the BBC received many complaints with John Reith having to step in and assure the public the 'revolution' was just a gaff. In fact, Ronald had made it very clear at the outset of the programme that it was 'a work of humour and imagination' and his style was quite obviously a parody of the then official manner of the newsreaders: 'Mr Popplebury, the Secretary of the National Movement for Abolishing Theatre Queues, has been urging the crowd to attack the National Gallery. The desirability of sacking the National Gallery is being urged by Mr Popplebury, Secretary of the National Movement for Abolishing Theatre Queues. One moment please. London calling; continuation of the news bulletin from reports which have just come to hand. The crowd in Trafalgar Square is now proceeding at the instigation of Mr Popplebury . . .'[9] and so on.

There was widespread indignation about the broadcast and Ronald came in for some stern criticism from Cardinal Bourne in the Catholic newspaper *The Tablet*. He wrote: 'Few literary deeds are more facile and more tiresome than the shoving of serious things into a droll context ... There are in England groups of hireling Communists who must have been enormously encouraged by the fact that many Britons were badly scared last Saturday.'[10] The *New York Times* accused the British of being naïve for being taken in by the spoof but of course the smile was on the side of the face when, twelve years later, Orson Welles terrified America when he broadcast the *War of the Worlds*. Far from putting the BBC off it encouraged Reith to order more of the same kind of programmes. Ronald was not put off either. He was delighted when he heard himself roundly abused by two men in a local pub over their beer. A few months later he delivered a parody of a popular scientific talk illustrating the sounds made by vegetables in pain.

The year of the great hoax, Ronald returned to Oxford and lived for the first and only time of his life in a home of his own. The Old Palace, Rose Place, was his house for thirteen years. By this time his reputation had spread far beyond the confines of St Edmund's,

London and Oxford. He was a speaker and preacher in high demand. People from all over the world consulted him on anything remotely related to Catholicism, and sometimes not even related. He had become, he complained, the wastepaper basket for crackpot ideas of people who wanted to change the world. He was too polite and generous a man to deny requests and he found himself increasingly depressed by his lack of personal private time. It was at about this time that he met Daphne Acton. Lady Acton had made it clear to her family after the death of her second daughter that she wished to prepare to be accepted into the Catholic faith. Lord Acton's brother-in-law, Douglas Woodruff, had come to know Ronald over the years and was now working as editor of *The Tablet*. He said he knew of no finer mind nor better priest to help instruct Daphne and so he set up their first meeting at his home at Stanford Dingley in Berkshire in 1937. In his biography of Knox, Evelyn Waugh wrote:

> He found a girl of strong and original intellect, certainly; a tall, elegant beauty, but one who looked younger than her 25 years; was as shy as himself and fermenting with a radical, spontaneous humour in which there were echoes of the laughter of his lost friends of 1914.[11]

Despite it not being Ronald Knox's first choice of holiday, he was so taken by Lady Acton that he agreed to join the party on a cruise around the Greek islands. To the other passengers' irritation he spent his time exclusively with her, getting to know her and finding complementary tastes and talents. According to Waugh 'they began the accumulation of common experiences, private jokes and private language ... Within a few days of sailing she told him that she wished to be received into the Church and asked him to prepare her.'[12]

Ronald was captivated and confided in her his deepest desire for privacy and 'his ambition to write something of permanent value.'[13] She listened while he outlined his ambition to translate the Old and New Testaments from the original Latin Vulgate. She was impressed and immediately suggested that he could withdraw to Aldenham to undertake this monumental task. They agreed, in a childish pact, that he would no longer write detective stories, which she did not enjoy reading, and she would no longer wear the lipstick that he disliked. So in a defiant gesture, Daphne Acton threw a copy of *Double Cross Purposes* and her lipstick into the Adriatic. With that their fates were sealed.

It took two years to get Ronald out of Oxford and into Aldenham. It was completed, furniture and all, by June 1939. He was happily ensconced in a study working on a book he had conceived in 1918 and learning Hebrew for a few hours in the day. He relished the peace and quiet of the countryside, the lack of any distractions other than beautiful views and head-nodding communication with the two gardeners who looked after the grounds. It was an ideal set-up in every possible way. But, like everything else in the summer of 1939, it was set to change.

Two months later the peaceful atmosphere of Aldenham was interrupted by the arrival of the sisters and pupils of the Convent of the Religious of the Assumption. The order was founded in Paris in 1839 by Anne Eugenie Milleret, who had the vision to transform society through education. She taught her nuns and pupils to live by the Gospel and to love 'the world and all peoples'. Based in Kensington Square, London, the convent ran the first Montessori school in Britain. It had catered for girls up to the age of thirteen, but in the war older girls were educated until they were ready to take their higher certificates.

In 1939, the building in Kensington Square was required by the ARP and the sisters had to find other accommodation for the school and the teaching nuns. Various offers of help came, including from Lord Acton, who had served at the altar at the convent's church at Kensington, while two of his sisters had briefly attended the school as teenagers. Lord Acton invited the school to Aldenham partly in an effort to ensure there would be an income for the estate while he was with his regiment, but also to see that Aldenham would not be requisitioned by the military. However, Lord Acton was resistant to the idea of a formal agreement, which caused the Reverend Mother Superior endless headaches. She wanted to know the extent of her rights and liabilities for a house that had not been permanently lived in for years. One of the problems at Aldenham was a leaking roof and fourteen attic rooms, where the sisters would live, which had neither heating nor any form of sanitation. On the other hand, the house did boast a lavatory on the first floor that flushed with hot water. It took almost three years to thrash out a legal agreement between the convent and the Actons but the basic points were settled before the nuns arrived in September.

On Thursday 31 August, Lord Acton received a telegram at his office of Barham & Brooks in Birmingham announcing that the convent would be moving in the following Saturday. In fact they arrived a day early on Friday. Ten choir sisters and five lay sisters travelled from Kensington by coach. The nuns, in their striking purple habits with white wimples and black travelling veils must have cut strange figures as they disembarked from their bus in front of the house. Rather wonderfully, there exists in the Religious of the Assumption house in Kensington Square a small archive box which contains papers and photographs from the war years, as well as a notebook. This is described by the author as 'The Annals of those of the Kensington Community who resided at Aldenham Park from Friday, Sept 1st 1939 to the date appointed by God for their departure.' In fact the book only goes up to February 1940, but for the first five months of the war it provides a priceless and at times funny record. Written by Sister Dominic, who was the school's games mistress as well as teaching French and history, and who had a delightful eye for the humorous as well as for detail, the annals give a vivid picture of life in the early days at Aldenham. They begin:

We were greeted on the steps by Lady Acton and Monsignor Ronald Knox. We were not greeted by Potiphar, who remained tied to his bench. It was only later on that we made his acquaintance; he slobbered over our aprons and soon seized Sister

Perpetua's blue sleeve, but did not chew it, D.G. [Deo Gratias].
Potiphar is fat – he cannot walk, he can only waddle. He sometimes hops like a frog. They <u>say</u> bull dogs are intelligent. He is
not.[14]

The following day their luggage, including bed frames and crates of
books, arrived from Kensington. There was much to do in order to
make the house fit for purpose and there were plenty of unexpected
surprises to contend with. Sister Margaret and Sister Clare had a
visit from four bats. Sister Clare screamed but Sister Margaret was
smug: '<u>I've</u> got my *bonnet de nuit* on!' she told her roommate. Sister
Clare was 'of a nervous disposition' and very anxious about the risk
of fire in the attic, so she persuaded the others to carry buckets of
sand up to all floors. As it turned out, there was a far greater risk
of leaks and flooding than fire. During a particularly rainy night
in November she had a long row of bowls in her room catching the
water that was pouring in from the leaking roof. Sister Dominic was
so tickled by the sight that she drew a sketch of it in the annals.

   Although the beds had already arrived from Kensington, the mat-
tresses had not. These came a fortnight later in a horse box:

> Unpacking is a hilarious business. Pelline with her hair in curlers
> watches it from the nursery window. Procession of mattresses,
> chairs, desks, beds, seems unending. When our beds appear, Sister
> Clare does a pirouette and Sister Margaret kisses her boards!
> Sister Francoise begins the superhuman feat of providing beds for
> mattresses and room for beds. Mattresses continue to perambu-
> late the house, propelled by invisible bearers.[15]

The day before the children arrived Sister Alethea had 'a nocturnal
visit from a RAT – or rather, of her companion rat, because <u>he</u> sat
up all night, pulling off strips of wall-paper. He made a lot of noise
walking round between the wall and the paper, in between moments
of chewing.'[16] The gamekeeper was summoned to block the rat's
hole but it was only a temporary solution and the rat made more

appearances during the autumn until they decided they had to lay down poison to get rid of it. Sister Dominic's description of the rat's end is as theatrical as anything else she wrote in the annals: 'His last fling was to jump upon Sister Clare (no joke for her of course) because she was standing in the semi-darkness near another of his HOLES in the children's refectory.' The following day she wrote: 'He has eaten the poisoned BREAD, has drunk the water, and must have retired to burst somewhere in secret. R.I.P!'[17]

Potiphar, the bulldog, was in no shape to chase rodents. He was generally found lying in the sun or sitting by the bench waiting for Lord Acton to appear. Whenever he saw the nuns he would amble over to them and lick their habits and try to chew their sleeves. Sister Dominic wrote: 'The objectionable Potiphar is due to go into camp on Saturday. Sister Clare's gratitude to Providence is visible. Perhaps our aprons will be cleaner now.'[18] The following day they caressed him and were chewed for the last time. 'At 7.15 he was taken into Lord A's car, sitting beside him on the front seat; and he has gone into camp with the British Army!'[19]

The loose agreement between the Religious of the Assumption and the family was that the tenancy would include the house, grounds, gardens and garden produce, with the exception of two rooms for the children and Nanny, who cooked for the youngest children in the day nursery and slept with them in the night nursery. One bedroom on the first floor was for Lady Acton and the sitting room on the ground floor to the left of the front door was shared by her and Ronald Knox. There would be no rent payable to the family but in return the convent agreed to pay the rates, lighting and the wages of certain employees, which meant the gardeners and Bazley, the estate handyman. In addition, they were responsible for cleaning the gutters and having the chimneys swept.

The financial outlay for the convent to live at Aldenham was £419 a year. At the outbreak of the war, the school fees were £30 per term, which had to cover the running of the school as well as the house itself. Lord Acton agreed the nuns would not have to pay for wear and tear related to the leaking roof and promised to get it repaired in July 1939, but it was still leaking badly in 1942 and a section of the library ceiling collapsed during a visit by the Mother General in 1945. Catherine Northcote, now Sister John-Mary, remembered the fuss that this accident caused and the desperate rush to find screens to hide the damage from their illustrious visitor.

The school was the senior school of the Assumption, the junior section being at Boxmoor, so Pelline, then aged seven, was taught with a handful of other younger girls whose parents had insisted on sisters being together at Aldenham. They were taught by Sister Alethea in the small drawing room. Hitherto she had been educated 'more or less successfully', she said, by Daphne and Nanny who had taught her to read. Sister Alethea introduced more formal teaching. 'She was very kindly and we all loved her. She used to make me write stories and illustrate them,' Pelline said.

Ronald Knox was initially dismayed by the arrival of the nuns and girls. His peace would be broken and he was daunted by the prospect of having to act as chaplain to the school, which he agreed to do only reluctantly. He was to receive no pay but get food, fuel and laundry in lieu. 'He stipulated only that a substitute should be found for him when he was asked to preach elsewhere and that he should not be expected to sing Mass or perform any ceremony except giving the ashes on Ash Wednesday.'[20]

He had to move out of the house as it would not have been seemly for a priest to sleep under the same roof as the sisters and a group of teenage girls. So he moved in with Bazley and his wife Gertrude, who lived in the original priest's house adjoining the chapel. He kept his desk in the small drawing room, a room that was declared a quiet zone and the schoolgirls were not allowed to make any noise that might disturb him at work. This was the only space he used in the main house and he shared it with Lady Acton, Pelline and sometimes a visitor. It was in here that he stored his reference library, laid out his patience cards, ate, typed and read. It was in this room, amidst the hubbub of school life rather than the peace and quiet that he and Lady Acton had envisaged, that the greater part of the Knox Bible was translated.

In the three weeks the nuns were busy getting the house ready for the arrival of the girls Ronald kept out of their way. The weather was glorious so he spent his days studying Hebrew and bathing in the Shore Pool. When the girls first arrived at Aldenham they barely noticed him, except in chapel or when he was teaching a class. He kept to his study and never walked through the house, although they would sometimes see him walking round the garden saying his office. On one early occasion he was coming out of the chapel when a rank two-girls wide strode towards him. Normally he would have expected the crowd to part and allow him through but they surged on and he found he had to leap to one side to avoid being mown down by this energetic female juggernaut. Sister John-Mary told me that after that he was very wary of groups of girls and developed the ability to hug the walls so as to become almost a shadow to avoid being careened into.

The inside of the house began to look more like a school with the refectory, formerly the dining room, and classrooms on the ground floor and dormitories on the first. The refectory, which had been earmarked before the war for Ronald, was emptied of his furniture and filled with tables and chairs from Kensington. The nuns were grateful for his generosity in offering the school any furniture of his that they could make use of. The tables sat six, except for the large table in the centre, and each girl had her own personal cutlery that was kept in the drawer in the table she habitually sat at.

The cooking and cleaning was done by lay sisters who also did the girls' washing on site. Alannah Dowling, who was a pupil at Aldenham, told me that they were only allowed to change their underwear once a week and that washing was equally infrequent. As a result, two girls sent their washing home and it came back in biscuit tins, sometimes with a cake. The uniform was a navy-blue dress with a white removable collar. In the early days of the school the dress material came from France but during the war they had to resort to blue serge.

Out-of-doors preparations for games facilities got underway. Bazley mowed a piece of land very close to the house which was to be used for senior games. 'Volley ball, over a net, with a net-ball. There's nothing big enough for net-ball or hockey without going a long way away.'[21] Meanwhile, Father Broderick from nearby Bridg-north helped to create a home-made gymnasium, begging a pole from the local builders to make a horizontal barre. 'It turned out to be too soft for the purpose, but he said that a very long broom handle is the right thing.'[22]

As the lay sisters were responsible for feeding the family as well as the school, they took charge of the vegetable garden and another large area of the land close to the house, which they worked with the help of the gardeners and the girls. It proved both vital and very productive once the planting got going and began to yield fruit and vegetables.

Aldenham's extensive gardens were soon ringing to the sounds of laughter and games' whistles as the schoolgirls enjoyed sport and leisure. The nuns had the pleasure of long walks around the gardens and the estate in the weeks before the girls arrived, making use of the shade of trees by Shore Pool to have picnics after their hard work bringing the house into use as a school. More used to life in the city, the nuns found themselves in trouble on their second weekend. They decided to have a picnic by the Shore Pool and gathered together and lit a fire under a big tree so they could bake damper bread, a traditional Australian soda bread typically baked in the coals of a campfire, so ideal for the picnic. Suddenly there were loud shouts of 'Get Out! Get Back!' in angry tones. 'A peppery colonel ordered us first in one direction then in other to get out of line of fire while they shot duck off the lake. Half an hour later, polite apologies all round, general explanations.'[23] The colonel was so embarrassed by his outburst in front of the nuns that he personally delivered a brace of duck to the kitchen the next day.

The countryside turned out to be full of hazards for the sisters, used to the more genteel life in Kensington Square. Shooting par-ties were one thing but then they had an encounter with a sow that scared them all so much that they had to climb several fences and leap over half-frozen marshes in order to get away from the dangerous hog. 'Sister Oswin landed in the mud, once, (and shrieked of course!) and Sister Anthony nearly left one of her galoshes behind.'[24]

The first-floor dormitories among others were called the Pink Dormitory, the Oak Dormitory, the Sacred Heart and Our Lady of Peace. Downstairs there was a further dormitory in what was known in the family as Uncle Peter's Room. It would have been Ronald Knox's bedroom in other times. The nuns lived in the leaky attic rooms which had fireplaces but no central heating and, initially this floor had neither electric lights nor lavatories, prompting a letter to Lord Acton begging at least one lavatory for the sisters. The infirmary was housed in the servants' quarters and sufficed until an outbreak of flu meant dormitories had to be used to cope with the number of sick.

Within days of arriving at Aldenham the nuns became convinced the house was haunted. There were several ghostly happenings which frightened them and the girls alike but Alannah remembers the nuns denying all talk of ghosts until they moved to the next school premises in 1946. Others, such as Sister John-Mary, recall the nuns making light of the subject. The first ghost was believed to be linked to a murder from the distant past that had taken place in the bedroom overlooking the stable yard where Sister Dominic had been sleeping before the girls arrived. First she heard whistling and then she heard a coach and horses coming up the drive at high speed and racing into the yard but when she looked out of the window there was nothing to be seen. Another happening was in the room next to the Pink Dormitory where a dozen girls who had not gone back to London because of the danger of bombing spent their holidays during the first year of the war. Alannah said: 'there was a room facing the drive that was really creepy – I remember well sleeping there in the holidays and on perfectly still nights the curtains flew right in, up to the ceiling, it was very scary!'[25] One of the sisters had experienced the same phenomenon, finding herself lifted out of her bed. The Turret Room, at the top of a spiral staircase leading from the library, was also haunted. Girls sleeping there occasionally heard someone walking up the stairs and past the bedroom. They believed it to be a former Lord Acton. The dormitory called St Christopher's overlooked the front of the house and on quiet nights they sometimes heard someone walking up and down on the gravel. He – it was assumed it was a 'he' – was referred to as 'the Night Watchman' and seemed to hold a particular terror as more than one girl had strong recollections of his night-time wanderings, even three-quarters of a century later.

By the end of September 1939, the house was swarming with girls, and for six years every corner of Aldenham was inhabited as the school expanded, including buildings that had been hitherto little used. The chapel, completed in 1837, was probably the first private Catholic chapel in England after restrictions were relaxed by the Relief Act of 1829, also known as Catholic Emancipation. It fell into disrepair but was restored by Lord Acton after he had made an excellent sale of a racehorse in early 1939. Perfect Part was tipped as the favourite to win the Grand National and the sale went through just before the race. For the record, the horse fell at the fourth fence and never raced again, but the chapel was repainted. Sister Dominic wrote: 'Visited the chapel – Our Lord was there already. Chapel very dank because unaired.' They rolled up their sleeves, shooed out spiders and dusted away the cobwebs, throwing open the windows to let the sunshine stream in. The chapel nave was approached down a set of steps and it was always a squash to accommodate the whole school, especially when the numbers of girls increased to more than fifty, but there were few complaints about it.

The pupils came mostly from London and some had been at the school before the war. Parents answered an advertisement in *The Tablet* and applied for their children to be allowed to attend, so that by the middle of the war the school was granted LEA (Local Education Authority) status, which it had lost in 1937 owing to a drop in numbers. Many of the families knew one another and a few were from old Catholic families. There were also local girls who attended as weekly boarders. Being invited to go home with a friend was a great treat for the London girls. During the first year of the war some girls stayed at Aldenham for the holidays, using it as a country house. Parents and other family members boarded at the Acton Arms in the local village of Morville. 'Skating on the pond in winter and burning the bracken in the summer holidays were major highlights of the year,'[26] one young girl recalled. On the whole, the girls loved life at Aldenham.

Nicola Macaskie, who was a pupil at Aldenham from 1940 with her twin sister, Claudia, told me that it had been a remarkably free and easy life. 'We did little enough work!' she said. 'You started the week with 100 points for conduct and none for work. You had to get up to eighty for work and not less than eighty for conduct. The biggest scare was spilling ink – that was a big conduct no-no. As was talking on the stairs.'[27] When I visited Aldenham in May 2015 the owner, Hettie Fenwick, showed me an ink stain on the floor in what had been the schoolroom. She told me that one of the girls had visited the house a few years earlier and had admitted it was her ink stain. I wonder how many conduct points she lost for that. Sister John-Mary remembered stricter rules than Nicola. She said that if a girl was late for a meal the whole dining room had to eat in silence and they were constantly lectured on wartime austerity such as shallow baths to save hot water, checking socks for holes every evening and turning off lights. Ten-year-old Jane Anton wrote in the *Assumption Chronicle* – the school's annual magazine – that her dormitory took these suggestions so seriously that they dressed and washed in the dark and wore their socks until they were more holes than sock.

The education followed the standard curriculum with plenty of scripture and religious tuition. The girls were fortunate to have Sister Alethea, a fine pianist, who played the organ in chapel and they even had the odd visit from actors from Birmingham. Dafne Bidwell remembered when the actor Robert Speaight, who was a regular performer on the wireless, came to stay with the Actons for the weekend. He gave performances of all the Shakespeare soliloquies from *Macbeth*, *Henry V* and *Hamlet*. She wrote in the *Assumption Chronicle*: 'His representation of Shylock in the *Merchant of Venice* was so realistic that one of the juniors began to cry. We are all very grateful for such a treat.'[28] I don't think she meant to imply it was a treat to see a junior crying.

On 30 September 1939, Lady Acton gave birth to her third child, Catherine. She arrived at 1:30am and the nuns were as delighted as the family. Ronald Knox was uplifted by the birth of the baby and celebrated the occasion by translating the first chapter of Genesis. Pelline, Lady Acton's oldest daughter, wanted the baby to be called Josephine but her parents settled on Catherine. Catherine's birth was recorded in the annals as was a funny exchange between seven-year-old Pelline and Sister Dominic: 'Pelline yesterday asked me, in a worried way: "Can you see any resemblance between her and Potiphar? Daddy says they are just like each other. Of course, her nose is a little flat!"' Two more babies were born at Aldenham during the war, Richard in 1941 and Charlie in 1943. Ronald baptised Richard in the chapel and he became the first Acton heir born in England since the eighteenth century and was probably the first heir ever baptised at Aldenham, all the other heirs having been born and baptised abroad.

Ronald was beginning to enjoy giving talks to the girls in a way that he never thought possible. Daphne Acton had shown him that youth was no different than it had been when he had been a chaplain at Oxford before the last war. He simply had to open his mind to the delights of young intellect once again. Although he never quite lost his shyness in front of the nuns he learned that the girls loved his sense of humour and he theirs. He told them that the call of 'Last bell, last bell!' was not very good for an old man to hear. He sometimes regaled them with stories from his past. Several girls remembered being told of the great BBC hoax, but they were far more amused by the story of the squeaking vegetables, which he told them while adding the noises of carrots and potatoes in pain for effect. His quick mind meant he could come up with witty puns and rhymes quickly. One of his aphorisms the girls remember with delight is 'a baby is a loud noise at one end and no sense of responsibility at the other'. He told them limericks that he had made up while he was at Oxford:

There was a young man who said 'God
Must find it exceedingly odd
To think that the tree
Should continue to be
When there's no one about in the quad.

Reply:
Dear Sir: Your astonishment's odd;
I am always about in the quad.
And that's why the tree
Will continue to be
Since observed by, Yours faithfully, God.

So what was it like having this extraordinary man in your midst? I asked the girls of the Assumption. 'Father Knox was incredibly significant to us. He always made you feel that he was preaching to you and you only,' one girl said. Nicola Macaskie added, 'We didn't realise how famous he was and I think in a way he rather liked that. My sister Claudia and I were used to grown-ups and we were not intimidated by him. He responded to that by being very friendly and open with us. The nuns were the people he was wary of!' She remembered that he was a great Scrabble player and of course keen on crosswords.

Ronald never lost his good looks, even into his sixties. His hair was grey by his fifties but his face maintained its youthful features so that he looked much younger than his fifty-one years. Although he often appeared solemn when contemplating a problem in the Bible or worrying about talking to the nuns, his natural expression with the girls was of suppressed merriment. There is a photograph of him taken at Aldenham showing him unsmiling but with his eyes twinkling and alive with life and probably mischief. When the Macaskie twins arrived at Aldenham they were given the traditional do-or-dare challenge by the sixth-form girls. Claudia, who was athletic, had to climb around the first-floor balcony over the main hall. Nicola, who they thought might fall off and hurt herself, was dared to knock on Father Knox's door and ask him if he liked pink blancmange.

She did not realise that there was a cordon of silence around his room so she walked boldly up to the door and knocked. He called her to come in and she asked him the question. He answered the question solemnly and then laughed. He realised she had been put up to the prank and had no idea of the rules surrounding his working space. That broke the ice and when she asked him about his work on the Bible he answered her questions with his engaging smile. She remembered how he always had a pipe either in his mouth or in his hand. His desk was covered in files with a typewriter perched on one corner; there were books on shelves and piled upon the windowsills, and there was a card table set up with patience. 'He told me that he always had patience laid out so that he could play it if he came to a very difficult bit in the Bible,' she said. She remembered him explaining to her that he ate his meals at the central table that had to be cleared of books and cards to be laid for his lunch or evening meal. Daphne Acton also had a desk in the room at which she dealt with her correspondence, so the two of them often worked in silence. She relied on him for more than just company and intellectual conversation: the family was always short of money and Ronald paid for items such as the children's shoes. They all had flat feet, Pelline explained, and had to have special shoes sent from far afield.

Nicola and Claudia became Ronald Knox's favourite pupils. He lent Nicola his bicycle, because she did not have one, so she could go off on rides around the estate or to nearby Bridgnorth. Once she was playing the role of a bishop in a Victor Hugo play and he lent her his vestments so that she could look the part. 'We did so many plays over the years and I think he came to all of them when he was there. The house had a great trunk of old uniforms which we could use as costumes. It seems extraordinary now how much drama we undertook.'[29]

The plays everyone enjoyed most were the ones written by the girls. Joan Ackroyd wrote *The Wizard Who Wanted Power*, a modern fairytale inspired by the war. The wizard was of course

Hitler and all the princesses he stole were from the countries invaded, so Princess Holland, Belgium, France and Greece as well as Princess Poland and Czechoslovakia. The wizard was finally defeated by Prince England with the help of Fairy America. It was so successful that they were invited to play it in the village where they had a packed house and a rapturous reception. The plays at Aldenham took place in the library. Pelline explained: 'It was empty by then, all the books from the first Lord Acton having been sent to Cambridge, and I'm sure the building was not structurally safe but needs must during wartime. The girls were forbidden from going up into the gallery but they used the ground floor for their plays and it worked very well.'[30]

Ronald Knox took a weekly sixth-form class in which he read some of his old, humorous papers to the girls. *French with Tears*, was a favourite. He described the agony he felt when he was expected to chatter away in French, something he found distasteful in any language. Not for him small talk about the weather or flowers. The inner schoolboy came to the surface and worried over the correct declension or past participle. He explained his discomfort: 'If I were going out for a country walk with a Frenchman, I should find myself immediately wanting to express more sudden and arresting thoughts. I should want to say, for example, "That cow looks rather like a parson I know" – I am merely suggesting that by way of illustration.' This is followed by three minutes of constructing the sentence which ends in '*Cette vache-ci a l'air d'un ministre de religion de l'église d'Angleterre*'.[31] By which time, he admits wryly, the cow has now disappeared over the horizon with its companions. So he says nothing and the Frenchman thinks him profound and inscrutable. When out with a German the situation is completely different:

If we meet with a cow on our walk, a sudden idea occurs to me; I point at it, so that there can be no mistake, and say '*Kuh!*' I am not sure that it ought not to have a couple of dots on its back, but it works all right; he bursts into a roar of laughter ... Then he makes a great effort, and says something like 'cow'. I take both his hands in mine, and we stand there, the tears starting in our eyes at this evocation of our Indo-European origins. We are brothers – because I never learnt any German, or he any English, at school.[32]

The girls loved him not just for his humour and entertaining lessons, but for his holiness: 'He explained the action of the liturgy as they had never heard it explained before, but it was in participation in his Masses that their understanding flowered.'[33] Faine Meynell, another pupil, spoke of Ronald Knox as an inspiring teacher giving wonderful sermons: 'I've never really enjoyed one since,' she said matter-of-factly, seventy years later. 'He wrote one a week for us. The sermons spoke to us, the children, and we thought "he is preaching to *us*".'[34]. They were magical. We found him very shy and he appeared to want to avoid us but actually he knew everything about us.'[35] The nuns also appreciated his sermons: 'We all, nuns and children, look forward to Monsignor Knox's weekly sermons, in which he expresses irresistibly his acute observation of our foibles and joins deep spirituality with so much interesting knowledge.'[36]

While many of his sermons were focused on religious topics, he sometimes diverted and addressed issues of the day. In 1942 he gave a sermon called 'Sword of the Spirit' in which he celebrated a positive aspect of the war: toleration between peoples of different nations and classes, which was new in England. The sermon made a big impact on the girls, especially when he urged them to see that there was 'relapse into the old selfishness. Foreigners must still be *real* people for us.'[37]

Although he was a brilliant speaker, able to extemporise on any given subject, Ronald Knox never gave a sermon without notes. 'You would not know that he was speaking from notes,' Alannah Dowling said. 'He spoke naturally, fluently but thoughtfully and without rush'. He spoke in the clipped upper-class manner of the time but he radiated warmth rather than authority. It was through his strength of personality which shows through his sermons that he won the girls' attention. They were all aimed at their level without in any way appearing to be diluted for their benefit. After the war, the sermons were published in a series of books entitled *The Mass in Slow Motion*, *The Creed in Slow Motion* and *The Gospel in Slow Motion*.

The Mass in Slow Motion, dedicated to Nicola Macaskie, was the first series of sermons he delivered to the girls and he described the twelve different parts of the Mass, emphasising the importance of the actions as well as the words:

> The Christian faith has a religious dance of its own; all the twisting and turning, and bobbing and bowing, and lifting and parting and rejoining his hands, which the priest goes through in the course of the Mass, really add up to a kind of dance, meant to express a religious idea to you, the spectators.'[38]

He teased them: 'Of course that sounds nonsense to you, because what you mean by a dance is the wireless in the hall playing revolting stuff and you lounging around in pairs feeling all gooey.'[39] They knew exactly what he meant and that made them laugh out loud.

The sermons are a delightful mixture of history, theology, liturgy and humour. None of the girls had imagined they might enjoy his sermons, still less to laugh during them, but they relished them. Over the months and years he came to know them so well and to enter into the life of the school that he even managed to adopt their speech and alluded to their routine in his sermons. In an article in the school's annual magazine, the *Assumption Chronicle,* one of the nuns commented: 'One expects a schoolgirl to be excited over many things on returning to school after two terms' absence. Constance Webber declared that one of her reasons for being so excited was the prospect of hearing Mgr. Knox's Sunday sermons again.'[40] Another girl wrote: 'Half-terms are so popular that very few go home.'[41]

In an article for the *Chronicle* Knox described how they should answer Mass. He wrote that he once said Mass for an elderly lady who was stone deaf and 'accustomed to answer a priest who took about five minutes less to say Mass than I do. So it was a bit of a scramble.' But he encouraged the girls to learn to work with the priest:

> If two people are answering Mass together (as at Aldenham) the senior should go ahead as if she were answering alone, the junior should chime in as best she can. Don't wait for one another, or hustle one another. Above all, when you come to a difficult-looking word in the Latin, don't both think simultaneously, 'That looks a bit of a stinker; I'll leave it to Mary-Jane.' *Laetabitur* is pronounced like 'late arbiter', not like 'later bitter'; it is *confitAY-bor,* not *confittybor,* and *PeccARtis,* not *PECCotis.*[42]

Ronald was always prepared to be self-deprecating to make a point. In one of his sermons he described how he was the conduit between their prayers and the Almighty. He gave this visual image:

> When you see me standing up there mumbling to myself and apparently taking no notice of you, all dressed up in silk like a great pin-cushion, you mustn't think of me as something quite apart, at a distance from you, uninterested in your feelings and your concerns. On the contrary, I am standing there like a great pin-cushion for you to stick pins into me – all the things you want to pray about, all the things you want for yourself and all the worries that are going on at home, are part of the prayer that I am saying, and I couldn't prevent them being part of my intentions in saying the Mass, even if I wanted to.[43]

Aldenham was not all about the Mass or Father Knox's sermons. The girls were there to learn, though all of them I spoke to commented on the laid-back attitude towards the education they were supposed to receive. 'I don't think any of us did very much work!' Alannah Dowling said but the examination results do not bear this out. While the school did not turn out a full fist of Oxbridge candidates, several went to university while others joined the services. The studies were broad: with the help of the Lady Acton's library at Aldenham, which contained not only Shakespeare and Milton but also a full set of *Punch*, which was particularly popular, the girls benefitted from small class sizes and great diversity. Pelline remembered the nuns often gave commands in French '*Depechez vous!*' and '*Taisez vous!*' being the ones she recalled most clearly. She didn't like learning French but she felt desperately sorry for the French teacher who burst into tears when she learned of the fall of France.

The proximity of beautiful countryside and the formal gardens, including the Shore Pool, meant that there was plenty of opportunity for outdoor activities. Faine Meynell had a pony at the school and Alannah Dowling borrowed one from the Meynell family, which gave them both great pleasure. Jane Dowling remembered that some of the weekly boarders came with their ponies as well so that there was quite a string by 1941. The girls eventually had netball baskets on the tennis courts for winter use, which were then returned to their intended purpose in the summer. They played tennis, croquet, rounders and swam in the pool in warm weather and skated in the winter. The Aldenham Guide Company was formed in 1940, and the camping excursions, lessons in Morse code, patrol drill and first aid were popular. They took guiding seriously, as girls did all over the country. A skipping display was no light-hearted undertaking. It had to last exactly five minutes; 'we had been practising for weeks to perfect even the most difficult steps'[44] wrote Jane Ackroyd. One of the badges they aimed for was the war service badge which required ninety-six hours of voluntary war work within one calendar year, such as salvage collection, gardening or potato picking. Even though Aldenham was remote some of the girls succeeded in clocking up the hours.

Lady Acton, the leader of the First Aldenham Guide Company, accompanied Lady Baden-Powell on an inspection of the Guides at Bridgnorth in 1943. She wrote a very complimentary letter to Sister Dominic, praising the Guides for being smart and well coordinated but 'not Prussian officers, which unfortunately is the tendency of the efficient Guiders.'[45]

The first June of the war enjoyed record sunshine and temperatures. In the strange contrast that was the war, the evacuation of over 350,000 British, French and Allied troops from Dunkirk was underway while the girls were lounging on the grass at Aldenham, enjoying picnics by the pool on their recreation days or working in the kitchen gardens. They helped the gardeners and nuns in the vegetable patch and ran an active rabbit club. This began in an ad hoc way with pet rabbits, which were allowed on account of the large amount of space at Aldenham. They were fed on carrots and rolled oats although everyone knew that animals should not eat human food during the war. Sister Dominic soon followed the national drive to keep rabbits and thereafter they were entitled to bran rations as an official club. Monica Lawlor, a pupil, wrote in 1941: 'There are about twenty of all breeds and sizes. Pat Bartlett had great success with hers and some of the baby ones are destined for the pot.'[46] Sister Dominic explained in her official notes: 'Being an integral part of the Ministry of Agriculture and Fisheries' Scheme for increasing the food supply in wartime, we feel that the Report of the Aldenham School Rabbit Club should consist mainly in statistics. Breeding does eight; number of young rabbits potted thirty-nine, of which twenty-four in the summer term. Next year ... we have hopes of doing some trade in Chinchilla skins.'[47] The girls were in two minds about rabbit keeping. Marie-Anne Zarine wrote: 'our moments of distress, when our pets must go into the pot, are forgotten when we enjoy their chicken-like meat in Sister Placid's famous rabbit pies.'[48] By 1945 the rabbit club was closed and Dean Swift wrote an epitaph:

> For rabbits young and rabbits old,
> For rabbits hot and rabbits cold,
> For rabbits tender, rabbits tough,
> We thank Thee, Lord: we've had enough.

Lady Acton kept pigs, starting with a single piglet but raising her herd to one hundred. She dispensed with skirts and started wearing dungarees, still cutting a striking figure. The girls remember her as being tall and very beautiful. Jane Dowling described the scene outdoors at Aldenham once Lady Acton had got started: 'Pigs grovelled in the sties, the stables, the orchard, the bracken, and some of us learnt to feed them, and – which needs much greater skill – to catch the escaped ones.'[49] The pigs eventually had pens in the stable block and they were separated according to size – rather like the school girls, Pelline observed.

Ronald Knox tried to learn the vocabulary of pig husbandry and read to Lady Acton out loud in the evenings from pig-keeping manuals and papers from the government. This was a change from his former quiet time with her when they would read religious works to one another. It marked a slight shift in their relationship. Where she had once been his most assiduous and successful pupil, he was now her somewhat less successful student. Practical matters were not his forte and the girls would watch him following her around trying to help in the garden or with the pigs. He gave up picking fruit when a ladder he was standing on to pick damsons slipped and he fell, spraining his ankle, but he continued to enjoy slashing nettles according to Pelline. The girls, on the other hand, were enthusiastic gardeners and helped locally with haymaking in June and the potato harvest each September. This was backbreaking and often very hard work, especially if the crop contained a lot of rotten potatoes, as it did in 1941. That year they were rewarded for their work by Lady Acton who presented the complete works of Kipling to the library, which was a treasured addition.

Mr Rowe, the Actons' gardener, was in charge of the kitchen garden and produced abundant vegetables in season. The nuns wrote that he 'works marvels in the kitchen garden and never fails to give a helping hand in any emergency.'[50] He encouraged groups of girls to plant their own beds of salad or vegetables. The Guides had beds of lettuce which appeared in large quantities, while Susan Wood grew tomatoes and Violet Lucchesi Palli's garden produce became famous,

according to the *Assumption Chronicle*. Bazley was a favourite with
the girls as he could solve most of the practical problems in the house
and gardens. 'Run and ask Mr Bazley' was the invariable answer to
such complaints as 'the electricity has fused'; the 'water is cold'; 'my
rabbit's ill'; 'I have no hutch for my new guinea pig' or questions such
as 'is the pond safe for skating?'

On feast days they would hold dances, swaying to the 'revolting'
music from the radio that Ronald teased them about. The dances
were very popular as Lady Acton gave them a dressing-up trunk full
of old family uniforms so that some of them could attend as men.
On another feast day they had 'an exciting game invented by Sister
Dominic, British versus Nazis [which] kept us very busy. The park
and house were filled with fighters; prisoners of war were shut up
and guarded, and one, wilder than the rest, escaped by a sheet to the
garden.'[51]

Reading this chapter it is hard to believe there was a war on but
the Aldenham inhabitants were aware of what was happening in the
outside world. The news was relayed to the schoolgirls via the nuns
and in letters from home. Sometimes they learned of friends and
family who had lost their lives in the Blitz and on the battlefields.
There were always prayers in chapel for those caught up in the war
and Father Knox regularly referred to the war in his sermons. It was
a grim reminder of the Great War in which he had lost so many close
friends.

For the younger Acton children, their father's leave was the only
reminder of the war, about which they had no real understanding.
As Lord Acton was not allowed to sleep in the house, he and Daphne
would stay with the Bazleys and Ronald when he had leave, so that
the younger children rarely saw him even when he was at home. In
1944 they were staying with their grandparents at Terling Place and
could see London burning during the V2 attacks, which made an
impression on the boys in particular.

Rationing affected the household as it did everyone in the country
and, despite the valuable addition of fruit and vegetables from the
gardens, the wartime fare was described as revolting. Pelline hated

eating rabbit, 'it has that horrible, musky smell that doesn't go away. My mother shot rabbits and sold them to the butcher but we got some on our plates too.'[52] Nicola Macaskie recalled that 'the bread was always stale, so you did not eat too much. There was spam, pilchards in tomato sauce and corned beef with lumps of disgusting yellow fat. Our sweet rations were sent from home and that was a high point. The only thing we all loved was Assumption tart. This we had on feast days. It was a triangular puff pastry tart covered with jam and it was delicious.'[53]

After the food, what the girls remembered most was the cold. The main problem with the house was that it had not been designed for so many inhabitants. The boiler frequently broke down during the bitterly cold winter of 1940, and the overriding collective memory was of freezing basins and gutters, arctic conditions in the dormitories and classrooms and of frozen towels in the bathrooms. 'We had to scrape the ice off the inside of the windows in the dormitories – they were freezing the first winter of the war, though the rooms on the ground floor were kept slightly warmer.'[54] Everyone got chilblains and in the mornings there was an unseemly race to the one radiator at the bottom of the stairs. Alannah Dowling remembered how 'we would make a bee-line for that radiator, the only hot one I remember, but there was always a nun there first. My chilblains burst and I was not the only one. They were extremely painful.'[55]

The damp, cold conditions brought with them streaming colds and outbreaks of flu every year. Two girls developed German measles but the most serious illness was the streptococcal infection. Nicola Macaskie remembered the night when her sister Claudia nearly died: 'Lots of the girls were poorly. Dormitories became make-shift sick bays. Claudia and I slept in the pink room with two others. She had an abscess in her throat and one night she woke up with a massive haemorrhage. She stumbled around the room trying to find something to stay the bleeding and when it was light the next morning the room looked like a battlefield: blood everywhere.'[56] Claudia was taken down to the sanatorium and there a kindly but unwise nurse gave her a warm drink which caused another colossal bleed. The doctor was called and pronounced her fatally ill. Father Knox was summoned and gave Claudia the last rites, the only time he administered them in his life. Nicola was sent in to see her sister and later sat with Ronald, who tried to assure her that Claudia might not die. The twins' mother sent a specialist ear, nose and throat surgeon from Birmingham to Aldenham who was able to lance the abscess and Claudia slowly recovered. It was probably the most dramatic incident that occurred at Aldenham and it was the only one that unsettled Lady Acton and knocked her off her usual intrepid stride. She took the children to her parents' house, Terling Place near Chelmsford, where Pelline remembered being warm and well fed: such a welcome change from the freezing-cold house they had escaped from. On another occasion the boot was on the other foot. The Acton children developed whooping cough and if any of them went out of the nurseries and into the corridors they had to ring a large hand bell, known as the 'Leper's Bell', to warn all the others to hide out of the way so they would not become infected.

The only time the school was seriously short of food was during the freezing weather of early 1940. On 28 January, there was an ice storm which the novelist Virginia Woolf described in her diary: 'Everything glass glazed. Each blade is coated, has a rim of pure glass. Walking is like treading on stubble. The stiles and gates have a shiny, green varnish of ice.'[57] It was one of the most extreme weather events of the century. The country was paralysed as roads turned into skating rinks, railway points froze solid and thousands of telegraph poles collapsed. For the animal population it was often fatal. Wild ponies in North Wales became entombed in ice and birds in Kent died in flight when their wings locked solid. All the pipes at Aldenham seized up, both hot and cold, water in the sinks froze and the lavatories were out of order. It was the severest storm of the century and people all over the country found themselves in difficult situations. The roads to and from Bridgnorth, five miles away, were impassable so there were no deliveries for several days. The shortage of bread became a problem and Sister Dominic described how: 'Lady Acton and Mgr Knox trudged to Bridgnorth with a sledge and brought out fourteen loaves in a suitcase. The next day there was no meat, for the same reason. The milkman drove up in a steam tractor, which he also lent us when they delivered the coal for the furnace at the bottom of the drive, and the men couldn't get it up. The VIth form went and dug out the coal-cart before the tractor came.'[58]

For six years the school thrived at Aldenham. The peak of joy was the midnight picnic, a reward for the tidiest dormitories. 'Sister Margaret, Sister Clare and Sister Francoise Irene with Anne Cecilia Baring set off early and we had to follow clues which led us miles round the park in the dusk. We found them hidden in the bracken, with a delicious supper. Night fell and the glow-worms came out in their hundreds, and we were loath to go in on such a perfect night.[59]

Joan Ackroyd summed up her years at Aldenham in an essay for the *Assumption Chronicle* in 1944: 'I see how different the atmosphere of this school is from any other. We are given great freedom and we are trusted by the nuns, who in return demand absolute trustworthiness and loyalty from us. This immediately transforms the school into something more like home.'[60] In the friendly atmosphere of Aldenham the school coped despite the wartime shortages. The girls continued to put on plays, learn from the nuns and enjoy the vast library that continued to benefit from new editions of books, thanks to the generosity of Lady Acton.

And meanwhile, the great life-work of Father Knox progressed. It took him nine years to translate first the New and then the Old Testament. The NT was published in 1945, having been translated over the space of just three years. It was a remarkable achievement and one that few thought could possibly be achieved. The delay in publishing the work had little to do with wartime paper shortages and everything to do with interference and criticism from scholars, priests and lay people alike. He wrote in the introduction to *Trials of a Translator*:

If you translate the Bible, you are liable to be cross-examined by anybody; because everybody thinks he knows already what the Bible means. And the form which these questions take is a very interesting one; nearly always it is, 'Why did you alter such and such a passage?' Why did I alter it? When you say you are going to translate the Bible, why do people assume that you do not mean to do anything of the kind? They think you mean to revise the exist-ing translation, with parts of which we are all familiar; changing a word here and a word there, like a compositor correcting proofs with a pair of tweezers. The more you plagiarise from the work of previous interpreters, the better your public will be pleased.

That was not what he was aiming for, of course. He wanted to intro-duce a new translation that would be a fresh interpretation of the original source. You can sense his frustration when he wrote: '"*Etre ou ne pas être, c'est bien la la question*" is not Shakespeare's "To be or not to be ...'"

The Knox Bible is still regarded by some academics, not least former Archbishop of Canterbury Rowan Williams, as one of the finest scholarly literary translations of the Old and New Testaments. It is little used nowadays, except of course by his former pupils at Aldenham, most of whom still own an original signed copy from 'Mr Translator'. It made a significant difference to the Church's finances, bringing in more than £50,000 in the first decade after its publication, about £3.6 million in today's money.

The war drew to its end and life at Aldenham was about to change once again. VE Days were celebrated by Victory Games in the rec-reation room and picnics for each form in a different room as the weather was miserable. The sixth form wrote up the account: 'We spent all Monday in anxious waiting for the radio announcement of peace, and by 9pm when peace and the two VE holidays were proclaimed our pent-up excitement broke out in prolonged cheers. Flags of all nations suddenly appeared from all the windows.'[61] The fifth form's play was entitled *What Really Happened to Hitler*. He was discovered to be hiding in the convent, disguised as a nun and was converted by the girls into an honest house painter. They played cricket and had an enormous bonfire on the school field. It was a last hurrah for the Assumption nuns and girls at Aldenham. The school had to leave and move to another house, Exton Hall in Rutland, as the buildings in Kensington Square were designated to be a new teacher-training college and the Acton family needed Aldenham Park for their own private use.

The Convent of the Religious of the Assumption's stay at Aldenham had secured the school for the future and given its pupils a far broader education than if they had remained in London. Neither the nuns nor the girls were in any doubt of that. Pelline, who had lived for half her life surrounded by the sisters and pupils, remembers what an enormous change it was for her when the school left Aldenham: 'The house was quieter now. I remember how loud the girls' footsteps were on the uncarpeted stairs and that was all gone. The rooms were returned to their former functions, our cousins moved in and a new chapter in our lives began.'[62]

Blenheim, the only non-royal stately home in Britain designated a palace, accommodated 500 boys and staff from Malvern College in 1939–40.

CHAPTER 4

Twice Removed

We arrived next day at School House, to find the doors wide open, and the house being inspected by bowler-hatted officials of the Ministry of Works, who were already giving instructions for work to be carried out. As yet war had not been declared, though Poland had been invaded, and no requisition order had been served.

H. C. A. Gaunt, headmaster of Malvern College,
1 September 1939

On 26 December 1938 an envelope marked 'Secret & Confidential' plopped onto the desk of the Reverend Canon Howard Charles Adie 'Tom' Gaunt, headmaster of Malvern College. In those days letters were delivered 365 days a year but with two rather than three deliveries on Christmas Day and Easter Sunday. It was scooped up and brought to him on a tray with the rest of his post. He explained in his memoir *Two Exiles*:

Following the admirable example of my predecessor, Mr F.S. Preston, I was accustomed in those palmy days of peace to have my correspondence delivered to me together with a cup of tea in my bedroom: a quick glance at the letters followed by a few moments of reflection during the morning toilet often saved valuable time a little later in the day. On Boxing Day the 26th December, 1938, among a number of envelopes containing Christmas cards one letter stood out among the rest. It was pale bluish grey, was marked on the outside 'Secret & Confidential', and bore the crest of His Majesty's Office of Works on the back of the envelope. Speculating rapidly on what single honour I was about to be asked to accept, I slit open the envelope. Inside was a second sealed envelope, this time marked 'SECRET To be opened only by HCA Gaunt Esq, MA, Headmaster of Malvern College'. I complied.[1]

The communication was not notification of a New Year's honour, but a letter from Sir Patrick Duff, a permanent secretary at the Office of Works, informing Gaunt that the government had 'under consideration the question of earmarking a number of large buildings outside London for national purposes in the event of war, and I am afraid it is my ungrateful duty to let you know that Malvern College is one of those so earmarked.'[2]

When government departments were contemplating moves out of London, one of the most popular places in the country was the beautiful spa town of Great Malvern. It is in an area of outstanding beauty, nestled below the Malvern Hills, and for the past two centuries at least has been a popular tourist destination thanks to its particularly fine natural water with its health benefits. The Ministry of Information took over the luxurious Abbey Hotel to house part of its staff while the Board of Trade decided upon the Girls' College as its initial wartime billet. Such was the obsession with secrecy within the civil service in the early months of the war that all correspondence had to be sent via London, to prevent any section of one department knowing the location of any other. This could mean that two offices of the same ministry might be housed in adjacent buildings but could not correspond directly with one another. 'When "Lord Haw-Haw" [William Joyce, Nazi propaganda broadcaster]

helpfully announced a full list of addresses of evacuated government departments, there was a collective sigh of relief from the civil
servants concerned, as the previous restrictions were listed,'[3] wrote
Norman Longmate in *How We Lived Then*.

Absolute secrecy was exactly what the government asked headmasters and headmistresses of public schools to maintain when they
broached the subject of requisitioning. Unsurprisingly, large public
schools in safe areas with their extensive accommodation were targeted by the Office of Works from early on. Moving government
departments out of London meant there was an appetite for buildings designed to accommodate large numbers of people, furniture
and equipment. Few buildings were as well set up for this purpose
as a school, especially one in a town such as Malvern that had
tourists all year round, which meant there was also plenty of other
local accommodation available. Some schools, like Marlborough
College in Wiltshire, were simply asked to 'double up'. They shared
their premises and facilities with the City of London School, while
Shrewsbury accommodated boys from Cheltenham College for two
terms. Others were not so fortunate. Malvern College had a particularly difficult time in both 1939 and 1942.

The college, sited in the hills above the town, occupied a large
sloping site of some 250 acres. Canon Gaunt received his Boxing Day
letter because the Admiralty had earmarked the school as a headquarters in the event of an emergency evacuation from London. The
town was in a designated safe area as it was thought that the Malvern
Hills – which run some nine miles north to south and are around
600 million years old – would act as a deterrent to low-level bombing. There was ample accommodation for civil servants and military
personnel in the town's hotels and boarding houses. It also had the
advantage of being close to other relocated ministries – though it does
seem a little ironic that the Admiralty should be housed almost as far
away from the sea as it is possible to be in Britain.

By the standards of British public schools, Malvern College was
relatively young. It had been founded by local businessmen in 1865
after the expansion of the railways and the prominence of Malvern

as a spa town. The population of the town rose from 819 in 1801 to 2,768 forty years later and by the middle of the century Malvern town was receiving over 3,000 visitors a year. The originator of the idea for the College was Walter Burrow, the manager of the Malvern Branch of Messrs Lea & Perrins of Worcester. It was in Burrow's dispensary that the formula for the famous sauce was developed. Two dozen boys and six masters in two houses soon expanded to six school houses and nearly 300 boys. Within twenty-five years, the school had over 500 boys occupying the magnificent main building which dominates the school's campus, Big School. Canon Gaunt became Malvern's seventh headmaster in 1937 at the age of thirty-five, taking over from the previous headmaster who had been in post for a quarter of a century. Gaunt had many plans for the school but moving out was not one of them.

The morning he received the letter, Gaunt sought permission from Sir Patrick Duff to speak to the chairman and vice-chairman of the College Council and to his second master of the staff, Major Elliott. This was granted but the need for secrecy was impressed upon him at every possible opportunity. It 'was a most serious hindrance, but it was of the highest importance to the Government, first that it should not be known that plans were being made at all, since war might not break out, and secondly that the nature of the plans should not be known, if it did.'[4] This placed him, as it did other headmasters and mistresses who received the same news, in the unenviable position of having to continue to run the school as if everything were normal while at the same time engineering visits to possible sites for the future. Secrecy was just as important from the school's point of view as revelations of this nature would make prospective parents unlikely to choose Malvern for their boys. Although a public school might seem of lesser importance than government offices in a time of war, everyone in the Department of Education and heads of schools realised the vital importance of education for the future of the country. It was not possible for a generation of children to be cut adrift: the country needed investment in the future.

Sixth formers from public schools in 1939–40 would be the junior officers, the scientists, the doctors and nurses of the next few years, not to speak of the lawyers, architects, journalists, bankers and farmers. To deprive them and the country of high-quality teaching would be disastrous, the department insisted.

At first Gaunt decided they should focus their search to the west, in Wales. Major Elliott was a keen fisherman, so it was perfectly natural for him to pack his fishing tackle into the back of his car and head off on a Friday. Some masters thought Gaunt was being a little indulgent, but nobody seriously questioned why his second-in-command was given so many opportunities to pursue his hobby in term time.

The search proved to be far more difficult than anyone had anticipated. Schools have very particular requirements which cannot easily be fulfilled by simply moving everyone and everything into a large home, hotel or camp. In addition to dormitory and kitchen requirements, there was a need for classrooms, laboratories, sports facilities and accommodation for the staff. Elliott found that hotel owners were expecting an influx of wealthy clients who would pay higher than normal rates to stay in safety away from the bombing so it would be unlikely the school could get a whole building to themselves.

By April 1939 they had still failed to find anywhere, so Gaunt and the vice-chairman of the school's governors, Mr Richardson, went to London to see Sir Patrick Duff and express their concerns about the lack of facilities and the lack of support from the Office of Works. Gaunt threatened to mention it to his MP, which ruffled the feathers of the otherwise very pleasant civil servant. They were preparing to leave the meeting, beaten and thoroughly down, when Sir Patrick mentioned somewhat casually that he had that very morning received a letter from the Duke of Marlborough offering Blenheim Palace but assumed 'it would not be large enough for what you want.'[5] Gaunt and Richardson exchanged glances and decided on the spot that it was worth making a diversion via Woodstock on the way back to Malvern. Sir Patrick telephoned the duke and an hour and a half later Gaunt heard that he was welcome to visit him the following day. 'The day was brilliantly fine, and Blenheim

Palace looked magnificent with its great façade of golden stone and the green spreading lawn on the south side.'[6]

The Duke and Duchess of Marlborough must have been relieved to think they would be potentially housing a school, which would mean they could have some influence over how the palace was to be used rather than having to hand over Blenheim to a ministry. They were gracious and hospitable as they showed Gaunt round the great palace and its enormous grounds. The size was impressive but would it be big enough to keep 400 boys washed, fed, slept and educated? Time was of the essence. It was clear that someone else would snap up the opportunity to take on such large premises as Blenheim and Gaunt had little choice but to make the decision. 'I was vividly aware of the grave deficiences in the buildings as they stood, and the appalling problems of dislocation and organisation which would have to be faced: but I felt that the moment for decision had arrived.'[7] He told the duke that he would be very grateful for the security of Blenheim as a temporary home for his school if war were to break out. He wrote later that the Marlboroughs were refreshingly welcoming after the provincial greed of the hoteliers they had been dealing with in Wales. A fair rent would have to be agreed but 'there is all the difference between a high profit and a fair return.'[8]

Over the next few months, Gaunt wrote to the duke on a number of matters so that he and Major Elliott were able to start making general plans as soon as the summer holidays began to move the college to the palace at Blenheim in the event of war. It was planning only, however, as Gaunt explained:

> Of course, we could not commit the College to heavy expenditure which might prove to be wholly unnecessary; and the Government, though it might have powers to requisition buildings for its own needs, had no power to requisition for the needs of others, and never has had. In fact the Government at this time had no powers of requisition at all, for although the necessary Act of Parliament was already framed, it was not actually passed into Law until September.[9]

The Duke of Marlborough's daughter, Lady Sarah Spencer-Churchill, turned eighteen in June and the duke threw a magnificent ball, 'perhaps the last great European ball' one commentator mused. A thousand people were invited and catered for by the palace kitchen and dining-room staff. That gave Gaunt the reassurance that he was not trying to attempt the impossible by believing the kitchens could cope with large numbers of hungry mouths to feed. The duke offered to leave the extensive equipment he had installed in the kitchens for the event and that really helped to boost the catering capabilities of the palace.

Gaunt wrote later that had the war broken out in the summer he would have happily housed the school under canvas at Blenheim while arrangements were made to prepare the palace for accommodation but this would not have been ideal in the winter. 'I do not mean that boys – certainly the senior boys – could not have existed quite happily under canvas even in winter: certainly many of them had to do so in the Services not very much later.'[10] War was declared on Sunday 3 September but by Tuesday the school had heard nothing, although people in Malvern whispered openly about the college being requisitioned. 'This was exasperating to the point of despair!'[11] Gaunt wrote. Those public schools who would have their buildings requisitioned were due to find out on 7 September but Gaunt did not hear formally until 2:45pm the following day. From that moment the planning began in earnest. Major Elliott was given the 'stupendous task of fashioning and installing the necessary equipment in the Palace and outside, and of making the place ready for the school to reassemble at the beginning of the new term which was to start on September 28th.'[12] This was clearly impossible to complete in three weeks so term was delayed until 12 October.

The day after the order was received, Gaunt wrote to the parents of boys who would be attending Malvern for the academic year:

I regret to have to tell you that His Majesty's Government have informed me that the houses and buildings of Malvern College will be required almost immediately for war purposes. Fortunately the government gave me warning of this probability sometime ago, and we have been able to make our plans in good time. I may add hitherto I have been bound by the government to the strictest security. The college will reassemble at Blenheim Palace, Woodstock, the seat of His Grace the Duke of Marlborough. The palace is large enough to house the entire School and many of the staff, and the facilities contained in the magnificent buildings and grounds will make it possible for all normal school activities to be continued. The Estate contains its own farm and vegetable gardens, which will supply the school. The State rooms are being converted into dormitories and classrooms, and the school will feed together in the Great Hall. At the same time the house units will be kept, and all boys will be under the care and supervision of their present Housemasters. Woodstock itself is in the heart of the country in a reception area (i.e. for evacuees) while the palace itself contains admirable shelter against air raids.[13]

The letter was intended to reassure parents and it worked. Only six families decided to withdraw their boys from the college. All the others felt the move to Blenheim was sensible and that the plans Gaunt had put in place were satisfactory. He asked parents only to write to him from thenceforth on matters of great urgency as a 'heavy task' confronted him and the Malvern staff in getting furniture, musical instruments – including twenty pianos – and books to Blenheim in time for the delayed start of term. A heavy task was no understatement. The great palace had plenty of space and was ideally suited to accommodate the numbers but it did not have the infrastructure to cope with the day-to-day running of the school. All this had to be thought through, planned, initiated and completed in the space of five weeks.

The then Duke of Marlborough was John Spencer-Churchill, the tenth duke. He was married to Alexandra Mary Cadogan and by 1939 they had three daughters and one son, John 'Sunny' Spencer-Churchill, who would go on to inherit the title from his father in 1974. The duke decided to remain at Blenheim with his wife and daughters, moving into the east wing and offering the rest of the palace to the college.

Blenheim Palace has been the seat of the Duke of Marlborough since the early eighteenth century. It was 'an epic gift of the nation to John Churchill, first Duke of Marlborough, whose victories over France and the subsequent Treaty of Utrecht in 1713 firmly established Britain as the pre-eminent great power, a leading position held until 1942.'[14] The architect of Blenheim was Sir John Vanbrugh. His great palace, designed in 1705, had gone through many stages of building and refurbishment as the vicissitudes of life under the various dukes waxed and waned. But by 1939 it was in excellent condition thanks to two marriages to wealthy American heiresses. As the work began to turn the Great Hall into the school dining room and the Long Library and state rooms into dormitories, historian Christopher Hussey, writing in *Country Life* in 1940, mused that its conversion to accommodate such a large number of boys 'certainly had not been visualised by Blenheim's architect. Yet Vanbrugh's ghost must have chuckled with delight in having his belief at last confirmed that Blenheim is not an inch too big.'[15]

The men undertaking the removal of school equipment from Malvern to Blenheim were organised by the Office of Works and lorries began arriving on 14 September with their cargoes. On the one hand this was good, as Gaunt did not have to worry about negotiating the transport, but on the other hand he and Elliott had no control over how the furniture and school treasures were handled or when they would be delivered to the palace. 'We had to be ready at all hours of the day to direct the contents as they arrived at the Palace steps to their proper destination, and the final blow came when on the second day the men announced that they had received orders to dump the vanloads on the steps and return to Malvern with the utmost speed.'[16] This meant that the contents of fifty-five vanloads had to be carried by the staff to their final locations. As the state rooms were not yet ready to take the school's furniture, everything had to be stored temporarily on the terrace, apart from items such as books which were piled up in the Great Hall. Fortunately that September Blenheim basked in warm, dry weather and the possessions stacked on the terrace came to no harm.

The duke watched over the conversion of the palace into a school with anxiety. It proved too difficult to move some of the art treasures in time, so he decided that the magnificent tapestries and the paintings should remain on the walls but must be protected. He told Gaunt that he was concerned that boys might be tempted to use the portraits of his ancestors as dartboards. The staff laid down very strict rules of behaviour and these were assiduously monitored, which succeeded in instilling respect in the boys for the glories of the palace. Gaunt wrote later, 'The Long Library alone contained, I suppose, over a thousand panes of eighteenth century bevelled glass. Two of these panes were broken during our stay, and both accidentally.'[17]

Screens of Essex board were fixed with battens around the walls, but not a nail could be driven into the walls or floors of the palace. Essex board is light, being made of layers of strips of paper, but strong enough to withstand wear and tear, with the added advantage that it does not bow in humid conditions. It can be cut with a saw or knife and does not produce rough edges, so it was the ideal material for the task. Hundreds of sheets of Essex board were required and the Office of Works helped to supply the palace with enough to cover the art works sufficiently to a height of eight feet. The damask curtains were sheathed in canvas covers that made them look like huge, hanging ghosts and felt padding was fixed to the mahogany doors to preserve the carved mouldings. It is difficult to make sense of the amount of material required to protect Blenheim Palace: 1,400 square yards of linoleum was needed to cover the floors and a further 1,000 square yards of matting. Taken together this would be enough material to cover half a football pitch. It took a lot of effort to get it into shape for the invasion of four hundred teenage boys.

One of these was James Roy, a seventeen-year-old Malvern College pupil who would go on to join the Royal Artillery, seeing active service in northern Europe, Egypt and Palestine. He attained the rank of captain by the age of twenty-two. For now he was about to enter his final year of school and wrote to his mother from Blenheim that he was sleeping in a dormitory with twenty other boys which was in fact a picture gallery. 'No ink is allowed so I am writing outside.' He described his journey to Woodstock by train and his delight at the beautiful grounds, ending: 'the address is No. 8 Malvern College, at Blenheim Palace.'[18]

The following week he wrote again, giving her a more detailed picture of life at the palace:

> All the state rooms on the ground floor are dormitories and the rooms upstairs are classrooms, which are 'house' rooms when not in use. There are not enough desks for the whole house. There is nowhere to put any clothes except in the trunks under the beds. The beds are 1'6" apart at the sides and nothing at the ends. A changing room has been made in a courtyard and the wash downs are in the cellars. A place for coats has also been constructed. We have to make our own beds and clean our own shoes [at Malvern, maids did the former and a boot boy (mature) did the latter]. We have to wash in shifts both morning and night. Sixty lavatories have been made in a large wooden shed.[19]

The kitchens, even with the extra ovens provided for the great feast in June, could not cope with the requirement to feed the school three meals a day. Additional cookers and steam ovens had to be acquired as well as extra sinks, shelves, plate racks and other kitchen equipment. This was not easy as the whole of Oxfordshire was in a state of upheaval thanks to the influx of over 37,000 evacuees, all with competing requirements. A further problem was that the ranges were run on petrol gas which soon became unobtainable as petrol was the first commodity to be rationed in the war. There was nothing for it but to lay a new gas main from Woodstock to the palace. 'A gang of masters heroically set to work with picks and spades to dig a trench, half a mile long, in the Blenheim limestone, and were not sorry when a pneumatic drill arrived to take over.'[20] The four-inch gas main took just three days to install. While the cooking facilities were being expanded and improved, new boilers were put in to heat the water in the temporary shower rooms set up in one of the internal courtyards. Another courtyard housed a changing room built out of wood and lined with the all-purpose Essex board, fitted out with seats, shelves and clothes racks sufficient to cater for the sports clothes of the entire school. Further huts, sixteen in total, were constructed to act as school rooms, reading rooms and recreation rooms for the boys, fitted with gas radiators and lamps. At Malvern, the boys had been used to eating their meals in their houses as there was no school refectory. At Blenheim this changed with all boys and masters eating together for the first time in the college's history.

A further requirement at Blenheim was the need to black out the entire palace. Nobody knew exactly how many windows Blenheim had but as there are 187 rooms in the main part of the palace it can reasonably be assumed there would be hundreds. In 1886, the eighth Duke of Marlborough was asked how many rooms he had and he replied: 'I am not sure but I know I paid a bill this spring for painting a thousand windows.'[21] He may have been exaggerating for effect but the task of covering every window where light might leak out was colossal. The state rooms all had heavy eighteenth-century shutters which were adequate to conceal the light from within, but the Great Hall and library needed to be blacked out as well as smaller windows in a multitude of rooms. Blackout material was supplied by the Office of Works and had to be stitched and sewn by an army of matrons and needlewomen from Woodstock in order to render Blenheim 'properly opaque' by the beginning of term.

While the palace was being overlaid with this armature of protection, the grounds were quickly converted into kitchen gardens and sports pitches. One boy wrote to his father in delight to tell him that 'we play football on cultured lawns'. Cultured they may have been, but Blenheim is built on solid rock and it took hours of work with crow bars and pick axes to plant the goal posts in front of the palace. The boys did PE in the main courtyard and often took their lessons out of doors when the weather was fine.

The press was interested in the new occupants of the palace and a photographer from *The Times* arrived on a blustery day to take pictures. The following day Gaunt and his staff were horrified to see two photographs of boys 'enduring intolerable conditions'. One picture showed a group of twenty boys sitting at desks in the open in a howling gale. The truth was that these boys, who had been on break and were aware of the photographers around the palace, saw the empty desks and thought it would be fun to sit at them and pretend this was where they were being taught. It caused mayhem for Gaunt who received a slew of letters, 'though not as many as I had feared' from anxious parents.

Gaunt was the first to admit that there were drawbacks at Blenheim: 'After all you cannot uproot people from a happy life and a home as beautiful as Malvern, and wrench them from cherished traditions and secure foundations, without considerable distress, discomfort and dislocation.'[22] Blenheim Palace was new to them all, pupils and staff alike. The familiar nooks and crannies of Malvern's school houses were replaced with endless corridors, labyrinthine basements and the Great Hall in which the whole school dined together. There were moments of despair, Gaunt wrote, when things went wrong and decisions that might have worked well in Malvern felt wrong in the vastness of Blenheim's palatial rooms. Forced out of the familiarity of its own school buildings, the boys and staff struggled in the first few weeks to maintain its sense of community. The older boys were determined to maintain the dozens of college traditions in order to cling to their school's character. In a new environment these seemed anomalous to the new boys who, homesick and cold, stared in disbelief as they were punished for minor infringements such as which hand they could have in which pocket when walking past a prefect.

However, the boys were, on the whole, very positive about their experiences in the early months of the war. Letters home described their pleasure in the magnificent surroundings. The school catalogued their stay in an album of beautiful black and white photographs which show the boys wandering around the gardens, reading on the lawns and sitting on their beds in the dormitories beneath the tapestries and paintings. Christopher Hussey summed up the conversion of Blenheim Palace in his *Country Life* article in 1940:

> Blenheim's history is built on battles … It was therefore in the Blenheim tradition that the latest episode in its history should have war as its background and determining cause, and surely the way in which this lightning campaign was conducted, undertaken by volunteer forces and fought against time, will ensure for it its own particular little place in Blenheim's annals.[23]

By the end of October 1939 life had settled down into something approaching normal school routine. Every possible outbuilding had been refashioned to service the school. The laundry was converted into physics and biology laboratories, although the boys went into Oxford by bus to use the university labs for chemistry lessons. The riding school became an assembly hall for concerts and entertainments as well as doubling as a gymnasium. The Church of St Mary Magdalene in Woodstock, a short walk from the palace of which it was a benefice, became the school chapel for the duration. It must have been a tight squeeze to fit the whole school into the church because the current seating capacity is about 250. Gaunt wrote that the Reverend Pickles was very generous and accommodating of the school which often held its own private services. 'But, we usually attended Morning Service on Sundays with the rest of the village, and contributed something in the way of singing. On one occasion the whole school sang as an anthem the "Hallelujah Chorus" – unaccompanied, as the organ failed at the critical moment.'[24]

James Roy appreciated the fine works of art at Blenheim Palace. He told his mother 'I sleep next to a £25,000 picture and there is also a £20,000 picture in the room.'[25] The picture James slept next to was a Marlborough family portrait painted by Sir Joshua Reynolds in 1777–8 for the fourth duke, and it still hangs in the palace today. It shows the famous Blenheim spaniels and the duke and duchess with their six children. The other painting in James Roy's bedroom was covered up by a sheet but he believed it to be by Gainsborough.

The editor of the December edition of the school magazine, *The Malvernian*, collected a series of first impressions from boys. One spoke of 'the first glimpse of the beech-girt lake, grey-blue in the early sunlight, its waveless surface gently veined by the fussy paddling of myriad coots', while another had enjoyed 'those quiet half-hours construing Sophocles astride a leaden sphinx amid the sunlit plashings and green formality of the lower terrace.' But the war was never far from the boys' and their teachers' minds. The editor wrote of 'using those powers of imagination credited nowadays to the military, to pretend, for OTC [Officer Training Corps] purposes, that the lake is the Upper Rhine and the palace a pill-box.'[26]

Each house – there were eight at Malvern at the time – had a hut which was used for relaxation and socialising after lessons were over. These were soon kitted out by the boys to be comfortable and personal, something that was impossible in their tightly packed dormitories. James Roy asked his mother to send his wireless and gave her strict instructions about how to pack it so that it would not be damaged in transit. It arrived the following week and gave good service to the hut, though it broke down all too frequently. The only shortage at this stage was bath huts. Each boy could have a bath once a fortnight and even morning ablutions had to be done in relays as there were so few sinks. The Office of Works was obliged to do something about the lack of washing facilities and by January 1940 there was a second hut with twenty baths, which was deemed adequate for 400 boys.

Living in the east wing of the house, the Marlborough family watched the school get organised over the autumn. The duke took an interest in the running of the school, and would invite the head of school and other senior boys occasionally to have supper with his family on Sunday evenings, as he liked his daughters, aged eighteen, sixteen and ten, to meet young men. These evening meals were a duty for some boys and a delight for others but always an amusement for the duke who enjoyed the company of the young men and would quiz them on what they had managed to discover about the palace during their stay. He was generous and enjoyed their enthusiasm. On one occasion he told them they could use the fine model railway in the orangery if they could get it going again. Predictably this was a popular challenge and the boys had fixed it in no time.

The winter of 1939–40 was bitterly cold with temperatures several degrees below the seasonal average and lows of -15°C not uncommon, making it the coldest British winter for fifty years and the coldest January in Oxfordshire for a century. The Great Lake at Blenheim froze with ice a foot thick and the boys were allowed to skate on it. 'The townsfolk skate on the ice, the Woodstock side of the Grand Bridge, we skate on the other,'[27] James Roy told his mother. The following week the ice was still a foot thick and it had snowed copiously, producing drifts of three to four metres in places, causing severe transport disruption. Despite the freezing tempera- tures, the sun shone and the boys made the most of the bright, white days. 'We had a terrific inter-house snowball match on skates, which was an extremely good pastime,'[28] James Roy wrote.

The cold weather took its toll, as it had done at Aldenham, and in the unheated school huts the boys went down with colds and flu with alarming speed. By the end of January, 146 boys were ill, so the Long Library had to be converted into a sick bay, mirroring the use the palace had been put to in the First World War when it was used as a military hospital for sick and injured servicemen. The boys who had been sleeping in the Long Library were moved to huts in the courtyard with disastrous results. Snow lay three inches deep all over the grounds and the cold air seeped up through the temporary structure and into their beds. The following week there were 170 in the sick bay. Four members of staff and several boys succumbed to pneumonia. Luckily the school physician, Dr Elkington, had access to the then new wonder-drug, M&B 693, a precursor of penicillin, which saved the lives of several boys and the school was able to emerge from the scare without loss of life, something that would have been unlikely even a few years earlier.

James Roy was sent to sleep in the duke's riding school, which was warm, light and had plenty of room so he managed to escape the flu. The biggest complaints the boys had besides the flu were chilblains. The sharp pain of blisters on toes, fingers, noses and ears is described in many letters home. The cure, they knew, was to avoid further exposure to the cold but that was almost impossible in the unheated classrooms and changing huts at Blenheim. 'Boys came into morning school wrapped in coats and rugs, to find that icicles had formed under the corrugated iron roofs during the night. As the temperature slowly rose, they melted and dripped onto the forms below.'[29]

Over all this period, the war had been merely a background rumble to the life of the school with the reminder of it only during Officer Training Corps practice or in chapel. The period from September 1939 to the spring of 1940, known as the Phoney War, had lulled many people into a false sense of security. In March, Gaunt wrote to the parents announcing the welcome news that the Admiralty had had time to build and equip vast underground shelters in London as well as a mass of hutments in Malvern, which would mean that the college could occupy its own school buildings from September.

During April the Germans invaded Denmark and Norway. The unnatural calm had been broken and the power of the Nazi aggression against the countries of western Europe was witnessed by British and Polish forces in Norway. On 10 May the Germans launched the Blitzkrieg against France, Belgium and neutral Holland. The British Expeditionary Force, which had been guarding the Maginot line, was rudely awoken by the monstrous German war machine that lurched towards them, creating panic among the civilian population. At home in Woodstock life too changed gear. Headmaster Tom Gaunt wrote to the parents of all boys over the age of seventeen announcing that they would be expected to undertake Local Defence Volunteer duties. He needed parental permission as the boys were underage. James Roy wrote to his mother asking her to return the form, duly signed, adding 'there will be a row if you do not agree.'[30]

One of the masters took on the task of giving the boys some extra tuition in the art of defensive warfare: 'under Mr Nokes' tutelage, we made Molotov cocktails in a quarry area in the north-east end of the lake. The wine bottles were filled with 1/3rd tar or bitumen, 1/3rd paraffin and 1/3rd petrol. Cotton waste was wired around the base of the bottle and ignited before it was thrown. As a reward for our efforts we were allowed to test the odd cocktail to destruction against the quarry face.'[31]

Stephen Brown, who was then in his first term at Malvern with his twin brother Peter, remembered an occasion at Blenheim that still makes him laugh. 'There were wild rumours circulating all over Britain that German soldiers were parachuting into Holland disguised as nuns. We had a scare one evening at Blenheim and the OTC was called into action and sent out on patrol to locate the parachutists. It turned out to be a hoax but it showed how jittery everyone had become since the Germans had set their eyes on the west.'[32]

Gaunt was only too aware of the war in the background. He wrote:

Day after day the sun streamed down upon the golden landscape of Oxfordshire, wild flowers and birds abounded in the Park, the gardens and shady nooks of the Palace grounds provided refresh-ing retreats, and the sound of cricket floated from the Great Lawn ... Elsewhere, however, more significant events were taking shape ... Night by night, almost hour by hour, we listened to the grim catalogue of events in the Great Hall, in House huts, in dor-mitories and in the open air. The voice of Mr Churchill sounded only too clearly the peril with which we were now faced.[33]

The summer of 1940 was as glorious as the winter had been freezing cold. The Met Office's summary was as warm as the weather: 'June 1940 will long be remembered for abundant sunshine and unusual warmth; it was also markedly dry.'[34] In Oxford, the mean maximum temperature was the highest for the month since 1881 with over 100 hours of sunshine in the first week. The school boys made the most of the weather, bathing in the ornamental pools and swimming in the lake. Years later, James Roy described an expedition that he and two others undertook:

> Another episode concerns the Grand Bridge designed by Vanbrugh to cross a precipitous valley through which trickled the Glyme stream and its tributaries and built between 1705 and 1722, supposedly there were 33 rooms in it. However in 1764 Lancelot Brown (Capability) built a dam to flood the valley and all the ground floor rooms were flooded with the result that the visible height of the bridge is now a great deal less than Vanbrugh intended. We were convinced that there was an underground passage from the cellars to the palace due north to the bridge, partly I think because there were some manhole covers on the line of the suspected tunnel. Very early one morning, I think three of us, attempted to swim out to the nearest buttress of the bridge containing two floors of rooms, starting from the south-east bank of the lake. Whether we were beaten by the temperature of the water or by the distance being greater than we thought, the attempt was a failure.'[35]

Life at Blenheim continued to be enjoyed by most of the boys over the last few weeks of the summer term, though all were aware of the contrast between the grim events on the continent and one of the most beautiful summers of the century. 'Cricket on the Great Lawn and swimming in the lake all took place under the same blue sky out of which, in France, the Stukas were swooping on columns of refugees. Even more incongruous it must have been at this moment of crisis in the nation's affairs, the school could return to its home in Malvern.'[36]

In early June a complete Canadian Armoured Division arrived and set up camp. The Canadians had declared war on Germany a week after Britain and they offered military support as they had done in the First World War, when 425,000 men had served. By late

December 1939, the 1st Canadian Division had begun to arrive in Britain and almost 330,000 Canadians passed through Aldershot camp where they were sent for training. 'In twenty-four hours the Park was festooned with camouflage nets over guns, anti-aircraft batteries, armoured cars, lorries and tanks; while vast spaces were covered with the tents, kitchens, stores and military equipment of six thousand men.'[37] The older boys were in their element and excited by the presence of real soldiers. Tom Gaunt wrote: 'For ten days this occupation lasted, during which time we entertained some five hundred men to a great open-air concert on the Palace steps, and a number of boys learned to play baseball. Then one evening the division began packing up, and by early morning the men were gone, leaving behind them hardly a trace of their invasion!'[38] Stephen Brown disagreed. He thought the Canadians had left plenty of evidence of their presence. 'They took Woodstock apart. The Bear [Woodstock's most famous inn] saw the worst of it.'[39]

At the end of the summer term the school began to pack up and the boys were sent to a camp in Worcestershire to support the war effort by helping with the harvest. It would be known as the Malvern College Harvest Camp at Oxstalls Farm at Evesham where the boys picked fruit for local farmers and were paid for their work. Once again, Gaunt wrote to the parents, this time to explain that the work was arranged under the supervision of the Evesham War Executive Agricultural Committee 'and is an important form of National Service'.[40] James Roy left Blenheim Palace for Evesham in early July. It was his last term of school and he would go on to study natural sciences at Sydney Sussex College, Cambridge for a year before joining the Royal Artillery.

The removal of Malvern College from Blenheim was managed with the same energy and organisation as it had been for the arrival in September the previous year. Lines of trucks drove into the great courtyard to collect beds, pianos, desks and chairs, books and sports equipment and take it back to Malvern ready to reopen the school at the beginning of September.

Blenheim was not to remain unoccupied for long. The Battle of Britain and the Blitz concentrated the mind of the government and many departments were moved out of the capital on a temporary, or sometimes permanent, basis. The Security Service MI5, which had expanded greatly at the outbreak of war, had failed to find office space in London to house its staff, so it had moved its headquarters to Wormwood Scrubs where it occupied part of the Victorian prison. The prison was hit by a bomb in September 1940 and most of the staff of MI5 transferred to Blenheim Palace, although some senior officers and counter espionage officers remained in London at the former MGM building in St James Street 'whose identity was camouflaged by a large "To Let" sign outside.'[41]

When MI5 moved to Blenheim they took with them almost 1,000 people. They worked in the state rooms, which had been altered for the boys and were now further altered as they were subdivided by wooden panels with filing cabinets and trestle tables to provide office space. A 'sea' of wooden huts was erected in the courtyards to provide further accommodation. Helen Quinn worked for MI5 in London and she recalled the move to Blenheim, which was ordered by Churchill after valuable documents had been lost during a bombing raid. 'We had three huts and were beside the courtyard which contained four squares of sacred soil brought back from the site of the battle of Blenheim. The Duke of Marlborough was insistent that nobody should walk on the soil, but he was not a match for the removal men who when they found that they were carrying cupboards full of ashes, walked straight across the sacred soil.'[42] Helen lived in digs in Oxford and caught the bus out to Woodstock every day. 'Though supposedly highly confidential, the nature of the palace's new occupants was not a very well kept secret. The conductors on the bus from Oxford to Woodstock used to call out in ringing tones when they reached Blenheim's gates, "Anyone for MI5?"'[43] After MI5 returned to London in 1944 the British Council moved in and used the palace as a base in which to plan their promotion of British culture in the postwar world.

*

When the boys and masters returned to Malvern they found it a completely different place from the sleepy little town they had left in September 1939: 'A contingent of the Belgian army had its HQ at the Abbey Hotel; the records branch of the Polish Navy and a small number of Greeks were in town, and on occasions we had visitors from Yugoslavia, Norway and Holland at the some of the dances and parties which were held.'[44]

The college, smaller in size than it had been pre-war with just over 350 boys, settled back into its old buildings and familiar routine. School life continued with boys contributing to the war effort in various ways, including salvage collection, potato harvesting and training with the OTC, which they all took seriously.

In November 1940, Gaunt was approached by the office of the Free French in London to see if he could accommodate sixty to seventy boys of some two hundred who had cycled to the coast of France when the Germans invaded and had managed to escape to Britain. Two boys had crossed the Channel in an open rowing boat and were photographed taking tea with Winston Churchill in the garden of 10 Downing Street before being sent to join the rest of their fellow escapees. They were to be trained by the Free French army for commission, but the colonel in charge of the boys' training was keen for them to be attached to a public school. In January 1941 sixty-three moved into No. 5 House and soon became a familiar sight in their red 'walking-out' cloaks. They joined in a number of school activities and used the classrooms, gymnasium and swimming pool.

For eighteen months life at Malvern College ran smoothly, but on 25 April 1942 everything changed again and this time there was no warning. A group of government inspectors arrived at the college, spent two hurried hours looking around the premises, and left without an explanation for their visit. Gaunt was sufficiently worried to go straight to London and present himself at the Office of Works: 'I began by apologising for troubling them over what might be a silly scare, and until that very moment I was half expecting to be walking out of the building ten minutes later... [but] within two minutes it became obvious that the situation was extremely critical.'[45]

The reason for the crisis was genuinely a matter of national security. Radar had been in development since the 1930s and Britain's research establishment was situated near Swanage on the Dorset coast. Both the Germans and the British had functioning systems by the outbreak of war and the use of radar during the Battle of Britain had proved the vital role this technology had to play in defence. A daring Combined Operations raid, Operation Biting, on the German radar station at Bruneval near Le Havre on the French coast in February 1942 had captured the vital components of a Wurzburg radar system and its German operator. These were taken to the Telecommunications Research Establishment in Dorset, known by its acronym TRE, the main organisation responsible for Britain's research and development into radar and radio navigation. Over the next few weeks, while TRE researchers were examining the German equipment, the British became increasingly worried that the Germans would retaliate in kind. Then came intelligence about plans for a heavy attack on TRE by aircraft and the landing of a large number of parachute troops during the next moon period. When Churchill realised how vulnerable the radar establishment on the coast would be he ordered that it be moved inland with all possible speed and certainly before the next full moon, which would fall on 11 May. Finding somewhere suitable for such a huge and important establishment, while maintaining absolute secrecy, was tricky and especially so at this stage in the war when most of the large houses and buildings that could be requisitioned were already in use. In addition, TRE needed certain specific geographical features for their work, including fairly high hills, a wide range of vision – twenty-five miles would be ideal – proximity to an aerodrome and, of course, a secluded place of comparative safety.

Records in the National Archives reveal the agonising debate that went on behind the scenes in the hurried attempts to find a suitable location. The War Cabinet held three secret meetings in the third week of April, presided over by the prime minister himself. Also involved in the debate were Secretary of State for

Dominion Affairs Clement Attlee, Minister of Production Oliver Lyttelton, Home Secretary Herbert Morrison, Sir John Anderson, Ernest Bevin, Air Vice-Marshal N. H. Bottomley, the Deputy Chief of the Air Staff and nine other RAF officials. On the 20 and 21 April 1942, this committee came to the conclusion that either Malvern College or Malborough College in Wiltshire should be requisitioned. Over the course of the next few days there was a great deal of buck passing. The Ministry of Supply claimed that this was the government's responsibility, not theirs, while president for the Board of Education R. A. 'Rab' Butler weighed in with a hefty argument about the probable disruption to the pupils' education. He wrote a three-page memorandum to the War Cabinet which is stamped in red ink: 'TO BE KEPT UNDER LOCK AND KEY'. He argued that while the warning given to boarding schools in 1938–9 enabled the headmasters or mistresses to find alternative suitable accommodation, this current situation was unsatisfactory as any school with over 150 pupils would be unlikely to find a building large enough to accommodate them en masse. He cited the recent example of Wycombe Abbey School for girls that had been forced to close when it was taken over earlier that year. Some thirty percent of pupils at Malvern College were in the 'higher' stages, that is to say studying for entry into university. His impassioned argument claimed that if boarding schools such as Malvern College or Marlborough were forced to close there would be a generation of young people who had an inadequate or defective education and 'the general morale of the nation will suffer by throwing out of school at short notice large numbers of pupils without providing reasonable opportunities for carrying on their education.' This, in turn, would lead to a drop in the number of qualified and trained boys and girls 'for commissioned rank and for technical posts [which] is vital for the war effort'[46]. It is a reminder that officers were still drawn, in the main, from the public schools and that the class system continued to dominate society. It also reminds us that war consumes mainly younger people at the peak of their fitness and potential. He went on:

The results are serious enough for any pupil, but they may be disastrous in the case of those with abilities of a high order. The need for competent boys and girls to enter the services with advanced qualifications, especially in science, has never been greater. The effect of closing a school at the present time is that boys and girls have their studies interrupted, sometimes at a vital stage in their career, and have to continue their advanced work often with overcrowded and totally inadequate facilities. The handicaps on advanced work are particularly crippling where premises not designed for education purposes have been taken into use.[47]

He pointed out that the other, perhaps less obvious, reason that school evacuations should be avoided was the issue of national security. It was inevitable, Butler wrote, that the wholesale evacuation of a school at this stage in the war would lead the public to assume, quite rightly, that the premises were required by the government for some secret military establishment. 'By giving the strongest presumption that an important government establishment was involved, the object of the removal might, in part, be defeated.'[48] These minutes provide a fascinating and detailed insight into the different and legitimate concerns the government had to weigh up when considering a course of action such as the movement of a major department from one place to another, with all the fallout that would result.

The need to house TRE safely away from the coast and in the proximity of similar establishments, such as the Air Defence and Research Development Establishment, made sense. There was already a strong presence in Malvern as the Ministry of Aircraft Production Research Establishment had acquired land in the town which they used for a Signals Training Establishment, housed in one-storey prefabricated buildings. In the end that appears to have been the overwhelming reason for the move even though bringing TRE to the town would require substantial premises to house hundreds and eventually over a thousand researchers and other staff.

Gaunt was told that the irresistible reason for this choice had to do with the most basic of human needs: sewage disposal. Marlborough's drainage system was barely adequate for the existing residents so that the idea of increasing the population by 2,000 would put it under extreme stress. Furthermore, evacuating Marlborough would mean evacuating two schools totalling 1,100 boys as the City of London School had been sharing the premises of the Wiltshire public school since the beginning of the war. Malvern, by contrast, had only one third of that number.

So Gaunt and his council, staff and boys were once again to be made homeless but this time with one week's warning and coming at the worst possible time for the senior boys, as they prepared for summer exams. Stephen and Peter Brown, now about to enter their final term at school, were told by telegram that the start of the term would be delayed and they would find out where they would be going in due course. For two boys about to sit their Higher Certificates this was an unwelcome disruption.

The Office of Works suggested relocating to Berkeley Castle in Gloucestershire but it had no proper water supply, then they proposed a half-built Canadian camp near Hereford. It was a heartbreaking time for Tom Gaunt and at times he feared the break-up of his school which he believed would be final and fatal. His only hope, he wrote later, was to join up with another school. 'But I also knew that most schools were far too full even to contemplate taking us.'[49] At one stage he even considered splitting up the school by house and asking headmasters of other public schools around the country to accommodate one or more houses, but that would have proved to be a logistical nightmare. Then by a stroke of good luck he learned that Harrow School had suffered an alarming drop in numbers, owing to its proximity to London during the Blitz. The number of pupils had gone down from 500 to 330 in eighteen months and the ensuing financial crisis had already made it necessary for the school's governors to close four of the houses. So when Gaunt picked up the phone and called A. P. Boissier, the acting headmaster of Harrow, he was pushing at an open door. Gaunt explained his plight and ended with the question: '"Can you do anything for us?" Boissier had listened to my recital in silence, and his reply was brief, "I think so; come and have lunch."[50] That afternoon, Thursday 1 May 1942, Gaunt sat in Boissier's study and they hatched a plan to accommodate both schools. Of the five houses offered, only one was empty and the rest would have to be vacated by the beginning of the 'new' Malvern term on 28 May. 'The Coldstream Guards were in Westacre; the Ministry of Health had a hospital in Newlands; a London insurance company had rented Deyncourt as temporary offices during the Blitz period.'[51] To its credit, the Department of Education, led by Butler, got things moving and three houses were empty by the middle of the month.

The need to get Malvern cleared for TRE quickly was intense and the chaos that ensued over the weeks before the school could open in Harrow was infinitely worse than the move to Blenheim. The Ministry of Aircraft Productions (MAP) which was in charge of the move to Malvern did not initially take into account the difficulties of simultaneously emptying a school and beginning construction work to convert the buildings to meet the needs of a completely different type of organisation. Gaunt felt he was in an almost impossible posi- tion: 'Requisitioning Malvern College was ... like asking the king to clear out of Buckingham Palace; in fact that would probably have caused less rumpus.'[52]

The removal to Harrow would be by rail, not road, but the rail- ways could not cope with thirty-eight containers of goods all in one transport. Major Elliott, who had learned a lot during the earlier move to and from Blenheim, took charge of the project while other masters worked as labourers, emptying the houses as quickly as pos- sible and loading up fifteen vans and thirty-eight railway containers. The bursar and Elliott had to work out a complete inventory for every item in every packing case. As this was happening, building contractors swarmed over the Malvern campus, installing hundreds of miles of new wiring, reinforcing floors, building a canteen to feed the staff and constructing huts on every piece of flat ground in the school grounds – with the exception of the 'Senior Turf', the school's cricket pitch, which remained sacrosanct even in a time of national crisis.

For twenty-four hours an indescribable bedlam reigned as vans from Swanage arrived and tried to unload in the college precincts at the same time as the containers heading to Harrow were being filled for departure. Then a rumour started that soldiers had begun to break up the college in an undisciplined rout. In actuality, a small number of soldiers who had been sent to help had got bored and discovered a few straw hats belonging to the boys which had been left behind. 'Intrigued by these novel objects, they had paraded through the grounds wearing them on their heads or dribbling them at their feet, a procedure that no doubt caused merriment to them, but aroused misgivings in the minds of others which swelled into horrific certainties a few hours later!'[53]

Meanwhile, the situation at Harrow was barely less chaotic. The housemasters had arrived from Malvern to settle into their new houses but only one was ready. The Coldstream Guards had begun to move out of one property, Westacre, but the Ministry of Health, who had promised to vacate a house called Newlands that was being used as a hospital, dithered before finally capitulating. The masters and their families were all temporarily lodged in the King's Head hotel where they ate all their meals, discussed the issues facing the school and waited for the buildings finally to become available. Gaunt wrote: 'The willingness of the hotel staff and the cheerfulness of our own people triumphed over the difficulties, and there were many moments of jest and gaiety as well as of perplexity and despair.'[54]

The bursar at Harrow offered Gaunt and his secretary, Miss Nicholls, a room in his office. It had previously had just one occupant but now it had two and a steady string of people coming in to ask questions: 'The entire day, from 9.00am until 6.30pm and often later, was one of constant interruption, and the queue of attendant questioners sometimes reached down the stairs and into the street. Indeed, much of my own consultation was done in the street, for the weather was mercifully fine and there was more room outside!'[55]

Finally, four weeks after the planned start of term, the boys arrived in their new surroundings. Gaunt and Boissier had discussed and agreed it was essential that each school maintained its own independent character and that cooperation, though encouraged, should not mean traditions were lost.

There would be no sharing of lessons or games but at the beginning, when both schools were depleted in numbers, there were joint chapel services, 'with the Malvern form of service being adopted for Matins and the Harrow form for evensong.'[56] This practice stopped when the growing numbers of boys in both schools meant that the chapel could not accommodate them all. The schools shared the sanatorium, the tea shop and the library, and the choral societies were combined under the leadership of the Harrow music master, but otherwise they were kept apart.

The school prefects had written a list of Malvernian customs which totalled 116 and down to the last detail. They specified when boys were allowed to walk with one hand in their pocket (except when they met a prefect) and when they could walk with both hands in their pockets *and* wear a white handkerchief in their top pocket. 'The very fact that these traditions were recorded and preserved made it considerably easier for the school as a community to adapt itself quickly and wholeheartedly to new ways. Time-honoured observances are treasured for their reminders of the duties, privileges, and responsibilities of a living social unit.'[57] The preservation of the school's traditions meant that it could maintain its own special character which differentiated it from Harrow at a time when public school rivalry was even more keenly felt than it remains today.

Some Malvern customs were lost forever, others merely given up for the time being. One that bit the dust was the tradition of swimming in the nude. Some thought this was because Harrow protested but in fact it was because 'women who worked in the NAAFI near the Ducker [Harrow's open-air swimming pool] objected to coming across naked sunbathers.'[58] Another custom that was lost was in the form of greeting masters which was less formal than the Harrow greeting which they had to adopt, namely doffing their caps.

For Canon Gaunt, the move to Harrow had been a logistical and emotional nightmare, but when he spoke to the boys on the first

morning they were all gathered in chapel he sought to present it from
a neutral standpoint:

> Let us consider this catastrophe in its right perspective, against
> the broader background of the war. Compare our sufferings with
> the perils and privations which our brothers are facing on land,
> on sea, and in the air. Consider the lives of those who fought
> at Singapore or who withdrew fighting week by week along the
> roads of Burma. Picture for a moment what our allies have to face
> in France and Poland and Greece. In the large picture of the war
> our sufferings and difficulties seem a small part.[59]

The school's proximity to London was a mixed blessing. It had
the advantage that boys and masters could enjoy the cultural possibilities as well as making it easier to invite distinguished speakers.
On the other hand, the boys experienced war first-hand when
Harrow was hit by incendiary bombs which 'were put out by the
fire-watching teams before they could do any serious damage except
to the tea-shop.'[60] The press reported on the incident referring to the
school as 'a famous one in London'. The *Daily Telegraph* regaled
its readers with the image of incendiaries showering down on the
school with 'a fire bomb falling through the roof of one of the school
houses, bouncing off the bed of one of the sons of a master. The boy
was dragged clear by a master.'[61] The reporter wrote that the boys
put out the fires so quickly and efficiently 'that the school was able
to carry on normally yesterday except for 90 minutes delay at breakfast – because the bombs had got among the rations.'[62] One family
had decided against sending their son to Harrow because of the risk
of bombing and had chosen Malvern instead. It was ironic that the
lad ended up in Harrow after all.

Twins Stephen and Peter Brown were two of only a handful of
boys who experienced both Blenheim and Harrow. Stephen said
that he had little to do with the Harrovians except when they went
down to the Ducker to swim. He recalled his time there as being
very happy, if brief, and he was impressed by how quickly the school

routine was up and running, despite the difficulties outlined above. 'I was gearing up to take my Higher Certificate and hoped to go to Cambridge so I suppose I did not see as much of the Harrow boys as others would have done.'[63] By the time the school returned to Malvern in 1946 only four boys had ever had experience of the life of Malvern College at Malvern not Harrow.

Malcolm Locock, who had arrived at Malvern College the term it was back in Worcestershire, spent four years at Harrow. He told his grandson: 'Once we had settled in it wasn't too bad, though initially a bit strange. Our house was quite some distance from school and we had to walk which meant getting up earlier each day.'[64] All the boys at Harrow and Malvern joined the Officer Training Corps, which was taken very seriously. Malcolm wrote: 'We were almost junior soldiers. We trained with guns and ammunition and still did night field exercises.'[65] On one moonless night the boys were crawling along the ground looking for the 'enemy' when one of the masters kicked what he thought was a boy, telling him to move forward smartly. 'As it happened it was a local cow which didn't appreciate being moved on and said so.'[66]

The schools received distinguished visitors over the course of the war including Churchill, who apologised to the Malvern boys for being responsible for the second evacuation. Addressing both schools, he said: 'You have visitors here now in the shape of a sister school – Malvern. I must say I think this is a very fine affair – to meet the needs of war, to join forces, to share alike, like two regiments that serve side by side in some famous brigade and never forget it for a hundred years after. I was very sorry that I myself had to be responsible for giving some instructions in regard to one of our establishments which made it necessary to take over Malvern at comparatively short notice.'[67]

He was booed by the Malvern boys not because of the school's forced removal to Harrow but because of the price differential policy at the Tuck Shop, which meant the Malvernians paid more for goods than the Harrovians. 'Rab' Butler came to Malvern's first prizegiving in July 1942, which meant a great deal to Gaunt and the masters who appreciated how much he had done to make their emergency move to Harrow happen by clearing bureaucracy from their path. A further visit from Herbert Morrison, then in his role as home secretary, in February 1944, acknowledged the sacrifice the school had made to the war effort.

Gaunt put the success of four years at Harrow down in large part to the boys and in particular to the senior prefects who formed an immediate and intelligent understanding with the Harrow monitors. They were always aware of the host–guest nature of the relationship and the seniors set an excellent example which filtered down to the most junior boys. 'There was a certain rivalry between the two schools but not as much as I had expected. On each side the different customs and manners of the other were viewed with interest and a healthy sense of superiority: for Malvern, at any rate, it was a stimulus to feel that the judgment of another great school was being formed day by day, as well as that of the residents and tradesmen on the Hill ... I never had any real anxiety about the school as a whole.'[68]

In the summer of 1945 a handful of Malvern boys who had been working on the harvest at a farm in Worcestershire were invited to visit their old school grounds. They accepted with delight. Most had never been there. They went into the sixth-form room which was being used by the superintendent A. P. Rowe as his study. Then they went into the chapel: 'and were convinced that our memories of its beauty were not exaggerated. We were not allowed into any of the houses but from the outside at least they looked the same as ever.'[69] When they got to the 'Senior Turf', the school's first XI cricket pitch a few of the present cricket XI decided to ignore the notices forbidding anyone to step on the hallowed turf and walked onto it. They were unceremoniously turfed off it by a policeman. Despite that, they were all deeply grateful to A. P. Rowe who had made it possible for them to return 'home' for an hour.

The original contract with Harrow stated that Malvern must vacate the houses it occupied within twelve months of the end of hostilities against Germany. The Ministry of Education had promised

Gaunt that he could return to Malvern in September 1945, which would have fulfilled this obligation, but unfortunately TRE seemed unwilling to leave its Malvern College site. It took a question in the House of Commons and exertion on the part of Ellen Wilkinson, the new minister of education, to get a partial derequisition of the site to allow Malvern to go back to Worcestershire in September 1946. So they returned. The dormitories were no longer partitioned, the grounds were littered with Nissen huts, TRE remained a presence on site but still it was a relief. Gaunt wrote: 'We shall be back at last – back to our own home and familiar surroundings – back to the open hills – back, pray God, for good!'[70]

TRE enjoyed remarkable success at Malvern during the war. When Gaunt visited his old school he was able to sense that the spirit of Malvern 'had not been wholly expelled by aliens' and this was down to the man in charge, eminent physicist A. P. Rowe, who superintended the entire operation. Rowe had, from the outset, engaged the local council in the secret project, who had listened to his explanation about the value of radar with 'rapt attention', promising their utmost cooperation and the maintenance of secrecy as the situation demanded. The only thing the townspeople knew for sure was that 'something unusual' was going on and the local community was generous in its cooperation.

The school grounds were surrounded with barbed wire fencing and existing buildings had exciting new names to describe the activities going on inside. The school house had the 'Centimeter Waveband Techniques' department, or 'radar counter measures'. The main school hall with its university boards and lists of alumni was taken over by Mr Dummer's Synthetic Aircrew Trainers and gained the nickname 'the Hall of Magic'. To give some sense of scale, the refectory completed on the school site could feed 1,500 people in one sitting, and the TRE Engineering Unit machine shop was said to be the largest electronics factory in Europe. TRE at Malvern was of such importance that the king and queen visited in 1944 and were shown around the Engineering Unit and other facilities.

TRE's work at Malvern enabled Britain to keep ahead of the

Germans in technology: the radar equipment developed there allowed Bomber Command to damage beyond repair Germany's industrial output and to allow 'the British and American bombers to blast the German defences on the French Atlantic and Channel coasts to pave the way for the Allied invasion.'[71] Among the instruments of war developed in the TRE laboratories of Malvern were some high-profile offensive devices such as 'Oboe', which made possible high precision bombing; 'H2S', which provided the bombers with accurate radar pictures of towns beneath them, leading in 1943 to the bombing of Berlin and other German cities. Another development was 'Window', invented by a brilliant scientist called Joan Curran. It comprised strips of metalised paper that were dropped from aircraft to disrupt the signals from enemy radar and so protect the bombers. This is still used today and is known as 'chaff'. The development of radar at Malvern which was used by the RAF from June 1943 onwards with great effect helped to spell the end of the U-boat threat, compelling Hitler to announce: 'the temporary setback to our U-boats is due to one single technical invention of our enemies.'[72] The Germans eventually came up with a device to fool radar but, as Rowe wrote, 'when 'Schnörkel' [a device to make submarines more difficult to locate] appeared our armies were advancing fast across Europe and the end was in sight.' TRE's main purpose, he always maintained, was to buy time. He said: 'In theory, nearly all radar devices could in time have been defeated by the enemy, provided that sufficient effort was put into countering them. The defeat of the U-boats serves to illustrate what we meant. The Germans were too late.'[73] In September 1944 the first German V1 flying bomb hit London and TRE scientists constructed a model at Malvern to measure the radar signature so that 'the anti-aircraft Radar AA No7 MK1, codenamed "Rugger Scrum", could be linked to Bofors guns to shoot them down.'[74] At this stage in the war, TRE ran courses in radar and electronics for both service and civilian personnel but immediately postwar the work focused on an altogether larger project: the Atom Smasher. A world first, it was built at Malvern in 1946 and was the predecessor to the Large Hadron Collider.

While such work was going on close by, the school resettled in its old buildings and began to grow and thrive as Gaunt had envisioned when he took over a decade earlier, and what to him must have seemed a lifetime ago. For a man whose temper must have been sorely tested for weeks and months on end it is extraordinary that he was able to be so generous. He was an optimist and summed up the impact of the second move of the war in typically positive fashion: 'If we remember with pain the agony and frustration of the early days of May 1942 and the long exile, we none the less appreciate our intimate connection with the men of TRE and its great achievements, and shall be proud to echo the words of a high official [A. P. Rowe], spoken to me in 1944, that the war against the U-boats and the war in the air had both been won on the playing fields of Malvern.'[75]

Howick Hall in Northumberland was the home of the Grey family for over 200 years. It was used as a convalescent hospital in both world wars.

CHAPTER 5

Lady Grey's Guests

Those years at Howick brought me out of my shell and did me the world of good.

Joan Hannant[1]

Late on the afternoon of 27 February 1941, Margaret Cook arrived at Howick Hall in Northumberland in her Austin 7. She had driven through the worst snowstorm she had experienced in her life and was relieved to stop in front of the handsome eighteenth-century Hall and get into the warm. The snow fall at the end of February was described by the Meteorological Office in its monthly summary as 'abnormal, particularly in north-east England and south-east Scotland and in some places it was probably the heaviest fall of the century.'[2] Twenty-nine and a half inches or seventy-five centimetres of snow fell in Newcastle in two days. Miss Cook was lucky to get to Howick at all. She was to stay there for the next four and a half years, during which time she never witnessed such extreme weather again but she gained a lifetime's experience in her job as the secretary-bookkeeper at Howick Hall Hospital.

On her arrival she met Lady Mabel Grey, who was to be the commandant of the military hospital set up for the second time in her home. Already in her mid-fifties at the outbreak of the Second World

War, Lady Grey had been awarded the CBE in 1919 for her work at the Red Cross Hospital at Howick during the Great War and in between the wars had continued her work with the organisation.

During the First World War there was an acute need for hospital accommodation in Britain. Country houses from northern Scotland to Cornwall were taken over to provide beds for anything from specialist units to general convalescent homes. In all, almost 2.7 million sick and wounded arrived in Britain, brought back from the continent and other theatres of war further afield, for treatment. Before the war there were 7,000 equipped beds in military hospitals. By the Armistice in November 1918 there were 364,133.

Previous experience had shown that mixing civilian and military patients was not a wise move. This had to do with the maintenance of records and the aftercare of the sick and wounded as well as the maintenance of military discipline, rather than with the nature of their treatment. A very large proportion of the beds made available during the First World War was provided and equipped by voluntary aid organisations and private individuals. All offers had to be submitted to the Red Cross for approval and they reported to the Army Council if they thought the accommodation would be of use. Some 1,600 large and small hospitals were accepted, ranging from one with six beds to the largest with more than two hundred. 'Voluntary hospitals were designated auxiliary hospitals and were entitled to a per capita grant for each military patient admitted to them for facilities for treatment. Those with a trained personnel and suitable equipment were designated Class A auxiliary hospitals and those suitable only for convalescents were Class B.'[3]

The Ministry of Health estimated that a similar need for hospital and convalescent beds would arise in this next war and they hoped that the Red Cross would once again run auxiliary hospitals that would 'fulfil the two-fold purpose of freeing beds in casualty hospitals for those who really needed them and of providing emergency medical service patients with suitable accommodation for convalescence.'[4] Lessons, both good and bad, had been learned from the experience of hospital care twenty years earlier when great advances had been made in the treatment of the sick and injured. These were taken forward into the current crisis and, as social researcher Richard Titmuss pointed out, 'the frame and pattern of the hospital services at the end of the war were due as much – if not more – to the kind of war that was expected as to the kind of war that happened.'[5] He went on:

This is an important historical fact. The estimates of the Air Staff, the translation of these into figures of casualties and hospital beds, and the prevailing mood of fear and alarm about the character of a future war had largely determined, by the end of 1938, the way in which the medical services of the country were to be organised eventually. The outline of Britain's first attempt to create a national hospital service was clearly pictured before the war began.[6]

Joined-up thinking was not something that had been widely experienced prior to the war, yet in so many spheres, out of necessity in a time of national emergency, even rival institutions agreed to work together for the common good. However, the idea of treating civilian and military patients together was still not accepted. It appeared that a major issue for the War Office was that they believed service patients would not be sent back to duty as quickly if they were treated in hospitals not under military control. So the situation remained largely as it had been during the First World War, that military patients were treated and convalesced in separate establishments. The War Office estimated they would require 20,000 beds, a substantial drop on the previous war, but in the end demand was lower. In August 1944, the Red Cross reported that there were over 14,000 beds available in 230 country houses, and the occupancy was 72 per cent.

Howick Hall had been the first stately home in north-east England to enrol as a First World War hospital. It opened on 23 October 1914 with thirty-one beds for convalescent servicemen, and ran for eighteen months. In line with the usual procedure it was funded by the

Red Cross but run by the owners on a voluntary basis. Lady Sybil Grey, daughter of the fourth Earl Grey, had been the first VAD [Voluntary Aid Detachment] to be accepted by the Royal Victoria Infirmary in Newcastle at the outbreak of the war. She threw herself energetically into the work of the Howick Hall Convalescent Home of which she became commandant. She was helped by her sister-in-law, Lady Mabel Grey, who went on to become a prominent member of the Red Cross. Lady Sybil, meanwhile, was part of a British party that set up a Red Cross hospital in Petrograd, on the initiative of Lady Muriel Paget, in response to the news of terrible Russian casualties in 1916. She remained in Russia until the revolution and her father's illness made it impossible for her to stay any longer. She was awarded an OBE for her work.

A large number of the patients at Howick in 1914 were Belgian and their letters of thanks in French to Lady Sybil contain poems, drawings and photographs. Their stay had transformed their opinion of British hospitality, one soldier wrote to her. Another letter starts 'My most noble lady, I have so much pleasure in writing you this short letter to thank you for your wonderful, maternal care of me while I was at Howick.'[7] The British soldiers' letters were equally warm in their thanks but also full of self-deprecating humour. One contained a photograph of a football team called the Howick Cripples. Another man wrote to say that after he had returned to France he found himself sleeping on a stone floor in January with just one blanket to keep him warm. 'I could not help thinking of Howick Hall and my surroundings and companions … I shall always have pleasant memories of the happy time and the many kind ways in which I was treated at Howick and once again I thank your Ladyship from the bottom of my heart.'[8] The correspondence was not only one way. Lady Sybil responded to many of the letters and sometimes initiated the exchange. It would appear the hospital had been a great success.

In 1926 a catastrophic fire had destroyed the interior of the main house and all the contents of the top two floors. The fire was discovered by Lord Grey who was woken up by the noise of the second-floor ceiling falling in onto the floor below. He roused the household and rang the alarm bell outside the hall. Men and women from all over the estate and Howick village rushed to help out, as did the police and the local fire brigade, who were informed by a telephone message sent by Mr Hale of Howick Grange. Howick Hall did not have a telephone until after the Second World War but the press got hold of Lord Grey's daughter, Molly, who was staying with her aunt Sybil in London. They asked her if she knew that Howick Hall had burned to the ground and Lord Grey with it. She was just nineteen years old and it gave her a terrible shock. Lady Sybil immediately phoned through to Mr Hale to find that Lord Grey was alive and in charge of the fire-fighting.

Unfortunately it was a foggy night and the local fire engine took three hours to cover the twenty miles from Ashington and the hall's own fire engine proved to be of no use. Volunteers had to carry pails of water from the burn at the side of the house until the fire brigade arrived.

People who were not fighting the fire helped the Greys rescue as many of the treasures as they could from the house before the flames took such a hold that it was no longer safe to enter the building. Lady Grey, who the press delighted in reporting was 'clad in a dressing gown' directed volunteers to the most important corners of the hall. She and Bob Nicholl, the gamekeeper, rescued books and other treasures while Billy Meakin, the estate's carpenter, saved all the family portraits from the blaze by cutting the canvases out of their frames and bringing them out to safety. Soon there was a huge pile of furniture, books, paintings and other treasures on the front lawn. Billy watched the men hauling buckets of water to cool down the walls in order to save the ballroom and the west wing. When the fire died down and the damage was assessed, the drawing room, breakfast room, dining room, library, central hall and eight bedrooms were completely destroyed. The main reason the damage was so extensive was lack of a nearby water source to fight the blaze. The ornamental pond that now stands in front of the hall is a fire pond, constructed to provide water close at hand in the event of another fire.

Howick Hall was rebuilt by Sir Herbert Baker who introduced a portico above the front hall in order to make the house smaller. 'Disciples of Georgian architecture are not amused'[9] said the present owner Lord Howick. However, Baker's redesign gave the family opportunities to introduce modern conveniences such as bathrooms with hot water and electricity. There was even a basic central heating system installed in the house, though the family still relied on fires in the library and the other large downstairs rooms to keep warm.

The Grey family has an eminent and varied history. The first Earl Grey was the general who introduced marching in step on manoeuvres as an efficient method of moving an army around quickly. This had not been done since Roman times. His son, Charles, the second Earl Grey, lent his name to the famous tea. It was blended for him by a Chinese civil servant using bergamot to offset the taste of lime in the water at Howick. Lady Grey served it when she was entertaining guests in London and it immediately caught on as a fashionable and sophisticated drink. 'It proved so popular that she was asked if it could be sold to others, which is how Twining came to market it and it is now sold worldwide. Sadly the Greys, being unbusinesslike, failed to register the trade mark and as a result they have never received a penny in royalties.'[10] The second Earl Grey became prime minister in 1830 and was most famous for introducing the Great Reform Bill of 1832. He was vigorously opposed by his predecessor, the Duke of Wellington, but he prevailed, thus taking Parliament on its first step towards modern parliamentary democracy. He was also active in the march to abolish slavery. Grey married Mary Elizabeth Ponsonby in 1794 and between 1797 and 1819 eleven sons and four daughters were born and survived. He also had an illegitimate daughter, Eliza Courtney, who was born to Georgiana Cavendish, the Duchess of Devonshire, before the earl's marriage to Mary. His oldest son, Henry, who became the third Earl Grey, remembered with great affection his father reading out loud to the family almost every evening. He lived at Howick Hall for forty-four years, dying in 1845 at the age of eighty-one. Unlike his father, Henry Grey had no children so the estate passed to his nephew, Albert, fourth Earl Grey, in 1894. Albert was married to Alice Holford whose father, Robert Stayner Holford, created the great arboretum at Westonbirt in Gloucestershire. Their son, Charles Grey, married Lady Mabel Palmer and together they laid out the gardens at Howick, transforming them from a formal Victorian design into the sweeping, informal gardens that are still to be seen today.

At the outbreak of the Second World War, Countess Mabel Grey was president of the British Red Cross Society in Northumberland and she immediately suggested Howick should again be a convalescent home. She had enjoyed her experience of working with the soldiers during the First World War and knew that the newly refurbished hall was even better suited than it had been twenty years earlier.

Although Howick had been accepted by the Red Cross, it was not called into use for the first eighteen months of the war as the requirement for beds for service personnel had been far lower than the original estimates. Lady Grey was informed at the beginning of 1941 that they could expect their first patients in early March. She was eager to get cracking and Margaret Cook's arrival on that snowy day helped to encourage a sense of purpose. As the hospital stores arrived they were piled up in the hall waiting to be distributed. The Red Cross not only sent medical supplies but also beds, tables, chairs, recreation equipment, games, books and deck chairs. Lady Grey oversaw the transformation of the hall personally.

Slim and of average height, Lady Grey had brown wavy hair parted in the middle and a kind face but her appearance hid a tireless and steely determination. Her grandson, Lord Howick, remembers her as a Victorian lady. 'She was very religious and there were rules that had to be obeyed. She always went to church and there was no shooting on a Sunday, except for rabbits on the croquet lawn.'[11] To the outside world, and to the hospital staff during the 1940s, she was efficient and well connected and Margaret Cook, working in the office, was constantly glad that Lady Grey was on her side. As she put it, 'She knew what we needed [at Howick] and she could persuade the Red Cross Committee to let us have it.'[12] Lady Grey could also be very warm and sympathetic. Joan Hannant was just eighteen when she volunteered to become an auxiliary nurse. She was desperately upset to be sent to Howick as she had never been away from home before. As an only child she was not used to mixing with other people but, she said, 'it turned out to be one of the happiest times of my life.'[13] When her mother was ill, Lady Grey sent her home for the weekend with a bunch of daffodils and a box of fresh eggs. Joan never forgot that kindness.

Lady Grey not only had a hospital to run but also an expanding household. Her younger daughter, Elizabeth, was married to Lieutenant Colonel Ronald 'Ronnie' Dawnay, an officer in the Coldstream Guards. The couple had four children born between 1933 and 1938. He served between 1939 and 1942, being mentioned in dispatches, but was taken prisoner at Tobruk. Lady Elizabeth died on 25 February 1941 of a brain tumour, two days before Miss Cook arrived at Howick. She was just thirty-two years old and had been living in Canada since the outbreak of the war. The children were effectively orphaned as their father was abroad so they came to live at Howick in 1942. Lord and Lady Grey lived in two rooms in the main house and the children stayed in the west wing, which is now the family home. Despite the great sadness of losing her mother, Anne Dawnay has very happy memories of the war years at Howick. She, her sister and her two younger brothers were looked after by a governess and a nanny called Scottie. When she was old enough, Anne went to the local school in Howick village on the bus, but the focus of her life was at the hall where she had her dogs and ponies.

Margaret Cook, Lady Grey, the nurses, quartermaster, matron and general service members of the Red Cross worked round the clock to get the hall ready to take the first patients. The general service members were to work in the kitchen and as cleaners for the hospital. There was roughly one Red Cross or St John auxiliary nurse to every ten beds, which meant some half dozen nurses at any one time. Overseeing the day-to-day running of the hospital was Matron. There were two at Howick over the course of the war, Matron Reid and Matron Railton, and they were feared and respected in equal measure. The doctor was a civilian who came in as and when he was needed but most of the men needed nursing rather than medical intervention.

While the hospital staff was focused on preparing the hall for the patients, Lord Grey was anxious to protect the hall and its treasures from damage. He called on the ever-reliable estate joiner, Billy Meakin, who had helped to rescue the family portraits during the great fire fifteen years earlier. Billy had lived at Howick Hall since 1918 when his father, Charlie, took the job of coachman to the fifth earl. It was a time of change: the family was switching from horses to motorcars so Charlie became the family's chauffeur, but he spent part of his day taking the Grey daughters out riding and looking after the remaining horses in the stables. Billy, who was fifteen, was initially engaged as a pantry boy but he seems to have 'twisted the stems off so many wine glasses, they couldn't afford to have him in the pantry so he became apprenticed to the estate joiner, Mr Richardson.'[14]

Although Billy Meakin's title was 'house joiner', he acquired the skills necessary to keep a house and estate the size of Howick in order. He taught himself to restore antique furniture, to regild and French-polish furniture, but also wheelwrighting and glazing. He learned how to construct barns, make garden furniture and repair doors and windows. In the mid-1930s he was badly injured in an explosion. It damaged his hand and he nearly lost his eyesight. Lord Grey organised for his eye surgeon to take over Billy's care and his sight was saved. However, the injuries rendered him unfit for war service. By the outbreak of the Second World War he was installed in the old dairy where his son, Arthur, remembers 'the little books of very thin gold leaf, the sweet smell of new planed wood, the stable smell of animal glue heating gently in the glue pot . . . the type of glue that took seventy-two hours to dry.'[15] The workshop was located in the west courtyard which had huge gates that were supposed to keep the male staff isolated from the female servants who slept in that corner of the house. As soon as Lord Grey heard that the hall would

be accepted as a convalescent home he asked Billy to help with alter-
ing the interiors to make them suitable for the purpose. All this had
to be undertaken quickly and with limited materials as the Office
of Works did not offer to help out, as it had done for other properties. Billy took great pride in saving Lord Grey money and would do
anything to avoid having to bring in outside contractors. As well as
being an outstanding and inventive joiner, he was also an able metal-
worker. During the war he won a contract with the War Office to
manufacture episcopes (a kind of slide projector). Lord Grey could
not afford to give him a pay rise so he gave him half a day off a week
to allow Billy to make them.

The hospital occupied the new part of the house which was cen-
trally heated and had plenty of bathrooms and hot water upstairs.
Two extra bathrooms and a sluice room were put in for the patients
on the ground floor, the whole of which was used except the central hall which was piled high with stored furniture and closed off
from the staff with partitions and wooden doors, all made by Billy
Meakin. A sign on the front door sent visitors to the left if they
wished to enter the hospital and right to reach Lord Grey. Margaret
Cook described the changes:

> The dining room and library became wards each holding about
> fifteen beds. The drawing room became the recreation room,
> complete with grand piano and table tennis table and a door lead-
> ing out on to the terrace. Lord Grey's study became the nurses'
> sitting room where we also had all our meals (the nurses, sister,
> QM and myself). The butler's pantry became the surgery, the wall
> cupboards with sliding glass doors being perfect for instruments,
> and the heated steel cupboards for keeping food hot being excel-
> lent for airing bed linen, shirts etc. The Servants Hall became
> the men's dining room and a small room where the butler used
> to sleep was used as a massage room and contained a massage
> couch and lamps for ultra-violet and radiant heat. In the library
> the books were left in their shelves which covered the walls, and
> the whole shelves were covered with a beaver boarding, so nobody

ever knew they were there. The men also spent a lot of time playing billiards in the billiard room.[16]

The fire escape at Howick was a rope slung from a top-floor window
and escaping meant abseiling from sixty odd feet above the ground.
The Australians, who were the most enthusiastic at sport, enjoyed
fire practice but others were not so keen. It is difficult to imagine
how sick men could have been efficiently evacuated using this adven-
turous method of escape.

The administration office was in Lady Grey's sitting room where
there were three desks, one for Lady Grey, one for Margaret Cook
and one for Miss Hale, the quartermaster. Hers was a voluntary
post and she usually had three VAD nurses living with her as lodgers
at the Grange. It was her family that had had the only telephone at
Howick when the fire broke out in the 1920s. Margaret was amused
that Miss Hale 'spent a lot of time downstairs giving out stores etc
and as little as possible at her desk coping with Food Office returns
and ration books.'[17] Anne Dawnay remembers Miss Hale as a
woman who was full of advice on what 'was done' and 'what was
not done', especially when it came to manners and speech. But she
was an enthusiastic horsewoman and that was something she and
Anne had in common. Anne, the most passionate of the four children about horses, had been taught to ride by her mother and now
Miss Hale took over as Anne's riding instructor.

The top floor of the hall had smaller rooms which functioned
as additional wards to the dining room and library wards downstairs. The hospital kept the pre-war names of these rooms: Cherry,
Spotted, Hayfield, Day Nursery and Night Nursery. 'You can imagine what the men's faces were like when they arrived and were told
they were sleeping in the night nursery!'[18] When the weather was
fine beds would be set up outside so those who were unable to walk
could enjoy fresh air and the gardens. Those who could walk were
encouraged to make use of the grounds and the photograph album at
Howick is full of pictures of men sitting in deck chairs, playing cards
around a garden table or lying in the long grass, reading or sleeping.

Fitter men took advantage of the croquet lawn and some even tried fishing in the river.

Howick Hall Hospital opened officially two weeks after Margaret Cook's arrival. She wrote afterwards:

> We opened on March 12 1941 with one patient, five VADs, a Matron, the QM, myself (the secretary book keeper), four RC general service members in the kitchen and four Red Cross general service members to do the house work. You can imagine how the one patient enjoyed himself! Next day there were two more, then five more and then they began to come and we were really going.[19]

By the summer of 1941 they had over forty patients and the routine at the hospital had settled down and was running smoothly under the direction of Matron Reid. The men were allowed in the main gardens but other areas, such as the kitchen gardens, were out of bounds, presumably so they would not help themselves to the fruit. The children each had their own vegetable patch which they tended enthusiastically under the eagle eye of Mr Woodman, the head gardener, who, presumably under instruction from Lady Grey, had put the beehives next to the strawberry beds to stop them from helping themselves to the strawberries. Margaret Cook remembered fruit trees growing along all four walls of the kitchen garden. These were unusual walls as they were hollow so they could be heated to grow espaliered fruit that would not otherwise have survived the harsh climate. Half the kitchen garden had been dug up for potatoes and the rest produced fruit and vegetables for the kitchens to bulk out the rations supplied by the Red Cross.

As president of the Women's Land Army as well as the Red Cross in Northumberland, Lady Grey was entitled to additional petrol rations, so she would take her grandchildren with her and drop them off somewhere for a picnic while she visited hospitals or hostels and then collect them on the way home. There was usually little opportunity for getting around in wartime so the children loved those outings and looked forward to Lady Grey's official work visits. She remained in her Red Cross role throughout the war, supporting the county director, Miss Maude Williamson. In her December 1941 county director's report, Miss Williamson wrote that three auxiliary hospitals had opened in the county and 'are running very successfully. Ford Castle forty-five beds, Callaly Castle 100 beds, Howick Hall fifty beds.'[20] The hospitals were staffed entirely by Red Cross officers and members and at Howick the number of beds rose to sixty over the course of 1941. Two further houses were taken over in the county, Pallinsburn with forty beds for women's services and Wallington with fifty.

Howick Hall Hospital took soldiers, sailors and airmen from the ranks. It is said that they were preferred to officers as they were generally better behaved. Howick had convalescent patients from all over the world, not just members of the British armed forces. Margaret Cook wrote:

Besides British patients we had a few Canadians, Australian, one American, a few Dutch, French, Polish etc., a few merchant seamen, including one Lithuanian marine, and practically every regiment in the British Army! Quite a lot of sailors, and a few RAF though they were usually nursed in their own sick quarters until they were fit for duty. The sailors were frightfully useful and good at polishing floors. And they were always washing their collars and pressing their trousers.[21]

Lady Grey's guest book of Howick Hall is an exceptionally valuable resource. Every man who went through the convalescent home as a patient was asked to sign the book in his own hand, giving his name and home address including country, so it is possible to see when the Australians arrived or the Norwegians left and what overlap there was. In September and October 1942, for example, they had men from Greece, France, the Netherlands, Republic of Ireland and Norway. The weather was wet and windy with a dozen severe thunderstorms that kept the men indoors. The billiards' room came into its own when the weather was foul and the men were encouraged to take up a range of activities with material supplied by the Red Cross.

One of the jobs assigned to Lady Grey was the missing lists. These were supplied by the Red Cross to official searchers, of which she was one. Nothing, short of a death notice, was more cruel than to receive an MIA (missing in action). She took this responsibility very seriously and did everything she could to establish for the families the actual fate of MIAs. In the summer of 1940 there was a good chance that a man had been taken prisoner on the continent, but sometimes it was a question of identifying where he had died. A few of the patients at Howick were able to give her news about men on the missing list. Some were able to give her detailed informa-tion which she could pass on to the Red Cross and it was Margaret Cook's job to keep the lists up to date crossing out names of those accounted for from a list of amendments. The news was not always good. She wrote in her memoir: 'One day I came across the name of an old patient of ours who had been killed – a young and brilliant actor who had been with the Birmingham repertory company and had entertained us a lot the previous Christmas.'[22]

The convalescent hospitals were designed to relieve pressure on the general hospitals by taking patients as soon as they were fit enough to travel by ambulance. There were, therefore, few bedrid-den patients at Howick except at pinch times, such as after D-Day, when all the major hospitals in Britain were overwhelmed with emergencies. There was little actual nursing to be done at Howick so that girls who wanted more experience tended to go to Plymouth or Haslar where they joined major military hospitals and dealt with more serious cases. At Howick the men were recovering from anything from fractured limbs to operations for appendicitis and hernias. They had cases of jaundice, tonsillitis, bronchitis and gas-tritis. Auxiliary nurse Joan Hannant described doing general jobs on the wards: 'giving bed baths, doing dressings and giving pills. Sometimes we'd take the patients for a bit of exercise, even down the Long Walk to the sea for a paddle.'[23]

There was only one operation ever held at Howick, which was to

The Prince Regent's suite was created by Lady Melbourne, at the request of her lover the future George IV, with fashionable Chinese wallpaper and a red and gold pagoda bed.

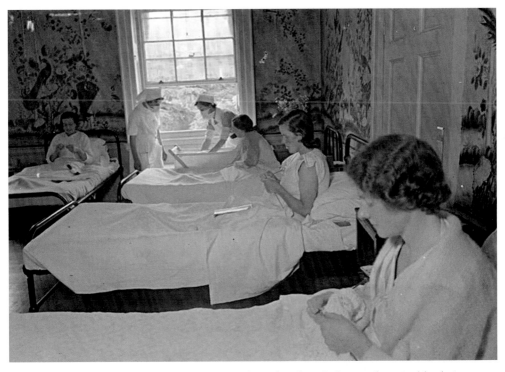

Mothers recovering from childbirth knit for their babies in hospital beds in the lavish surroundings of the Prince Regent's suite, stripped of its furniture for the war. © *Imperial War Museum*

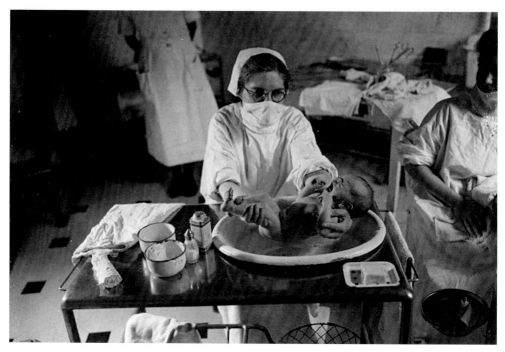

A student midwife bathing a baby in the bathroom located in a tiled room next to the wine cellar at Brocket Hall. All nurses wore surgical masks to reduce the risk of spreading germs. © *Imperial War Museum*

Alan Brocket Lowe, seen here with his grandmother, was the first baby to be born at Brocket Hall on 3 September 1939. His mother gave him the name Brocket to celebrate his place of birth.

© *Alan Lowe*

Children accompanied by nurses
coming down the steps and
across the South Parterre,
at Waddesdon Manor, 1941.
© *Fox Photos Ltd*

Evacuee children cluster around
a gardener on the North Front,
Waddesdon Manor, 1941.
They loved the sound of the
lawnmower as it reminded them
of home. © *Fox Photos Ltd*

The Cedar Boys, Waddesdon Manor, 1944, *l-r standing* Gert Hermann, Ulrich Stobiecka, Otto Decker, Lilly Steinhardt, Rolf Decker, Irwin Freilich, *seated* Peter Gorta, Walter Kugelmann, Helmuth Rothschild, Hans Bodenheimer, Guenter Gruenebaum. © *Helga Brown*

Dorothy de Rothschild, though childless, opened her home and her heart to orphaned children from London and Frankfurt, while working hard on behalf of the Women's Voluntary Service. © *Waddesdon Manor*

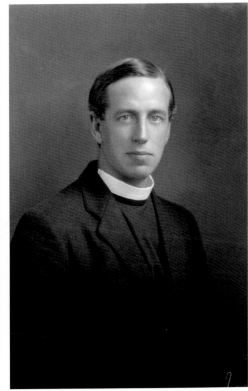

The Nuns of Assumption shared Aldenham Park with their fifty-five schoolgirls and Monsignor Ronald Knox (right) who translated both books of the Bible during the war.

© *The Religious of the Assumption and National Portrait Gallery (Knox)*

Daphne Lady Acton was the mainstay at Aldenham Park. She managed to juggle entertaining Monsignor Ronald Knox with intellectual conversation while playing go-between to Lord Acton and the Mother Superior when they had discussions over the upkeep of Aldenham Park. © *The Acton Family*

Boys from Malvern College used the Long Library at Blenheim as a dormitory. In autumn 1939 some boys posed at outdoor desks as a joke and the photographs appeared in *The Times* a day later, shocking parents who thought their boys had lessons inside the palace. © *Getty Images and Times Archive*

The task of moving Malvern College into Blenheim Palace in September 1939 was an immense one. Among the items transported were twenty pianos and 400 beds. © *Malvern College*

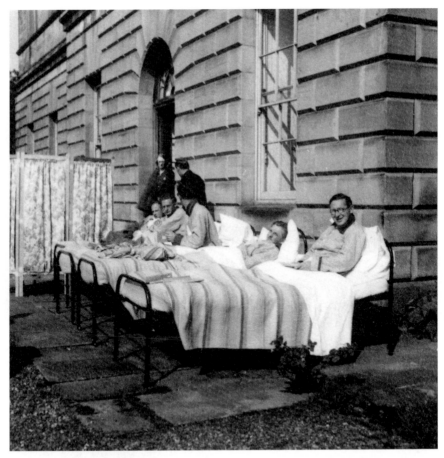

Australian soldiers enjoyed the peace and quiet of Howick Hall convalescent hospital. © *Howick Hall Estate*

Walter Samuel was Chairman of Royal Dutch Shell and worked for MI6 during the war. The Long Gallery at his country home, Upton House, was used as a banking hall.

© *National Portrait Gallery and* © *Solent News & Photo Agency*

In the event of an invasion in the summer of 1940 the life expectancy of a British stay-behind saboteur was thought to be about fifteen days. They were trained at Coleshill House in the art of ungentlemanly warfare. © CART, Coleshill

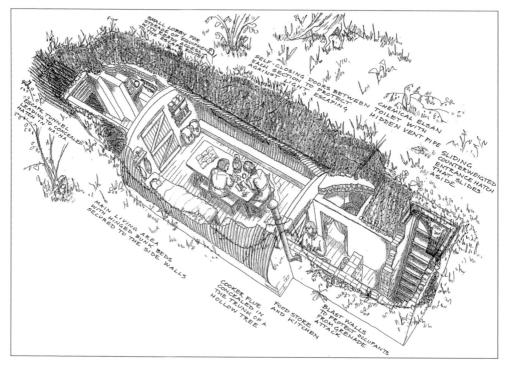

Over 600 operational bases were built for the stay-behind parties from where they would launch sabotage attacks. The location for each base was top secret.

remove a piece of cartilage from the knee of one of the household. Margaret Cook related it in her memoir with evident relish:

> There was great excitement! Matron was longing to have an oper-
> ation! The massage room was scrubbed up and the doctor came
> to operate bringing his partner to give the anaesthetic and every-
> body watched – including all the VADs and Lady Grey! The house
> member, Florence Bickerton, did not seem to mind and thor-
> oughly enjoyed a week or two in the guest room recuperating![24]

Howick lies on the coast of Northumberland some forty miles north of Newcastle. The village is ancient but the seashore is older still. In 1992 the earliest footprint ever to be discovered in Britain was found on the Howick seashore. The prehistoric amphibian dates back 350 million years and caused a great stir in the world of archaeology. Not long after that there was an even more remarkable find: the remains of the oldest house in Britain were uncovered a few hundred yards away. 'It was thought until the find that the population of Western Europe had been nomadic in 8,000 BC. But here in Howick it became plain that families had built houses and settled down in an organised community.'[25] The ancient coastline and the sea air was a tonic to the recovering patients. The extensive gardens and the woods leading down the Long Walk along Howick Burn between an avenue of beech trees were full of wildlife, while the sea beyond had its own rugged beauty, even on stormy days. Margaret Cook wrote: 'The patients really had a lovely time while they were convalesc-ing. Howick is a beautiful spot with lovely grounds famous for its daffodils and enormous trees. It was only 1/4 hours' walk to the sea. The coast is rock rather like the coast of Cornwall and there was a nice beach.'[26]

The men who were fit enough to walk the six miles to Alnwick were allowed to do so as often as they liked, and those who could not were taken into the market town on Tuesdays on a specially organised bus where they went to the cinema. For men who had been fighting abroad life at Howick must have seemed blissful. 'They could bathe, play tennis, croquet (which was very popular), clock golf, walk in the woods, play billiards, table tennis, have dances, whist drives, ENSA shows and films, read books and have a really good holiday.'[27]

On the surface the regime of the hospital was relaxed. In addition to the various pursuits available to them, the men who could would help out by making their own beds or offering to chop wood. Some took joinery lessons from Billy Meakin and others took advantage of the peace and quiet to paint, stitch and write. Embroidery was a popular pastime and Margaret Cook was amused by the craze for embroidering their regimental badges on pieces of linen which they then had framed. 'Some of them were beautifully done, even by those who had never used a needle before. They also made a lot of string bags and belts, and some made leather handbags for their wives and rugs for their homes. We were able to get materials quite easily for all this through the Red Cross.'[28] One soldier embroidered a piece of canvas the size of a pillowcase with a beautiful picture of Howick Hall and gardens. Many of the men wrote to Lady Grey when they left the hospital telling her how much they had benefitted from their stay. 'They really did seem to enjoy themselves and the whole place had a very happy atmosphere and very little discipline.'[29]

Behind the scenes, however, the hospital was run on strict lines. Lorna Granlund joined the Women's Royal Naval Service at the outbreak of war and got a job at Howick looking after the patients. She said: 'I had two weeks training at the RVI [Royal Victoria Infirmary in Newcastle] and then I was set to work looking after the wards, cleaning, keeping the patients cheerful and making them cups of tea.'[30] Matron Railton, who took over from Miss Reid in 1942, was a stickler for the rules and everyone was wary of her. Anne Dawnay remembered her as a formidable character. 'She was the Überboss, she was god and ruled everything but she was very kind.'[31] Some VADs stayed for long stretches but most did short stints so that the turnover of nursing staff was high and often gave Matron something to complain about. She could be brusque with the young nurses and some found her strictness too much to take.

The girls had to wear blue overall dresses with an apron over the top and a 'nun-like head covering'. Lorna cycled two and a half miles from the village of Embleton to Howick in her blue knee-length dress, but her headdress and apron had to stay at the hall. Matron did not approve of Lorna's dress. It was far too short in her opinion. 'She said to me: "you might let the man in the next bed see your knickers!" I replied very cheekily "I don't keep my knickers down there."'[32] Matron was not amused by the remark and gave Lorna the lowliest jobs she could find. One of these was to sweep the floors. 'Lady Grey used to sweep as well,' Lorna said, 'but not with a brush! She would sweep into the hall and go through the green baize door through which we were not allowed to go.'[33] The hierarchy of the hall was further underlined by the seating at mealtimes. 'The cook was Mrs Robertson and the table was laid in such a way that where you sat reflected your grade.'[34] Lorna did not stay long at Howick as she found the work of an auxiliary nurse dull. She joined up in 1941 and the following year was at Portsmouth with the Wrens.

The Joint War Organisation (JWO), which had responsibility for paying for the convalescent hospital beds, had two separate rates depending on occupancy and one of Margaret Cook's jobs was to keep a tally of the number of occupied and unoccupied beds. There were endless rules that had to be complied with to satisfy the army as well as the Red Cross and JWO and Margaret had to make sure that all these were followed. Some were easier than others. The men were not allowed to stay at Howick for more than three weeks, after which they were returned to their regiments or, if still unfit, they were either invalided out or sent to another holding camp. They were not allowed to wear anything but their hospital blues so that they were instantly recognisable in Howick or Alnwick and could not go 'walkabout' without permission. 'All their khaki was handed in when they arrived and put in the pack store (above the stables) in numbered pigeon holes. I had to deal with this at first and give them receipts for everything they handed in, but later the army provided a full-time NCO which was much better. Later still they also provided a PT instructor, but PT was never really popular with the majority of the men.'[35]

The men were entitled to bus and railway warrants, thirty-five free cigarettes a week from the Red Cross and ten shillings a week from their army pay so they could buy cinema tickets or pay for any other little expenses. On Mondays and Thursdays Margaret ran a canteen in an attic room that sold NAAFI cigarettes, matches and chocolate. She worked flat out from morning to night filling out endless forms for the Ministry of Health and the army. 'The army's love of forms is something we had to get used to but it sometimes seemed overwhelming,' she said. Margaret was also asked to organise pantomimes for the men at Christmas time. *Snow White* was very popular, she recalled, as were *Aladdin* and *Cinderella*.

Anne Dawnay remembered the lively atmosphere at Howick. The soldiers' presence made a real difference to the house:

> I think there were about thirty or forty of them and most of the main house was taken over. For their dining room they took over the servants' hall, which is now part of the tea room with the fireplace (my grandmother was allowed £1 per soldier per week for food). On the whole, our convalescents were recovering well. So it was good fun for us children to join in with some of their activities. We saw films on the home cinema – I recall *Mrs Miniver* – and we'd be allowed to sit in when ENSA concert parties visited. They brought some quite big names to Howick.[36]

Anne had ponies and dogs at Howick; her favourite was Chang, a Pekinese that she was given as a puppy for her tenth birthday. He was a great character and the men used to enjoy playing with him and teasing Anne. Chang used to lie on the bottom shelf of a trolley and growl at passers-by. Once he went missing for two days and was found by a local farmer who brought him safely back to the hall, but the event that sticks most firmly in Anne's mind was Chang's abduction by one of the soldiers. A group of men were leaving Howick and after they had gone Matron looked round and could not see the little dog. She marched down to the bus stop at the end of the drive and found him hidden in the greatcoat of a departing soldier. Chang was returned to Anne and after that she kept a more careful eye on him when parties of soldiers were leaving. The presence of the children at Howick was a tonic for the men and they enjoyed seeing them around. They were a reminder, one of them said, of their own families at home and of why the war needed to be fought and won.

Life at Howick was not all about the war and the hospital patients. Family life continued with visits from various relatives as well as friends. Lady Sybil Middleton, Lord Grey's sister, who had been so active in the First World War, lived at Lowood in the Scottish Borders. She was widowed in December 1941 and visited Howick several times over the course of the war years, making annual donations to the hospital even though she was involved in Red Cross work in her own area. Her hand-written diaries record her views on the war in brief but honest detail. She wrote on 10 June 1940: 'Italy declares war – Dirty Dogs!' Later in the year she described going with her brother to see four huge craters made by bombs that had landed near Howick. They made such an impression on them that later in the afternoon she wrote: 'We took Mother and we took a number of photographs of the craters which were over thirty feet across and fifteen feet deep.'[37] Sometimes she would accompany her sister-in-law on her official business around the county. In January 1944 they visited Cornhill, Pallinsburn and Ford hospitals and then played a round of croquet.

Christmas at Howick was a joyful occasion and the staff made every effort to give the patients a happy time. There was a huge decorated tree in the hall, a gift from Lord Grey, and Margaret Cook was in charge of preparations from pantomimes to presents: 'Every Christmas the men each received a Christmas stocking – a long white knitted operation stocking – filled with all sorts of odds and ends from Woolworths, as well as sweets, cigarettes, matches, writing paper, shaving cream etc.'

They had visitors at Howick, some official from the Red Cross and the army, others informal, but the men were not permitted visits from family members as they were not on leave. One stood out in everybody's memory and that was the visit of Princess Mary, the

Princess Royal, in July 1941. As commandant-in-chief of the Red Cross and a former trained nurse, she came to inspect the hospital. She was accompanied by her lady-in-waiting and Helen, Duchess of Northumberland, who lived at Alnwick Castle. The Princess Royal came again two years later with her entourage. On that occasion the men, including a pair of Australian soldiers, organised a guard of honour. Twenty patients were fit enough to stand for a photograph with the Princess, the Duchess of Northumberland, Lady Grey, ten nurses, Matron and Margaret.

For the next two years the convalescent hospital functioned almost to full capacity with upwards of fifty patients at any one time. In January 1943 Lady Sybil and her son Harry arrived at Howick to find 'Mabel, Charlie, the 4 Dawnay children, 63 men in hospital.'[38]

The numbers increased after D-Day and then gradually began to slow down over the early months of 1945. In August there were nine patients, all British. Over the course of the war, a total of 14,135 patients were treated in Northumberland's five hospitals, with a far greater number passing through Howick Hall than had done during the First World War. Lady Grey wrote in the foreword to her 1944–45 official Red Cross branch report for Northumberland: 'Our five hospitals were then in full operation, and now that they have all closed down we can look back and see what a really satisfactory piece of work they accomplished. During the whole war they were busy – but for the six to nine months after D-Day they were crammed and the staffs rose most gallantly to the occasion.'[39]

The last patients left Howick in September 1945 and the family, including the grandchildren, moved in and took over the Hall once again. The rooms downstairs were reinstated, the boards removed from the library bookcases and Billy Meakin was busier than ever, restoring damaged furniture and moving paintings back into position. He managed to 'procure some field telephones in handsome leather cases plus some huge drums of cable. He worked out the circuitry and ran cables around the hall, stables, gardens etc. So by winding a handle and depressing certain switches, the estate was in telephonic communication for the first time.'[40] Billy's son, Arthur, remembers that not everyone was happy about the introduction of modern communications to Howick. Some of the estate workers didn't like feeling they could be got at on the other end of a telephone line, Arthur Meakin explained. The telephone system did good service and was still in use at Howick until the 1960s.

Margaret Cook helped to oversee the packing up of the Red Cross material and clearing up Howick Hall. At the end of October she gathered her bags and papers, and left the Hall for the last time in her Austin 7. It was a wet and windy day but mild, in contrast to the day she arrived in the snowstorm four and a half years earlier. She wrote her four-page memoir of her time at Howick in 1946, concluding: 'I feel I was very fortunate to have had such a happy and yet useful job to do during the war years.'[41]

Upton House in Warwickshire belonged to Walter Samuel, the second Baron Bearsted. During the war it housed the family's bank and all the bank's staff.

CHAPTER 6

Dear 'K'

*Your connections in Washington being what they are,
you will no doubt be able to give us on return a good
picture of the political situation there and the general
opinion from outside of the OSS organisation as a
whole.*

Instructions to Lord Bearsted on a visit
to the USA for MI6 in 1943

On 31 August 1939, Peter Samuel, a director of his family's London based bank, M. Samuel & Co., sent a telegram to the staff at the family's country house near Banbury in Warwickshire: 'War imminent STOP CONFIDENTIAL Prepare Upton House STOP No Time To Lose PETER SAMUEL'

The reply came back: 'Staff Ready'.

Upton House in Warwickshire had been the family's country residence since 1927, when Peter's father, Walter Samuel, purchased the house after his father's death. He had come into an immense inheritance and the title of second Viscount Bearsted. He and his wife Dorothea extensively remodelled Upton over the next few years. It was a house more associated with pleasure than work, designed to accommodate Lord Bearsted's collection of art and porcelain. For their three sons, Richard (Dicky), Peter, and Anthony (Tony), Upton provided a wonderful contrast to their home at 1 Carlton Gardens in London. Here they could enjoy everything the countryside had to offer, from hunting and shooting to weekend parties and dances. Peter Samuel was a keen huntsman and regularly rode three horses in a day and then returned to Upton to play a vigorous game of squash.

Walter Samuel's wealth came from his father and uncle who were in business together. His father, Marcus Samuel, born in Whitechapel, had begun his business life as the owner of a small company trading in painted shells and other curiosities. In 1890 the company began shipping petroleum and by 1897 had its own oil wells in Borneo. The Shell Transport and Trading Company was formed that year, the name taken from Samuel's first business. Ten turbulent years later, Shell was amalgamated with Royal Dutch to form Royal Dutch Shell. The group rapidly expanded and became one of the world's leading energy companies. Marcus Samuel was ambitious, passionate and keen to be accepted in society. He took his civic responsibilities seriously and was a prominent figure in the City of London, becoming Lord Mayor in 1902. During the First World War he threw himself and Shell wholly behind the war effort, eventually convincing the Royal Navy to switch from coal to oil, advocating the internal combustion engine as the best form of propulsion for its fleet. He turned his house, The Mote, near Maidstone, Kent, into a hospital for non-commissioned officers and took a close personal interest in their welfare.

Marcus Samuel retired from the board of Shell in 1920 announcing that 'the weight of this gigantic business must be carried by younger shoulders and when the time comes it is a matter of much gratification to me to know that I and every member of your board will have great confidence in my son, Captain [Walter] Samuel, who will, I hope, succeed me and who has all the qualifications necessary.'[1] The announcement was greeted by cheers from the shareholders who were pleased to have continuity on the board. A year later Marcus Samuel was created a life peer, choosing the name Bearsted from a village close to his home in Kent. He was not a vain man, his biographer called him 'uncommunicative about the past', but his elevation to the House of Lords gave him great satisfaction. He told friends who visited him in his study shortly after the announcement: 'You can't think what pleasure it gives me to put the "Honourable" on my children's envelopes.'[2] By the time he died in 1927 Shell had a capital of more than £26 million or about £11 billion today.

Marcus Samuel brought up his four children to believe that with great wealth went equal responsibility. With his eldest son, Walter, he set up the Stepney Jewish Lads Club, to give young people a chance to enjoy sports, drama and outdoor activities which they might not have been able to do with their parents. Walter's younger brother, Gerald, had no desire to go into the family business but he took a great interest in the club, eventually giving up his luxurious life in the West End to move to Stepney and be more involved in the lives of the boys the club supported.

At the outbreak of the First World War Walter Samuel joined the Queen's Own West Kent Yeomanry, serving in Gallipoli. From there he went to Egypt with the regiment before returning to the Western Front in spring 1918. He attained the rank of captain, was mentioned twice in dispatches and was awarded the Military Cross in 1918 for an 'act of exemplary gallantry during active operations against the enemy'. Gerald went out to France and was killed at Verdun in 1916, a tragedy that affected Walter very deeply.

Walter's two sisters also lost their husbands in the war, so that he was the only male of that generation of the family to have survived. In 1908 he had married Dorothea Montefiore Micholls and over the next ten years they had three sons. Like his father before him, he was an intensely private man. When the first Lord Bearsted died there had been what his biographer described as a 'documentary massacre' when all personal papers were destroyed and very little is known about the private life of the family.

As well as being a businessman, the second Lord Bearsted was an art collector and a philanthropist. The New York Times described him as rich in possessions but a man who spent unostentatiously and wisely. He was shrewd in his judgments and managed to maintain 'a happy balance in his life between sympathy and recreation'[3]. He had begun collecting art at the age of twenty-three and had an excellent eye. He continued to indulge his passion for the rest of his life, forming one of the most important private collections of the twentieth century, including works by George Stubbs, El Greco, Pieter Brueghel, William Hogarth and George Romney, as well as many other famous artists. At the age of forty-one he donated a vast collection of Japanese art, which included some of the famous wood blocks by Hokusai, to the Maidstone Museum, necessitating the construction of a new wing, which his father funded. The collection remains one of the best Japanese collections in the country, rivalling the British Museum and the Victoria and Albert Museum's holdings. He had sound judgment and bought works that he liked rather than because they were by artists fashionable at the time. His taste was respected and he served as a trustee of the Tate Gallery, the National Gallery and the Whitechapel Art Gallery as well as being a major benefactor to the Ashmolean Museum in Oxford with a donation of £18,000 in 1938. During the war he continued to play an active role on the various museum boards.

At some stage over the summer of 1939, he and Lady Bearsted decided they would have to move the valuable contents of their London home to Upton for safe-keeping. They offered the magnificent 1 Carlton Gardens as a gift to the nation and it was accepted by a grateful government. It is now an official ministerial residence normally used by the foreign secretary.

When Lord and Lady Bearsted handed over the property they moved into the Dorchester Hotel. This became the chosen home of many wealthy people and a favoured meeting place during the war. It was known to be the safest building in London as the basement, which is one third of the size of the hotel above ground, is made of reinforced concrete. The eight upper floors are supported on a massive three-feet-thick reinforced concrete deck that forms the roof of the first floor of the building. When the Blitz began, the dining rooms were moved downstairs into the Gold Room and the ballroom to avoid flying glass. One Canadian diplomat, Charles Ritchie, compared the surreal atmosphere of dining at the Dorchester during the Blitz to cruising on a luxury liner with the remaining members of London's high society in the midst of a hurricane. Despite the danger of the nightly bombing there were residents who eschewed the communal air-raid shelter in the basement as it was insufficiently exclusive. They chose the less secure option of the hotel's underground gymnasium and Turkish baths where at least they could sit with like-minded friends. It all seems a little absurd from today's perspective and indeed some thought so at the time. Cecil Beaton was scathing. He described the hotel as 'a building in which the respectable and the dubious mixed by the thousand, knocking back cocktails and indulging in careless talk.'

In 1944 General Eisenhower moved out of Claridges and became a resident of the Dorchester because he wanted more peace and quiet in order to plan the Normandy invasion. He moved into two rooms on the first floor today called the Eisenhower Suite. Winston Churchill also had rooms at the Dorchester and had a wall built on the balcony between his and the one next door to afford him privacy. Many politicians, aristocrats, socialites and hangers-on enjoyed a hedonistic atmosphere of dancing, drinking and gossiping but that does not appear to have been the lifestyle that the Bearsteds sought. It seems strange that they, with their focus on philanthropy and public service chose to live there but as wealthy members of society they would have known many residents and besides, they needed a London home.

Peter Samuel left London to join his regiment, the Warwickshire Yeomanry at Thorseby Park in Sherwood Forest, two days after sending the telegram to the butler at Upton House. Meanwhile, his parents made their way to Warwickshire to oversee the alterations which would allow their home to become the headquarters of M. Samuel & Co. – the merchant bank owned by the family – for the duration. The intention was to move the entire operation including all the essential staff to the countryside so that the bank could continue to function.

The central block of the house dates from the late seventeenth century and was altered over the centuries with additions and removals. The twentieth-century alterations include two wings and extensive redecorations, some in the art deco style, including Lady Bearsted's bathroom which is lined with aluminium leaf. But the real glories of Upton – apart from the art collection – are the gardens. Lady Bearsted took a great interest in the development of the gardens and employed the designer Kitty Lloyd Jones to make sweeping changes, including a paved garden, to be seen from her bedroom, a blue and yellow herbaceous border by the kitchen garden and bog gardens to the west of the house. At the bottom of the garden is the beautiful and picturesque Mirror Pool which reflects the sky and trees around it while the main lawn has a stand of magnificent cedars, which Peter Samuel recalled when he was out in the middle of the desert in 1943:

> I would give all the world to be lying under the cedar at Upton in the summer and smell the unforgettable smell of grass and new-mown hay and hear the lazy humming of the birds and bees, and looking and seeing everything calm and green and cool, and then close my eyes and do absolutely nothing. One day I shall do that again and it will be heaven.[4]

The staff at Upton House had their work cut out to prepare the house to provide suitable accommodation for a London bank within a matter of days. The man in charge of overseeing the changes was George Smith, the head butler. He worked day and night to get a house which normally had a handful of residents and weekend guests ready for almost two dozen bank workers, more than half of whom were women, with just a skeleton staff to help him. By the time the bank was running at full strength there were twenty-three bank employees working in the Long Gallery and the main hall. The dining room, with its precious collection of china and the magnificent paintings by Stubbs, was off limits to the banking staff except by special invitation of the Bearsteds.

Dormitories were set up on the first floor with two, three or four beds. The female staff was quartered in rooms overlooking the back garden while the largest men's dormitory looked out over the front drive. One of the bank clerks, Barney Adler, who was twenty-three at the outbreak of war, described Upton as being run like a holiday camp 'but a little more austere'. The rooms for the men were basic and comfortable but the women's rooms had an ensuite bathroom, an untold luxury in comparison to life back home. Lord and Lady Bearsted's rooms remained closed to the banking staff, Lady Bearsted's exquisitely decorated bathroom being deemed too fragile for general use.

Downstairs, the Long Gallery became the banking hall with a dining area at one end. Barney Adler wrote: 'The meals were taken in the Long Gallery, which was full of magnificent paintings and the finest collection of Chelsea china in the world. The food I remember most of all was rook pie and stewed rabbit.'[5] Furniture from Shell House at 55 Bishopsgate arrived by lorry and was quickly set up. Tables with typewriters for the secretaries were ranged along the garden wall, with the clerks and managers at the far end of the gallery on individual desks. The senior secretary was Miss Diana Hazlerigg. At five feet eight inches tall she was a striking young woman. George Smith described her as 'a cut above – not a run of the mill typist. She had blonde hair and was beautiful. She was very smart and imposing.' Diana Hazlerigg remained at Upton until Christmas 1941 when she left to join the ATS, enlisting at Oxford on 10 January 1942, a week after her twenty-eighth birthday. She returned to M. Samuel after the war and worked there until she married Robert Hope-Falkner in March 1946. Her son Patrick wrote: 'My imperious grandmother shortlisted her as a candidate for introduction to Dad after he was demobbed – one of six!'

It was only Miss Hazlerigg and Mr A.C. McCarthy, the company secretary, who had telephones. At a meeting held in London on 5 September the board confirmed that 'the name of Mr A C McCarthy is added to the list of special signatures for the war period.' Albert 'Mac' McCarthy had had a long association with the bank. In the First World War he had fought with the King's Royal Rifle Corps, attaining the rank of corporal before he was invalided out in 1916. He was brought back to Britain and after hospital treatment was sent to convalesce at the Mote, the large country house in Kent owned by the first Viscount Bearsted. Lord Bearsted senior was taken with the young man and offered him a job as a footman at the Mote. However, he soon realised that McCarthy had a great deal more to offer so he was moved to Bishopsgate where he worked his way up to become chief secretary to the bank in his forties. During the late 1920s he spent time working on Wall Street but returned to M. Samuel after the crash. With war looming, Mac joined the RAF as a pilot officer but he was soon discharged as unfit for service due to the trauma he had experienced in the previous war. He returned to the bank and was immediately put in charge of the move to Upton. On 11 September 1939 he wrote to Lord Bearsted: 'Everyone is comfortable and happy at Upton.' His only concern was that during the short days and longer evenings the staff might get bored. Mac lived at Upton during the week but at weekends he joined his wife at a house in South Bar near Banbury Cross.

Bank records show that he was paid £1,000 a year working as the most senior member of staff at Upton. He was responsible not only for the day-to-day running of the bank but also for the welfare of the staff, all of whom were younger than he was, and some of whom found the isolation from London trying. He encouraged the younger staff to make the most of the beautiful grounds. In the early mornings before going to work they swam in the pool that the Bearsteds had had built in 1936. They took walks around the extensive gardens and roamed further afield at weekends. Lord Bearsted bought wellington boots for all the staff and bicycles so that they could explore the countryside beyond the estate. The gardens were not greatly altered during the war, although the borders were turned over to grow fruit and vegetables but the two large pools, the Mirror Pool and the Temple Pool, had to be drained as they shone like glass in the moonlight and it was feared that they might be used by the Luftwaffe to map their routes and find targets more easily.

Barney Adler embraced life in the countryside with relish. He wrote to his fiancée, Joyce, a month after he had arrived telling her how much he enjoyed swimming in the late summer. He had managed a swim almost every morning before work, he told her. It was such an enormous contrast to his life in London just weeks earlier. Two months later he learned to cycle for the first time in his life. 'The old Chief Accountant gave me a push off and I rode quite a long way until I fell off.'[6] The first few rides were a bit wobbly but he soon got the hang of it and spent most of his weekends riding around the Warwickshire countryside visiting antique shops, having been inspired to take an interest in art and porcelain after admiring Lord Bearsted's collection. Barney and Joyce soon married and moved into a bungalow about three quarters of a mile from Upton House. He wrote in his memoir: 'It was a wonderful war for us and we were very lucky. We cycled 3,000 miles during the summer of 1941 and bought all sorts of antiques which we stuffed into the bungalow. One day, Joyce cycled to Stratford on Avon to see a play, but they wouldn't let her in because she didn't have a gas mask, so she went into Woolworth's and bought a case for 6d and stuffed it with paper. She saw the play.'[7]

The bank had a real role to play during the war supporting commerce by funding government projects. Two schemes that M. Samuel & Co. became involved in were providing loans for acquiring supplies of parachute silk and credits for purchasing eggs from Hungary. The company's board minute books list other items such as the provision of credit for the Ministry of Supply who needed to buy 10,000 sets of leather equipment in October 1939 and quantities of American beer destined for the NAAFI in Egypt. In May 1942, board members were informed that the company held over 2 million sterling 3.5 per cent War Stock as well as Baltic, Bolivian and astonishingly, given the circumstances prevailing at the time, Japanese government securities, reflecting the areas where Shell Company had been active in the 1930s.

Stephen Howarth, author of the company history of Shell, *A Century in Oil*, wrote that 'Shell Transport entered World War II in an uncompromising mood.'[8] It is hardly surprising. The experience of the First World War had shown how vitally important oil would be in any future conflict. An army can march hungry, albeit inefficiently, but tanks and battleships cannot run without fuel. Petrol was the first commodity to be rationed and the government exercised complete control over its distribution throughout the war.

As far as the board of Shell was concerned, the greatest role they would have to play in the war was to secure sufficient oil whenever and wherever it was needed:

> Under Shell Transport's leadership, the creation of the Petroleum Board, or 'the Pool', symbolized the nature of the British wartime oil industry. Planned during 1938, it was activated at 'time zero', the last second of Britain's first day at war: midnight on the night of 3–4 September 1939. Following the plan, the Pool was ready to continue its work for as long as the war continued.[9]

Shell was one of the four largest distributing companies that dominated the Pool. Ninety-four smaller companies were also involved and all had been rivals pre-war. They agreed to suspend their competition and work together as a group for the duration of the hostilities. Lorries with the logos of both Shell and BP were used to deliver petrol around the country. The Pool's board's headquarters was in Shell-Mex House on Bishopsgate, which had air-raid shelters in the basement and a comprehensive duplicate telephone system with their lines re-routed – some to the Strand, some to Embankment – so that if one or other telephone exchange were put out by enemy action they would still be able to communicate. Shell also installed a teleprinter which had a dedicated phone line, giving it extra security. This machine was for the Pool nationwide but it was also linked to the three armed forces and was in constant use, twenty-four hours a day, handling as many as five thousand messages a day. Although there is no documented link between Lord Bearsted's work for the Secret Intelligence Service and this close relationship between Shell, the government and the armed services, it is hard not to imagine that he was at the very least a highly regarded individual who could be trusted with information close to government.

The Pool was not responsible for fuel rationing, merely for its distribution, but it proved to be a highly successful and effective relationship which was mirrored on the high seas by a working relationship with the Royal Navy and their convoys:

> Shell tankers served in every part of the world. In the latter part of the war they acted as oilers for the British Pacific Fleet; they brought fuel to Malta and, through the Murmansk convoys, to Russia; they were present on 6 June 1944 at D-Day ... not only carrying millions of gallons of fuel but also distilling and providing fresh water, that other essential for armies on the move; and throughout the war they brought oil to Britain on the core transatlantic routes.[10]

With Walter Samuel as its chairman and the majority of Shell's directors both Jewish and proud to be British, the rumours of Jewish persecution in Nazi Germany gave an added urgency to decisions taken by the board. Immediately after the declaration of war one of the first actions of the company was to furnish the British intelligence services and the RAF with all the available information on Shell's refineries and oil fields in Germany. 'Though easily seen as a correct decision, it was nevertheless depressing, because it was a clear invitation for the bombing of Shell installations and Shell personnel; yet the alternative was too awful to contemplate.'[11] By the end of the war it was discovered that the oil establishments in Germany most comprehensively destroyed were those belonging to Shell.

Lord Bearsted also suggested putting the Shell Film Unit at the disposal of the government. The film unit had been set up in 1934 to take advantage of a new kind of cinema: documentaries. Cinema-going was at its peak in the mid-1930s and Shell spotted the opportunity for high-profile advertising. Their first film for public screening was called *Airport*, which depicted a day in the life of Croydon Aerodrome. 'The film lasted only seventeen minutes, but nothing could quite compare with aircraft, and everything associated with them, for excitement. Many people had never seen an aeroplane (of if they had, only at a great distance) yet everyone recognised the exotic glamour of flight.'[12] *Airport* was a critical success and it cleverly positioned Shell at the 'vanguard of modernity' while providing high-quality entertainment and education. The technical quality of the Shell films, often using techniques such as mechanical animation, were so innovative that one critic raved over a film with the unpromising title *Transfer of Power* as 'most exciting and beautiful ... a short but dazzling demonstration of the human genius for invention.'[13] With such a pedigree it is easy to see why the government accepted the offer with alacrity. Over the next six years, forty-seven films were made for the Admiralty, the Ministry of Home Security and the Ministry of War Transport – some aimed at boosting public morale, while others focused on secret instruction and training.

Shell's involvement in the war went far beyond the transport of oil for the war effort. As a petrochemical company it was constantly innovating and many of its products were used in a variety of fields, from flexible pipelines for transporting oil or water to acetone which was used in the manufacture of Perspex for aeroplane hoods. On 18 January 1943, the Ministry of Supply asked Shell if a suitable waterproofing material could be made to coat up to 150,000 vehicles that would be landed off the beaches of Normandy:

> The challenge was uniquely daunting. First and foremost, the material had to provide 100 per cent water-proofing efficiency, 'to enable a vehicle to wade in sea water' to a depth of three feet with eighteen-inch waves on top. It had to be easy to use, so that comparatively unskilled personnel could apply it with a high degree of reliability. It had to be a good insulator; it had to be rigid up to 200 degrees Fahrenheit, and to survive exposure to that temperature for long periods without either sagging or

hardening and cracking, and without showing any oil separation whatever; it had to smear easily and 'take' on slight greasy surfaces, without being tacky or clinging to the operators' hands; and it had to be something which could be provided soon, in enormous quantities.[14]

By 24 February, after just thirty-seven days, Shell was ready to trial Compound 219. An engine was covered in the material, placed in a water tank, warmed up, immersed in salt water and when it was turned on it worked. There was jubilation after the trials and the company was proud to record that over 24 million pounds of Compound 219 was used at D-Day. The secretary of state for war told the board that 'despite the fact that many of them went ashore through five feet of water in heavy seas, less than two out of every thousand of the vehicles, or 0.2 per cent, were "drowned" off the beaches.'[15]

Lord Bearsted took a keen interest in all the developments within Shell's chemical products but he could not hide his dislike of the purpose to which they were put. He said in 1942, 'We look forward to the time when the manufacture of all these materials for war purposes is no longer necessary; they will, however, each be able to play a more constructive part in peacetime.'[16] He never expressed the slightest doubt that there would be anything other than an Allied victory when peace finally returned.

Lord Bearsted also took a close personal interest in Shell's personnel during the war, particularly the tanker-men who were the lynchpin to everything else the company undertook. They were constantly under threat from U-boat attack when they made their way in the convoys across the north Atlantic and through the Mediterranean. When the crew of the *Ohio* arrived in Malta in a dramatic and critical operation which so very nearly failed, to his great delight the crew was decorated. The captain, D. W. Mason, was awarded the George Cross and the chief engineer, J. Wyld, the DSO. Other members received between them five DSCs and seven DSMs. At the end of the war, Lord Bearsted could count over 300

Shell employees who had been given medals, citations, mentions in dispatches and other recognition. Probably the most famous of them all was Sir Douglas Bader, who flew for Shell after he was invalided out of the RAF in 1933 having lost both legs. He rejoined the RAF in 1939 earning both the DSO and DFC in 1940 before taking command of a squadron in 1941. He was shot down in France later that year and captured. Repeated escape attempts landed him in Colditz. After the war he rejoined Shell, becoming manager of Group Aircraft Operations and the first managing director of Shell Aircraft in 1958.

The highest decoration of all was awarded to former Shell employee Major Robert Cain when he and his men came under heavy attack from Panzer tanks during the Battle of Arnhem. 'Taking an anti-tank launcher Cain left cover alone, shot at the leading Panzer, immobilised it and then, though wounded, co-ordinated its destruction by Howitzer. For this and other subsequent acts and examples of extreme courage and leadership he was awarded Britain's highest military decoration, the Victoria Cross.'[17] He had been a manager in Nigeria and after the war resumed his employment with Shell working in East Asia and then Africa, dying of cancer in 1974. His daughter, Frances Cain, was unaware of her father's Victoria Cross until after he died because, according to her ex-husband, Jeremy Clarkson, 'he'd never thought to mention it.'

Lord Bearsted was as quick to show his pleasure for small promotions as he was for the award of high military honours. When two of the bank's junior members of staff, Barney Adler and Harry Bluglass were made assistant and chief accountant respectively, Lord Bearsted gave a lunch in the dining room at Upton for his newly promoted employees. There was a 'royal feast' with roast turkey and two different wines. Barney Adler recalled later: 'It so happened that Turquand Youngs, the auditors, arrived by chance at the same time, so they sat down to lunch too. They had a new articled clerk with them – Drysdale – he looked amazed and asked me if we ate like this every day. I said "Yes". He was delighted and he wasn't to know that we had rook pie again next day!'[18]

In the summer of 1940, the tranquillity of Upton was rudely disturbed by the Battle of Britain which roared and exploded above the country. Members of the bank staff took it in turns to be on fire watch and ARP duty. The Blitz on Coventry and other provincial cities that autumn focused Lord Bearsted's attention on the precious paintings and china at Upton. The most important consideration for him after the safety of his banking staff was the preservation of his art collection. Pictures from 1 Carlton Gardens had arrived along with the bank's furniture and files in September 1939 and were stored in the cellars, in spaces on the walls and in the long corridors on the first and second floors. Initially he had believed Upton House to be a safe distance from London and in a sufficiently remote location to remain unthreatened by bombing. Now he was no longer confident that the house was as safe as he had thought. As a trustee of the National Gallery he was aware that plans had existed since 1934 to evacuate the national collection out of London in the event of war. In the summer of 1940 there had been plans to move the entire National Gallery collection to Canada but when the director, Kenneth Clarke, who was worried about submarine attack, suggested this solution to Churchill he met with a blunt response: 'Hide them in caves and cellars, but not one picture shall leave this island,' the prime minister thundered.

The National Gallery's collections had been stored in various sites in Wales such as Penrhyn Castle, the National Library of Wales at Aberystwyth and the University of Wales. However, the feeling was that these were not immune from enemy bombardment either, so Assistant Keeper Martin Davies searched Wales for a better venue and finally settled on Manod Quarry, a disused slate mine above Blaenau Ffestiniog. Lord Bearsted was sufficiently worried that he wrote to Kenneth Clarke, asking whether he might send a selection of his paintings for safekeeping in Wales too. He wrote: 'The present position is that every picture I have is now at Upton. I originally considered Upton as safe as anything but now they have built an aerodrome quite close. As you know, most of my pictures are comparatively small and I should be very glad if I could send a few of the best to the Quarry.'[19] Kenneth Clarke agreed to Lord Bearsted's request in recognition of the importance of the collection at Upton. Forty small paintings were chosen and spent the rest of the war in Chamber 5 in Manod Quarry with works from the king's own collection. The press heard rumours regarding the whereabouts of the National Gallery's treasures and Lord Bearsted offered advice: 'I see no harm in the *Daily Telegraph* saying that the pictures are stored in a bombproof cave in a mountain, which is very vague. The only question which occurs to me is that, if such a statement were made, we might have a lot of enthusiastic journalists trying to find out where the mountain was. I do not think Wales should be mentioned in any way.'[20]

While thinking about his works of art and his employees at the bank and at Shell, Lord Bearsted was also busy working behind the scenes to help his country at its time of greatest need. In the febrile atmosphere of the late 1930s, the British Secret Service underwent an expansion and metamorphosis that would have a great impact on the war. While Hitler was rearranging the map of Europe with his incursions into the Rhineland, Austria and the Sudetenland, activity in and around a small area of west London was on the increase. The Secret Intelligence Service (SIS), or MI6 as it became known in the Second World War, was so secret that its existence was not acknowledged until 1994. As M. R. D. Foot, the historian and authority on Special Operations put it, 'Governments like to keep up with each other the pretences that no such bodies exist, though without one no strong regime can stand for long.'[21] SIS was created in 1909 and from 1921 was under Foreign Office control. It formed part of the UK's intelligence machinery and its job was to secure secrets from abroad. The security service, MI5, was responsible for guarding secrets at home and came under the auspices of the Home Office.

SIS had offices at 54 Broadway, near St James' Park, and was undertaking the purchase of a house in Buckinghamshire that would be the wartime home of the Government Code and Cipher School, Bletchley Park. The head of SIS, known simply as C within Whitehall, was Admiral 'Quex' Sinclair. By 1938 it had become

clear that war was imminent and that some form of subversive tactics would be called for in addition to 'normal' military warfare.
In April, C 'borrowed' an officer from the army to work for him
in a yet undefined capacity. Major Lawrence Douglas Grand was
seconded to SIS and told to start up a new section, at first called
IX, later known as D. His task was 'to investigate every possibility
of attacking potential enemies by means other than the operations
of military force',[22] yet at first he was forbidden to initiate any overt
action. His was to be purely a research role and to make a report
and recommendations to SIS. 'Examining such an enormous task',
Grand wrote after the war, 'one felt as if one had been told to move
the Pyramids with a pin.'[23]

Lawrence Grand was described by Bickham Sweet-Escott in
Baker Street Irregular as having some of the traits that have come
to be expected in a secret service leader: 'He was tall, handsome,
well-tailored, with a heavy dark moustache; wore a red carnation;
smoked cigarettes, almost without cease, through an elegant black
holder; had an equally elegant wit. He was brimful of ideas and
energy and he had a rare gift: he gave full trust to those under him,
and backed them up without question against outsiders.'[24] He was
to be responsible for the civilian arm of this new branch of intelligence, while parallel to his department another was set up to focus
on military intelligence and the potential for disruptive sabotage
and guerrilla warfare. This branch will be discussed in the next
chapter.

Set up in a little office in 2 Caxton Street with only limited funds
and a brief 'to *do* nothing but to think', he had a small full-time staff
but expanded his team by recruiting men on a 'territorial' basis, that
is to say unpaid, to be trained and then co-opted as full-time intelligence officers in the event of a war. In the first instance these new
recruits, mainly civilian businessmen from the City of London with
wide commercial and foreign experience, were asked to produce
intelligence on a wide range of activities within their own spheres.
By the end of the 1930s, SIS had a network of intelligence gathering
agents who were in effect spying on behalf of Britain.

When Lord Bearsted was recruited to SIS by his friend Stewart Menzies, he was already exceptionally well connected and keen to lend his support to this small branch of intelligence. He had no illusions but that there would be another war. That Shell had refineries and factories in Germany meant he had already observed the worrying signs emerging from that country. Menzies, who had been working in SIS since the end of the First World War, would go on to play a prominent role in the organisation.

As the war progressed, so SIS's influence and therefore funding grew, and Menzies became closer to Churchill than any other head of an intelligence section. He was eventually responsible for the Government Code and Cipher School, which famously, with considerable Polish and French help, broke the naval Enigma code, Germany's secret communications system, for which he was knighted and created a KCB (Knight Commander) in 1951.

Thanks to the brilliant fiction of Ian Fleming, the image of a spy as a dashing, gun-toting, martini-swilling bachelor with the flashiest of cars and the gadgets of schoolboys' dreams has become hard-wired into the public's mind. There was unprecedented collecting of intelligence, otherwise known as spying, during the Second World War and much of it was done by people ostensibly going about their everyday lives and far from the profile of the cinematic legend 007. Lord Bearsted was one such businessman, who was known in the secret world of MI6 by his code name K. Lord Bearsted and others similarly recruited would provide all important contacts but they could also act as a conduit for secret funding and this was key, especially abroad, where channelling hush-hush funds from Britain was more difficult.

Lord Bearsted was re-commissioned as a lieutenant on the 'special list' of the Territorial Army (TA) Reserve and asked to sign a copy of the Official Secrets Act, which he did on 23 September 1939. In order to give the officers recruited by SIS some official status and legal protection during wartime, from 1940 recruits were given a formal army rank, with a choice of appearing either on the General List or the new intelligence corps. By March 1940 Lord Bearsted held the rank of acting colonel and had become involved in the development of resistance networks in Scandinavia. According to Malcolm Atkin, the author of *Fighting Nazi Occupation: British Resistance 1939–1945*, he put Royal Dutch Shell in Scandinavia at the disposal of Section D and instructed the company's office to provide full funding to the agents aiming to recruit and build intelligence gathering networks in Sweden and Denmark. As a trusted officer Lord Bearsted was permitted direct communication with the Section D's agent in Scandinavia, Gerald Holdsworth, ensuring he had the necessary funds to carry out his secret work in Norway and Sweden.

Lord Bearsted was also involved in one of Lawrence Grand's more convoluted schemes to send and distribute black propaganda in Germany. He obtained the loan of the 'addressograph' facilities at Shell, complete with two trained operators, and persuaded the company to buy three stencil-cutting machines from the USA. Once Section D had compiled a mailing list, the equipment was used to send propaganda material into Germany which 'apparently' emanated from the USA. Eventually this had to be stopped in case the Americans found out what Section D was up to. It was felt it would not be a good thing to discover in an election year that a foreign government was using its 'signature' to send subversive material into another country, enemy or not.

Meanwhile, back in the real world of business and civilian life, Lord Bearsted had to keep up the perfect disguise of being himself. He was in almost every way ideally suited to the double-sided life of businessman and member of the secret services. He was scrupulously polite, modest and reserved and with a dry wit, appearing to some unapproachable, but this hid an extremely generous philanthropic side to his personality. Despite the fact he was leading a double life he never would have thought of himself as duplicitous; he was a true patriot and proud of his country. The summer of 1940 was a time of the greatest imminent danger to Britain. A German invasion looked likely and as a prominent Jewish figurehead and as chairman of Shell, Lord Bearsted was a key Nazi target. He figured not once but twice on the infamous German 'Black List' of Britons who would be arrested in the event of invasion.

Section D's activity was at its zenith, with Lawrence Grand energetically setting up arms dumps all over the country for stay-behind sabotage parties to access in the event of an invasion. Lord Bearsted was put in charge of the Home Defence Service (HDS). This was the part of Grand's scheme that would be responsible for intelligence gathering after the Germans had landed and would be able to feed reports from behind enemy lines back to the regular armed forces who would still be in the unoccupied sections of the country. His exact role in this intelligence gathering has never been made clear but John Warwicker, the historian of the stay-behind parties, the Auxiliary Units, suggested in his book *Churchill's Underground Army* that he may well have been the 'overlord' of the Special Duties Section in charge of 'civilians . . . trained to collect and communicate intelligence. In a nutshell they were to be spies.'[25] He wrote: 'On just one occasion in the otherwise typewritten Section D closing report, the name "Bearsted" is added in pen and ink . . . It is understood – and it will be no surprise if true – that intelligence corps may simply be cover for his role for the Secret Intelligence Service as overlord of the SDS.'[26] After the high point of anxiety in that summer, when the threat of invasion began to lessen, Lord Bearsted was seconded to the newly formed Special Operations Executive again on the intelligence gathering side. This was a significant move as the Auxiliary Units continued to operate, as we shall see in the next chapter, until late 1944 but clearly Lord Bearsted was deemed to be too valuable not to be used in the more ambitious organisation that was developing to place trained men and women into Nazi-occupied Europe.

As part of his undercover reconnaissance work, Lord Bearsted travelled across the Atlantic several times, ostensibly on Shell business. In November 1942, he was informed that the Minister of Economic Warfare had organised for him to visit Washington 'in connection with the JIC [War Cabinet Joint Intelligence Sub-Committee] on the Far East'. In a letter addressed 'Dear K', Lord Bearsted was instructed to report back on the relationship between the newly formed American Office of Strategic Services (OSS) – the US equivalent of the UK's Special Operations Executive (SOE) and the US intelligence service. There was clearly some friction within the US intelligence service, as there had been within the British equivalent and he was to garner the opinion of the two highest-ranking officials in the US military intelligence as well as the Director of National Intelligence as to how things were developing. In the fullness of time the US and British would be working together and it was key to know what was going on.

In a long and colourfully worded report Lord Bearsted answered all the points requested of him and then summed up the situation as he saw it in Washington: 'Generally I found Washington a domestic bear-garden. There are far too many inter-services and inter-departmental jealousies. There never seemed to be any central body to whom one could go where all information on any subject was collected and filed for reference.'[27] It would be difficult not to imagine someone from the outside would have made a similar assessment about the state of the British secret services in the summer of 1940.

On 6 October 1943, Lord Bearsted wrote to Stewart Menzies announcing his decision to return to civilian life and to relinquish the special commission he had been granted in 1939. This was agreed on 18 October and a note from a senior SIS official read: 'The matter, we understand, was discussed at a high level and is quite in order.'[28] Lord Bearsted was given the honorary rank of colonel in recognition of his valuable contribution towards the war effort.

The history of Section D and the activities of men like Lord Bearsted are usually relegated to single sentences or footnotes in the official histories. This is not a slur on their work but the vicissitudes of life and of official paranoia. Section D suffered in the mass but haphazard obliteration of material relating to the secret services during the war. There was, for example, the destruction of sensitive documents in the summer of 1940 for fear that they would fall into Nazi hands in the event of a successful invasion. After the war there was a further purge of secret papers and this was followed by a fire in Baker Street that destroyed many more records. Ironically, the cover name for Section D had been the Minimax Fire Extinguisher Company, a name well known to taxi drivers and German agents as the home of Britain's secret intelligence service.

And of course there was a reluctance in the first place to keep records on secret missions, which explains why there is so little material available for historians on the early months of the Auxiliary Units, as we will see in the next chapter. In 1949 the secret services carried out another 'weeding' of historical records and finally, during the Cold War there was absolute silence maintained on all secret service activities. Lord Bearsted did not live long enough to see the era when it was considered acceptable to write or speak of clandestine wartime activities. His behind-the-scenes work within SIS will never fully be known or celebrated, but it is likely that he would not have wished it to be. He would have seen it simply as part of his patriotic duty to his country in the same way as it had been to ensure that the Shell Transport and Trading Company kept the engines of democracy oiled.

The other side of his life was philanthropy which he had fostered with the same degree of energy and modesty that he did his secret work. The list of organisations Lord and Lady Bearsted helped over the years, and especially during the Second World War, is long and varied. They supported many Jewish charities including the Bearsted Memorial Hospital at Stoke Newington, on which construction began in 1939, and a daughter hospital, begun in the same year, which was a maternity home near Hampton Court. But Lord Bearsted was prepared to cross religious fault lines. He supported Christian organisations such as the YMCA to which he and Lady Bearsted gave financial support both before and during the war. Between them they helped children's charities, orphanages, boys' clubs, prisoners' aid, the Red Cross, and many other groups who needed support. Locally they were active and many small organisations near Upton House benefitted from their generosity including the local Women's Institute, the Girl Guides and the Volunteer Fire Brigade. Lady Bearsted had been alarmed to see children walking to school along the main road in the late 1920s and had a footpath created so they could make their way safely, and she provided a bus to take children from the local area to Banbury Grammar School. At the height of the Great Depression when Lord and Lady Bearsted bought Upton House, Lord Bearsted wrote to the local community and said: 'Any man who presents himself at my house at 9am on Monday morning shall find work there.'

In 1936 Lord Bearsted had travelled to the United States with Sir Simon Marks and Sir Herbert Samuel to raise money for German Jews. The three men travelled extensively throughout the States, giving speeches and persuading the Americans of the desperate situation in Germany. As things got worse for the Jewish children, in particular those who were orphaned or having parents in concentration camps, Lord Bearsted and Anthony Rothschild secured an enormous loan from the Prudential Insurance Company of £365,000 (the equivalent of around £14 million today). This helped to fund the Kindertransports, which brought some 10,000 child refugees, of whom 7,500 were Jewish, by train from Germany, Austria, Czechoslovakia and Poland between December 1938 and September 1939 to safety in Britain. About half the children lived with foster families and the remainder stayed in hostels, schools or on farms throughout the country. Later, after the Allied victory in North Africa, when refugee Jews were rescued from Spain and Portugal, he helped to work towards a peaceful accommodation in Palestine.

There is no doubt that through his generosity and genuine concern for men and women of all faiths Lord Bearsted touched many thousands of lives and probably saved a number of them as well. The bank staff at Upton House were among those whose lives had been changed by Lord Bearsted's thoughtfulness in keeping them out of London. When they returned to 55 Bishopsgate in 1945 they found the building had survived the war unscathed though much of the surrounding area had been badly damaged in the Blitz, including St Helen's Place, just 350 feet away from the Shell building.

After the war, Upton House once again became the Bearsteds' family home. The Long Gallery was rehung with the works of art that had returned from the quarry in North Wales and the rest of the porcelain and art taken out of storage. The Temple and Mirror Pools were refilled and the borders planted with herbaceous shrubs. The three Samuel sons all returned from the war with distinguished records, the two older boys having fought in Africa while the youngest, Tony, had, like his father, been involved in secret operations. Dicky and Peter went back to work in the city while Tony became a highly successful race-horse trainer in Warwickshire. The bank's wartime senior staff Albert 'Mac' McCarthy and Barney Adler both worked for M. Samuel & Co. until they retired. Lord Bearsted was reunited with his art collection and spent the rest of his life living at Upton House.

Coleshill House, home of Lord Radnor's sisters, Katharine and Mollie Pleydell-Bouverie, was used to train stay-behind saboteurs.

CHAPTER 7

Secret Saboteurs on the Home Front

*At the time of Stand Down, volunteers were told that
'no public recognition would be possible due to the
secret nature of their duties' and that, since no written
records of service had been kept, they were not eligible
for the Defence Medal.*[1]

John Warwicker

Two young men, Bob and Tony, piled into the back of a fifteen-hundredweight truck and were driven out of the back gates of Coleshill House into the Wiltshire countryside. It was midnight and pitch black; the moon and stars obscured by clouds. They drove for about fifteen minutes and then the truck stopped and they were ordered to jump out. The truck sped off into the night leaving them on the side of the road with the roar of the engine ringing in their ears. Bob felt for a packet of cigarettes but Tony signalled to him to put them back in his pocket. He cocked his finger, indicating that Bob should follow him into the wood where they could whisper. Their task was to find their way back to the house undetected. 'We were given a general map of the area and left to find our own way in pairs,' Bob Millard explained. 'We had to make a mark in chalk on one of the vehicles abandoned in the grounds to prove we had got back unseen and unchallenged.'

They set off in the direction they had worked out from the plan and made their way back towards Coleshill. They knew there were at least two patrols out and they had to sneak past them to reach the woods on the outskirts of the estate where the cover was better and they could hide. Every leaf seemed to crackle beneath their feet and even their breathing sounded loud in the windless, silent night. Key to being undiscovered was learning how to stand still if they heard a sound close by and melt into the background as close to a tree as possible. 'If you stay dead still they [the enemy] can pass right close to you and not see you. They might know you are there but they cannot see you,' Bob explained. Crawling through the undergrowth close to the wall they managed to avoid being spotted and within two hours they had made it back into the grounds and reached the vehicles. Bob took a piece of chalk out of his pocket and marked his sign on the side of the lorry. He grinned at Tony who looked dishevelled, his blackened face smeared with sweat and his knife still between his teeth. He took his cigarettes out of his pocket, lit one and drew on it with satisfaction. They had done it. 'It was all good boy scout stuff,' he recalled sixty years later.

Bob Millard was just nineteen years old when he went to Coleshill House for the first time in 1941 – not that he ever set foot in the mansion. He and his fellow trainees slept and ate in the stables and used the grounds for night training in order to learn techniques of sabotage, unarmed combat and night patrols. Bob had volunteered to become part of a secret organisation of stay-behind parties sited all over Britain who would aim to slow the progress of a German invasion by targeting their fuel dumps, ammunition stores and basic infrastructure, such as bridges and railway lines. These 'Auxiliary Units' were called into being in the summer of 1940 when the threat of invasion was at its most intense. They were so secret that many of the men who volunteered only found out fifty years later that someone they had known well was in a neighbouring patrol. 'Our sergeant, Jack Wyld, had a contact outside of the patrol because he came along with things we had to do. But we knew nobody else. In fact, with patrol members, there were two or three one only knew by Christian name or nickname.'[2]

The men who volunteered to be involved in the stay-behind sabotage parties represented a cross-section of the Britons that would never willingly submit to being ruled by an invader. They formed a slice of village life from earls, vicars and doctors to gamekeepers, boy scouts, poachers, and farm labourers. They were people who knew the land around their village like the back of their hand and who would quickly learn how to live off it when called to. Their training, like everything else about their patrols, had to be secret and the location of Coleshill House as their base was ideally located close to Swindon with its excellent railway network, but so well hidden within its grounds that its true nature was never uncovered. Without signposts the recruits did not know where they were, so circuitous were the routes taken by the drivers when picking up men to drive them to the house.

The last invasion of Britain had been by revolutionary France in February 1797 during the War of the First Coalition when the French landed at Carregwastad Head in Pembrokeshire. The Battle of Fishguard lasted for three days from 22 to 24 February when the French were beaten back and forced to surrender by a hastily assembled mixture of British Forces and the civilian population. It was short-lived but a painful memory nevertheless. The threat between June and September 1940 was of far greater moment and on 4 June the prime minister made his rousing speech in the House of Commons promising that Britons would fight on the beaches, in the fields and in the streets. He is purported to have sat down after the speech and muttered to a colleague 'and we'll fight them with the butt ends of broken beer bottles because that's bloody well all we've got!'[3]

Is that really all Britain had? No, of course not, but the retreat from Dunkirk had seen the British Expeditionary Force obliged to abandon the majority of its kit and equipment (from vehicles to weaponry large and small) while 60,000 men were taken prisoner, including whole battalions at St Valery. And yet, despite the initial disarray, Britain had not only the remains of the British Expeditionary Force but, over the next few weeks, it acquired a large number of foreign servicemen who would stand by Britain and fight on behalf of the Allies for the rest of the war. These were men from Poland, Czechoslovakia, France, Holland and other countries, numbering in the tens of thousands, and their contribution was essential.

Churchill's oration motivated the British public and engendered a spirit of singular focus so that when volunteers were called for to create an ad hoc stay-behind-the-lines fighting force to hold up the Germans should they invade, there was no shortage of applicants.

War is about killing. Kill or be killed. And the Second World War was a period of almost limitless development in the art of killing human beings, following just two decades after the First World War in which mechanised warfare made unprecedented advances. Increased variety and methods of extermination led to atrocities against civilian populations as well as the military, escalating from the aerial bombardment of cities and devastating U-boat attacks in the Atlantic to the ultimate horror of the atomic bomb. The annihilation of millions of men, women and children in concentration camps lent a new dreadfulness to the word holocaust.

The British sought to exploit brilliant minds to come up with inventive ways of sabotaging the enemy's powerful war machine. The development of technology was critical and the race was on to keep ahead of the enemy. Radar, code-breaking and intelligence were some of the methods developed and used. Guerrilla combat, or as Churchill called it, the art of 'ungentlemanly warfare', was just another arrow in the government's quiver and it was not new. In the early nineteenth century, the first irregulars to tackle an army were Spanish *guerrilleros* 'who fought their "little war" against Napoleon'. Later, the French had their own irregulars known as *francs-tireurs* (free shooters) 'who took on the might of the Prussian army during the war of 1870–71 and had a lasting effect on the psyche of the German soldiers in both the First and Second World Wars.' [4] The term 'guerrilla' was widely used for the first time in the Second World War.

Within the British Army's experience there was a tradition of sub-versive tactics developed by T. E. Lawrence during the First World War and the IRA during the Troubles in the 1920s. These methods were expanded during the Second World War by the British to equip amongst others the Commandos, the agents of Special Operations Executive (SOE) and the Auxiliary Units. Guerrilla combat was ide-ally suited to a mobile war and its strategy of subversive disruption, distraction and sabotage made it a useful tool for the Allies.

At the same time that Lawrence Grand, head of Section D of MI6, was studying guerrilla subterfuge, a separate committee was formed to examine and analyse campaigns in Spain and China where such tactics had been used. It had a secret brief as well, which was 'to consider how British support might be provided to resistance efforts in Europe should the German Army march and conquer east.'[5] This was called GS(R) – General Staff (Research) – and was run by Lieutenant-Colonel J. F. C. 'Jo' Holland. Older than Lawrence Grand by a few months, Holland had seen service in the First World War and in Dublin during the Troubles, where he was badly wounded. He had admired the technical skills of his Irish guerrilla opponents even if they had been used against him. By 1938, declared unfit for war service, he joined the War Office and chose to research irregular warfare. Initially he was the only officer in GS(R). Historian M. R. D. Foot wrote: 'Holland's Irish experiences led his lively imagination well outside the normal range of military thinking at the time.'[6] In early 1939 Holland's section was renamed MI(R), standing for Military Intelligence (Research), and a quote from a minute from the section's war diary introduc-tion reads: 'I have introduced a research section directly under me. This section must be small, almost anonymous, go where they like, talk to whom they like but be kept from files, correspondence and telephone calls.'[7]

The need to keep a lid on the secret nature of his work meant that Holland felt safest recruiting men who were, if not personally known to him, at least known to be like-minded. Each new recruit was given a specific task, such as securing intelligence from prisoners of war, developing code names or inventing secret gadgets. Holland's section worked alongside Section D, and agreed 'on a rough division of labour: MI(R) would cover tasks that could be tackled by troops in uniform, while Section D would look into undercover, unavowable work.'[8] Eventually these two groups, along with the propaganda arm of the Foreign Office, amalgamated to become Special Operations Executive, or SOE. This highly secret organisation, so secret in fact that it was never referred to by its name during the war, but by its cover name, the Interservices Research Bureau, helped to bring down Hitler and Mussolini, as well as fighting against the Japanese in the Far East before it was quietly wound up in early 1946.

One of Holland's recruits was his friend of twenty years Colonel Colin McVean Gubbins, an army officer with a distinguished First World War record and a holder of the Military Cross. It is this man who arguably had the greatest direct impact on the development of underground warfare both in Britain and in occupied Europe. Gubbins was born in Japan in 1896 and from the age of seven lived with his maternal grandparents and maiden aunts on the Isle of Mull, the beautiful Scottish island due west of Oban. One of the aunts, Elsie, believed in toughening up young boys. He was told that 'Scottish boys were harder than English and should never admit to being hungry or cold: "Run around the house twice if you are cold" was the cure for that,'[9] he said, years later. He did not see his own parents for five years but he described his childhood as blissfully happy. These early years gave him a love of all things Scottish and particularly of the Highlanders whom he trusted implicitly. Although he attended the Royal Military Academy at Woolwich he was always considered by the military as something of an outsider. He was particularly impressed by men he encountered in the Territorial Army and he appreciated their constructive criticism of military procedures and practices. 'While many soldiers, sceptical of civilians, might have discouraged such comments, Gubbins encouraged them.'[10] He disliked bureaucracy and hide-bound ways of thinking, so he was in most ways the ideal fit for the role of a training instructor in subversive techniques. The only outward expression of his willingness to ignore the rules was the fact that he usually wore a kilt, which was now against army regulations.

Just before the outbreak of the Great War, Gubbins was in Heidelberg learning German and had to make a frantic dash back to Britain to avoid arrest. He succeeded by disguising himself as a child and later wrote: 'My escape from being imprisoned in Germany was entirely due to the kindness of the Englishman, a complete stranger, who lent me £1 on Cologne platform.'[11] Gubbins was at Ypres for the first and second battles, then on the Somme where he won his Military Cross for conspicuous gallantry, organising a rescue party for wounded men who had suffered when one of his guns had been blown up. He was shot in the neck on the Somme in October and was in hospital for eleven days; he was gassed in 1917 and suffered from trench fever in April 1918, but was fit enough to join General Ironside, later commander-in-chief of the Home Forces, as ADC (aide-de-camp) on the autumn mission to Archangel in Russia to prepare a winter campaign.

After the war, aged twenty-three, Gubbins was sent to Ireland where he was given a three-day course in guerrilla warfare and, like Holland, observed the methods used by the nationalists at first hand. In 1923 he learned Russian and then went to India to learn Urdu. Promoted to major in February 1934, Gubbins was posted to the War Office and appointed general staff officer grade 2 in a new section of MTI (Military Training Instruction), which was the policy-making arm of the Military Training Directorate. In this role he was sent in 1938 to Czechoslovakia to oversee the withdrawal of Czech forces from the Sudetenland. It was something that he found exceptionally repugnant and it remained a matter of lasting shame to him for the rest of his life. It also gave him a first-hand view of the brutal force of Nazi expansion.

It was these experiences and his ability to command loyalty and affection, while communicating energy that reminded Holland that he would be ideal to explore the possibility of the British giving support for insurgents working against the Germans in any Nazi-occupied country. He chose Gubbins to be responsible for

organisation, recruitment and training, and recruited an expert in
explosives and demolitions for sabotage. Gubbins described his first
meeting with Holland in his new role:

> ... a cold hand took me literally by the back of the neck and a
> voice I knew said 'what are you doing for lunch today?' I whipped
> round – it was Jo Holland – and I replied that I was going to my
> regimental races at Sandown; there, beside me, were my field-
> glasses. 'No you are not,' he replied. 'You are to lunch with me;
> the CIGS says so.' We knew each other very well and I naturally
> agreed. In a private room at St Ermin's Hotel I found the real host,
> who was waiting for us there.[12]

The expert in explosives who joined them at the lunch was a 'somewhat eccentric and extremely able Sapper major' called Millis
Jefferis, who Gubbins also knew from earlier days. Jefferis was
to perform with distinction in Commando raids in Norway in the
spring of 1940 and later would go on to run 'Churchill's Toyshop'.
In that role he developed twenty-six different devices to assist with
regular and irregular warfare.

Holland, who was both far seeing and imaginative with a first-
class brain, was also a severely practical and down-to-earth man.
He asked Gubbins to write two pamphlets: *The Art of Guerrilla
Warfare*, and *The Partisan Leader's Handbook*. Jefferis wrote a third
pamphlet, *How to Use High Explosives*. Gubbins said later: 'My difficulty was that, strangely enough, there was not a single book to be
found in any library in any language which dealt with this subject.'[13]
Those three pamphlets became compulsory reading for every would-
be agent and trainee guerrilla over the years of the Second World
War. He wrote them in 2 Caxton Street and was amused by the
eccentricities of Lawrence Grand and his obsession with secrecy but
he found the revolutionary nature of the work exhilarating. *The Art
of Guerrilla Warfare* begins with a statement outlining the general
principles: 'The object of guerrilla warfare is to harass the enemy in
every way possible within all the territory he holds to such an extent

that he is eventually incapable either of embarking on a war or of continuing one that may already have commenced.'[14]

The military elite found the idea of this type of activity distasteful and Gubbins' popularity did not improve as a result. There was a residual dislike of the idea of guerrilla tactics which were seen among some of the older officers as unfair or unsporting. Some of the methods Gubbins was to go on to recommend were nothing short of murderous but he was unapologetic: the foe was pitiless. Gubbins was under no illusion that guerrilla warfare would win the war, but he understood that it could prove to be a useful additional weapon in Britain's armoury. He also recognised that expertise in this kind of attack could greatly boost the morale of underground resistance networks in occupied countries. This expertise could be passed onto men and women on the ground and SOE could further back them up with supplies of weapons and communication equipment which would make a significant difference in the long run.

Gubbins was described by his biographer and the woman in charge of the Secret Intelligence Centre in the Cabinet War Rooms, Joan Bright Astley as:

... quiet-mannered, quiet-spoken, energetic, efficient and charming. A 'still-waters-running-deep' sort of man, he had just enough of the buccaneer in him to make lesser men underrate his gifts of leadership, courage and integrity. He was a man-at-arms campaigner, the fires banked up inside him were as glowing as those round which his Celtic ancestors had gathered. He was dark and short, his fingers square, his clothes immaculate and in peacetime he wore a carnation in his buttonhole.

Holland's department expanded over the summer of 1939 and Gubbins was given a free hand to pick whoever he thought fit to work in clandestine work: Polar explorers, oil executives, British expat businessmen and regular army officers with specialist experience or expertise.

In early August 1939, Gubbins was sent to Warsaw to make contact with the Polish intelligence where he met Stanislav Gano, head of the Deuxième Bureau, who was described as 'a brilliant agent'.

The Poles had the best intelligence services in Europe, not least because they had spent so much of their time squeezed between enemy neighbours. Douglas Dodds-Parker wrote of them: 'with generations of clandestine action behind them, they had educated the rest of us.'[15]

The Polish Cipher Bureau had already cracked the code of the German Enigma machine in December 1932 with the help of French intelligence and had been reading much of Germany's military and political communications for more than six years. The British were incredulous. Just before the war broke out the Poles, fearing an invasion and the loss of this priceless intelligence asset, sent replicas of Enigma to Britain and France with detailed instructions on how to use it.[16]

Gubbins had the great skill of making good and trusting friends quickly. 'My appointment to Warsaw in the event of war had been arranged in July with the DMI, so that I had two roles, the official one as Chief Staff Officer, and the unofficial "to stimulate and assist the Poles and Czechs in Guerrilla warfare."'[17] He returned to Britain on 19 August with the intelligence that in all likelihood Germany would invade Poland before the end of the month. Four days later, Molotov and Ribbentrop signed the German–Soviet Non-Aggression Pact in Moscow. The fate of Poland was sealed as far as Holland, Gubbins and everyone in MI(R) was concerned. Gubbins's role was now to get the MI(R) element to Warsaw before the German invasion took place. He realised he needed to return immediately and set out overland for Poland, via France, Egypt and Romania as the direct route led through hostile countries and was far too dangerous. Arriving in Bucharest on 1 September he heard that the Germans had bombed the airfields around Warsaw, so he and his delegation took taxis to the border and travelled by train to the capital. He spent ten days in Warsaw talking to contacts in the security services but the mood in the country was gloomy. The army was at a loss in the face of overwhelming aggression from the Luftwaffe and the Wehrmacht. Gubbins was forced to withdraw, heartbroken. He described their retreat:

Lunch had been arranged for us at a hotel in Lyublin and we sat inside, still wearing our civilian clothes as our country was not at war. While having our meal we heard on the radio that Britain had declared war on Germany. I immediately ordered my officers and men to put on their uniforms and we went out into the town square to rejoin our buses. The square was completely filled by a huge crowd, cheering and shouting 'England is beside us. Long live England.' We were each of us lifted bodily into the air and carried into our buses already loaded with flowers. My heart was filled with sadness and foreboding.[18]

The mission arrived back in Bucharest on 14 September only to be forced to leave a week later when Romanian prime minister Armand Călinescu was murdered. Gubbins finally returned to London on 4 October, having spent a week helping General Carton de Wiart VC, one of the most striking figures in the British Army, write up a report on the Polish campaign. Two vital items came back from Poland. Gubbins brought a time-pencil – a fuse designed to be connected to a detonator – which would be so useful for SOE, and the Enigma machine, which the Poles had been working on had been sent to Bletchley Park and would prove vital in helping finally to break the naval Enigma code.

Back in London, Holland gave Gubbins the task of trying to establish contact with the Polish and Czech underground forces. For the next few months he worked on this project, spending time in Paris with the Polish and Czech general staffs who were established there at the invitation of the French government. The contacts he made would prove useful in the medium term but events began to change rapidly as the German advance of spring 1940 transformed the face of Europe in a matter of weeks.

By March, Gubbins was back in Britain on Holland's orders. He was put in charge of preparing and training selected assault troops who would make amphibious raids on Norway's western seaboard, an initiative keenly advocated by Winston Churchill, then First Lord of the Admiralty. Gubbins realised that battalions would be too large and unwieldy and he recommended small raiding parties which Holland proposed to name Independent Companies, forerunners of the Commandos. These companies would be armed and equipped to operate independently for up to a month. Crucially the men were volunteers from the regular army, as Gubbins and Holland recognised their roles would put them in great personal danger. Ten Independent Companies, each comprising twenty-one officers and 268 men, were formed in mid-April and moved to Scotland to train. The soldiers were drawn from the Signals, the Royal Engineers and the Infantry. Gubbins joined the trainees in Scotland and on 2 May was given command of SCISSORFORCE, comprising four Independent Companies. His brief was to prevent the Germans from occupying three Norwegian towns: Bodø, Mo and Mosjøen. These missions in Norway ultimately failed, but Gubbins gained first-hand experience of fighting the Wehrmacht and he was deemed to be the man of the moment. He showed himself to be a bold and resourceful commander of these small groups and was awarded a DSO for his leadership. Crucially his experiences had taught him the importance of thorough training and preparation for guerrilla warfare. He had also learned how single-mindedly ruthless the Nazis were prepared to be. He wrote: 'This was total war, and total war is a very cruel business indeed.'[19]

The Blitzkrieg, launched on 10 May, the day that Churchill succeeded Chamberlain as prime minister, followed three weeks later by the evacuation from Dunkirk, shook Gubbins as it did everyone. He said that the sight of Germans on the French coast caused him the first real shock of the war. Everyone from Churchill down feared an imminent invasion, probably within six weeks. The focus for those involved in secret training was to put the methods learned to good use in defence of the country. 'By mid-June the numbing incredulity produced by the Dunkirk evacuation and the arrival of German forces on the Channel coast had given place to a sense of frantic urgency to prepare a virtually defenceless Britain for an invasion which at the time appeared inevitable.'[20]

On his return from Norway, Gubbins was put in charge of preparing home-grown guerrilla units which would have one mission: to attack, sabotage and disrupt the invaders in any possible way. The idea now was to train small groups of civilians as stay-behind resistance fighters. Gubbins wrote:

> The immediate circumstances necessitated the highest degree of
> decentralization from the start ... they must be very small units,
> locally raised, and able to melt away after action. So there was no
> need for transport, and wireless too was out of the question. The
> highest possible degree of secrecy must be maintained.[21]

Some stashes of arms and explosives had already been left by Lawrence Grand's D Section officers in various dumps around the country in anticipation of invasion. On his instructions, drawn up in a briefing document on 31 May 1940, before the evacuation from Dunkirk was complete, thirty regional officers distributed incendiary weapons for stay-behind parties to use in the event of invasion. It was ad hoc and not carefully planned. M. R. D. Foot wrote: 'Combining haste with secrecy led too often to muddle. D Section's attempts in midsummer 1940 to arrange stay-behind parties, to disrupt the communications of a German invasion that was expected shortly, caused such confusion that the whole project was handed over to Holland.'[22] Nevertheless, it was an extraordinary effort, as a more recent historian, Malcolm Atkins, has pointed out. It took Lawrence Grand just a matter of days to lay the basis for an entire network of civilians prepared to undertake guerrilla activities.

Holland told Gubbins that his task was to create order out of chaos and to organise small bands of men to work in patrols against the invaders. Groups were overseen on a county or area basis by regular army officers given the cover title of intelligence officers, even though they were not part of the Intelligence Corps. These officers worked round the clock to find the men and women who would be trusted to work in the new companies. Some of the youngest were under military age while others were considerably beyond. Only men were to be trained in guerrilla tactics to work in the Auxiliary Units. The women, some of the boys and the older men were recruited to work as observers. These recruits belonged to the Special Duties Section (SDS) and their job was to learn how to recognise high-ranking German officers, to memorise number plates and to count passersby inconspicuously. There were over four thousand civilians involved in this type of intelligence work.

Civilians would be expected not to flee in the face of invasion but remain in their ordinary jobs having been trained to collect and communicate intelligence. Within the SDS there were agents, coast watchers and runners. These last, often boy scouts, were tasked with passing information from agent to radio operator via secret or dead-letter drops. They were taught how to use hollowed-out and sleeved door-knocker studs or the hinges of otherwise derelict five-bar gates. These were installed on the direction of a man called Douglas Ingram, an SDS intelligence officer in Norfolk, whose brother was in MI6. His favourite DLD (dead-letter drop) 'was the identifying number plate pinned into a telegraph pole. Once the plate was first removed it was straightforward to hollow out the core of the pole and fit a sleeve to take the rolled-up message. Once the DLD had been set up, the runner knew it held a message from the agent if the number plate was upside down.'[23] It didn't stop there. The runner had to take the precious hidden message to a local garden refuse dump and find a tennis ball with a cut in the cover. The message was slipped inside the ball and taken to the stump of a beech tree. 'This had been carefully sawn horizontally and fitted with an off-centre pivot. When rotated by someone in the know, a hollow section was disclosed and this married with a terracotta water pipe passing downward into the ground.'[24] At the other end of the pipe was a radio operator in a hidden bunker. She would take the message from the tennis ball and pass on its contents via her radio transmitter. 'The coded messages were received directly, or through relay stations, at in-stations situated at local army HQ, assessed by an intelligence officer and passed upward to the CO if neces- sary.'[25] Runners had to learn to be inconspicuous; radio operators inscrutable when going about their work and the letter drops had to be checked regularly to make sure they remained fully functional but undiscovered. In all there were some 200 secret radio transmitters operated by trained civilian signals staff working for the SDS.

The men who were chosen to carry out sabotage were the type who would not stand out in their community. They had to be able to fade into the surroundings once they had carried out an attack so no one questioned by the Germans would be able to point at an individual and name him. The majority of them, like Bob Millard, had served in the Home Guard. His friend, Anthony Bentley-Hunt, 'Tony', asked him one evening if he wanted to join something that was a bit more exciting than the Home Guard. Bob replied immediately '"Yes, I'm willing to try anything". So we went to a house in Bathwick Street where we met a chap called Jack Wyld. He asked us all about our families, about our knowledge of the neighbourhood, our knowledge of weapons. He produced a 9mm Barretta, I remember, which he field-stripped in front of us and said, "Can you put that back together again?" Fortunately, being of a practical nature and watching what he was doing, I could. "Right-ho," he said, "come back in a week".'[26]

Jack Wyld checked out the two boys and when they returned the following week he asked them whether they would like to join the Auxiliary Units.

'Our job will be to go underground if there is an invasion, bob up behind the Germans, and act as saboteurs.' Well, to a teenager, it sounded very interesting, so we said 'Yes, we would'. Before that though, before he mentioned it to us, he said, 'If you are going to join, I'm going to have to swear you to secrecy.' So we were sworn to secrecy and had to sign the Official Secrets Act before we were told any details.[27]

All the men who joined were warned that if they were caught by the invading Germans they would be treated as agents: tortured then executed. They were also told that the life expectancy of a stay-behind fighter would be about fifteen days if the Germans invaded.

Although they were told the job would be a dangerous one they probably had no idea just how vulnerable they would become if the invasion occurred. 'To be fair to the powers-that-be, nor did anyone else,'[28] concluded John Warwicker.

On 16 July Hitler showed his hand. In his Führer Directive No. 16 he set out his plans to his senior Nazi colleagues and the military planners:

> As England, in spite of the hopelessness of its military position, has so far shown itself unwilling to come to any compromise, I have decided to begin to prepare for, and if necessary to carry out, an invasion of England.
>
> This operation is dictated by the necessity of eliminating Great Britain as a base from which the war against Germany can be fought, and if necessary the island will be occupied.[29]

Herman Kindred was a farmer in Suffolk when he was recruited that month. He was conducting routine duties with the Home Guard when he was taken to a local village hall and asked if he would be prepared to 'join something special'. Like Bob Millard, he was warned it might be dangerous and he would have to keep it absolutely secret. Kindred considered the offer and, like Millard, thought it sounded more interesting than standing around with the Home Guard so he accepted, albeit cautiously. The man interviewing him, Captain Andrew Croft, told him:

> You may be the man we are looking for. We have already started work along the south coast and are now in a hurry to sort out East Anglia. You will be checked out. Could you get another five or six men you can absolutely trust? They have got to be patriotic and determined and, above all, must know the land like the back of their hands. You see, the Germans are coming and they are a ruthless lot. We have to make special preparations *because they could invade at any moment.*[30]

Croft, who was the intelligence officer in charge of Essex and South Suffolk, was a distinguished member of Gubbins' team. He had been the deputy leader on an Arctic expedition to Nordaustland for which he had been awarded the Polar Medal. He was said to be able to make himself understood in ten languages, but, most significantly, he had witnessed the burning of the Reichstag in Berlin in 1933 when he was there studying German. He had no illusions about the Nazis' methods and knew that an invasion would be brutal.

When the Germans invaded Norway, Croft was in Bergen. He succeeded in evading them by walking over the mountains and reaching the evacuating British Forces. It was there that he met Gubbins. By the end of the war Croft had been involved in many missions with SOE and had himself led over twenty sorties into enemy territory. For now, he was busy recruiting suitable men for the Auxiliary Units. It is a mark of how serious the situation was in the country that people of such calibre as Andrew Croft were involved in screening would-be stay-behind saboteurs.

Recruiting was undertaken by the intelligence officers in the first instance but the vetting was done internally within the patrols. If a new member was judged not to be pulling his weight or refused to turn up for training in bad weather, for example, he would find himself rejected by the core members with the threat ringing in his ears that if he ever spoke about their work he would face a grim and swift reckoning. In this way the patrol could get rid of leaders as well as rank and file men. Men of one patrol would not know the identities of men from adjacent groups. Nor would they know where the neighbouring operational bases were. This was designed to lead to foolproof secrecy in the event of capture.

However secret the operating units had to be, they needed to be trained to a certain standard and in clandestine activities that could not easily be taught in the local drill hall. Colonel Gubbins needed to find a suitable property for training exercises. As men and women would be travelling from all over Britain, it was crucial to have a secret base in a central part of the country that was sparsely inhabited but within reach of public transport.

As well as being close to the rail hub of Swindon, Coleshill House, near Highworth in Wiltshire, was entirely surrounded by its own parkland and had extensive woods, fields and streams, with a quarry located on the edge of the wood for explosives training. In and around the quarry a few old army trucks and armoured vehicles were used as targets. The great advantage was that the house and grounds were not overlooked by any other property other than Coleshill's own lodge so it was truly a secret location. In addition, there were extensive outbuildings which could be put to good use as accommodation for the trainees, lecture rooms, offices and the obligatory NAAFI. The kitchen for feeding the Auxiliary Units was set up in the old brewery. In the early days some of the officers' wives were obliged to sign the Official Secrets Act in order to have access to the site to help out with the cooking.

Coleshill House was purportedly the first house in England to be built for a 'minor' gentleman in the classical manner. It was the work of the architect Sir Roger Pratt to a design influenced by Inigo Jones, for his cousin, Sir George Pratt, and was completed in 1662. The house remained in the family throughout the next 275 years and had the unusual fate of remaining virtually unaltered. Also, some aspects of the original design meant that the house was already fairly suited to the style of living in the eighteenth and nineteenth centuries. For example, the house had central corridors running through all three floors which meant that the main rooms were private rather than having to act as passageways as was the norm in older large houses. The other novelty was a servants' staircase, which became very useful during the war when the house was occupied by the officers of the Auxiliary Units. One of Pratt's other architectural innovations was the matching storeys. Many larger houses built in the period were in the Palladian manner with a *piano nobile* as the first floor, with grand state rooms, and smaller rooms with lower ceilings above.

While the exterior of Coleshill was handsome, symmetrical and all of one style, it was the interiors that were most noteworthy. The handsome central staircase sprang out of the hall for two storeys and was lit by a beautiful cupola. The hall and staircase were further lit by huge windows, so that the sense was of a brightly lit space with carefully placed detail. Nine niches in the wall in the entrance hall were filled with portrait busts. These niches, it was said, would be filled by nine spectral cats if the family were ever threatened with evil. No one who occupied Coleshill during the war ever mentioned the cats so it is safe to assume the family was not threatened by the guests from Gubbins' Auxiliary Units.

The interior decoration in the main rooms was lavish: great carved wreaths of flowers and fruit adorned the staircase and some of the walls, while the ceilings in most of the ground-floor rooms were deeply coffered with fine classical motifs carved into the recesses. Each room had a different style of carving, some Dutch, others Italianate or French. The main drawing room was filled with family portraits and had the most elaborate coffered ceiling of all. A magnificent chandelier hung from the richly decorated oval above the centre of the room. The first floor had suites for the family and above them, on the second floor, there were thirteen bedrooms, designed for use by the servants.

When Sir George Pratt died his sister inherited Coleshill. She was married to Thomas Pleydell and their only daughter, Harriet, married the Hon. William Bouverie, Viscount Folkestone and Baron Longford. He was later created Baron Pleydell Bouverie and 2nd Earl of Radnor in 1765 and the conjoined name stuck. The principle Radnor seat is Longford Castle near Salisbury and by the early twentieth century Coleshill House, with some forty rooms, was occupied by the Earl of Radnor's sisters – the renowned English potter Katharine Pleydell-Bouverie, and Mary, or 'Mollie' – and their dogs.

Katharine, known always as Bina, had trained as a potter with Bernard Leach at his pottery in St Ives, but in 1925, at the age of thirty, she set up a studio at Coleshill where there was an abundance of clay, water and trees to provide the large quantities of wood to fire the double-chamber kiln that she had built in the grounds. She used ash glazes prepared from wood and vegetation from the trees and plants growing at Coleshill. This gave her work a particular look which had a similar style to Bronze Age English pottery. Cole Pottery, as the style was called, remained active until the outbreak of the Second World War when it had to close in order to comply with blackout restriction. As the firings took thirty-six hours it was not possible to confine them to daylight hours.

Bina and Mollie remained in residence throughout the war. Their first visitors were forty evacuees from the Isle of Dogs and although they did not stay for long, the boys remember being taught sword fighting by Bina. She had an infectious laugh and was very self-deprecating, sympathising always with the underdog but she was great fun and the boys enjoyed sparring with their eccentric host. From the beginning of the war she agreed to become the local Red Cross commandant and would go to Shrivenham regularly to help give the wounded hot drinks when they were brought in on their way to hospitals. When the estate was taken over in the summer of 1940 the sisters were told it was to be used for Home Guard training and they asked no questions. It is said that their dogs were so distressed by the explosions and goings on in the grounds while the Auxiliary Units were training that they had to be fed on aspirin and brandy by their mistresses. For the Radnor estate it must have been something of a relief to have had the house requisitioned as the War Office's contribution towards the upkeep of Coleshill would have been a considerable help.

Once Coleshill had been requisitioned the next task was to develop the house, outbuildings and particularly the grounds. The officers lived and messed in the house itself while the soldiers initially slept in the stable block. This was unheated and full of rats so eventually two Nissen huts were erected with heaters and the men found that much more comfortable. The house, while large and opulent, was not as luxurious as it might at first have seemed. There was no central heating, no electricity and a very poor water supply. Water was pumped from a main reservoir well below ground level and ran through a series of cellars and tunnels. 'This, and the ancient appliance – man-handled and pumped by half a dozen men either side of a master lever – was the only protection against fire hazards.'[31] Eventually the army installed a generator so they could at least have light. The temporary cables hung well below the ceilings so as not to damage the ornate plasterwork, with light shining into corners that had remained in the shadows for over two hundred years. Soon after the Royal Signals provided the house with a switchboard. Prior to that there had been only one telephone – Highworth 85. Corporal Eric Grey of the Royal Army Service Corps (RASC) was at Coleshill for two years and was one of the regular drivers. He remembered having to enter via the servants' staircase into the house if he needed to speak to one of the staff officers as the front entrance was still the preserve of Bina, Mollie and the dogs.

The routine for training Auxiliary Units at Coleshill was fixed from the word go. Recruits would arrive on Friday nights, usually by train. They were given very few instructions but one of them was to report to the post office in Highworth, the closest village to the house. In a gloriously understated and very British manner, they would have to ask for Mabel Stranks, the post-mistress, who would check their identity and then phone to the house for a car to collect them. Soon a car or an army vehicle would arrive to take them up to the house by a winding route so that they would not be able to pinpoint Coleshill's location were they ever caught. Mrs Stranks always refused to answer any questions posed by the recruits and she was regarded as a local character. 'Even when obviously genuine military convoys arrived at the Highworth post office the post-mistress always refused to direct them to Coleshill House, instead telephoning ahead to announce: "Some of your lot are down here."'[32] She had worked at the post office for twenty-five years and was nearly sixty when the war came to her village. She refused to be fazed by anything. To Bob Millard she looked immeasurably old.

The Auxiliers spent the weekend at Coleshill living in the stables on bunks made of chicken wire with straw palliasses and army-issue blankets. Bob Millard described the set-up:

Behind the clock house was the stable yard, which was quite a large cobbled yard with big buildings and stables around three sides of it. People who came there for training would work in this area. As I recall we did that on the first floor of the building, which was a large room that had bunks down either side and tables down the middle and we would sleep, you would eat and work in that room, get our lectures and talks in that room. I think too that in the stable yard in those days there was a wooden building, a wooden kitchen, and we used to go down and collect our meals and take them back up into this upstairs room and to eat. But, as you can imagine, the training was very, very intensive and you didn't get much sleep.[33]

At night they would do exercises in the grounds, such as stealing up on sentries, guarding dummy aircraft or practising unarmed combat. Gubbins called it 'scallywagging' but it was deadly serious and the intense training was intended to turn men with little or no previous military experience into highly efficient saboteurs in a very short space of time. It is greatly to Gubbins' credit and vision that he was as successful in accomplishing this as he was, even though the Auxiliers were thankfully never put to the test. On Sunday evenings they dispersed, either by train or car. Those going back to Scotland were driven to Leighton Buzzard so as to avoid having to go via London to return home. Bob Millard remembered going home buzzing with excitement about everything he had learned and keen to pass it on to the other members of his patrol who had not been on the course. 'But the biggest thing about Coleshill was the comradeship it gave you, knowing you could rely on the man next to you. And the self-confidence.'[34]

Gubbins had a very clear idea of how he wanted the Auxiliary Units to work. The units should be small: just six to eight men. They would be trained in guerrilla tactics and to use explosives. They were also encouraged to make sure they knew their patch like the back of their hands: 'We walked miles, both through the open countryside and also through the urban areas. We wanted to establish quick routes, possible places where one could lay up in the town, where each alleyway went to, possible doors into gardens and houses, short cuts and things like that so that if we had to move about the town we knew it backwards.'[35]

Gubbins had as his second-in-command at Coleshill a larger than life figure, Major (later Brigadier) Geoffrey Beyts, known as Bill or Billy, who was in charge of drawing up the guidelines for the country-wide intelligence officers and designing 'lecture notes and training schedules and facilities for Coleshill'.[36] While he was preparing the courses his wife, Ruby, was in charge of cooking. She and Oonagh Henderson, the wife of one of Gubbins' senior aides, Major the Honourable Michael Henderson, the Auxiliary Unit's quartermaster, manned the kitchens. Later the Army Catering Corps arrived and Mrs Beyts and Henderson were relieved of their onerous duties, cooking for upwards of seventy people each weekend.

Major Beyts had been born and brought up in India and was the third generation of his family, who were originally of Dutch extraction, to lead the Third Battalion, Sixth Rajputana Rifles. At the age of just twenty-two he was allotted an area of Burmese teak forest and a list of 100 rebels to seek out and capture or kill. After nine months he and his company had accounted for every man on the list and for this he was awarded the Military Cross. He subsequently saw action against Waziri tribesmen and the Japanese army. By the time he arrived in London in September 1939 he was just thirty-one. His biographer, Ian Trenowden, wrote of him: 'He was no stranger to the truism that if you want to establish something where nothing has previously existed: you will have to do most of the work yourself.' Gubbins, who knew of Beyts' reputation, asked Beyts to visit him on his return from a quickly aborted visit to France on 9 May 1940. He offered Beyts the rank of major and asked him to become his second-in-command, with responsibility for training at Coleshill. Within a short time, Beyts had worked out the forty-eight-hour crash course in unarmed combat, night stalking, the use of petrol bombs, hand grenades and high explosives that served as a template for the weekend courses for the Auxiliary Units and which needed very little alteration over the next four years. The main emphasis was on the use of explosives in order to attack the enemy's supplies, transport and communications rather than their ground troops.

Any weapons the Auxiliers were issued with were intended for defence rather than attack. The British stay-behind forces were the first to be equipped with the Thompson sub-machine gun, phosphorous grenades, the PIAT (projector infantry anti-tank), plastic explosive and time-pencil delay devices based on the one that Gubbins had brought back from Poland in 1939. In some cases these new weapons were still at the experimental stage and the men in the weapons research and development section of the Ministry of Defence, known as MD1, run by Lieutenant-Colonel Millis Jefferis, and nicknamed Churchill's Toyshop, used the Auxiliers to test new devices. Special stores for the Auxiliary Units personnel included 0.22 inch rifles with telescopic sights and silencer – easily capable of killing a man 100 yards away. These were primarily intended for picking off German officers and tracker dogs. They also had rum rations which were only to be used in the final emergency. However, intelligence officer Captain Ian Benson, who worked at Coleshill in 1944, handed back several gallon jars of rum only to be told they contained cold tea. He was completely perplexed and only found out after the war how the sergeant had managed to get at the rum while leaving the jars sealed. 'He explained how he got a red hot razor blade, ran it around the seal, banged the bottom of the jar with the manual of military law, out popped the cork and they resealed it after the tea went in by rubbing oil round it.'[37]

Auxiliers tried out booby-trap lines, detonators, hand grenades, smoke bombs, time-pencils and a plastic explosive called Nobel 808, which was green and smelled of almonds. Eric Grey remembered the weekends as being exceptionally noisy with the firing ranges in full operation and 'bangs' being set off both in the grounds and in a nearby quarry where recruits were taught how to set explosives.

Beyts' speciality, learned in the forests of Burma and in Waziristan, was teaching men to move absolutely silently and unnoticed through the night. Under his direction, they learned to accept darkness not as a hostile element but as their best friend: 'anyone who remains still is invisible' was his mantra.

> It may properly be claimed that, in his teaching, Beyts formalised irregular, even illegal warfare, for what was seen then as a totally worthy and justified cause – the national interest. At the same time, he created an example of terrorism as it has since developed worldwide – sometimes justified by the perpetrators from the very highest moral standpoint and, at others, with no justification at all. It all depends on whose side you are on.[38]

After Beyts left Coleshill in 1942 to become chief of staff to Colin McKenzie in India, his training role was taken over by a former prep school headmaster, Major Bill Harston. 'He made his new pupils pretend to be German sentries, and he then demonstrated how they could be approached silently and stabbed before they had time to cry out.'[39] One Auxilier, speaking in 2012, told an interviewer that he had been taught to kill sentries, cut open their stomachs and spill their intestines next to the body in order to demoralise the Germans.

At Coleshill, Auxiliers trained in demonstration Operational Bases – underground bunkers built in secret locations and carefully disguised where the units could hide in preparation for attacks following the invasion. Peter Fleming, writing under his pseudonym Strix, described them in *The Spectator* in 1966:

> In order to stay behind, we needed somewhere to stay: and by sucking up to the Sappers we had already brought into being what might very loosely be called a network of subterranean hide-outs in which not only the striking force – Strix and about fifteen other idiots – but our far-flung, hand-picked collaborators in the Home Guard, would bide their time before emerging to wreak, in a variety of ill-defined ways, havoc among the invaders.[40]

The one still remaining in the woods at Coleshill is typical of the design used throughout the country. It is some twenty feet long and over eight feet in diameter (6.4 × 2.45m), lined with curved corrugated iron sheets and known as an elephant shelter. Each tunnel-shaped bunker had benches on which the men could sit and sleep, housing three to six men. Over time they developed a design that meant the shelters would be watertight and yet have some form of ventilation. When Captain Ian Benson dug his first OB on the Suffolk coast he did not think of how the water table might rise. As a result the base flooded and he had to find another more suitable site. Sometimes existing structures, such as caves in Scotland and coal mines in Northumberland, could be adapted, but more often than not they were dug by Royal Engineers who helped to fit them out. The entrance hatch was a trap door which had six inches of earth on the lid so weeds could grow to help with the camouflage. It was closed by a carefully constructed balance mechanism. The main chamber had either a concrete or railway sleeper floor, and the sheets of rust-proof iron created a rounded, hut shaped roof that was very strong. At one end was a wall with the entrance hatch and rungs to climb down from the outside. At the other end was an opening that led to an escape tunnel, usually less than one square metre in diameter and several metres long. By the time the units were disbanded there were thought to be some 600 OBs throughout the length and breadth of Britain. The bases, like the Auxiliary Units, were set in rural locations because it was believed that the Germans would invade by sea and thus into the countryside rather than towns. Also, it was likely that the patrols would be fighting not the Wehrmacht but small groups of enemy forces sent ahead to set up bridgeheads en route to the bigger towns and cities.

There were strict rules: for example, only ten to fifteen minutes of smoking per hour was to be permitted, partially to protect the air in the OBs but also because the smoke or fumes might give their position away. Some tips were practical – it was suggested that lights were turned out ten minutes before Auxiliers emerged into the darkness so their eyes would adjust quickly. They also recommended keeping the OB ship-shape as much for morale and psychological well-being as for practical reasons. The twenty-four-hour routine of an OB started at 14:30 with reveille followed by a meal, planning for night patrol and then eight hours out of doors between 20:45 and 5:45 and back to bed after a hot meal by 7:00.

Gubbins realised that certain men could not attend the weekend courses at Coleshill, some being prevented by travel and others by the fact that their cover such as air-raid wardens or Royal Observer corps duties would not permit them to get away for a whole weekend and keep down their regular jobs. This problem was solved by the appointment of Captain Benson as training officer for the Auxiliary Units in their entirety. Born in 1920 he was usually the same age and often younger than the men he was training. It was a job for a young man, however, as there was such a lot to be done. 'From the Outer Hebrides to the Dorset coast I travelled all round the bloody place,' he said. For eighteen months he toured the country working mainly at night time.

One or two wives felt suspicious of their husbands going away at the weekends or training on week nights. If it was out of character with their usual habits some came to suspect the involvement of another woman. The authorities became aware of this and gave the men Home Guard uniforms to wear when required to be out on patrol. They concluded that no one would consider it strange to see a man cycling in uniform with a Lee Enfield rifle. He was clearly doing his bit and it would seem unlikely that in such unglamorous gear that he was off to see a lady friend either.

By the end of August 1940 there were a total of 371 cells comprising more than 2,000 men with access to over four hundred arms dumps and explosives. The emphasis was on stealth and surprise. Had the Germans invaded, the Auxiliary Units would have gathered in their OBs and put their plan into action. They would have the upper hand initially which would, they hoped, allow them to set explosives on enemy supplies, tanks and aircraft, thus disrupting the enemy's advance, and then melt away in the darkness and make their way back to the OBs. That was the theory. John

Warwicker concluded: 'They would have performed well in the short term but all the long-term evidence is that they didn't have sufficient back-up or resources or reinforcements to enable them to take part in a long-term campaign as was conducted on the continent.'[41] When Ian Benson was asked how he felt about his role as an intelligence officer who would have stayed with his patrols he said: 'I never thought it had a great future attached to it! It was just part of the role.'[42]

Over the course of the four years it was used as the Auxiliary Unit's training HQ, Coleshill had several commanders. Gubbins left in November 1940, recalled by the War Office to lead another new organisation, the Special Operations Executive. He was succeeded by an officer with a confusing name. He was Colonel C. R. 'Bill' Major and must, at various periods, have been Lieutenant Major and later Major Major. He was in charge from the autumn of 1940 until February 1942 when he was replaced by Lord Glanusk, a Territorial Army colonel, who arrived at Coleshill in a Rolls-Royce with a complete entourage that included a young wife, a staff of Guards' officers 'with public school accents and double-barrelled names' and a string of thoroughbred race horses. His complete wine cellar was available for sale in the officers' mess. It was a far cry from the early days when Ruby Beyts prepared meals for seventy guests and the Coleshill staff from scratch.

In addition to the officers in charge, the instructors, drivers and other male support staff, about eight members of the Auxiliary Territorial Service (ATS) worked in the office at Coleshill. Corporal Joan Welborn was fifteen when the war broke out and by 1943 she was in the ATS working as a secretary to the former training officer Captain Benson. She remembered above all the cold: 'Although we had electricity the office was very cold and I use to type wearing woollen mitts.' During the week, when there were no courses, she and her fellow ATS members would be allowed some free time and she remembered lovely walks through the woods picking primroses in the spring. Joan's experience of life at Coleshill was on the whole a positive one. As a young woman in her first job she was as keen on her leisure time as she was on the work:

> Our working day was 8.30 to 17.00, so at 5pm we climbed into the back of a 15 cwt truck to take us back to our billet which was Hannington Hall in the village of Hannington north of Swindon, a journey of about 5 miles. It was home to the Fry Family of Fry's Chocolate. We slept on the second floor. At weekends we would cycle, or go to the cinema or to a dance. I met my future husband who worked at Highworth Station at a dance in the school at Highworth. It was October 1943 and we married on the 9th August 1947.

Hannington Hall was in the charge of Beatrice Temple, who was the senior commander of all ATS personnel in GHQ Auxiliary Units, Coleshill and Special Duties Branch. She earned the nickname 'the Queen-Bee of the hush-hush party' and was an impressively energetic woman who was described as having 'a natural friendliness and a pretty wit'. She had a staff of four officers, a driver, three corporals and eleven privates, including the cook and orderlies. The latter remained at the hall to keep the billets up to scratch while the other women were working at Coleshill.

Senior Commander Temple was thirty-four when she arrived at Coleshill in November 1941. Two and a half years earlier she had been touring Europe and was in Vienna when the Germans invaded Austria. A few days later she was on her way to Italy passing through a small Austrian town when she heard that Hitler was due to visit. She was invited to watch from an upstairs hotel balcony as the Führer passed slowly by on the street below. At the outbreak of the war she joined the ATS because she wanted to drive lorries but that never happened. She was snapped up and in only five days became an officer, learning to drill with sergeants in the Guards and studying military law. She was made a captain and given the job of ATS company commander attached to the Seaforth Highlanders.

In November 1941 she was interviewed by Colonel Major and

asked to take command of the ATS element at Coleshill House. She joined Major Petherick and his small team of officers who ran the Special Duties (SDS) Branch at Hannington Hall. John Warwicker described Petherick as 'a shadowy figure if ever there was one'. However, Beatrice Temple wrote in her diary in January 1942 that he was very amusing, friendly and helpful: 'Really improves on acquaintance.' Petherick's service in the First World War with the War Office at the age of just twenty-two and his subsequent career as an MP from 1931 to 1945 might well have been a cover for a full or part time association with MI6. He was certainly an excellent choice as leader of the SDS. Beatrice Temple wrote of her arrival at Coleshill: 'Arrived Highworth. DR led to HQ Coleshill House – met by charming Colonel Beyts. Tea with Colonel Major who then led the way to Hannington Hall which turns out to belong to friends of a fellow officer. Butler opened door and maid asked if she could unpack any cases. The Fry family still had fourteen servants. All but a few left eventually to engage in war services.'[43]

Her role, apart from commanding the ATS girls who worked at Coleshill, was to interview prospective candidates for secret signals work. These interviews took place in Harrods' tea rooms and were followed by a voice test. It was only when the girls had passed the test, proving that they could speak clearly and be audible over radios, and signed the Official Secrets Act that they were told to report to Coleshill. Beatrice wrote of one group who came for a training session: 'much slower lot than last – not such good manners + how did Clifford pass voice test, can't think!'[44] Their job was to run the clandestine radio network and remain behind the enemy lines once the Germans invaded. They would be just as vulnerable as the male Auxiliers and experience showed later that the Germans took a harsh approach to radio officers, often shooting them on the spot if they were caught. A historian of Coleshill House wrote: 'As most of the candidates were well educated, spoke well and [were] generally attractive, they eventually became known as the "Secret Sweeties" but they were to undertake a highly dangerous task – relay messages from our spy network.'[45]

Unlike the Auxiliary Units who were to practise in the field with no support at all, the signal control stations around the country were set up and maintained by Royal Signals personnel. 'Each station consisted of a "hut" and a secret underground bunker each with a radio. Each would be linked to a series of "outstations" sending them reports.'[46] The idea was that the radio operators, usually two or three ATS subalterns, would work in the huts, but once the invasion came they would go to the underground bunkers to avoid detection. Their main task was to link up with the out stations but they were also encouraged to listen out for broadcasts by suspect agents. They were so secret that when an RAF officer came across a member of Special Duties transmitting from a wireless hidden in a wood he called in back-up from soldiers who were intent on killing the operator as an enemy agent. They were dissuaded at the last minute.

Temple was exceptionally thorough. She would inspect stations once a month and she was constantly on the move around the country. Her responsibility was not just to keep an eye on the radio operators' skills but she was also in charge of their welfare. She checked that they were properly billeted, paid and in touch with the right military commanders. Her diary is an extraordinary log of life on the road and brushes with various members of the secret service, some of whom she liked more than others. She travelled by train and car, sometimes having to be rescued when her own car broke down. In early 1942 she was, '"Run in" by stern + stupid young Policeman in Basingstoke who thought GPO address bogus & took me to Police Stn for "further enquiries". Returned to HH.'[47]

If all else failed she was happy to hitch a lift with lorry drivers to get to where she needed to be. On Monday 23 February 1942 she had a staff car and was to drive welfare items to Canterbury. She wrote at the bottom of the entry: 'other news: Uncle William got Canterbury'. She was now the niece of the Archbishop of Canterbury. Two months later to the day she wrote: 'Installation of Uncle at Cathedral'. Eight weeks after that she was back in Canterbury helping out with rations and bedding as the ATS billets there had been bombed and they were now homeless.

Beatrice Temple had boundless energy and a great deal of compassionate common sense but she was also somewhat clumsy and accident prone. In March 1942 she went for a stroll with her junior commander, Barbara Culleton, and fell into the ice-covered fish pond, injuring her wrist. That summer she went to a Home Guard sports day outside Winchester where two of the Coleshill officers tried to get her to throw a Mills bomb. 'Knowing her throwing she declined!' her younger sister wrote later.

As secrecy was everything for the Auxiliers and members of the Special Duties Section under Gubbins' tenure no paper records were kept. It seemed there was simply not the time or the inclination for any unnecessary formal administration. The quantity of ordnance and the size of ammunition dumps in the countryside was all unrecorded and, 'any attempt to catalogue the first issue of firearms to the Auxiliary Units is just a minefield of confusion. The intelligence officer simply gave them whatever he could get his hands on.'[48]

This has been frustrating for historians of the Auxiliary Units who found, at best, notes scribbled on the backs of envelopes by the intelligence officers and others involved in recruiting and shaping the early units.[49] Colonel Major took a different view and ensured that records were kept and that the Auxiliary Units had some affiliation with the Home Guard, something that had been considered troublesome at the outset owing to the pressing need for confidentiality in the face of the threat of invasion. 'With these changes, much of the absolute secrecy previously demanded from every participant in these highly secret units was thrown away and replaced by War Office standardisation.'[50]

Some people's lives were cover enough but others needed a more elaborate story in order to carry out their work. One observer was the secretary of the local beekeepers association. He was given extra petrol coupons and special rations of sugar – that all-important ingredient for a successful apiary and so short during the war – and with that he was free to visit anywhere he desired. He could scout around and not attract attention to himself.

Another who was involved with secret activity was Ted Jefferies. He was a boy scout and carried messages for the Auxiliary Units at Coleshill House to the Highworth post office and back. Too young to sign the Official Secrets Act, he had to give the scout's oath as he was sworn not to breathe a word about what he was asked to do. As a boy scout, he was unlikely to attract suspicion or attention from the invading Nazis. Ted used his roller skates to race up and down the hill between Coleshill and Highworth and the only thing that singled him out from the other keen roller skaters was that the rubber on his wheels was replaced when it wore out. That was something other boys could only have dreamed of after the fall of Singapore when Japan gained control of the majority of the world's rubber.

The Auxiliary Units were stood down at the same time as the Home Guard on 30 November 1944. 'A skeleton staff of physically low-grade officers and men were sent out to seal or destroy the Aux units Operational Bases and recover all the explosives. This process was hurried and piecemeal. The men were expected to continue with their ordinary lives and to keep secret, forever, their wartime activities.'[51] The courage of the men and women who were prepared to stay behind enemy lines in the event of an invasion is an extraordinary testament to the spirit of wartime Britons. Although the existence of the Auxiliary Units was not made public until the 1990s and the men and women who had been involved remained secretive about their wartime activities, there was a letter published in *The Times* on 14 April 1945 quoting the farewell message of General Sir Harold Franklyn, commander-in-chief, Home Forces:

I realise that each member of the organisation from the first invasion days beginning in 1940 voluntarily undertook a hazardous role which required both skill and courage well knowing that the very nature of their work would allow no public recognition. This organisation, founded on the keenness and patriotism of selected civilians of all grades, has been in a position through its constant and thorough training, to furnish accurate information of raids or invasion instantly to military headquarters throughout the country.[52]

Would the Operational Bases and their keen personnel have made an impact on the advancing Germans had Operation Sea Lion succeeded? Peter Wilkinson, a close colleague, friend and later biographer of Gubbins, thought they would have been nothing more than a 'flea-bite behind the enemy lines.'[53] The Auxiliers were never intended to be compared with the resistance movements in occupied Europe. They were a short-term harassing force. 'As the men in the Operational Bases were isolated from the outside world, including the military one, it meant that the only order they could follow was the last one given by their intelligence officer – something like: 'Mount an operation against the enemy every night until you are killed, captured or relieved by counterattack.'[54] As each of the OBs had just a fortnight's rations, it is not difficult to conclude from this their likelihood of survival and their life expectancy.

Had the Germans invaded and had the units carried out sabotage there would have been reprisals and they would have been appalling. Captain Peter Fleming, who was a pioneer of the XII Corps Observation Unit, wrote that 'reprisals against the civilian population would have put us out of business before long. In any case, we would have been hunted down as soon as the leaf was off the trees.'[55] There are many examples of Nazi brutality when their forces came under partisan or guerrilla attack. In the village of Tulle in France the villagers still remember the day when storm troopers hanged ninety-nine local men from lampposts in a reprisal for the killing of forty Germans by members of the Resistance. Two days before, the Germans had shot eighteen men. A further 101 local citizens never returned from Dachau concentration camp where they had been sent after the hangings. In any tit-for-tat battles the Germans exercised extreme violence and it would have been no different in Britain.

Each Auxilier was given a pistol and a letter which he was

instructed to open only in the event of his being trapped behind enemy lines. The letter contained instructions to 'eliminate' certain people on their patch, such as the chief constable, who might know more than he ought to and who would be a danger if caught and tortured by the enemy. They were told to keep the final bullet for themselves. On no account were they to be taken alive. 'Would you have done that, killed people you knew?' Geoffrey Devereux was asked in 2012. 'Oh yes,' he replied, 'we had to be extremely hard in our outlook.' Geoffrey Devereux was just seventeen when he was recruited by an intelligence officer.

Indeed, every man who was interviewed about his role in later life claimed that he would have undertaken the sabotage willingly and with fervour. In 1957 Peter Fleming sounded a note of caution:

> Yet legend plays a large part in their memories of that tense and strangely exhilarating summer, and their experiences, like those of early childhood, are sharply rather than accurately etched upon their minds. The stories they tell of the period have become better, but not more veracious, with the passage of time. Rumours are remembered as facts, and – particularly since anti-invasion precautions continued in force for several years after the Germans had renounced their project – the sequence of events is blurred.[56]

The story of the Auxiliary Units remains one of the Second World War's lesser known stories of bravery and patriotism. Coleshill House, the backdrop for top-secret training, was stood down in late 1944. As the dust settled and grass grew over the tyre marks in the lawns, the Pleydell-Bouverie sisters resumed a quieter life. Katharine remained at the house until a year after the war when she moved to Kilmington Manor. In 1946 the house and estate at Coleshill was sold to Ernest Cook, one of the founders of the travel agents Thomas Cook & Son, to be handed on to the National Trust on his death.

Arisaig House was the HQ of the highly secret Special Operations
Executive training in northern Scotland.

CHAPTER 8

Guerrillas in the Mist

*While SOE was at work no European politician could
be under the illusion that the British were uninterested
or dead; he might have had reason to believe that they
were incompetent or sinister, but he was bound to take
account of them.*[1]

William Mackenzie

In the rugged terrain of hills and sea lochs thirty-five miles to the
west of Fort William lies the remote fishing village of Arisaig, on the
edge of Loch nan Ceall – 'the loch of the churches'. Its inaccessibility
by land is of no concern for the myriad wildlife that abounds in the
crystal-clear waters and on its shores. Sea otters tumble and dive,
playing games with one another or floating on their backs while seals
heave themselves onto the rocks to bask in the sun. Round the corner
are the Silver Sands of Morar with a sublime shorefront of white
beaches and stunning views across a sea of brilliant turquoise to
the isles of Eigg and Rum. At other times powerful forces of nature
unleash some of the wildest weather in Scotland on this land and
seascape. Waves pound the beaches and winds whistle round the
rocks, tearing at the machair grass clinging to the sand dunes.

This epic landscape with its stark beauty that impresses itself indelibly on the mind of any who journey into the mist and mountains, rock and heather is full of military history. Bonnie Prince Charlie left Scotland for France from Borrodale Beach, to the west of Arisaig, following the failure of the Jacobite rising of 1745. The clan Fraser of Lovat settled in Scotland in the late twelfth century and their heirs fought with Robert the Bruce at Bannockburn and later against the French in North America. In 1900, the fourteenth Lord Lovat, a former soldier and owner of almost 182,000 acres of the Highlands, put together a mounted infantry unit comprising 150 stalkers and ghillies from his own and neighbouring properties, eventually expanding to take in volunteers from across the Highlands, to serve in South Africa. The Lovat Scouts served with distinction in both world wars. In the 1940s Arisaig played a critical part in the secret world of guerrilla warfare. Its remoteness and challenging environment were ideally suited to the task of putting men and women through the toughest training in personal survival.

A handsome granite manor house taking its name from the village was to become the hub of a top-secret training facility. This time the trainees were volunteers who would become agents to be dropped into Nazi-occupied Europe and carry out sabotage and intelligence gathering, making contact with the resistance organisations in their native countries. Arisaig House was built in 1863 by F. D. P. Astley, a wealthy industrialist from the Midlands, as a shooting lodge. The architect was Philip Webb, the so-called father of the Arts and Crafts movement. A fire razed the house in 1935 which meant a complete rebuild. It was finished in 1939, and as a result the house was furnished with mod cons and was comfortable, with handsome wood panelled interiors and beautiful views from the generously sized ground and first floor rooms.

The location of a specialised training school for agents who would fulfil the highly dangerous roles expected of them had to be set up in a location that was easy to keep secret and which offered varied facilities. A number of houses in unrevealed locations in Hampshire, Essex, Buckinghamshire and other counties were chosen for specialist purposes and as 'finishing schools' for the agents, but it was the choice of northern Scotland for outdoor training, field craft and sabotage that was particularly satisfactory. The Highlands were remote and west of Fort William was an area served by a railway running the length up to the fishing port of Mallaig over the picturesque Glenfinnan viaduct. The Admiralty was persuaded to annex the whole area for use by the military. This meant that it would be possible to maintain a check on who went in and out at all times. Even the local inhabitants had to show their permits whenever they entered the region. A great benefit of this was that agents, instructors and high-ranking visitors from London could visit the special training centres and secrecy would be maintained.

Peter Kemp, one of the most active and successful of all SOE agents, arrived for a summer course with MI(R) in the area in 1940 and was immediately enchanted: 'the shores of Lochailort and the Sound of Arisaig reveal a wild, bleak beauty of scoured grey rock and cold blue water, of light green bracken and shadowed pine, that is strangely moving in its stark simplicity and grandeur.'[2] Others who arrived when the weather was anything but lovely were far less pleased with what they saw, complaining of incessant rain, mist hanging low over the hills and clouds of midges who found their way into every nook, cranny and orifice. One Dutch agent described it as 'a most depressing place'.[3]

The Special Operations Executive had been developed by combining Section D, MI(R) and the propaganda organisation of the Foreign Office, EH, named after Electra House, its headquarters. It was approved by the various heads of departments and the army high command and it was deadly secret. In fact, it was so secret that the organisation was never referred to as SOE by any of the operatives or staff involved in its organisation during the war. The title only became familiar when historians began to write about it decades after the war. Within Whitehall it was called the Interservices Research Bureau, but it was more often referred to simply as 'Baker Street', its home in London. The aim of the organisation was to train agents who could be flown or parachuted into occupied Europe to team up and work with resistance organisations on the ground. In the fullness of time SOE would be able to respond to requests for arms, communications equipment and ammunition, but in the first instance it was a question of selecting and training volunteers for this dangerous task.

The man in charge of SOE, appointed by Churchill, was Hugh Dalton, the minister of economic warfare. Although not a favourite of the prime minister, he had been backed in the War Cabinet by Clement Attlee and wrote in his diary on 11 July that Attlee had reassured him he would deal with Churchill, concluding: 'I am handling it, you can leave it safely to me.'[4] Less than a fortnight later Dalton wrote with evident satisfaction: '"And now," said the PM, "go and set Europe ablaze."'[5]

Dalton was ambitious and not trusted in all quarters. 'Being a socialist politician he was party to the fashionable left-wing view that all that was needed was to stir up the continental working class – the German working class as well – and they would rise and revolt against the invaders – the so-called "trigger" theory.'[6] However, this theory was not born out in practice. As historian Ingram Murray explained: 'the German working class thought Hitler was wonderful and so did a lot of French. The Communist party, which can be said to have been the most powerful embodiment of the working class had been completely bamboozled by the Nazi–Soviet Pact. Until the German invasion of Soviet Russia in 1941 – the game-changer – it was relatively quiescent.'[7]

Dalton was an energetic leader, nicknamed Dr Dynamo by his chief executive officer and undersecretary at the Ministry of Economic Warfare, Gladwyn Jebb. Jebb was a Foreign Office official put in place to smooth ruffled feathers if SOE's activities were to blight some aspects of British foreign policy. Joan Bright Astley, who ran the Secret Intelligence Centre in Whitehall and later co-authored Gubbins' biography, wrote that 'Jebb's incisive mind and exceptionally wide inter-departmental experience, coupled with Gubbins's tenacity and military experience, made them ... a formidable combination.'[8]

Dalton's ambition was to turn SOE into a major coordinating body for resistance throughout the occupied countries of mainland Europe. Only Czechoslovakia and Poland had underground resistance organisations in place; France, Belgium, the Netherlands and others further afield would take longer to get established.

By September 1940 the immediate threat of a German invasion had passed and Gubbins left the running of the Coleshill courses to Colonel Beyts with Colonel Major in overall charge. In November he was offered secondment to the newly formed Special Operations Executive but not before some serious internecine wrangling within the War Cabinet. Gubbins was hotly in demand. Dalton had met him the year before at a Polish dinner party and had been impressed by his quick mind and dynamic personality. He described the situation in his diary, offering a fascinating glimpse into the machinations in Whitehall:

I say [to Major-General John Kennedy, director of Military Operations at the War Office] that if he will release Colonel Gubbins I will not ask him for any more senior officers; also that I have been pressed to appeal to PM over case of Gubbins. DMO [Kennedy] says that he thinks it would be more difficult to succeed if I did make such an appeal, as the case against releasing Gubbins is very strong. The C-in-C Home Forces [Lieutenant General Sir Alan Brooke] is most anxious to keep him, but, I gather, the CIGS [Chief of Imperial General Staff, General Sir John Dill] is prepared to let me have him. DMO still thinks it doubtful whether I need a DT [Director of Training], but I say that if I get Gubbins, he can do this as well as other duties.[9]

Dalton prevailed and 'got Gubbins', to his evident satisfaction. He sent him to Scotland, newly promoted to acting brigadier, with the brief to keep him informed of the steps he would be taking to settle on a training programme that would turn ordinary men and women into extraordinary agents. By early December Dalton was delighted with Gubbins' progress and wrote in his diary: 'He also gives a good account of **preliminary steps taken for training** [emphasis mine]. He is evidently getting a move on and, as I anticipated he would, doing very well.'[10]

The paramilitary training that would be put in place over the course of the summer of 1940, and developed over the next four years, was based to a large extent on Gubbins' two handbooks, *The Art of Guerrilla Warfare* and *The Partisan Leader's Handbook,* as well as Millis Jefferis' pamphlet, *How to Use High Explosives.* It was evidently these publications as well as the excellent first impression which reassured Hugh Dalton that Gubbins was the right man to move SOE forward and with the kind of dynamism he demanded. From SOE's perspective, they could not have had a better man than Gubbins in charge. It was written of him that his:

> creative spirit made him a natural leader of the young; and he delegated generously to those whom he trusted, both men and women. Above all, he was a dedicated professional soldier. With his quick brain, the imagination and energy necessary to transform ideas into action, and his force of will, he might have held high command in the field had his abilities not been confined to special operations. As it was, he left his mark on the history of almost every country which suffered enemy occupation in the Second World War.[11]

SOE was so secret that it had no formal identity. It had no agents, no aircraft, no communications, no doctrine and, at first, no resources. SIS and the regular services were always suspicious of SOE, not least as their requirements were directly competing. Ingram Murray wrote: 'SIS needed peace and quiet to reconstruct its networks and to collect intelligence; SOE needed public and noisy evidence to demonstrate Allied support for resistance to the invaders.'[12] Initially SOE was housed in 2 Caxton Street, then on a floor in St Ermin's Hotel next door, but they were soon too small for the growing staff so SOE took over 64 Baker Street. At first there were a dozen telephone lines but these never appeared in the London telephone directory. When these grew to 200 lines they were distributed over three exchanges. Letters appeared either without a letterhead or were sent from the Ministry of Economic War Office or one of the three service disguises – 'MOI (SP) at the War Office, NID(Q) at the Admiralty, or AI10 at the Air Ministry; or that of the Inter-Services Research Bureau, one of SOE's cover titles (devised to account for the multiplicity of uniforms); or that of some quite bogus firm.'[13] By the end of its life, SOE had requisitioned buildings all round Baker Street and Gloucester Place under one of a variety of pseudonyms.

In the 1930s, the west Highlands were sparsely populated. The local characteristic was discretion and people were still mistrustful of answering strangers' questions in English. With few exceptions, they appeared willing to turn a blind eye to the paramilitary activities taking place in the dozen Commandos and SOE training schools which were to share the landscape for the best part of five years. The west Highlands have a historical link with warfare which might explain further the acceptance of whatever was happening in the glens and on the beaches around Loch Ailort and Loch Morar. The latter is the deepest body of freshwater in the British Isles and the fifth largest in Scotland. Naturally enough for such an imposing loch it has a monster, Morag, who was first 'sighted' in 1887. She is purported to be about thirty feet long with three dorsal humps and a head a foot wide. There were no reports of Morag during the war but the loch and its surrounding hills provided a harsh and haunting environment for SOE training.

The Lovat Scouts, originating from this area and mentioned above, had become a lasting feature in the British Army. Their specialist skill was 'unorthodox' fighting, to which they made their own contribution 'in observation, field craft and sharp-shooting'.[14] Lord Lovat, the founder of the Scouts, had died suddenly in 1933 and was succeeded by his son, Simon, who went on to become one of the most successful Commandos in the war.

Inverailort Castle was the first house to be commandeered on 30 April 1940. Mrs Cameron-Head, an eighty-one-year-old widow, was in London when she received a letter from the British Army's Highland HQ in Perth. She was informed that Scottish Command in Edinburgh had received notice that her two properties – Inverailort and Glenshian – 'were urgently required by the War Office for unspecified military purposes.'[15] By the time Mrs Cameron-Head arrived at Lochailort station she was dismayed to learn from two officers that the castle had already been half-emptied in preparation for its new role and that she would not be able to return to it. She wrote to her close friend, Sir Donald Cameron of Lochiel:

> The whole of the furniture has gone to store in Fort William. There seems to be no one really in command here except a nice Captain Stacy who can do nothing except order the men to proceed with the clearing of the two houses. The officers are going to live in the castle and there are some seventy to eighty tents for the men as well as Glenshian House ... They are planting their tents all over my ground and breaking down fences and walls and leaving gates open so that the beasts get out and all the Hotel cattle will get in and have a good feed on growing crops. Surely there is some redress for this ...?[16]

Soon she learned that her boat house and four dinghies had also been requisitioned.

Inverailort was known as 'the Big House'. It was situated in the shadow of a fine, steep-sided 814-metre cone called An Stac. At the time of writing the house is in a state of almost complete collapse, but it must, in its heyday, have been an imposing if somewhat forbidding castle. The land in front of the house and leading down to Loch Ailort is flat, ideal for the erection of tents, and it is easy to see why the early pioneers of the commandos and SOE thought it an excellent spot. By the end of June 1940, according to Stuart Allan author of *Commando Country*, there were 203 personnel capable of training 100 officers and 500 soldiers.

There were fifty-five instructors but that number increased and included, by the end of June 1940, six civilians (identified – three of them at least – as 'ghillies' or sportsmen's attendants from the nearby highland estates). Thirty mules and ponies were borrowed with staff to look after them. A further twenty-seven instructors with additional admin staff could train 150 officers and up to 2,500 ORs [soldiers]. The Local Home Guard was also roped in, often as the 'enemy' in guarding targets or pursuing students across the hills.[17]

During that summer the focus of the training was on British Army volunteers who were being prepared to be part of the Independent Companies, which would later become the Commandos. Men arrived by train, often in the middle of the night. Major R. F. Hall recounted his memories of arriving at Lochailort:

We were sitting comfortably there in the train and all of a sudden it came to an abrupt halt. We were all thrown forward and kit bags came off the luggage racks and the place was a shambles. Then we realised that the train was under fire and there were explosions going off all around us. Then instructors leapt out of holes in the ground and shouted at us, 'Get out of the train, get out of the train, grab your kit and follow us!' And so of course we all scrambled out, grabbed everything we had, and we were doubled, and ran from there all the way to the Big House clutching our belongings.[18]

It was typical not only of the introduction to the courses but of the surprises that would be unleashed on them over the next few weeks. The training at Lochailort was tough. There was a sense that they had to be ready, day or night, to expect the unexpected. With little or no warning the trainees might be ordered to climb the steep rock-face leading on the slopes of An Stac, or wade across the river Ailort to huts erected on islets where they would sit in wet clothes listening to a lecture. There were long tramps across the hills and glens carrying heavy packs. Their map-reading skills were tested to the limit when the sea mists rolled in or the rain fell so hard they could barely make out the shape of the landscape around them. It was designed to be arduous, especially in the bitter cold and snow of winter or the midge-filled summer weeks when the little critters would find every possible way onto any human skin left bare. The training was hard on the instructors too as most of them took part in the exercises.

The early instructors at Inverailort were a mixture of extraordinary men of adventure – some of them hard men experienced in extreme conditions who relished the prospect of a spell in the west Highlands. There were four holders of the Polar Medal, including Murray Levick, who had been with Captain Robert Falcon Scott on the Terra Nova Expedition to the Antarctic in 1910–13. Another famous character was the mountaineer Freddie Spencer Chapman, who was writing a book about his first ascent of the 7,326m Tibetan peak Chomolhari in 1937. He brought not only climbing skills but also much practical assistance to the early training; introducing rubber footwear, lightweight tents and a mountaineering rucksack which proved valuable given the nature of the terrain they were being trained in. He also suggested the use of polar rations which were made of concentrated food stuffs such as pemmican, a high-energy mixture of fat and protein loved by some and loathed by others. Spencer-Chapman was sent to Australia and from there, in September 1941, to Singapore. After the Japanese landings three months later, he was sent to Kuala Lumpur 'expressly to organise and lead reconnaissance and operational parties behind enemy lines.'[19] That he evaded capture for over three years makes his one of the most remarkable stories of the Second World War. Two other men with distinguished adventure careers behind them and a great deal of war in front of them were David Stirling, the founder of the SAS (Special Air Service) and Simon Fraser, Lord Lovat, who went on to lead a remarkable Commando raid in Norway in 1941. He was described by Peter Kemp as 'a brilliant instructor as well as a superb fighting soldier, he taught me in the three weeks I was with him all

I know about movement across country and the principle of natural camouflage.'[20]

In the early months, the restricted area of the Highlands set aside for training was used for the Independent Companies, which comprised groups of soldiers specially trained to carry out raids. As the training programme developed, it was clear that Inverailort should become the focus of training for British forces that would end up on sabotage missions in Norway.

The Independent Companies became the Commandos and by March 1942 their training had moved to the ancestral home of Mrs Cameron-Head's friend, Sir Donald Cameron of Lochiel, Achnacarry Castle. There the army developed an intensive programme to put British Army recruits through their paces in the toughest of conditions. By 1943, over 1,000 men were being trained on six-week courses at Achnacarry, sleeping in tents on the lawns in front of the castle. It was set up exclusively for training British military personnel and had nothing to do with the Special Operations Executive except for the nature of the training and the type of methods they would use in their sabotage work in the future.

Gubbins' 'Bods', as the SOE agents were known, would require a separate establishment. These men and women who came up to the Highlands for training were taken further up the line to an area focused around the handsome granite manor house of Arisaig, a few miles north of Inverailort, which also had its own railway station. The house belonged to Miss Charlotte Astley-Nicholson who was the primary landowner in the area. Unlike Mrs Cameron-Head, Miss Astley-Nicholson had several properties so that she was able to move out of Arisaig and into another of her houses – although most of these were also taken over before the end of the year.

SOE recruits were often civilians from the occupied countries of Europe: France, Belgium, the Netherlands, Poland, Czechoslovakia, Norway and so on. Others had served in their country's armed forces before occupation. Recruits were often given service ranks and uniforms as part of their disguise. The qualifications required to become an agent were never written down as the need for secrecy on the one hand and the voluntary nature of the job on the other meant that open recruitment was out of the question. A gift for languages was essential and bilingual men and women were particularly desirable. Patriotism and a hatred of the Nazi occupiers were required, but the most indefinable aspect of the agents was their personality. Out and out bravery could prove dangerous to their fellow agents but so could someone who cracked under pressure. Maurice Buckmaster, in charge of Section F (France) of Special Operations Executive summed up the dangers:

> In no other department of war were men and women called upon to die alone, to withstand agony of mind and of body in utter solitude, to face death, often ignominious and pain-racked, uncertain whether they might not have saved themselves by the revelation of petty secrets. In no other department of war were civilians asked to risk everything in order to conceal a man whom they had never seen before and might never see again.[21]

The would-be agents were selected carefully at a preliminary interview that took place in a variety of different locations. Those interviewed for Section F were summoned to a bare room in the Northumberland Hotel. Later, one-to-one interviews were replaced by an assessment board composed of psychologists. Once they had been thoroughly interviewed and investigated agents were sent on a three-week course in one of a dozen English country houses. This was a test in physical fitness, elementary map reading and some weapons training. There was always plenty of alcohol available in these houses as it was vitally important to know how agents would behave after they had had a drink or two. The most famous of these houses was Wanborough Manor in Surrey where the commandant, Roger de Wesselow, never failed to take part in the early morning run even though he was over sixty. Those who passed this course – and not all did by any means – were sent to Arisaig for the paramilitary-style training that would be necessary to equip them for the most dangerous role they would probably ever play.

The recruits were all volunteers drawn from every conceivable walk of life and every strata in society. They ranged from poachers to policemen, ladies from the leisured class to women brought up in poverty, artists, peasants, sons of ambassadors, daughters of forces personnel and many more besides. The best agents were the strong, silent types with the strength of character to keep a clear head and remain calm in extremely dangerous situations. M. R. D. Foot described the way the recruiters worked out whether an agent would be worth training: 'SOE's training system can be compared to a set of sieves, each one with a closer mesh than the one before. Recruiting and training intermeshed; one of the objects of the training system was to sieve out the unsuitables before they could wreak havoc abroad.'[22]

Arisaig became the training headquarters in the Highlands and was where most of the instructors and commandants lived. It was also the house used by Gubbins and his official visitors if they wanted somewhere to stay when they made periodic visits to the STS, or Special Training Schools. The ground floor comprised a spacious hall with a staircase leading to the first floor, a wood panelled dining room with a large fireplace, a drawing room with views of the sea loch, a 'smoking' room and 'business' room that doubled up as a bar and sitting room and was much used during the training weeks. Beyond the business room was the library leading to other rooms approached from the cloakroom area for brushing boots and, in former times, flower arranging. The wing beyond the dining room belonged to the servants or, during the war, the quartermaster's team and catering staff. The kitchen, scullery and housekeeper's room remained unaltered but the pantry was renamed the washing room. Below stairs, the servants' hall and store rooms were given over to the NAAFI while the largest store room became an indoor pistol range. There was also a cobblers' shop, a barber's shop and a wood store in place of the wine cellar.

On the first floor were the dozen large main bedrooms and two bathrooms with separate WCs, a great luxury in comparison to other large houses. The second floor had eleven rooms including the billiard room (the notations on the wartime map say 'no table' – this must have been withdrawn for safety).

All the formal gardens were given over to vegetables, as with everywhere else in Britain, but the field below the house was used for exercises and three huts on the edge of the field became ammunition stores. The house still stands today. It is built on three sides of a courtyard. The west wing comprises the main house; the south wing is now the family's accommodation and kitchens, but during the war served to provide extra bedrooms and the servants' quarters. The north wing has an arch that leads through to the service area, gardens and duck pond. The gardens directly behind the house are formal, with a rose garden and sunken lawns and beyond are rolling fields leading down to the sea loch, Loch nan Ceall. On a sunny, midge-free day it is hard to conceive of a lovelier spot.

On Christmas Day 1940, Gubbins and a lady driver accompanied Hugh Dalton to Arisaig. The minister did not record what he thought of the house but he found the remoteness of the location excellent for the purpose of training. He wrote in his diary for that day: 'I do not think I have ever before seen a "deer forest", having always regarded Scotland as a rather second-class foreign country which came low down on the order of one's preferences.'[23] The following day he and Gubbins spent the day motoring around the area beyond Arisaig, identifying possible stations or houses to be commandeered for training or accommodation. At one point he suggested to Gubbins that they should get out and walk rather than drive between the properties, despite the fact it was pouring with rain for the last mile or so of their journey. 'Dalton lost a shoe in the mud and talked incessantly, saying afterwards that he had "thoroughly enjoyed himself".'[24]

More houses were acquired over the next few months, a number from Miss Astley-Nicholson and two from Lord Brocket, which drew anguished protest from the peer, who had already lost Brocket Hall to babies. Hugh Dalton sent a reply from the Inter Services War Bureau, one of the many covers for SOE, in which he was politely sympathetic. He did not feel sorry for Brocket, whose Nazi sympathies were well known, and wrote in a memorandum: 'This young Lord appears to own a large number of alternative residences in various parts of the British Isles and I cannot believe that he is suffering undue hardship.'[25]

Agents of different nationalities were kept in separate houses, such as Traigh House or Camusdarach on the west coast opposite Eigg. Rhubana Lodge lies on the westernmost end of Loch Morar where the water leaves the loch and joins the river Morar, which has the distinction of being one of the shortest rivers in the British Isles, flowing for just one kilometre at high tide. Swordland and Meoble Lodge were also on the side of the loch. In these properties, foreign agents were looked after by a staff speaking their language and it depended on the numbers being trained at any one time which property was used by which country section.

The only houses that did not change role were Arisaig, the headquarters of SOE training; Swordland on Loch Morar which was used for boat work and ship sabotage training and Glasnacardoch, whose specific function was foreign weapons training. 'At their fullest extent of development attained during 1943, the Group A schools along the road to the Isles and Loch Morar taken together could train up to seventy-five students simultaneously ... Between them the schools had sixteen officer instructors and twenty-six non-commissioned officer instructors.'[26]

By the time Gubbins arrived in November 1940 as director of training, many of the early instructors, such as Colonel Spencer Chapman, had moved on and others had replaced them at Loch Ailort. The first class – consisting of Norwegians, Belgians, Frenchmen and one Scot – had completed its course a month earlier. Few instructors taught both the Commandos and SOE but one exception was a duo known affectionately – but in regard to their speciality, distinctly incorrectly – as 'the Heavenly Twins'. William Fairbairn and Eric Sykes were two retired policemen who had worked in the Shanghai municipal police in China, then the most dangerous city on earth. Confusingly, Fairbairn was known by the name of Dan and Sykes as Bill. During his career in China, Fairbairn had witnessed appalling levels of violence when many policemen were killed, so he developed a new approach to policing which he called 'shooting to live'. Training took place in a specially constructed shooting gallery and was much more hands-on than the previous target practice had been:

> In near darkness the policemen reacted to a series of surprises from pop-up targets, firecrackers and other hazards; this was the original 'Mystery House', the direct forerunner of the range created beside Inverailort. The intention was to inculcate with split-second decision-making and reflexes, where the pistol was drawn at great speed and fired at a target by instinct, without a deliberate aiming action or use of sights, much as one would point a finger at someone or something without thinking about it. Two shots were to be delivered to the target, to ensure that in the real event none were returned.[27]

Fairbairn was born in 1885 so by 1940 he was already fifty-five. He had served in the Far East with the Royal Marine Light Infantry and joined the Shanghai police as a constable in 1907. He rose to the post of assistant commissioner in 1935 and held that post until his retirement in February 1940. 'Bill' Sykes was born Eric Anthony Schwabe two years before Fairbairn. He was described by one of the younger instructors as looking nothing like his Dickensian namesake but rather having the appearance and voice of a bishop 'but was endowed with enormous hands with which he taught students how to throttle people.'[28] Although born in Lancashire, his name came from his German father and he changed it to Sykes in 1917 as so many people with German origins did in the First World War, for both self-preservation and in a show of patriotism. He worked for Colt and Remington in Shanghai and met Dan Fairbairn sometime in the mid-1920s. Under his guidance Sykes became a volunteer constable and was believed to have been in charge of the sniper division. He retired at the same time as

Fairbairn and the two men sailed back to Britain and, on arrival, offered their services to the War Office. They were immediately given the rank of captain and sent to Brickendonbury House in Hertfordshire where they taught close combat to trainees from Section D. They travelled all over the country teaching 'their brand of mayhem'[29]. From there they were sent up to northern Scotland to teach the skills necessary to equip both Commandos and special agents for clandestine warfare. One officer remembered vividly his first encounter with the duo:

> On the first morning we met 'Dan' Fairbairn and 'Bill' Sykes. We were taken into the hall of the Big House and suddenly at the top of the stairs appeared a couple of dear old gentlemen (we later discovered one was fifty-six and the other fifty-eight). Both wearing spectacles and both were dressed in battle dress with just a plain webbing belt. They walked to the top of the stairs, fell tumbling, tumbling down the stairs and ended up at the bottom, in the battle crouch position, with a hand-gun in one hand and a fighting knife in the other – a shattering experience for all of us.[30]

They practised this stunt on most recruits and with the same result. Now that they had the respect of the trainees they could bring their experience of the combined martial arts to bear and teach all manner of silent killing and unarmed combat. Where they advocated the use of weapons it was sparingly. Probably their most famous and lasting contribution to the British-trained guerrillas was the F-S [Fairbairn–Sykes] fighting knife. This was developed in association with Wilkinson Sword. Fairbairn and Sykes found the British Army issue dagger with its knuckle-duster hilt too large and clumsy to be of much use. So they arranged to meet the head of the Experimental Workshop, Charlie Rose, and Jack Wilkinson-Latham, the managing director of Wilkinson Sword. The meeting took place at number 53 Pall Mall on 4 November 1940.

The company, founded in 1772, had long been suppliers of weapons such as bayonets and other knives to the armed forces as well as

more recently flak jackets for pilots. Charlie Rose had been working at the company since 1926 and as early as 1931 had developed
a design for a prototype stiletto knife, which was now dramatically
altered and redrawn to match Fairbairn and Sykes' requirements.
The first pattern of the F-S fighting knife had a double-edged seven-
and-a-half inch (nineteen centimetre) blade and a brass hilt with a
chequered grip, for maximum hold, which slid into a leather scab-
bard. The beauty of the design was that it could be worn either
strapped to the user's calf or on a belt. The brass hilt was deliberately heavy so as to give the knife the perfect balance. As brass was
a restricted and controlled material this was to change as the knife
went into mass production with the third pattern. The knives were
initially made by hand and the first ones went into production just
ten days after the meeting in Pall Mall. The first order was for 1,500
knives, which were hand-ground, so that every knife was unique.
Fairbairn and Sykes first got to see one of 'their' knives in January
1941 and were delighted with it. It was conceived as a survival knife
and as a slashing weapon, 'but its principal application was in the
practice of "silent killing", above all to their recommended method
of despatching sentries and other unwary targets by a thrust to the
carotid artery in the neck.'[31]

The knife was used by agents and Commandos from Britain
to Belgium to the USA. It has been described as the Spitfire of the
knife world. It features in the insignia of the British Royal Marines,
the Belgian and Dutch Commando corps – all three founded in the
Second World War – but also in the Australian and US corps. It was
by no means the only weapon used by SOE agents, but it was possibly the most iconic.

Despite the intense security and need for secrecy around Arisaig
and the other houses (no part of the training syllabus was allowed
to be discussed in any way, for example, with the press or anyone
without the Official Secrets Act), Fairbairn committed himself to
paper. In 1942 he published a guide to unarmed combat called *All-In
Fighting*. It was an illustrated manual with shockingly violent lessons
which he justified thus:

Some readers may be appalled at the suggestion that it should be necessary for human beings of the 20th century to revert to the grim brutality of the Stone Age in order to live. But it must be realised that, when dealing with an utterly ruthless enemy who has clearly expressed his intention of wiping this nation out of existence, there is no room for any scruples or compunction about the methods to be employed in preventing him.[32]

Some of the methods of unarmed combat taught by Fairburn and Sykes were so dangerous that they carried a warning as to how to avoid accidents, urging great care when practising holds, throws and blows. It was based on Fairbairn's purpose-designed technique which conflated jujitsu, karate and holds he had used in Shanghai. Stuart Allan quotes the key sentence in *Commando Country*: 'On NO ACCOUNT should the Chinese "rock crusher" be practised over the heart.'[33] Despite these warnings there were accidents, which was inevitable given the violent nature of the training the recruits were undertaking.

The teaching had an enormous impact on the men and women who learned various skills from the two former policemen. George Langelaan, an American journalist from the *New York Times* dropped into France, was eloquent in his admiration for what the training in silent killing had given him. He wrote, without naming him, that Fairbairn:

> ... gave us more and more self-confidence which gradually grew into a sense of physical power and superiority that few men ever acquire. By the time we finished our training, I would have will-ingly enough tackled any man, whatever his strength, size or ability. He taught us to face the possibility of a fight without the slightest tremor of apprehension, a state of mind which very few professional boxers ever enjoy, and which so often means more than half the battle. Strange as this may seem, it is understand-able when a man knows for certain that he can hurt, maul, injure, or even kill with the greatest of ease, and that during every split

second of a fight he has not one but a dozen different openings, different possibilities, to choose from. One fear has, since then, however, haunted me: that of getting entangled in a sudden row and of seriously injuring, or even killing, another man before even realising what is happening.[34]

Away from silent killing, recruits were taught survival techniques and how to live off the land. They learned how to move across an open landscape unseen, an art often taught by skilled deer stalkers from the neighbouring estates. They were introduced to high explosives, sabotage and firearms, including foreign weapons that they might encounter in the field. It was quite possible that they would have to steal a pistol or rifle and use it in self-defence so the instructors tried to find a wide selection of non-standard weaponry. For every aspect of the training there were dedicated experts drawn from many walks of life, including prisoners. A former convict was released under a special arrangement in exchange for offering his expertise to the war effort. He had been in and out of Barlinnie and Peterhead prisons before the war for breaking locks to get into safes. His knowledge of setting small charges was put to good use. A forger was brought in to teach the students about secret handwriting and how to recreate others' signatures for passes or other documents. He was simply known at Arisaig as the Forger and nobody knew if that was his civilian profession or not.

One of the most colourful individuals to live and instruct at Arisaig was Captain Gavin Maxwell, who would later gain international fame as the author of *Ring of Bright Water*. He was by no means the most important instructor but he was such a fascinating character that I chose to focus on him rather than on some of the other excellent tutors. Maxwell had a complex personality and was a misfit in the regular army but working with the agents he found himself surrounded by like-minded people who were going to be living and working in the shadows and on the fringes of society, a place he to some extent inhabited for most of his life.

In August 1939 he joined the Scots Guards but within three weeks he became seriously ill with the first of many duodenal ulcers and was sent back home on sick leave. When he recovered he was posted to Ground Defences at RAF Kenley and took a course in sniping. His biographer, Douglas Botting, wrote that he showed such a natural aptitude that Evelyn Waugh, who he had met at Carlton Towers earlier that summer, and who was now a lieutenant in the Royal Marines, invited him over to Bisley to lecture about it to the troops under his command. During the Blitz, Maxwell was stationed at the South Metropolitan Gas Works on the riverside of the Thames in London, close to the Blackwall Tunnel and thus right in the target zone for German bombers. One evening he returned to his billet covered in dust and announced: 'If I'm alive when the war's over I'm going to buy an island in the Hebrides and retire there for life; no aeroplanes, no bombs, no commanding officer, no rusty dannert wire.'[35] In fact, in a sense his war was over. Struck ill again he was declared unfit for active service and downgraded to Category C which meant home service, something that did not sit well with the prickly character of a man of action, as he saw himself.

Maxwell was born in July 1914 and never knew his father, who was killed in the first German artillery barrage of the First World War three months after his birth. His mother never married again. She was Lady Mary Percy, the fifth daughter of the seventh Duke of Northumberland. Gavin's early childhood was spent running barefoot around the hills above Elrig, his home in what was then Wigtownshire, just north of Port William. 'Between the ages of seven and ten I was wonderfully, gloriously happy. This is when I became identified with the countryside, with other living creatures, and with my home at Elrig.'[36] He claimed only to have met ten other children before he left home to go to boarding school. Not unsurprisingly he hated school but he did make one lifelong friend, Peter Kemp, already mentioned here, who became a guerrilla fighter and secret agent. Maxwell suffered all his school years from a delicate physique and contracted a mysterious illness in his late teens which rendered him bedridden and in the care of his mother for the best part of fifteen months. When he recovered he was determined to challenge himself and wrote:

> ... shooting became a passion with me – and, later on, wild-fowling, the toughest blood sport in the world. To be out on an estuary – out on the salt-marsh and mud-flats of Wigtown Bay – completely on one's own in the early hours of the depths of winter was hard beyond belief – the conditions were so tough you'd think nothing could survive out there at all, least of all a human being. These were challenges I deliberately sought out. After my illness, after being a weakling for so long, I wanted to prove myself physically, I wanted to prove I could do macho things, that I was a man of action.[37]

This toughness led him to desire a life of excitement and adventure. At Oxford he was a rebellious student who ignored his studies and only passed his second-year exams by stealing the exam papers the week before he was due to sit them. He was a successful member of the Oxford University gun team and was reckoned by many to be one of the best dozen guns in the country. He also had a passion for fast cars. At Oxford he had a Bentley and would race his friend, Mike Wills, who owned a sports car and had boasted he could drive it up the Woodstock road at 100 miles per hour. Maxwell would find out when Wills was demonstrating this feat, lie in wait in a lay-by, and roar after him and overtake him at 113 mph.

In August 1941 Maxwell left his regiment and, via a former Stowe school friend, Captain Alfgar Hesketh-Prichard, obtained an interview at Baker Street. It was clear that he would never be fit enough to work as an agent but his reputation as a marksman and a sniper, his expertise in field craft and camouflage gained before the war, and his ability to teach seemed reason enough to offer him a place as an SOE instructor. He arrived in Arisaig in January 1942 and was immediately happy. He said later that he felt as if he were coming home. This part of northern Scotland, with its mountains, forests and sea lochs, with its magnificent coastline of white beaches and tempestuous seas, inspired awe in the twenty-seven-year-old Maxwell. It is one of the most beautiful landscapes in Britain and it sang to him.

He excelled as an instructor and was praised by the senior commandants for his expertise in field crafts as well as his knowledge of weapons. He had arrived at Arisaig with two large metal trunks full of firearms and ammunition from his own extensive collection, made during the 1930s and early 1940s. Some of the weapons were modern, state of the art German examples, a valuable addition for the trainees who got to handle pistols that might be used against them in the future. This would form the bulk of the foreign weapons training collection at Glasnacardoch Lodge, set up in the autumn of 1943. He taught the students how to strip, reassemble, load, fire and maintain firearms in the dark, a vital skill for an agent in the field. He provided the live ammunition which he fired over the students' heads from a Bren gun when they were negotiating the assault course. They knew to be wary of Maxwell. He could be moody and difficult but on the other hand he had respect and affection for his students and most of them for him. He had something of the devil-may-care approach to life which they needed to learn themselves, but he was also reflective, often to be found reading poetry under the shade of the rhododendrons in the gardens at Arisaig, and that marked him out as different from the other instructors. If Maxwell was an eccentric, he was not alone at Arisaig. Botting wrote:

Gavin found at SOE Arisaig a rather odd collection of people, many of them larger than life. One of them (a Norwegian) was a world champion ski jumper, another (a Russian) a world champion wrestler; one had been a Fascist at Cambridge and fought for Franco in the Spanish Civil War; another had been a Communist at Cambridge and a member of the Apostles group that had included the Soviet spies Anthony Blunt and Guy Burgess.[38]

Maxwell had a strong affinity with the land. He taught students how to collect mussels and limpets off the rocks on the seashore and eat them raw if they had no means of cooking them. In another demonstration of survival, he killed a seal, removed the blubber and strained the seal oil through blotting paper. This he proceeded to drink, showing that there were some improbable by-products of wild-life for use in extremis. He showed them basic butchery, cutting up a warm deer carcass, which shocked some of the raw recruits who had not acclimatised to Maxwell's extreme survival techniques. On one occasion he challenged a group of students to bring back a bird and whatever it was, he would eat it. Clearly hoping for a treat such as a plump grouse he was probably dismayed, although he did not show it, when they turned up with a jackdaw. He ate it with as much relish as he could muster. He taught them to relieve themselves in the open telling them: 'You drink the water higher up the burn and do big jobs lower down the burn. No toilet paper please. Dangle from the branch of a tree and use a smooth pebble dipped in water like the Arabs do.'[39]

One of Maxwell's stunts was to interrupt a ping-pong match by bursting into the room and shooting the ball mid-air with a Colt.45. Dr James MacDougall, one of the doctors at Arisaig with the brief to keep an eye on the psychiatric health of both the instructors and the trainees, described Maxwell as a 'creative psychopath'. Like Churchill, he went on, these people have a personality composed of absolute opposite characteristics:

> They can be simultaneously friendly and unfriendly, truthful and untruthful, bold and fearful, loyal and disloyal ... It was [my] view that Gavin was emotionally retarded, almost certainly because his sexual and emotional development had been put on hold at the age of sixteen, when his nearly fatal illness cut him off from all but his mother.[40]

This complex, exciting, dangerous man made a deep impression on his students, especially when he was trying to make a point about cour-age. One evening he was sitting drinking whisky with some French agents, and a fellow instructor Hamish Pelham Burn. It was late in the evening and the conversation had got round to the inevitable question about what they should do if they were caught by the Gestapo. They had all been indoctrinated to give nothing away even under torture but the French said they were not worried; they would just bite on their cyanide capsules. Pelham Burn witnessed the reaction:

'Oh no you wouldn't!' retorted Gavin. 'You'd try and survive it. Like this!' He was going to stub out his lighted cigarette on his bare thigh, he told them (he was wearing a kilt), and they could watch his eyes and see what effect it had on him. So he took a puff on his cigarette and then ground out the burning end on his thigh. I watched his face and there was not a flicker of reaction to the pain. It didn't do his thigh much good, but the French were very impressed. He'd made his point – as he always liked to.[41]

Although he got on well with the students and they respected him, even if some did not like him, he had a poor relationship with some of the colonels in charge of the training programme. A number lived at Arisaig and he described one or two of them as 'very objection-able and unpleasant people' who 'had got there simply by influence'. The situation got out of control when his senior commander, Colonel Jimmy Young, 'spluttered with outrage' when Gavin asked for compassionate leave after receiving a telegram from his mother informing him that his flamingos had flown out to sea. Colonel Young was exasperated by his refusal to adhere to the military dress code. Gavin insisted on wearing his family kilt, not an army one, and he wore a Texan scarf under his battledress. Those who were prepared to trust him to get on with his job he had no objection to. The reports on him reflect the fact that not everyone found him easy. 'Quite a cheerful person but rather self-centred' was one comment, while another thought him likely 'to create problems for himself and worry over them'. 'I didn't get on with my superiors,' he said bluntly. Eventually he moved out of Arisaig and into a small house on a hill near Glasnacardoch, six miles up the railway line towards Mallaig. It suited him better not to be under the same roof as the senior officers who irritated him.

Very few agents returned to Arisaig to vouch for Maxwell's instruction. Peter Kemp, his old school friend, thought him 'a tremendous teacher' but it was the independent view of a young Frenchwoman, Suzanne Warren, which gives perhaps the most descriptive view of Maxwell. She had been working in France for a Paris-based network helping Allies evade capture and escape to Britain. Her first husband was the treacherous double agent, Harold Cole, who betrayed many of his friends who were later murdered by the Nazis. Suzanne was captured by the Gestapo in January 1943 and brutally interrogated for two months. She refused to talk, despite being tortured, so was sent to prison at Castres. She escaped in September and, remarkably, joined another resistance network as a courier before being picked up from the Brittany coast by a Royal Navy gunboat in April 1944. She was carrying important papers for the French in London. After she had recovered her health she was sent to Arisaig as one of the last intake of resistance fighters to be trained there. She said later that Gavin Maxwell reminded her of the poet Byron, but nicer than Byron. 'He was one of the few people in my life who were like shining stars – something really special.'[42]

She spent the whole of July at Arisaig and spoke of it as a process of great peace and healing, even though she was being trained to fight for her life. 'I used to go out with Gavin in his lobster boat and explore the coves and islands along the coast, and the seals would follow us and the birds swoop around us and it was all so beautiful and wonderful after the nightmare of the Gestapo.'[43] She described his technique with the students:

We were an unruly mob of different nationalities but he never used a rod of iron, he was not a run-of-the-mill officer, he didn't go by the book. He was a rebel, like me. He exercised leadership by the sheer force of his personality. And he created such a happy atmosphere that there was no resentfulness, no rebellion, even though we were all confined and cooped up and couldn't go anywhere. I don't like people telling me what to do, but *he* could, and I didn't resist it. He made you feel you were part of a team, so he got far more out of us. He wasn't soft – we had to work damn hard.[44]

By the summer of 1943 Maxwell had been given ever more responsibility. He was made commandant of another training school, STS 24 at Knoydart and he was also the chief instructor at the Foreign Weapons School at STS 22a at Glasnacardoch. It was an intensive life by any measure and the instructors, as well as the students, needed to let their hair down. There was a constant supply of whisky at Arisaig – it was important that the agents learned to react to any surprise situation that instructors would throw at them, even when drunk. One fellow instructor and friend of Maxwell's, Matthew Hodgart, described the hedonistic life in the excited, sometimes intoxicating, atmosphere at Arisaig: 'We used to drink like fish in the evenings after the day's work and talk about everything under the sun. Looking back, that's what it was all about – being young and alive in the most beautiful place in the world.'[45]

Another account described the evenings at Garramor, another of the special training centres five miles up the coast from Arisaig, when trainees would eat salmon caught after being stunned by plastic explosives thrown into the rivers or venison shot 'accidentally' and gutted by an instructor, probably Maxwell. The students read John Buchan novels and drank copious quantities of whisky. A journalist researching the house recounted this story in the *Daily Telegraph* in 2000: 'Finally, when lurching through the darkened corridors towards their beds, they might be confronted by one of Garramor's 'surprises' – a thunderflash, an open trap-door or a dummy springing from the shadows dressed in a raincoat and Homburg, so loved by the Gestapo. Whatever state they were in, they had to blast the dummy with a double-tap before they brushed their teeth.'[46]

Accidents did happen during the agents' training, both to property and personnel. The pier at Swordland on Loch Morar was severely damaged when too much explosive was used during a sabotage training exercise. Occasionally Limpet mines were stuck to the sides of the wrong boats, much to the indignation of the fishermen of the local fleet, while a party of over-enthusiastic Czech saboteurs very nearly destroyed the rail track to Fort William. This would have been awkward as the line was the main link with the outside world, and was relied upon far more than the single track unmetalled road that ran from Fort William to Mallaig, for delivery of rations, trainees and visitors from London who periodically arrived at the training centres to check that everything was exploding to plan.

To relieve the pressure SOE training put him under, Maxwell would slip away for the odd weekend between courses and ride down the coast on his motorbike to watch birds or he would disappear in his lobster boat, the *Gannet*, to explore the crinkly coastline and spot seals, otters and other wildlife. Occasionally he would go deer stalking and on Sunday evenings he might meet up with fellow instructors in the Morar Hotel. However, the favourite watering hole in the area was the Lochailort Inn run by an extraordinary character who became great friends with Maxwell. She was called Uilleamena MacRae, 'an eccentric, warm-hearted, striking-looking, Lewis-born woman in her early forties, with a Bonnie Prince Charlie hairstyle and a big, swishing Inverness cape. She ran her wartime inn like a private home for her friends and her horde of pets.'[47]

Special relationships naturally formed in such a rich and intense environment. Maxwell, who described his sexuality as rather more *Death in Venice* than *Anthony and Cleopatra*, developed a close bond with an intelligent young instructor who had also been in the Scots Guards. His name was Michael Bolitho and he was killed in November 1942 in Algeria having been dropped behind enemy lines. His body was never found and he was eventually commemorated on the Medjez-el-Bab Memorial in Tunisia. When Maxwell heard of Michael's death he was absolutely devastated and, according to Hodgart, began drinking ever more heavily.

*

So who were these agents who were being trained in such lethal arts in the depths of the Scottish Highlands? The instructors never knew the identity of their trainees, nor did they know what they were being trained for. Nor, for that matter, did the trainees. Their missions were given to them only after they had left Arisaig and done their intensive parachute training at Ringway outside Manchester. After that they might be sent to Beaulieu in Hampshire or another house for finishing training and held in one of the fifty or so country houses requisitioned for the purpose, such as Audley End, while their futures, their aliases and all their paperwork were gathered together and the final nature of their task disclosed. So it was that the instructors only learned much later and by accident that two of the young Czechoslovak soldiers they had trained at Arisaig had been responsible for the assassination of acting Reichsprotektor Reinhard Heydrich in Prague in May 1942. Their story is told in the next chapter.

George Langelaan, the former *New York Times* journalist and later author, wrote an autobiography in 1959 entitled *Knights of the Floating Silk*, in which he described in detail his experiences of the training at Arisaig. He wrote about the Forger, 'No one ever dared to question him about his past and to this day I do not know whether he was a real crook who had come to some fantastic agreement with the legal and military authorities, or whether he was merely a very efficient expert doing a very unusual job.'[48] The Forger talked incessantly about swindles and swindlers he had known while he taught them to reproduce signatures perfectly with the aid of an egg, how to alter figures or change the date of a document and 'the art of extracting a letter from an envelope without opening it and, far more difficult, of putting it back again afterwards.'[49] He alarmed the students by producing perfect imitations of all their handwriting within a week. Langelaan was fascinated by the tools of the Forger's trade. His attaché case was a treasure chest of stationery items including pens, pencils, stamps, rulers, rubbers and inks of various colours. He had fountain pens stuffed into his waistcoat pockets that reminded Langelaan of 'cartridge cases out of a Cossack's shirt.'

From Bill Sykes he learned how to roll off a moving train and escape into the countryside: '"Now watch! This is what you have to do!" and rolling off the foot-board, he barely touched the ground, came up on his feet, doubled up and somersaulted down the grass bank.'[50] By the end of the exercise all the recruits were confident they could escape from a train moving at anything up to forty miles per hour. Sykes also taught them how to use their hands in combat – never closed but open, using the base of the palm. 'By making us hit trees and even a brick wall, he also showed us that one could hit much harder in this way than with a closed fist full of very fragile bones.'[51]

Langelaan learned from other instructors how to blow up buildings, bridges, trains, dams, lock-gates, ships and locomotives. He enjoyed becoming a hard man, swimming in the icy waters of the Atlantic, climbing cliffs and ropes for hours on end and dealing with sleep deprivation. He concluded: 'Thus, in less than three months, we had acquired a store of highly practical but most immoral and even criminal knowledge which few people (including criminals) ever acquire in a lifetime. And physically we were as fit as a world champion should be on the morning of his big fight.'[52]

George Langelaan was given the task of forming a network called UKULELE, part of the French Resistance network. Concerned that his strong features made him easily recognisable, he underwent painful plastic surgery to have his ears reduced in size and pinned back, saying they stuck out 'like taxi doors' before the operation. He was dropped by parachute near Argenton-sur-Creuse, 100 kilometres east of Poitiers, on 6 September 1941. Unfortunately he was caught at Châteauroux within a month and was condemned to death by the Nazis. On 16 July 1942 he succeeded in escaping from Mauzac camp and got back to England via Spain. He returned to France in 1944 with the British army in the D-Day landings. After the war he resumed his career as a writer and journalist, publishing his most famous work *The Fly* in 1957.

Nancy Wake was another Arisaig-trained SOE agent. Her code name was White Mouse and by the end of the war she had won the

George Medal; the Croix de Guerre with palm (twice); the Croix de Guerre with star; the Médaille de la Résistance (a rare decoration for a foreigner) and the US Medal of Freedom with bronze palm. When the war broke out 'she seemed nothing more than the frivolous young fiancée of a wealthy Marseilles industrialist'.[53] By the end of the Second World War she was on the top of the Gestapo's most wanted list.

In the 1930s she had personally witnessed the Nazi brutality towards the Jews in Vienna and resolved 'there and then that if I ever had the chance I would do anything to make things more difficult for their rotten party.'[54] In 1940 she drove an ambulance but after the fall of France she went back to Marseilles with her husband, Henri Fiocca, and she worked as a courier for Captain Ian Garrow, a Scot, 'who had helped to create an escape route for officers and airmen from Vichy France across the mountains into Spain.'[55] Henri Fiocca supported the enterprise financially. He grew to be concerned for his wife's safety when she became known to the Nazis and suggested she should make her way to England where he hoped he might join her. At one stage she was arrested and beaten up for blowing up a cinema but she was helped to wriggle out of that and was set free. Getting to England was fraught with difficulties and she was thwarted several times before eventually leaping from a train window and, dodging German bullets, escaping through a vineyard. She finally arrived in June 1943 and joined SOE to become a fully trained agent. She was described in the official SOE history of France as having 'irrepressible infectious high spirits [which] were a joy to everyone who worked with her.'

Nancy Wake was parachuted back into France in April 1944 and built up various Maquis – rural bands of guerrilla French Resistance fighters – that eventually numbered 7,500 men and women. She was in control of communications with London and allocated the arms and equipment that were parachuted into France. When her lines of communication were cut by a powerful German counter-attack after the Auvergne Maquis had launched an assault on factories in the area, Nancy Wake made a 320-mile round trip from Auvergne to Châteauroux through German-held territory on a bicycle in just seventy-two hours. She was so saddle-sore after her epic journey that she could neither stand nor sit. 'When I got off that damned bike I felt as if I had a fire between my legs ... When I'm asked what I'm most proud of doing during the war, I say: "The bike ride."' She did a great deal more though, bringing her training to the fore in a murderous attack on the Gestapo headquarters in Montluçon which left thirty-eight Germans dead. She wrote later that it was 'the most exciting sortie I ever made. I entered the building by the back door, raced up the stairs, opened the first door along the passage way, threw in my grenades and ran like hell.'[56] She said later she was never frightened and that it had been a great adventure. 'When we were fighting we were fighting. When we weren't we were having a jolly good time. I never was scared.'[57]

Although Nancy Wake survived the war her husband did not. He was captured and tortured by the Germans and finally executed. When Maurice Buckmaster – head of Section F (France) of Special Operations Executive – was asked to justify using women as special agents he was indignant on their behalf:

> Those of us who know of the work done by women like Violette Szabo, Noor Inayat Khan, Denise Bloch, among those who died, and by Lise de Baissac, the sisters Jacqueline and Eileen Nearne and Nancy Wake among those who survived, can only feel anger and contempt for those who try to denigrate Baker Street by questioning the ability of women to fight alongside men ... These women did an invaluable job and one for which, whatever people may say, they were admirably suited. Coolness and judgement were vital qualities; none lacked them. Courage was their common badge.

Roosevelt suggested in 1945 that the efforts of SOE and the American OSS had shortened the war by six months, and there are certainly spectacular examples of resistance fighters and Commando parties harrying the enemy and causing serious disruption. Perhaps the most famous of these was the raid by SOE-trained Norwegians on the German's heavy-water plant at Vemork in south-central Norway. The mission, called Operation Gunnerside, was led by Lieutenant Joachim Rønneberg and took place in February 1943.

The agents met up with a team of Norwegian scouts who showed them how to get into the plant without crossing the booby-trapped main route via a 660-foot ravine that the Germans had judged impassable. Not for SOE, however. Once into the building, Rønneberg and his fellow explosives expert, Birger Strømsheim, placed their charges and Rønneberg lit the fuse. The explosion succeeded in destroying more than 1,000 pounds of heavy water and the equipment needed to make it, thus curtailing the Germans' nuclear programme. It was finally put completely out of action by further raids, both bombing and agent sabotage, in November of that year as the ferry *Hydro*, carrying a shipment of heavy water was sunk by SOE. A highly fictionalised version of the raid, *The Heroes of Telemark*, was released by Columbia Pictures in 1965, starring Kirk Douglas and Richard Harris.

Operation Gunnerside was SOE's most high-profile and successful mission, but others were equally important as a morale boost to resistance groups operating underground in France, the Netherlands, Poland, Czechoslovakia and further afield. Although the operations with the French Resistance are among the best known, probably because of the sheer number and scale of them, there were teams active in more than a dozen countries in Europe, as well as Egypt, Abyssinia, the Balkans and, later in the war, the Far East. There was even SOE presence in Germany and Austria, but, as the SOE historian M. R. D. Foot put it: 'There was no chance of successful guerilla action in a country in which so large a slice of the public took the opposite side.'[58]

In October 1944, the order came to close down Arisaig and the other SOE training establishments. The instructors dispersed and the houses were handed back to their owners. Some men prepared to rejoin their regiments, while others were anxious to get back to their wives and families. Maxwell was happy to explore the seas on his boat. 'Gavin put his unique collection of foreign small arms into two metal trunks, loaded them on his lobster-boat and took them out to sea, where he dropped them overboard. It was the end of his war.'[59] It was during these trips to sit among the puffins or watch seals or catch lobsters that he first saw a basking shark, which was to take his life in a new direction. He got himself declared medically unfit and moved into the dining room of Morar Lodge on the edge of the loch where so much of the training had taken place. His biographer, Douglas Botting, wrote of him: 'In SOE he had spent his time among congenial people who liked and respected him, living a secure, regular and purposeful life, working at the things he could do best in the area he loved most in the world. Now he was returning to the doubts and uncertainties of private life.'[60]

In all about 3,000 SOE agents were trained in northern Scotland. Of the 470 that were parachuted, inserted by water or dropped by light aircraft into occupied France, almost a quarter lost their lives. Of the 118 who failed to return, one disappeared and the remainder were killed. The same sort of statistic, though smaller in number, applied to other countries throughout Europe, the Middle East and, later, the Far East.

As SOE left, so the houses were returned over the next months and years to their rightful owners. Some bore the scars of war, others survived more or less unscathed. Mrs Cameron-Head never returned to live at Inverailort. She stayed with her sister in Inverness and died in 1941, having been deeply saddened to see her home and land so abused. Between 1940 and 1945 Inverailort had been an SOE training centre, a specialist commando training school and was finally used by the navy. Her son, Francis Cameron-Head, was paid £200 in 1944 by the War Office 'in compensation for damage to surfaces, dykes, fences and buildings caused by military training and War Department contractors' operations between 1940 and 1942.'[61] It took a further four years before compensation of £6,300 was received under the Compensation (Defence) Act of 1939 in the family's claim against the Admiralty.

The present owners of Arisaig House still find unexploded ordnance and empty cartridges in the rockery and behind the north wing of the house as well as in the fields. A few years ago, bomb disposal engineers had to be called in when five unexploded bombs were found in an area being dug for a duck pond. It is a reminder of the serious nature of the training being undertaken at and around Arisaig.

Aston Abbots Abbey, forty-nine miles from London, was the war-time home of the exiled president of Czechoslovakia, Edvard Beneš.

CHAPTER 9

Three Lime Trees

A conquering army on the border
will not be stopped by eloquence.

Otto von Bismarck

The lime tree is the national emblem of the Czech Republic and Slovakia. In old Slavic mythology, the 'Linden' or 'Lipa' is considered a sacred tree. A lime tree is planted to mark an event or as an honour to a town or village. So how extraordinary to find not one, not two but three commemorative lime trees planted in the Buckinghamshire village of Aston Abbotts in the Vale of Aylesbury. The story of why they are there is the subject of this chapter and the three houses at the heart of the story are Aston Abbotts Abbey, the wartime home of the Czechoslovak president-in-exile, Edvard Beneš; Wingrave Manor, four miles down the road from the abbey, which housed his chancellery; and Addington House, a safe-house for the heads of the military intelligence unit-in-exile.

We hear the oft-repeated cliché that after the fall of France Britain stood alone on the edge of Europe, implying isolation and lack of support. Britain was alone in the sense that the majority of mainland Europe, including the countries of all our erstwhile allies, was occupied by the Germans. In the literal sense, however, we were not alone. Czechoslovak and Polish armed forces, battle-hardened and experienced in a way that the British Expeditionary Force was not, were of great support during the summer of 1940. There were also Dutch, French, Australian, Canadian, and later Greek, American and others working alongside the British and Commonwealth armed forces and, later in the war, men considered enemy aliens in 1940, such as German nationals living in Britain, were accepted.

In 1940, the majority of foreign fighters were Polish and Czecho-slovak, who numbered in the tens of thousands. Their pilots flew in the Battle of Britain, helping to thwart the Luftwaffe's attempt to crush the Royal Air Force and render it useless prior to Hitler's planned invasion. They were there to help the citizens of Coventry when the city was bombed in the Blitz and a number trained to become SOE agents and were parachuted back into their home countries to help the resistance.

Czechoslovakia's place in the Second World War is inextricably linked with the Munich Agreement of September 1938 and the invasion of Bohemia and Moravia by the Nazis in March 1939. It is all too often passed over as a footnote in history, which does it a great injustice. In addition to the contribution of its soldiers and airmen, Czechoslovakia's intelligence service had two high-quality agents within Germany and produced some inordinately valuable information about the enlargement of the Luftwaffe in the 1930s and Germany's plans for the invasion of both their own country and Poland in 1939. Czech agents carried out the only successful assassination of a high-ranking Nazi officer, which led to a dramatic political U-turn by the British and French governments who had betrayed Czechoslovakia by agreeing to the terms of Munich but who now condemned the German reprisals after the assassination. Why and how this all happened is less well-known today than it was at the time but it constitutes a very important chapter in the history of the war.

The Republic of Czechoslovakia was created after the collapse of the Habsburg Empire at the end of the First World War and was officially proclaimed independent on Wenceslas Square in Prague on 28 October 1918. The new republic was an alliance of the Czechs from Bohemia and Moravia, who had been ruled by the Habsburgs and the inhabitants of Slovakia which was until then part of Hungary. It was considered by some interested parties as 'the major blunder of many blunders made at Versailles'.[1] However, by others it was deemed a success. Its first president, Tomáš Masaryk, appointed Dr Edvard Beneš as his foreign minister as he had been responsible for the lion's share of negotiations for the formation of the republic in Paris during the war. On Masaryk's death in 1935 Beneš became president. By 1938 he presided over a country that had developed heavy industry with an enviable record of workers' rights: 'an eight-hour day; sickness and employment insurance, government aid for housing, pensions for old soldiers and their dependents, a good system of wage arbitration courts, and protection of the tenant.'[2] In Bohemia, where the majority of the Czech population lived, illiteracy was only just over 2 per cent. As to the German minority in his country: Beneš could point to the fact that more money was spent per head on the education of German children and the same applied to German students in Prague. The Sudeten Germans, however, did not see things in the same positive light. During the dismantling of Austria-Hungary after the First World War they found themselves no longer part of Austria but part of the new country of Czechoslovakia.

Czechoslovakia quickly became a thorn in the side of the Nazi party. Lieutenant-Colonel František Moravec, the head of the intelligence service, saw the danger right from the beginning of Hitler's reign. He wrote in his autobiography:

In 1934 it was not necessary to go to history to see the German danger. By jutting deeply into its territory, Czechoslovakia with its military strength and mature industry had been since 1918 the keystone of the post-war French alliance in the east. The moment Germany decided to implement the policy of expansion announced in *Mein Kampf* it would come up against the Czechoslovak state. It would be a military necessity to destroy it before any German aggression could take place.[3]

President Beneš was singled out by Hitler as the epitome of evil. 'Hitler hated Beneš and identified him, correctly as it happens, with the spirit of Czech nationalism that he was determined to crush.'[4] In September 1938 he challenged Beneš to hand over the Sudetenland so that the ethnic Germans could be set free, accusing him of inventing 'the lie that Germany had mobilised her troops and was on the point of marching into Czechoslovakia.' Far from being oppressed, as Hitler maintained, Beneš believed the Sudeten Germans to be well cared for, despite, as he put it, 'their innate sense of social superiority'. He wrote later that Hitler needed to take control of Czechoslovakia for strategic reasons and the Sudetenland question was just a screen for his ultimate plans, which were to gain control of the Czech armaments industry. The French aviator, writer and politician Henri de Kérillis agreed, writing in a journal called the *Époque* in 1938: 'Bohemia and Slovakia are a bastion, a great junction that commands all the roads of Europe. With Czechoslovakia under her rule, Germany will be able to encircle Poland and Hungary, and gain an outlet to the reserves of oil and wheat in Rumania and Russia. If Hitler takes Prague, he will, in fact, have become master of Europe.'[5]

Hitler was implacable and every time Beneš spoke out about his country the Führer became more angry. Two weeks after he challenged Beneš publicly to hand over the Sudetenland he made a speech in Munich:

> I can say only one thing: now two men stand arrayed one against
> the other: there is Herr Beneš, and here stand I. We are two men
> of a different make-up. In the great struggle of the peoples while
> Herr Beneš was sneaking about through the world, I as a decent
> German soldier did my duty. And now today I stand over against
> this man as the soldier of my people! ... With regard to the prob-
> lem of the Sudeten Germans my patience is now at an end![6]

Three times Hitler ordered Beneš to meet with him and three times the Czechoslovak president refused. By the third time Hitler, who

Beneš described as an 'animalesque', was beside himself. The president told his officials he would agree to go to Berchtesgaden on one condition: that he would be carrying a pistol in one pocket and a hand grenade in the other. His advisers were fearful but in 1944 he was asked what he would have done. He replied:

> I am considered in Central Europe almost a human symbol of that democracy which Hitler loathes. He and I were living in two different worlds. There could be no mental link between us. Very well, he would have begun to shout at me, and so offend me. He would have been boastful and disgusting. I would not have tolerated that. Therefore my conclusion was: if I went it would end in disaster because I should never accept his insults. I should have to answer him, and as such a creature is impervious to reason the only answer would be to take a hand-grenade in my pocket and when he started to shout simply to throw it at him.[7]

The meeting of course never took place and Hitler pushed the head of the Sudeten Germans, Konrad Henlein of the Sudetendeutsche Partei, to draw up an eight-point plan to put to the Czechoslovak government. Henlein had been set up and funded as a troublemaker by the Nazis to provide an excuse for invasion on the grounds of the mistreatment of the German nationals. The plan included making reparation for post-republic damage caused to German estates, full self-government for the German-speaking areas and, most sinister of all, 'Full liberty to profess German nationality and the German National Socialist political policy.'[8] Beneš was prepared to give several concessions to Henlein in the pursuit of peace.

On the last point of expressing Nazi political policy, however, Beneš refused to negotiate. His country represented the most liberal democracy in Central Europe and he was not prepared to surrender that freedom the people had won over the last twenty years. It was this that infuriated Hitler the most.

Some thought he had gone too far in his actions but, as his biographer Compton Mackenzie, who interviewed Beneš extensively in 1944, wrote:

> Beneš was in the same position as every other European statesman. He might feel positive that it was useless to appease Hitler, but to assume that and provoke war was to face a moral responsibility beyond the courage of any man. He believed it to be his duty to the world to make the utmost sacrifices for peace, and of this belief the British and the French governments took advantage.[9]

Neville Chamberlain promised in his negotiations with Hitler that he would seek agreement from the Czechoslovak government that it would give up all lands to the Third Reich with 50 per cent ethnic Germans or more. For this concession, Hitler was prepared to discuss peace in Europe. Chamberlain presented his idea to the House of Commons in front of the French foreign minister and wrote to Dr Beneš to request him to agree to the terms and to do so quickly so that he could discuss the issue with Hitler on his next visit to Berchtesgaden. Dr Beneš personally wrote a long, poignant and dignified note in reply turning down the 'offer' and explaining eloquently why changing her borders would in effect be 'a mutilation of Czechoslovakia' and lead to the balance of forces in Central Europe and Europe being destroyed. 'It would have the most far-reaching consequences for all other states and especially for France.'[10] This reply was never published in London or Paris. President Beneš was effectively abandoned by his erstwhile allies. That France had refused to stand by Czechoslovakia hurt Dr Beneš personally and when friends visited him in late September after the Munich Agreement permitted annexation by the Nazis of portions of his country, he was a broken man. He said to one of them in a barely audible voice: 'We have been disgracefully betrayed.'[11]

Winston Churchill recognised this and wrote on 21 September: 'The acceptance of Herr Hitler's conditions constitutes the prostration of Europe before the force of the Nazis, who will gain very important advantages thereby. It is not Czechoslovakia alone which is menaced, but also the freedom and the democracy of all nations. The belief that security can be obtained by throwing a small nation to the wolves is a fatal delusion.'[12]

Churchill was ignored, Hitler was appeased and Czechoslovakia was forced to surrender part of its territories. As the government was reconstructed at the beginning of October, President Beneš felt he had no option but to resign. He gave a broadcast on 5 October in which he said: 'In these difficult times I have tried to safeguard the interests of our State and I have tried to do what is right for Europe in order to preserve the peace ... As a convinced democrat, I think it better to go. We remain democrats and we shall try to continue to work with our friends, but my resignation is imperative in order to accommodate our State to the new circumstances.'[13] He wished his fellow countrymen the best of courage for their future and urged them to stand together. He made special mention of the armed forces with whom he 'would remain in spirit'. With that he left his official residence and moved out to the country.

On the same day Churchill stood up in the House of Commons and predicted a terrible future for Europe. He spoke of the five years of 'futile good intentions', of a search for the line of least resistance and for years of neglect of air defences. 'We have been reduced in those five years from a position of security so overwhelming and so unchallengeable that we never cared to think about it. We have been reduced from a position where the very word "war" was considered one which would only be used by persons qualifying for a lunatic asylum.'[14]

In the middle of October, Bohuš Beneš, the president's nephew, arrived in Prague and urged his uncle and aunt to flee to London as they would not be safe in Czechoslovakia. On his way to his uncle's house, Bohuš Beneš spoke to a taxi driver who told him how brutal the Nazis had been in the short time since the president had resigned. He said: 'The people are suffering from hurt like unto that of a watch dog which has been whipped unjustly for having guarded the security of Europe.'[15]

Czechoslovakia was left to become a victim of the Third Reich:

It was a bitter moment for Beneš as it was for all Czechs. He was under great pressure from the army to reject Chamberlain's mediation and to fight Germany alone but decided that this would simply mean the annihilation of his country. It was a controversial decision and one which many held against him ever afterwards, for in handing over the Sudetenland with its frontier defences Beneš left Prague at the mercy of Hitler.[16]

It took a week to complete the preparations for Dr Beneš' departure from Czechoslovakia. He flew out of Prague on 23 October 1938 and landed unannounced at Croydon airport later that day. His nephew, who lived in Putney, gave the Beneš family a home. The president retired to bed for two weeks and, once rested, began the next stage of his work in earnest. He maintained total silence in London, while his name was abused in his old country. He was to blame for every-thing and the Germans fanned the flames of fury. He said later that 'I had to be careful not to make myself *persona non grata* in Great Britain by indiscreet public utterances.' Early in 1939, the president accepted an invitation to go to the United States to give a series of lectures on democracy at the University of Chicago. He arrived in February to a warm welcome, which both surprised and delighted him and his wife.

By the late 1930s Czechoslovakia possessed one of the best intel-ligence organisations in Europe, run by the highly able head of the military intelligence service, Lieutenant-Colonel, later General, František Moravec. This was to have a powerful influence on sub-sequent events. Moravec had been part of the entourage who had entered Prague to celebrate the newly independent Czechoslovakia in 1918 and thirteen years later he was posted to the intelligence sec-tion of the First Army in Prague. He was an excellent networker and formed strong and trusting relationships. The British had had an SIS man in Prague from 1933 called Major Harold 'Gibby' Gibson, an officer with immense experience of intelligence gathering who specialised in running 'deep cover spies'. He worked under the cover of passport control officer, a post that was recognised throughout

Europe as synonymous with intelligence gathering. Gibson proved to
be an important friend to the Czechs and was affectionately known
later among the exiles as 'Moravec's Englishman'.

Moravec had two key agents working with him. The first, known
as A52, was a 'brush-haired Prussian type with a monocle'[17] called
Major Selm. He told his contact in the intelligence service in Prague
that he was heavily in debt and needed large sums of money to keep
his lifestyle going. For handsome payments he was prepared to offer
detailed information about the build-up of Goering's Luftwaffe,
including 'numbers of planes of the various fighter, bomber and
dive-bomber types, the nature and training of the pilots and their
support crews and their battle tactics.'[18] He also listed the locations
of airfields and the expansion plans. It was prime data much needed
by London and Paris as the estimates of German aircraft strength
available to the Allies were inaccurate. In total, Moravec paid him
over 2 million Czech crowns, the equivalent at the time of £150,000
(and around £6 million now). He warned Selm not to spend lavishly
as he would draw attention to himself. His advice was ignored and
Selm was tracked by German counter-espionage who arrested and
beheaded him in 1936.

A year later, Moravec met his most impressive agent of all, a
high-ranking Abwehr officer who called himself Karl. He was given
the name Agent A54 and the material he produced was of such high
quality and of such a reliable nature that it gave the Czechoslovak
government-in-exile top-class intelligence from inside the Reich.
From March 1937 until October 1941, A54 supplied information
about Germany's intentions, including the invasion of the Soviet
Union, and its order of battle. In December 1937 he gave the Czechs
the cipher keys used by the SS signal regiments in the field and told
them that the secret password on the night before the Munich agreement was *Heil 15 März*.

At the beginning of March 1939, A54 warned Moravec of the
German intention to invade Prague on 15 March. The two men met
in a secret location in the city with a few of Moravec's most trusted
men. He described the scene:

The master spy stood facing me, stiff and erect. The suppressed emotion in the room was almost palpable and found its expression in rigid formality. We were all standing – almost to attention – as we listened to A54's report, which made it perfectly clear that in exactly eleven days our country would cease to exist.[19]

He gave them details of the plans of attack and even the names of the officers who would be commanding the four divisions. Chillingly he also brought with him an original document, an order for the Gestapo to arrest all Czechoslovak intelligence officers and subject them to interrogation 'with great severity' in order to learn the identity of their source agents on German soil. A54 asked Moravec what he would do next and when Moravec hinted that they might go abroad, he assured him he would find the Czech intelligence officer wherever he went and would keep supplying information.

The next day Moravec warned the Czech Parliament of the coming invasion by the Germans. At a secret meeting of the cabinet the foreign minister told them in his opinion the fears expressed in the report were wholly unfounded. The following week Moravec tried again to convince the government of the situation. He was told by the foreign minister: 'I know that you are a good intelligence officer and that you mean well. But if anything of this kind were happening, I, as Foreign Minister, would be the first to know about it. Calm down. And bring us better news in the future.'[20] It was the most humiliating experience of his life, Moravec said later.

Major Gibson, who had been working closely with Moravec for the best part of a decade and had already made it clear that British intelligence 'had a great interest in preserving co-operation' with the Czechs, organised for Moravec and ten others to be flown secretly out of Prague on 14 March with the most valuable intelligence files and archives. They stopped over in Amsterdam and then flew anonymously into Croydon airport. As Moravec flew out of Czechoslovakia and into German airspace Gibson watched him bury his head in his hands and weep. At six o'clock the following morning the Germans made their move. Moravec, safely in London, wrote to Beneš, 'informing him of our arrival and placing myself and my staff at his disposal as the natural leader of any nascent movement.'[21] He was invited to head up the Czechoslovak military intelligence in exile. The team worked out of the radio shop of a British agent called Reg Adams in Rosendale Road in Dulwich, as a cover for their work. The shop was bombed in September 1940 and they were only just able to rescue the precious secret files smuggled out of Prague by Gibson and Moravec. The radios were all lost.

After the German takeover of Bohemia and Moravia in March 1939, Beneš was recognised as the voice of free Czechoslovakia and its natural leader. In April he was formally invited by representatives of the Czech National Alliance, the Alliance of Czech Catholics and the Slovak National Alliance, to accept the leadership of what was to become the Czechoslovak National Council.

Dr and Mrs Beneš returned to London and moved into a villa in Gwendolen Avenue, Putney in July 1939. He was fired up by his welcome in the United States and three months later by French prime minister M. Daladier, who recognised the Czechoslovak National Council and agreed to the reconstitution of the Czechoslovak Army.

Beneš was embarked upon a project to promote the Czechoslovak cause in the free world. In due course he would be successful in gaining recognition from other countries: Lord Halifax confirmed the British government's recognition in December and on 23 July 1940 His Majesty's Government recognised the Provisional Czechoslovak Government. With Chamberlain out of office and Churchill in power, Britain had gone from betrayal to becoming an ally. It was an extraordinary turnaround. A year later, 'on 18 July 1941, Great Britain accorded full recognition of the President of the Czechoslovak Republic and of the Czechoslovak Government, and the king accredited to the President of the Czechoslovak Republic his Envoy Extraordinary and Minister Plenipotentiary.'[22] This did not mean they made life easy for the Czechs in London. Quite the opposite; President Beneš and his ministers found themselves frequently confounded by Whitehall mandarins who were uncooperative and treated the Czechs with little respect. However, the

British government's intelligence arm, MI6, was very keen to court the Czechs.

Meanwhile, A54 continued to supply the Czechs with reliable information and this gave President Beneš a strong hand with the British government. Moravec and Gibson carried on working closely together, making use of the Czechoslovak network within the Third Reich. This relationship would have positive repercussions for the future. Moravec was also in touch with Colonel Gubbins in Paris and Captain Peter Wilkinson in London in early 1940. 'Through these channels Czech intelligence kept the War Office "generally informed" about the operational plans of the underground, passed on requests for weapons and received tactful military advice.'[23]

A54 remained an enigma and his true identity unknown to the Czechs, MI6 or the Russians for a decade after the war. But the Germans knew who he was and caught up with him in October 1941. Such was the protest at his arrest, as a highly decorated Nazi Party veteran, that the Gestapo was forced to release him. He was rearrested the following March and imprisoned without trial. It is alleged he was murdered by his SS guards two weeks before the end of the war but not before he had succeeded in significantly damaging Germany. His name was Colonel Paul Thümmel, a Dresden-based high-ranking member of the Abwehr and no one has ever worked out the motives behind his treachery. He received payment for his intelligence but nothing like enough to compensate for the danger he put himself in and indeed the quality of the material he was handing over to the Czechs. Some believe he was disenchanted with the Nazis because they looked down on him for coming from a working-class family. Whatever the reason, his information was of vast importance and it helped to give the president-in-exile a much-needed lever in London.

Despite the quality of the material coming through from A54, the British attitude towards the Czechs, with the exception of the intelligence services, was unhelpful. President Beneš had an intermediary at the Foreign Office called Robert Bruce Lockhart, a former diplomat and journalist who had got to know the president well in Prague and was sympathetic to his cause. He had worked for SIS in

Russia before the war and wrote a book about it. From 1941 he ran the Political Warfare Executive (PWE) and was close to the foreign secretary Anthony Eden. Lockhart was equally frustrated by the attitude and over the next years did his best to ease the relationship between the Czechs and the British. After A54's arrest, however, that was not as easy as it was when the information was flowing freely. With this and other arrests SIS was virtually wiped out on the continent and it was partially as a result of this that a plan was hatched within the Czech intelligence service to deliver what might today be called a 'Spectacular'. Hugh Dalton met Beneš in 1941 and agreed that a small number of Czechs could be trained for special operations.

To go back to 1939, as Beneš was in London promoting his country's cause, the servicemen in his once great armed forces in Czechoslovakia had to decide whether they should remain in their occupied country or whether they could better serve their fellow countrymen by leaving and finding friendly territory. The Germans had raided the Czechoslovak armed forces, taking 48,000 machine guns, 1.5 million rifles, 2,500 guns of different calibres, 4.5 million rounds of ammunition, 600 tanks and 1,000 aeroplanes. They raided the Czecho-Slovak National Bank's gold reserves, seizing 18 million pounds of sterling – now worth some £6 billion.

Most Czechoslovak servicemen were influenced by memories of 150,000 Czech and Slovak volunteers who had fought alongside the French in the Great War. Now many chose to leave Prague to fight in other countries, some getting out while sympathetic customs officials looked the other way while others posed as Sudeten Germans and got passes to Austria. Most ended up in France where they joined the Foreign Legion.

The French high command seemed to know little and care less about the welfare of its Czech allies. The troops lost their smart Foreign Legion uniforms and were issued with kit which had probably done service with French recruits in 1914. Weapons were

few and antiquated. There were no boots and the soldiers had to
wear wooden clogs. There was increasing frustration and bitter-
ness with the situation amongst men who had travelled across
Europe at great personal risk to fight, only to find themselves
relegated to the margins of the allied war effort.[24]

Others had remained in France after 1918 and were integrated in
French society, marrying into French families. Some fighters had
joined the International Brigades fighting in the Spanish civil war.
They were known as *Spaniěláci* and held strong left-wing, some even
Communist, views. Those who could not return to Czechoslovakia
had been living since the end of the conflict in a large camp in the
Bas-Pyrénées. At the outbreak of war in September, they were
allowed by the French to join other Czechoslovak soldiers who gathered at Agde Camp on the Mediterranean coast.

Czechoslovak pilots saw action during the Battle for France, but
it was too late to save France by the time the ground troops were
brought into the fight near Paris in June 1940. As the situation unrav-
elled and France surrendered, Czech troops made their way back to
the Mediterranean coast. It was anything but orderly. Some lucky
pilots were able to fly direct to Britain, other men escaped south-
wards in small groups, a few ended up in North Africa. In the chaos
that followed the collapse there was no systematic withdrawal. It was
a case of each group of men for themselves. As they had no food for
the long walk back to the south they had to forage in deserted houses
and gardens in order to eat. Franz Kaplan was with a small party of
officers and men who made the journey on foot. He explained what
happened in an essay in 2000 to mark the sixtieth anniversary of the
arrival of Czechoslovaks in Britain.

Those who had families in France were released from their service
commitments: for them the war was over. The rest, mainly those
who escaped from their homes in Czechoslovakia and risked
being arrested by the Germans as traitors, congregated in Sete
and embarked available ships bound for England, via Gibraltar.[25]

The majority of the Czechoslovaks who were to end up in Britain in July 1940 were rescued in this way. Soldiers piled into any vessel that would take them, such as the *Northmoor*, a British registered coal ship, which had just unloaded its cargo. The rescued men arrived at Gibraltar covered in coal dust. They were transhipped to *The Viceroy of India* where they sailed in a little less discomfort and arrived in Plymouth at the beginning of July. The last contingent to get away from France sailed in an Egyptian vessel on 27 June, joining at Gibraltar on 2 July and sailing up the Mersey and into Liverpool a few days later. A few stragglers arrived on other vessels and family members and dependents who had managed to escape from France were also soon to arrive in Britain.

> Our group consisted of approximately 40 officers and men, some Czechoslovak airmen and civilians escaping from Paris whom we picked up on our way through France ... We arrived in Bordeaux the day the ceasefire was signed between France and Germany. Due to that, we had to travel to Le Verdon at the mouth of the Gironde estuary where we persuaded a willing captain to take us out of France. We eventually landed in Liverpool and our intro-duction to the British way of life began.[26]

Once Kaplan and his fellow Czechs docked in Liverpool they were taken to the landing stage from the ship in small craft where the beautiful sight of a long array of tables laden with sandwiches, cakes, tea and soft drinks greeted them. 'It was the first decent food we had had for weeks and we were encouraged to help ourselves to as much as we wanted. The last time we had so much attention and genuine willingness to help lavished on us was before we left our homes.'[27] After the feast they marched to Lime Street railway station. People in the streets cheered and pressed chocolate and cigarettes into their hands. It was an extraordinary experience for them and one they savoured as they made their way in comfort to Bunbury, a small vil-lage in rural Cheshire, almost equidistant from the railway junction at Crewe and the ancient Roman city of Chester. The journey by train was a joy, Kaplan wrote. Their previous journey across France had been either on foot or in the back of cattle trucks. This train had 'proper, soft covered seats for each of us – utter luxury! As we passed through the countryside, we saw bunkers and plane-landing obstacles in fields. From what we had experienced since we landed, everyone agreed on one thing – this country cannot lose the war.'[28]

When they arrived at Bunbury they decided to walk the five or so miles to Cholmondeley Castle and in Czech fashion they sang as they marched. In contrast to the reception they received in France in 1939, the Czechoslovak forces were warmly welcomed by the local villagers. To their surprise and delight children waved flags and cheered as they marched in their rag-tag combination of uniforms – British battledress with French-style helmets. Kaplan recalled that 'people were coming out of the houses as we passed, slightly bewildered, anxious to see what all the noise was about but smiling and clapping.'[29]

Cholmondeley Castle is the ancient seat of the Cholmondeley family who have lived there since the twelfth century. The current castle was built in the nineteenth century in true fortress style with castellated towers and gothic windows. It stands on a hill dominating immaculate gardens and an extensive estate. During the war, the castle was used by various authorities but most importantly as a Royal Navy Auxiliary hospital treating men suffering from nervous breakdowns. The Czechoslovak troops were housed not in the castle but in the grounds in a city of tents.

Long hot days and dry ground made the tented encampment a pleasure to inhabit, although Kaplan complained that when they first arrived they had to fumigate the tents as the previous occupants had left them flea-ridden. As they settled down to life at Cholmondeley, the spelling and the pronunciation of which caused endless mirth among them, they got organised into units. The soldiers became a Czechoslovak Independent Brigade, a force of some 3,000 men. They were given new uniforms, new equipment and above all, as Franz Kaplan wrote, 'a new resolution to carry on after the demoralising events in France.'[30] Their pilots, who had fought bravely in the battle for France, were quickly picked out by the RAF and integrated, along with the Polish pilots who equally had experience of fighting the Luftwaffe. These two groups would soon play a key role in the Battle of Britain.

The first problem the Czechoslovaks came across was how to cook the food they were supplied with. Their cooks had little experience of ingredients supplied by the British Army. 'On one occasion, there was a delivery of some flat, smelly fish. Our cooks had no idea what to do with them but, in the evening, they started to glow in the dark! Not long after, a procession formed and marched in the dark, down the tree-lined drive, singing and carry 'fish lanterns' aloft on sticks, which the English military personnel quickly advised how to transform into delicious kippers.'[31]

It took the soldiers a little time to get used to the friendliness of the locals. In France it would not have been possible for a girl to be seen with a soldier, especially a foreign one. Cheshire families had no such inhibitions. They welcomed the Czechs into their homes for tea, for dinner, for weekends, and gradually the men began to feel human once again. Franz Kaplan wrote: 'After all, most of us were civilians in uniform who had a job to do which necessitated being in the army. The local people, with their friendship and understanding were responsible for restoring our morale which had been so badly shaken by our experiences in the latter days of our stay in France.'[32]

The *Spaniěláci* who arrived at Cholmondeley, numbering just over 500, were not happy to be absorbed into the British Army. While the Soviet–German Non-Aggression Pact was in place they were presented with a dilemma. Most were committed Communists and objected to fighting with the Imperialists against their Communist brothers in Russia. The British solution was to intern them, first in Oswestry, then at York race course and finally at Sutton Park near Birmingham. At the beginning of October, as the bulk of the Czechoslovaks were being sent to Leamington Spa, 460 of the *Spaniěláci* were sent to Ilfracombe and formed two Czechoslovak Pioneer Companies. The remaining seventy soldiers were sent to Scotland and in early 1941 were released into civilian life. The

German invasion of the USSR changed the political reasoning of the pioneers and a large number of them rejoined the Czechoslovak Brigade. A small number of Czechoslovak fighters were hand-picked at Cholmondeley to be trained as secret agents by SOE to be parachuted into the Protectorate to operate with the Resistance behind the scenes in due course.

Richard Beith, author of *The Postal History of the Free Czechoslovak Forces in Great Britain 1940–1945*, described the situation that now faced them: 'As the Czechoslovak government-in-exile was now based in London, it was not long before the forces were on public display with the aim of emphasising the exiled government's determination to contribute to the Allied war effort and, eventually, to ensure that the pre-Munich borders and integrity of Czechoslovakia were restored.'[33]

Two events took place at Cholmondeley, the first being a troop review by President Beneš on 26 July 1940. Local people watched the event and there are photographs of village children cheering and waving flags, just as they had done the day the soldiers marched through their villages a few weeks earlier. The second took place on 28 September 1940 for the St Wenceslas Day celebrations. The foreign minister, Jan Masaryk, unveiled a memorial carved by František Bělský, at the time a nineteen-year-old gunner who went on to become a sculptor of international renown. It remains at Cholmondeley as a permanent memorial to the presence of the Czechoslovak forces in Cheshire that summer. Not long after these celebrations the Czechoslovaks left Cholmondeley and went to Leamington Spa where they had winter billets.

On 8 August 1940, at the height of the Battle of Britain, President Beneš had lunch with Churchill in Downing Street. They had known each other during the First World War but this event was in acknowledgement of the valuable contribution offered to the RAF by the Czechoslovak Air Force. Nearly ninety pilots would fly Hurricanes with 310 and 312 (Czechoslovak) Squadrons during the battle, while a number served with other fighter squadrons. They earned a reputation for bravery and aggression in aerial combat. They claimed almost sixty air kills over the course of the battle and of the eighty-six Czech and two Slovak pilots, nine were killed. The top Czech flying ace was Sergeant Josef František, serving with the Polish Air Force. He was considered ill-disciplined and potentially dangerous to his fellow pilots but he was undoubtedly extraordinarily brave. He claimed seventeen confirmed kills over the course of just one month, making him one of the highest scoring Allied pilots in the Battle of Britain. He died on 8 October 1940 when his aircraft crashed in Surrey during a landing approach.

In the early days of the war, the Republic of Czechoslovakia's government offices were at 114–115 Park Street in London, but they were destroyed during the Blitz so the President's headquarters were moved to 9 Grosvenor Place, a stone's throw from Hyde Park Corner and overlooking Buckingham Palace's walls. President Beneš was still living at Putney but in the autumn of 1940 a bomb landed in the garden and another destroyed the house opposite. A move was necessary. President Beneš was clear that he wished to pay his own way rather than relying on the British government to fund his residence. The story goes that his foreign minister, Jan Masaryk, organised the move to Buckinghamshire through his Rothschild contacts who were involved in the Whaddon Chase hunt. Masaryk was the son of the first president of Czechoslovakia, Tomáš Garrigue Masaryk and his American wife, Charlotte, and had entered the diplomatic service becoming ambassador to Britain in 1925. He spoke fluent English, was engaging and popular, embracing the British lifestyle with enthusiasm. Anthony de Rothschild was on friendly terms with Mary Eveline Stewart-Freeman, Countess of Essex, who was in charge of the hounds for the Whaddon Chase hunt and also with Captain Harold Morton, and was able to negotiate the rent of two properties close to one another in the Buckinghamshire villages of Aston Abbotts and Wingrave.

President Beneš, his wife, their nieces who lived with them, and their household staff, including his Alsatian, Toga, moved to Aston Abbotts Abbey near Aylesbury before Christmas. It was a village of just 400 inhabitants and the Abbey belonged to Captain Morton and his wife, Beatrice, who leased it to the Beneš family for twenty guineas a week (about £850 in 2016). The Mortons moved into the White House, the second largest house in the village, and the two families spent time together. Captain Morton was invested with the Command in the Order of the White Lion by the president in recognition of his duties in the Home Guard protecting the Czechs and his generosity towards Czechoslovakia during the war.

The abbey had belonged to St Alban's Abbey during the Middle Ages and stood on the edge of the village at the end of a long drive guarded by a thatched gate lodge, making it an ideal home for the president and his entourage. The accommodation comprised eight bedrooms, six reception rooms and extensive outbuildings. President Beneš set up an office in the library and his wife had a private sitting room on the ground floor. The drawing room and dining rooms were handsome, light rooms ideal for entertaining. The large, mature gardens and lake were both beautiful and practical from the point of view of security as the property could not be seen from the road. However, this did not stop the Ministry of Agriculture and Food requisitioning land around the abbey from the middle of the war. The croquet lawn was well used and Compton Mackenzie, who began to visit President Beneš regularly in 1944, noted with amusement that the croquet hoops had all been widened at the base. 'I was told with a smile that the "dear Benešes" could not bear to see the efforts of their guests thwarted by the severely narrow and exclusive apertures of hoops *de rigeur* for match play, and I reflected that even the croquet hoops by the President's standards had to be democratic.'[34]

The president's office was a comfortable room full of maps and books with a large armchair that Beneš used to sit in to read or talk to guests. He could become very animated and enthusiastic, waving his hands to emphasise his point. He had a habit of removing his spectacles and swinging them by one of the shafts so they span round his hand. Mackenzie spent many hours in the office talking to him for the biography he planned to write, which was published in

1946, a year before his giddily intoxicating wartime classic, *Whisky Galore*. He said that Beneš reminded him of a well-preened chaffinch. 'He was then on the edge of his sixtieth birthday; but the effect of his personality was of a man ten years younger at least, and this impression of comparative youth was sharpened by the care with which he always dressed ... his ties and his shirts and his suit always appeared to have been chosen deliberately to get on with one another.'[35]

Beneš spoke fluent English but with a thick Czech accent overlaid with an American lilt. He was short – a few inches over five feet tall – and sensitive about his height. He disliked having anyone over six feet tall in his retinue. By the time he was living in England he was balding and his moustache, which he wore short, was grey. His high forehead and bright blue eyes under dark eyebrows gave the impression of a man with great energy and strength. He described himself as a natural optimist and a man who never lost hope, despite being caught up in difficult, not to say at times impossible, political situations. He said: 'In politics I always behave as though I were playing tennis. When my opponent is "forty" and I am "love" and the next ball may be the last I am still convinced that I can win the game!'[36] In contrast to Compton Mackenzie's easy relationship with Beneš, Robert Bruce Lockhart found that he was 'a difficult man to know well' for his mind was 'machine-like in its compact tidiness and his reserve ... almost impenetrable.' His conversation was 'factual and entirely unemotional. Each point was marshalled in its proper place and, when dealt with, was marked off on his fingers.'

The president had a routine that seldom changed. Three days a week or so he would leave Aston Abbotts in a Daimler, driven by his chauffeur, accompanied by a body guard and, more often than not, Mrs Beneš. She was the honorary president of the Czechoslovak Red Cross and often had meetings in the capital. They would arrive at Grosvenor Place at 10am and leave London at 6:30pm arriving home in time for dinner.

The president's chancellery officials and his private office staff, which included his secretary, Edvard Táborský and his chief of staff Dr Jaromír Smutný, moved to the Old Manor House in the neighbouring village of Wingrave. Other inhabitants were Mr Leopold Matouš, caretaker and major-domo of the house, and General Oldřich Španiel, the president's military adviser. The manor belonged to the Countess of Essex, who received twenty pounds a week for the house. The manor, a Victorian half-timbered pastiche of a house near Wing called Ascott House. It was sufficiently grand to be used by the Czechs to house visiting dignitaries. The house commands a magnificent view over the Vale of Aylesbury and has large gardens, which during the war were used to provide a kitchen garden and pens for farm animals for the household. The staff kept chickens and rabbits for the pot, and three pigs named after the French collaborators: Pétain, Darlan and Daladier. The Wingrave stable block housed the government's two Austins and Jan Masaryk's bicycle. Although most drove the four miles to Aston Abbotts and back, the foreign minister preferred to cycle.

The everyday detail of the life of President Beneš' household is presented in a photographic book compiled by Neil Rees giving an exquisite insight into his establishment at Aston Abbotts. The British government permitted Beneš a permanent guard of fourteen Czech soldiers for his personal security. Their numbers were increased by thirty men from various regiments on a three-week cycle, who came from Leamington Spa. They lived in Nissen huts which they built with the help of Italian prisoners of war. The soldiers guarding the president were paid 2/6d a day (about £15.50 now) and a 5d (£2.50) clothing allowance. They had a daily newspaper called *Naše noviny* (*Our News*), printed in Leamington Spa and distributed to all Czech bases around the country. The soldiers fortified the village with forward and defensive active positions with light machine guns, anti-aircraft positions and Tommy guns. A military map of Aston Abbotts shows that the local residents were very well protected by the presence of the Beneš court and their guards.

The Czechs were popular in Aston Abbotts, Wingrave and the surrounding villages. Beneš regularly walked Toga from the abbey towards the village of Weedon. The route took him along a shoulder overlooking the Vale of Aylesbury and he told Compton Mackenzie that the view reminded him of the corner of Bohemia where he had lived as a boy. On one of his walks he met a lady from Weedon who asked him who he was. 'I am the president of Czechoslovakia,' he replied, much to her surprise. The Czech guards were regular customers in the Royal Oak Inn in Aston Abbotts, run by Bill and Audrey Williams. Some Czech soldiers married local girls and there were a number of weddings during the war. Another popular pub in the neighbourhood was the Bull and Butcher, which the soldiers visited when they were off guard duty. It was there that some of them learned to play darts.

President Beneš received many distinguished visitors during the Second World War. These included King Haakon VII of Norway who had been forced to flee his country, having taken a strong stand against the German demand to end resistance and appoint a fascist prime minister. He had initially been a guest at Buckingham Palace but moved to Bowdon House in Berkshire in September, while the Norwegian government-in-exile's official headquarters were at 10 Palace Green in Kensington. Another royal guest was Queen Wilhelmina of the Netherlands, an immensely impressive figure described by Churchill as 'the only real man among the governments-in-exile in London'. She had a country house at South Mimms but travelled extensively during the war, spending part of 1942 in the USA and 1943 in Canada. Politicians came too. Charles de Gaulle of Free France was based at nearby Ashridge Park in Hertfordshire, and General Władysław Sikorski of Poland who was based at Iver in Buckinghamshire enjoyed hospitality at the abbey.

Despite the delights of their domestic situation, the Czechoslovak president was consumed by the desperate situation 800 miles to the east. Reports coming out of the Protectorate via military intelligence were deeply worrying. The Reichsprotektor, Konstantin von Neurath, installed by Hitler in March 1939 was replaced in September 1941 by Acting Reichsprotektor Reinhard Heydrich who came to rule Bohemia and Moravia with particular brutality. Within three days of his arrival in Prague he had had ninety people executed. He told his aides he intended to 'Germanise the Czech vermin'. Nicknamed variously the Butcher of Prague, the Hangman or the Blond Beast, he systematically terrorised the population, arresting thousands of citizens on trumped-up charges. Those who were not executed were sent to Mauthausen-Gusen concentration camp. Only 4 per cent of those who were sent there survived the war. It was referred to by the Reich Main Security Office as the *Knochenmühle* (bone-mill) and was reserved for 'the extermination through labour of the intelligentsia'. Beneš knew that Heydrich was dealing with the Czechs mercilessly and that terrible reprisals followed any signs of insubordination. Nevertheless, he was aware that the Czechs were determined not to be crushed and that the resistance movement, small and fragmented though it was, would not be annihilated.

As a result of the understanding between Gibson and Moravec, Czechoslovak military intelligence became an accepted part of the government-in-exile's activity. It ran a wireless transmission station at Woldingham in Surrey, and in 1942 SOE set up a new station on a farm at Hockliffe, near Leighton Buzzard, supplied with equipment from the Special Communications Unit at Whaddon Hall, in Buckinghamshire. The station kept in contact with Czechoslovak embassies in neutral countries, the Czech resistance and paratroop mission radio operators. The safe house for the Czech secret service was twelve miles from Aston Abbotts in the secluded village of Addington. Moravec and his staff occupied Addington House, next to the village church, and the stable block and outbuildings belonging to the house.

After the capture of A54, the Czechoslovak intelligence service had the very real concern that they were no longer of first class importance to MI6 or the Russians. By the autumn of 1941 it was obvious to Beneš that, 'if the Czech national cause was to survive and flourish, words must be backed with actions by the summer of 1942, whatever the human cost.'[37] Occupied countries were judged by the success of their underground resistance's contribution towards the war effort. Czechoslovakia was at a disadvantage over France, for example, because of the greater distance from Britain. Flights took longer and it was difficult for the RAF to support Czech Resistance with air drops. Since the installation in September 1941 of Reichsprotektor Reinhard Heydrich, the Czech underground had been more or less broken and Czechoslovakia had fallen to the bottom of the list for MI6. So Beneš and Moravec hatched a plan to land trained paratroop agents into the German-occupied Protectorate of Bohemia-Moravia, where they would link up with what was left of the underground resistance and plan subversive activities comprising sabotage and assassination – including of the Reichsprotektor himself. 'The purpose of this action was two-fold,' Moravec explained after the war. 'First, a powerful manifestation of resistance which would wipe out the stigma of passivity and help Czechoslovakia internationally. Secondly, a renaissance of the resistance movement by providing a spark which would activate the mass of the people.'[38]

Moravec approached Gubbins asking whether he could help out with providing facilities for training and supplying weapons to the agents. Gubbins agreed but not without hesitation. He warned that an attempt on Heydrich's life, whether successful or not, would result in all likelihood in a round of widespread reprisals. Then he learned that Heydrich 'took a particular and personal interest in rooting out resistance in northwest Europe, which Gubbins saw as a direct threat to SOE.'[39] Heydrich was due to be posted to Paris imminently and that must also have been a factor that influenced Gubbins' thinking. So he changed his mind, though he 'decided to restrict the knowledge of the Czech approach, and above all the identity of the probable target, to a very small circle.'[40] The Germans had broken into an SOE cell in Belgium and were stepping up their efforts to infiltrate cells in other countries. It was in his and his organisation's interest to see the Czech plan succeed. He sought no ministerial support or approval as political assassination fell within SOE's charter but he did inform his superior, Lord Selborne.

Over the late summer of 1941, ten young men who had arrived at Cholmondeley the year before were handpicked to be trained and then flown into the Protectorate. They spent six weeks at Arisaig learning the basics of survival, sabotage, silent killing and weapons' training before returning south to the safe house where they would receive their orders, falsified documents, clothing and every possible detail that would convince a guard running a spot search that they were bona fide Czech citizens. Unfortunately, the one item of kit that would immediately give them away as coming from Britain was the Sten gun they were carrying. It was issued to agents as it was easy to put together and remarkably reliable. Of the ten who were trained, two were chosen to carry out this audacious and historic assassination attempt of acting Reichsprotektor Reinhard Heydrich. Their names were Jozef Gabčík, a Slovak and Jan Kubiš, who was a Czech. The mission was codenamed ANTHROPOID.

Gabčík was twenty-nine years old and an orphan since the age of ten. He had been in the army since the age of twenty and had been awarded the Croix de Guerre in 1940. Moravec described him as having 'a round face, blue eyes and brown hair ... his demeanour pleasant and unassuming. He was frank, cordial, enterprising and full of initiative. A natural born leader.'[41] Kubiš was the opposite of Gabčík but Moravec felt they were ideally suited as a pair. This was underlined by the report sent down to Addington House by Dan Fairbairn from Arisaig who described them as near perfect at jujitsu and artists with small weapons. Shortly before they left, Moravec interviewed them each separately asking them to be clear in their minds that this mission would probably lead to their deaths. He wrote later: 'Gabčík said he viewed the mission as an act of war and the risk of death as natural. Kubiš thanked me for choosing him for a task of such importance. Both said they would prefer death to being captured by the Gestapo.'[42]

Kubiš and Gabčík parachuted into the Protectorate on 28 December 1941 with five other soldiers on two separate missions. There were problems from the start. The pilot had been unable to find the drop site, near Plzeň (Pilsen), and had landed them to the

east of Prague. However, they managed to link up with their contacts and go on to Prague where they would live with underground
supporters and plan their attack. SOE had equipped them well. They
had 'two pistols, a .38 Colt – with four full spare magazines and
a hundred bullets – six armour-piercing bombs filled with plastic
explosives, two magazines of fuses, two model Mills grenades, one
Tree Spigot bomb launcher with one bomb, four electric fuses, one
Sten Mk.II machine gun with a hundred rounds, 32lbs of plastic
explosives, two yards of safety fuse, four smoke bombs, a reel of
steel string and three timing pencils.'[43] Over the next five months, the
team contemplated how they could possibly guarantee the success of
their mission. The first idea mooted in London was to kill Heydrich
on a train but it was dismissed as too difficult. The second plan was
to force his car to stop in the forest en route from his house in the
country to Prague but that did not work so they had to go with a
third plan which was to assassinate him in the city.

The Czechs on the ground realised that under Heydrich the human
cost of any action against the Nazis would be immense. Many of the
underground leaders in Prague had seen the response of previous
German reprisals and feared a hideous backlash if the assassination
were attempted. They even contacted London and tried to persuade
Beneš to call off the operation, saying, 'The nation would be the
subject of unheard-of reprisals. At the same time it would wipe out
the last remainders of any organisation.'[44] Acknowledging that Beneš
might have political reasons to do with national interest the message concluded: 'If for reasons of foreign policy the assassination is
nevertheless essential, the nation is prepared to offer even the highest sacrifices.'[45] Moravec was disappointed. He had told Gabčík and
Kubiš that they should not under any circumstances make their intentions known to the underground.

Kubiš and Gabčík's chance came on 27 May 1942 when Heydrich
was on his way to Berlin for a meeting with Hitler. He usually drove
in an open-top Mercedes in a defiant gesture to prove his confidence
in the occupation and in his government's effectiveness. On this
day the hood was down and his driver, Johannes Klein, was at the

wheel. The assassins had chosen a hairpin bend on the Dresden–
Prague road in the suburb of Libeň where drivers had to slow
down to negotiate a steep turn. Kubiš was armed with the specially
modified type 73 anti-tank grenades and Gabčík had the Sten gun.
Both men were carrying their pistols. As the Mercedes approached
it duly slowed down. Gabčík lifted his overcoat to reveal his Sten
gun and fired but the gun did not go off. In the split second that
followed, Heydrich ordered the driver to stop, apparently believing
that Gabčík was a lone gunman. As they reached for their weapons
Kubiš hurled his grenade at the car. It exploded against the right
rear wing of the Mercedes causing the tyre to burst and blowing
a hole in the side of the car. Heydrich was wounded. He and his
chauffeur opened fire and Kubiš, who had suffered injuries from
flying debris from the bomb, fled through the small gathering of
Czech witnesses. Heydrich pursued him but soon had to stop as he
was weak from shock. He collapsed. Kubiš had hidden a bicycle
nearby and was able to find it and pedal to safety. The chauffeur,
Sergeant Klein, was ordered by Heydrich to chase Gabčík and for
a few minutes there was a running pistol battle which ended in a
doorway when Gabčík wounded Klein in the leg, after which he was
able to make good his escape.

Heydrich was mortally wounded, although Gabčík and Kubiš
were unaware of this, thinking that he had merely been slightly
injured and that their mission had been a failure. His spleen had been
damaged by the blast and he contracted blood poisoning from the
shrapnel, the seats' splinters and the horse-hair filling in the upholstery. Hitler was incensed by the attempted assassination of one of
his great leaders and ordered the SS and Gestapo to find Heydrich's
killers. He was also angry with Heydrich, who he described as
an 'irreplaceable' man who should never have put himself in such
danger by driving in an open, unarmoured vehicle. At first he wanted
10,000 Czechoslovaks rounded up randomly and executed but he
was persuaded that this would have a deleterious effect on the work
force that was so needed to help with motor manufacture and other
war-related industries. Heydrich, meantime, was lying in hospital in

great pain. Shortly after a visit from Himmler on 2 June he went into shock and fell into a coma from which he never regained consciousness. He died two days later from septicaemia.

Gabčík and Kubiš remained hidden in Prague for almost three weeks. Kubiš was hiding in a safe house provided by a family called Novak. He had abandoned his bicycle outside a shoe shop but unfortunately when Mrs Novak thought it was safe to send her daughter to collect the abandoned, blood-stained bicycle, the girl was spotted and reported to the Gestapo. Gabčík was in hiding at another safe house, owned by Mr and Mrs Fafek, who were resistance fighters. Opálka and Valčík, two of the other soldiers who had parachuted into the Protectorate in December were also safe. As the dust settled, the resistance group managed to piece together what had happened and brought the four men together with a view to helping them to escape Prague.

The Gestapo had offered a million Reichsmarks to anyone who could help lead them to the assassins. Not long after Heydrich's death the Gestapo captured Karel Čurda, another member of the resistance team trained in Britain, who was in hiding in his mother's barn in southern Bohemia. He betrayed his contacts and took the bounty: 'First, on June 13, 1942, he wrote a traitorous letter in which he identified Gabčík and Kubiš as the assassins. Čurda then betrayed to the Gestapo everyone he knew personally who had assisted the paratroopers, not only in Prague but in Pardubice, Lázně Bělohrad and Plzeň. Through his betrayal he caused the deaths of Czech patriots and their families.'[46]

The following morning the Germans stormed the flats of the resistance fighters, torturing and murdering some while others took cyanide pills before the Germans arrived. Kubiš and Gabčík took refuge with the other parachutists in the Church of Saints Cyril and Methodius but Ata Moravec, too young to have been issued with a cyanide pill, whose mother was an active member of the resistance, gave their location away under severe torture. He was then executed. On 18 June 1942 over 800 members of the SS and the Gestapo stormed the church and were held off for fourteen hours by the parachutists.

Opálka died in the choir of the church and Jan Kubiš suffered multiple gunshot and grenade wounds and died of blood loss. The Germans realised the others were hiding in the crypt. They brought in the traitor, Čurda, to try and persuade them to give themselves up but their defiant response was gunfire. The hunted men held out, picking off soldiers who were sent in to storm the crypt. The Germans tried to flush them out using gunfire, tear gas and eventually by flooding. As nothing worked they had no option but to blow up the stairs to make an entrance. The other Czechoslovaks, their ammunition exhausted, committed suicide, rather than surrendering to the Germans. Josef Gabčík ended his own life with a pistol shot.

In all, fourteen Germans had been killed in the fight and many others injured. There would be more deaths. Even while Heydrich was lying in hospital there had been hideous reprisals. In addition to the underground resistance fighters who had committed suicide rather than face the Gestapo, there had been 135 murders of people believed possibly to have been affiliated with the attack. But much worse was to come. The villages of Lidice and Ležáky, which the Germans wrongly linked to the assassins, were completely destroyed by the Nazis on 10 and 24 June respectively. All males over the age of sixteen were murdered, as were all the women in Ležáky. In Lidice, 173 men were shot in the garden of a farm. The women and children were taken to the local grammar school. Three days later the children were taken from their mothers and, with the exception of those selected for re-education in German families or babies under a year, were poisoned by exhaust gas in specially adapted vehicles in the Polish extermination camp at Chełm. Eighteen died in that way. The remaining women were sent to Ravensbrück concentration camp where most perished. A thousand Czech Jews were rounded up and sent to their deaths in SS extermination factories on 9 June. Two more transports of a total of 3,000 Jews followed. One man only survived – he jumped from the train. In all more than 13,000 people were arrested in the wake of Heydrich's assassination and 1,300 died.

The Germans' boast that Lidice was erased from the map was soon proved wrong. Several towns around the world renamed themselves 'Lidice' in memory of the Czechoslovak massacre. It was one of the most brutal reprisals meted out by the Nazis but Gabčík and Kubiš became national heroes.

President Beneš always denied that he had known about the detailed plans for the assassination of Heydrich but he cannot have been disappointed by the impact the reprisals had on the British and French governments. The success of Operation Anthropoid finally gave Britain and France the excuse to renounce the Munich Agreement. On 5 August 1942 Foreign Minister Anthony Eden sent a note to exiled Foreign Minister Jan Masaryk stating that the government regarded itself free from the arrangements settled in 1938 and that they acknowledged the Sudetenland should be restored following the surrender of the Third Reich. Two months earlier, Beneš had passed a resolution which committed the government to prosecute those guilty 'for all the German crimes committed on Czechoslovak territory or against Czechoslovak citizens.' He named Hitler and members of his government, all representatives of the German Government and administration and traitors within the population. The resolution promised to track down all criminals wherever they might be after the war and to 'punish the culprits with extraordinary and most severe sentences.'[47]

Operation Anthropoid remained the only successful assassination of a top-ranking Nazi officer during the Second World War. In 1944 President Beneš planted the first of the three lime trees in the coppice behind Aston Abbotts Abbey to mark the link between the little Buckinghamshire village that hosted the wartime Czech president-in-exile and one of the most audacious of all SOE missions.

Bignor Manor was a secret stopping-off point for agents of the French Resistance who were flown in and out of Tangmere aerodrome between 1942 and 1944.

CHAPTER 10

Birds of Passage

*I hate this time when we're just waiting for the
telephone and everyone pretends they're not and then
when it rings there's suddenly an icy feeling of tension
and everyone stops breathing.*

Barbara Bertram

Not all country houses requisitioned in the war were large. The
minimum size designated in 1939 was a property with four rooms
downstairs. In the event, many smaller properties were taken over
for a variety of purposes and used at times for any number of functions from anti-aircraft bases – such as a private house in Elsworthy
Road, St John's Wood, which had a secret dug-out passage for the
ARP onto Primrose Hill, with its spectacular view over London, to
offices for the Ministry of Food in Aylesbury High Street. But it was
a modest manor house in Sussex with an unusual wartime story that
caught my eye. Bignor Manor had four bedrooms, a sitting room,
dining room and kitchen. Over the course of three years during the
war the house often had to accommodate up to fifteen overnight visitors, and sometimes for more than one night, and on top of that they
had to do it secretly. Once, the house was crammed to bursting with
twenty-one overnight guests. This was a clandestine safe-house for

French Resistance couriers on their way from London to France and back via Tangmere airfield near Chichester.

The French were in a different position from the other countries represented in London. The Czechs, Poles and Norwegians, to name but three who were involved in SOE, had governments-in-exile. France did not. It had an organisation that grew from scratch in the summer of 1940 headed by General Charles de Gaulle, a man of extraordinary vision, drive and height. He stood at six feet seven and had a distinguished record from the First World War. During the battle for France he led an armoured division which launched a counter attack against the invaders and he was appointed Under-Secretary for War. However, when France fell he refused to accept his government's decision to sign the armistice with Germany and, in danger of arrest, he escaped to London on 17 June 1940. It had not been an easy decision and he knew many in the French army saw it as a betrayal. This strengthened his resolve to stand up for France and to prove that he had a belief in a free France. He met Churchill on the afternoon of his arrival and the next day made a broadcast on the BBC when he urged people not to be demoralised and to fight the occupation.

From that day onwards he worked tirelessly to expand his Free French forces, starting from a tiny base in St Stephen's House in Victoria. He was a difficult guest for the British government as he was frequently at odds with what they expected of him. Churchill supported him from the outset in his aims to rally the French but their relationship was constantly under pressure as de Gaulle never really trusted the British to treat him as an equal. He said once of their relationship: 'When I am right, I get angry. Churchill gets angry when he is wrong. We are angry at each other most of the time.'[1]

By 1942, when the story of Bignor Manor comes into play, the Free French had established themselves as the legitimate representative for France in London and had moved to 4 Carlton Gardens. They had greatly expanded in strength and were in the business of building intelligence to help establish resistance networks on the ground. Much as he would have liked to function without the help of the British, de Gaulle realised he could not. He required the assistance of SOE, the RAF and all the infrastructure in between to get his agents safely into and out of occupied France.

Bignor Manor's story involves a chief conducting officer for the Free French; his wife, a partially deaf mother of their two young boys, Tim and Nicky; a goat called Caroline; Duff-the-dog, a Dalmatian; Peter the cat; two rabbits; a dozen hens and two beehives. The visitors were known as the 'Hullabaloos', named by Tim and Nicky who could not understand the excited French language they would hear in the house. All had a role to play – apart from the cat.

Barbara and her husband Major Anthony (Tony) Bertram had lived at Bignor Manor since their wedding in 1929. It was his wartime work that shaped the life of his family between 1942 and 1944. Barbara wrote an account of this time immediately after the war and it was finally published in a slim volume in 1995. It is an account of three years of activity working for the French Resistance, in which she provided sustenance, great kindness, beds for the night and endless practical help to hundreds of French men and women who were strangers to her. The book, written in 1946, is a carefully constructed narrative that gives a vivid picture of the facts and a little sense of the drama.

Barbara's was a strange role. Although she was not herself in danger, the agents she welcomed as guests were some of the most high profile of the Free French and their lives were at permanent risk from discovery by the Gestapo. Barbara Bertram was aware of this and she felt a sense of responsibility towards their security. The need for absolute secrecy and therefore a great deal of lying to friends, family and neighbours on her part, put her under pressure. Barbara also wrote a 'stream-of-consciousness' memoir, presumably in preparation for the book itself, which gives a breathless account of the same story but punctuated with moments of raw emotion: terror, despair, dread of being found out and thus putting agents lives at risk, combined with the pressure of hard work, little sleep, working round the rations and then, occasionally, the odd moment of joy and respite. It is the freshness and honesty of this account that makes it so compelling.

On the outside Madame Barbara, as the French agents called her, appeared calm and under control but the memoir shows that inside her head there were swirling emotions, some understandable, others irrational, copious lists and anxious thoughts as she tried to cope: 'Why am I always smoking?' 'I must dig up leeks – Oh it's not good just thinking, I must write it down after breakfast.' Or 'What can I wear? I wish I didn't hate myself in trousers then I needn't wear stockings.' It offers a vivid picture of the little things that mattered to women in wartime that remind us that they were human, despite playing a key role in the war machine, whatever their exact job.

Tony Bertram, in the foreword to his wife's published memoir, made it clear that it was she who had been on the front line, that her life had been shaped by the vicissitudes of his work as a conducting officer within the French Resistance and it was she who had been brave. Barbara, for her part, put it down to the fact that she found lying easier than her husband. Once, an elderly lady, new to the village, was collecting for the Red Cross and called on the Bertrams. As she walked up the garden path a French agent opened the window and fired his pistol. Barbara was sent out to offer an explanation and started an apology when the lady said, 'Don't worry my dear, don't worry. I know that anything can happen in a war.' With that she collected her pennies and walked away, never mentioning the incident again. Barbara knew that people wondered what was going on at the manor. She wrote of her neighbours: 'Poor Armstrongs they would love to know all about what we are doing. It's awful the way I tell lies so easily and they believe me. I wonder if anyone guesses what we're doing.'[2] The only people who were consistently frustrated at being put off by her excuses when they wanted to visit were a cousin who sold savings stamps and her mother, who came to think that her daughter had become very rude since the war began.

Barbara Bertram had grown up in Bignor, a stone's throw from the manor house. She was born in Chichester in 1906 and was just nine months old when her father died and her mother was left with little money and seven children under the age of ten. A friend lent the family a cottage in Bignor Park for half a crown a year (approximately £50 now), so they at least had a roof over their heads. At seven, Barbara was sent to Lincolnshire to live with a family who wanted a girl to be a companion to their daughter and to share the lessons from the governess they appointed. Barbara and two of her sisters received their education in this way, each in different families, and she said it was a great success. The sisters spent school terms with their hosts and returned to Bignor for the holidays. Barbara eventually went to school for three years at the age of thirteen and then became the stay-at-home daughter to look after her mother. She had a bicycle and as her mother was very sociable she had a good life with plenty of company. In 1919 she contracted scarlet fever and a severe ear infection meant that she had to have a mastoid operation that left her partially deaf. In the early 1930s she met Tony, nine years her senior, at a tennis party. He was a freelance journalist, writer and lecturer with special interests in the arts. During the First World War he was badly injured in the Battle of Cambrai and his life was saved by a German prisoner who saw him lying on the ground. The prisoner happened to be a doctor and realised Tony would die without immediate medical help so he and two other Germans got permission to carry him to a field dressing station where he was successfully treated.

In 1940, Tony Bertram was forty-three and Barbara thirty-four; their two sons, Tim and Nicky, were born in 1934 and 1936 and they had in addition three evacuee boys from Portsmouth who had been with them since September 1939 and were quite a handful. Over the course of the Phoney War, Barbara had increased the size of the kitchen garden and acquired her farmyard of domestic animals, which helped supplement the boys' diet.

Tony was in the Officers Emergency Reserve and was called up to join the Durham Light Infantry as he had been in the York and Lancaster Regiment in the last war. This did not suit him at all. He wanted to be with a local regiment so he could be close to his family. However, what he dreaded most was the prospect of spending the war in a depot doing some tedious desk job when others were putting themselves at risk and in harm's way. A young officer in his regiment saw that Tony was itching to do something more active and wrote to his brother-in-law who was working for the French in London: 'We've got an old man here. He's very bored and speaks fluent French. Can you use him?'[3]

Tony was interviewed by MI6 for an unspecified task but one that would involve secrecy. He told the interviewer that he did not relish the idea of 'all that lying'. The officer replied: 'Do you like all that killing?' On balance Tony felt that lying was probably better than killing and besides, he loved France and admired the French in their struggle against the occupying forces. He agreed to become a 'conducting officer' and in this role to escort couriers from the intelligence section of the French Resistance while they were in Britain. Conducting officers played a special part in SOE throughout the war. They were responsible for one or more agents and their overarching responsibility was the welfare of the men and women who were in their charge. They spoke their language and knew about the logistics of travel in Britain and the occupied country, providing practical help as well as emotional support. Tony wrote: 'The agent is a soldier, but with a difference. His work is individual and the constant strain on his nerves is not eased by the support of mass participation ... Mind and body must always be on the alert. The price of carelessness is torture, and I have never met a man who would not prefer to go with others into the most desperate attack than face torture alone.'[4] The ideal conducting officer was a returned agent who understood these strains but they were few on the ground initially.

Some of the men and women who were entrusted to Tony were working as secret radio operators or gathering intelligence on the ground in France and bringing it back to the Free French in London. They were not involved in sabotage or special operations duties but their roles were equally dangerous. Other were going out to France from London either with specific deliveries or the delicate but singularly dangerous job of managing landing grounds for incoming operations. Their lives depended on trust and impenetrable secrecy.

Tony was asked if he knew of a small house in West Sussex, not too far from Tangmere aerodrome, that they could use as a hide-out for French agents. Barbara wrote: 'He suggested our house, knowing I had had quite enough of evacuees and would welcome the chance to do something for the French.'⁵ She knew nothing of the specifics of Tony's new job but she accepted that it was something secret as she was invited to London to be vetted by MI6. When asked in 1999 what instructions or information she was given, she laughed heartily and said: 'None. None at all. All they said was "go and get ready". They never told me anything.'⁶ The only thing the officer who interviewed her over 'a very nice lunch' told her was that she should give up all her other war work and be prepared. So she dropped her Women's Voluntary Service (WVS) activities which had involved finding blood donors, and she sent her evacuees away to a new billet. She wrote later: 'How different the beginning of the war was. I prefer the French to evacuees, they don't bite and they don't wet their beds and they're much more interesting.'⁷

For three weeks she sat and waited anxiously to see what would happen next. She was worried that people in the village would ask why she had got rid of her evacuees and was apparently doing nothing to help the war effort. The story the Bertrams told friends locally was that they had been asked to provide a convalescent home for injured French servicemen. For show, two Frenchmen who had broken their legs during parachute training were sent to Bignor at separate times for a few days. 'They hopped about in plaster and looked most convincing,'⁸ she wrote.

When Tony finally told her what their work was about she was both relieved and afraid: 'I discovered that we were working with the Intelligence Section of the French Resistance. Not SOE, the saboteurs, who went out to France to blow up bridges and later to fight in the Maquis, but with men and women who went backwards and forwards from the autumn of 1941 to the liberation of France in September 1944 getting information.'⁹

Such was the need for secrecy that in 1943 they had to have a 'scrambler' fitted to the telephone so the operator at Sutton post office would not be able to listen in to and understand the messages.

There was the fear that if someone were to find out that the Bertrams were hosting French agents on their way to and from France there could be Nazi infiltration into resistance cells. The reprisals were well-known and rightly feared, as the revenge killings following Heydrich's assassination proved only too clearly. The French Resistance, being the largest in Europe, was constantly under attack from the Gestapo. The Germans employed double agents to try to break the links between Britain and France. On the continent they succeeded in penetrating cells, most notably in the Netherlands, so the Bertrams were justified in thinking they had to keep their work under wraps at all times.

As far as security for the French at the manor was concerned, Tony had been right to reassure the War Office that the house was remote. Bignor village lies in the middle of the South Downs, six miles south of Petworth and fourteen miles north-east of Chichester. It had a wartime population of less than a hundred and comprised fewer than forty houses. It is, however, far from insignificant. The handsome thirteenth-century Church of the Holy Cross is mentioned in the Domesday Book and its font dates from the eleventh century. Just up the road is a Roman villa which was excavated in the early nineteenth century and has been open to the public since 1814. The villa is said to contain some of the finest, most intricate and complete floors in the country.

Bignor Manor is located on the edge of the village with the churchyard on one side, farm buildings on the other and open fields behind. The front garden was some sixty metres long, leading down to a wall topped with a beech hedge which protected the house from the road. Nothing that took place in the house or garden could be seen by casual passers-by and, as the house itself was approached down the farm drive, there would be little risk of accidental visitors. While the location was perfect, the size of the house was not. It had four bedrooms, three of which were large enough to fit two beds but the fourth was a single room. The drawing room and dining rooms were large but the kitchen was tiny and equipped for four rather than fourteen. The one bathroom and one toilet were inadequate for so many

Suzanne Warren (left) worked as an agent in France. She was captured and tortured by the Gestapo. In 1944 she escaped to Britain and trained with Gavin Maxwell (right), who taught SOE agents survival, weapons training and fieldcraft. © *Getty Images (Maxwell)*

Training in Scotland was tough with obstacle courses built to add to the already challenging environment of the Highlands.

Major-General Sir Colin McVean Gubbins KCMG, DSO, MC was the head of Special Operations Executive. A man of the highest calibre, he received twenty-one foreign decorations over his lifetime and was feted in every country of Nazi-occupied Europe.

Gubbins and Hugh Dalton, Minister of Economic Warfare, talking to a Czech officer during a visit to Czech troops near Leamington Spa. Gubbins fostered Czech and Polish intelligence organisations.

Woldingham, Surrey 7th July 1940, on the occasion of President Beneš's visit to the Czechoslovak military intelligence radio communications station. © *Courtesy of Jaroslav Tauer care of Neil Rees*

Jozef Gabcik (left) and Jan Kubis murdered acting Reichsprotektor, Reinhard Heydrich, in May 1942, an act that had hideous repercussions for the civilian population.

Barbara and Tony Bertram (c. 1930) ran their home, Bignor Manor, as a safe house for Free French agents. Pilots at nearby Tangmere Airfield flew men and women into Nazi-occupied France. Their operations were planned in a cottage outside the airfield. © *Bertram family and Tangmere Military Aviation Museum*

Lysanders were associated with the lowest of aerial occupations: target-towing, or at best, air-sea rescue. But during the war hundreds of French agents were flown safely in and out of France in these little aircraft which could land on a field at night lit with just three flares or torches. © *Tangmere Military Aviation Museum*

The SOE Flight That Got Stuck by Douglas Littlejohn shows the night when Flight Lieutenant Robin Hooper's Westland-Lysander had to be pulled from mud by bullocks from a neighbouring farm. It was to no avail and Hooper had to burn the aircraft and await rescue. © *Douglas Littlejohn*

A Polish agent lays out the tools of his trade in a training exercise at Audley End, 1943 (left). Captain Alfons Maćkowiak, known always as Alan Mack, trained SOE agents at Audley End. He died on 31 January 2017 at the age of 100. © *The Polish Underground Movement*

Training at Audley End. Bicycles were expensive in pre-war Poland so many Poles learned to ride them for the first time during the war. © *The Polish Underground Movement*

A celebratory Polish dinner at Audley End. The screens of Essex Board, decorated with flags and portraits, hide the magnificent Jacobean hall and staircase. © *The Polish Underground Movement*

A Polish cartoon of a radio operator pursued by the Gestapo. Right: trainees on one of Alan Mack's obstacle courses. © *The Polish Underground Movement*

Trainee agents on the rope bridge across the waist deep muddy water of the River Cam at Audley End c. 1943. © *The Polish Underground Movement*

Melford Hall was burnt down by British officers during a night of revelling in 1942 and painstakingly rebuilt by Sir William and Lady Hyde Parker after the war.
© *National Trust*

Lady Hyde-Parker opened the hall to the public in 1955 and the National Trust took it over in 1960. © *National Trust*

guests and the water supply was not good: 'It was pumped up from a stream at the bottom of Bignor Hill. The stream was fed, in turn, by a spring. As we were the highest point in the village we were the first to suffer when it went wrong.'[10]

After the anxious wait it all began with a bang. Barbara wrote about her first experience of her mysterious role: 'Without warning, at about seven o'clock one evening an English officer, Captain John Golding, turned up with three Frenchmen and a girl driver.

"We want dinner punctually at seven-thirty," he said.

"What on earth do you think I'm going to give you at a moment's notice?" I gasped.

"I don't know. That's your job," he replied, cheerfully.'

With that he took the agents upstairs and left Barbara to concoct dinner for five in just thirty minutes. She rustled up a meal and placed it in front of them in the dining room. After dinner the phone rang and she was told the operation was off. What the operation was she had at that stage no idea. All she knew was that the conducting officer and the driver departed the next morning after breakfast and she was left with a bordello owner who had a chain of brothels in the south of France, a young man passionately interested in geology and an ex-prisoner of the Germans who had somehow escaped. She never asked and was never told how. In fact, she almost never knew the surnames of her guests and often she just knew the men and women by their code names.

From that moment on she was never without the wherewithal to prepare a full evening meal for any number of men and women at any time with almost no notice during the so-called 'moon period'. This was the two weeks when there was sufficient moonlight for aeroplanes to fly at night over the channel to drop their charges in France. The French couriers travelled in groups of three. Each group was escorted by a conducting officer, usually John or Tony, and a female driver to Bignor and on to the airfield. The drivers were from the Mechanised Transport Corps, a civilian women's organisation set up in 1939 to provide drivers for, amongst others, foreign dignitaries whose drivers were not used to driving on British roads. They looked after the maintenance of their cars, usually Chryslers, themselves. Some were married and one girl was already a war widow.

So if one contingent turned up that was five mouths to feed. Six Resistance couriers meant ten people staying, and sometimes there were nine French guests which severely tested Barbara's patience, accommodation and crockery. Fifteen people could just be squeezed into Bignor Manor. A snippet from her unpublished memoir gives an idea of the organisation required:

> Beds: Tony said it should be a double to begin with but you never can tell. That's six French, two drivers, Tony and probably John. Six and two's eight and two's ten and me eleven. That's three in our room, three in the guest room, the drivers in the drivers' room, us in the boys' room and John in the drawing room. No, I think I ought to be kind and put two French in each room and Tony and I can muck in with John in the drawing room, there won't be much night anyway.[11]

When arranging the accommodation she always gave the three large bedrooms to the French. The women drivers camped out in the little bedroom, which was fine unless there were three of them, in which case they were very cramped. She, Tony and John slept in the sitting room, John on the sofa, which became known as 'John's bed', while she and Tony were on camp beds – 'uncomfortable cold things' she wrote with feeling. Occasionally they would receive a guest known only to her as a 'high-up' and he, for it always was a he, would be offered the sofa and John was relegated to a third camp bed. When Tony's boss came to stay Barbara was never told his name. He was simply referred to as KC.

At first Barbara slept in her own bed on evenings when agents were due in but one night she fell down the stairs when the phone rang so ever after that she slept in the sitting room on the sofa during the moon periods: 'I hated being woken by the telephone so, if I could, I always set my alarm clock for a little before the time the

Lysander [aeroplane] was expected back ... the Conducting Officer used to tell me when that was. The telephone was such an important and anxious thing that I still panic when it rings and rush to the instrument as though the house were on fire.'[12]

> About half an hour after ringing up, they would arrive. I always went to the front door to greet them and risked the light showing. It was lovely to welcome old friends who had been through the house before and I prided myself on always remembering them. In the later years of the war men would arrive and greet me by name – Madame Barbara they always called me – and ask after the boys by name. I would think that they had been before and that I had forgotten them and I would try to pretend I hadn't. Then they would laugh and admit that they had never been before but had been told all about the set-up at Bignor, while waiting in France for the Lysander.[13]

As the accommodation at the manor was barely adequate to accommodate parties of incoming and outgoing agents, Barbara and Tony decided to send their sons to weekly boarding school. It pained her to see them go away at such a young age. In 1942 Tim was just eight and Nicky six, but there was nothing she could do about it if she needed their bedrooms. During the holidays or at weekends the boys would be farmed out to friends and family at short notice. After some time the War Office realised that the Bertrams needed more space and built a Nissen hut in the farmyard. Barbara was delighted and thought immediately that she and Tony could use part of it for a bedroom. However, the cold reality of a winter's night in the hut soon sent her back to the warmth and safety of the fuggy sitting room. The Nissen hut was useful as a spillover for dining and recreation and did good service as both.

The RAF squadron devoted to the safe delivery of courier and agents into France was 161 Squadron, based at Tangmere, and like everything else to do with the Free French couriers, it was secret. The pilots were not allowed to use the Tangmere mess and 'mingle with the fighter boys, lest over a noggin of beer we were pumped too much and the odd secret allowed to slip.'[14] They had a building outside the perimeter fence of the aerodrome called 'The Cottage'. There they were looked after by the area security officer provided by the RAF and under the eagle eye of Squadron Leader John Hunt, who in peacetime was a concert pianist and friend of the Bertrams. He spoke fluent German and another of his roles during the war was that of interrogator. The cottage was a small house used as a reception centre, to plan missions and as accommodation for the pilots who did not have rented rooms elsewhere. It had six bedrooms upstairs with any number of beds for RAF personnel. One of the pilots, James Atterby 'Mac' McCairns, who flew agents to France, wrote a memoir immediately after the war and shortly before his death in a flying accident in June 1948, and described the cottage as being 'rather like a cheap Turkish hotel'[15]. It had a kitchen and two living rooms, one of which was the operations room and the other a dining room with trestle tables. The cottage was run by two flight sergeants, Steve Blaber and Bill Booker, of the Royal Air Force Service Police, who were described as Jeeves-like in their amiable adaptability. They were so successful in keeping the nature of the work secret that when the scrambler was fitted on the telephone at the cottage the grumpy engineer from the post office muttered: 'Mr Churchill's got one of these; Mr Anthony Eden's got one of these. I don't know why you young buggers want one of these.'[16]

Mac described how they were looked down on by the RAF and civilians alike for flying Lysander aircraft: 'For years during the war when we said that to friends we were greeted with upturned noses. Our Lysander unit was so carefully camouflaged and guarded that not even in the RAF did one person in 10,000 know of its existence and true functions. Lysanders were associated with the lowest of aerial occupations: target-towing, or at best, air-sea rescue.'[17]

A Lysander could carry up to a maximum of three passengers, so occasionally, if there were larger groups of couriers and three Lysanders were too much of a risk, a larger aircraft like a Hudson would be used. The Lysander, or Lizzie as it was known, had been designed originally for daylight operations in co-operation with the army and had been built to be able to land on short airstrips on rough ground, which made it ideal for the purpose for which it was now adapted, namely as a 'passenger' aircraft for the French missions. It was painted matt black in the belief that this would make it invisible at night. While that was true from the ground it was not the case from above and the night fighters' view on a moonlit night was of a dark silhouette flying below them against low cloud, so Group Captain Hugh Verity had the upper surfaces camouflaged in dark green and pale grey. The Lysander had a long-distance range of 1,150 miles at its cruising speed of 164mph, though at top speed it could make 180mph. A photograph of a cockpit at Tangmere RAF Museum has over sixty labels to describe the instruments, levers, dials and other functions the pilot would have to be familiar with.

Tangmere was a major RAF base during the war and it is remarkable that the activities of Squadron 161 succeeded in remaining completely secret for more than three years. Group Captain Hugh Verity wrote a book about his time as commander of 161 entitled *We Landed by Moonlight*, in which he described the highs and lows, fears and joys of being involved in the delivery of agents into occupied France. This is his description of a tense moment of landing one of these planes in France by moonlight and with the help of nothing but three flares on the ground in the shape of an inverted 'L' and a brief Morse code exchange with a fourth flare to confirm the pre-arranged signal:

> On my third approach I was lined up ... Apart from the pin-pricks of the torches ahead everything was black. I switched on my landing lamps. In their bright beams the slanting rain was lit up like a bead curtain, almost obliterating my view of the flare-path torches ... A moment of doubt, a bump and we were rolling on the meadow ... I did a U-turn just past the end of the 450-metre flare path, and taxied along it wondering if our fat rubber tyres would sink into the rain-sodden meadow ... Another U-turn by lamp 'A', pre-take off checks, and I could relax until takeoff.[18]

The Lysanders were on the ground for the shortest possible time, sometimes as little as ninety seconds, such was the risk of discovery by the Germans of the precious passengers and material that they were dropping off and collecting. Verity and the other pilots were entirely dependent on the agents in France finding suitable fields for them to land in. This training was done in Britain.

Major Tony Bertram spent half his time at RAF Tempsford near Sandy in Bedfordshire and the rest of it between London, Bignor and Tangmere. Tony, who felt he should practice what his agents were to learn, learned to parachute but he broke his pelvis on his fourth jump and spent almost a month in hospital in Manchester. Two weeks in every month was devoted to training agents, one of whose jobs after being parachuted into France was to find and send descriptions of likely landing grounds. This was necessary because on early flights some of the fields had turned out to be unsuitable and there were a number of near-misses. From April 1942 onwards, the Air Ministry refused to lay on any landings unless the agent in charge of the field in France had been trained by 161 Squadron's own pilots. Mac described what Tony's agents were looking for: 'Roughly speaking, they had to find grassland, reasonably level and free from stones and slopes, which would give approximately 600 metres in all directions, or at least into that of the prevailing wind. Our light, parasol-winged monoplanes did not like being landed cross-wind. Once the field was located they had to send a coded description of it by radio, which was not at all an easy matter.'[19]

The design for the Lysander landing strip was always the flare path of an inverted 'L' shape pattern of three lights, which had been drawn on a tablecloth at Oddenino's restaurant in London's Regent Street by an agent, Philip Schneidau, code name Felix, and Flight Lieutenant Farley for the first pick-up by Lysander in 1940. It was so simple but successful that it was not improved during the war.

Those nights when agents arrived from France were exhausting but exhilarating for Barbara. After all, a safe arrival was something to be celebrated. She would prepare what became known and loved as 'reception pie'. Sometimes it was a pie, as the name indicated, but other times it was bacon and eggs or a stew. For the incoming guests it was hot, welcome and always delicious. Sometimes she felt self-conscious serving the French with anything but haute cuisine but they never seemed to mind, she said. Most of them had been living on minimal supplies and welcomed the wholesome, home-made food that Barbara provided.

After they had all gone to bed Barbara would wash up and then turn in to steal a few hours of sleep before getting up the following morning. The day after the night before began slowly. The French would arrive downstairs in ones and twos between nine and noon to find a delicious breakfast of bacon, eggs and fresh coffee. To men and women who had been drinking acorn or barley coffee, this was a feast. One agent came into the kitchen when Barbara was grinding coffee beans, picked one up carefully in his fingers, sniffed it and ate it with a look of dreamy satisfaction in his eyes.

After breakfast was over there were debriefing meetings, 'incoming men or women would go into huddles with French high-ups or others,' she wrote. Those who were not involved would sit on the doorstep and clean their dirty boots. As they had been picked up in French fields they were often extremely muddy. Barbara would collect that mud together and grow mustard and cress on it 'so that I could offer salad grown on French soil to the next moon's French.'[20]

Barbara took great trouble to make the French feel welcome at Bignor. Every new arrival was greeted with a cup of tea and then shown their bedroom. In each room there were beds with fresh sheets and a bunch of flowers on the window sill or table. Cigarettes, matches and a fresh bar of soap were also provided. It was not always easy to find enough cigarettes and she worried constantly about supplies but she seemed to have a knack of having everything in place on the night. She was only too aware that those arriving at Bignor were in a state of extreme stress and excitement. Some of them dreaded their missions while others could not wait to get on with it and strode impatiently around the house in anticipation of the flight. She felt it was her responsibility to provide some normality and comfort for them. It was never easy but it was made less difficult by the fact that they were all so very grateful to her. They brought presents: wine and books for Tony, scent, silk stockings and some-times flowers for Barbara. She remembered being deeply touched by a young man called André who, returning from France, laid a bunch of lily-of-the-valley on her plate on May Day morning: 'They had been picked in France the night before, following the charming French habit of giving Our Lady's tears on the first of her month.'[21] It always amazed her that people on the run and in tremendous per-sonal danger would take the time and trouble to bring her something as a thank-you present.

The War Office paid Barbara £5 a week for rent (around £200 now) and £2 a week in salary (roughly £80). In addition, they supplied camp beds, sheets and blankets, but refused to send any crockery. The Bertrams were frequently short and had to wash up between courses, a job often undertaken by her guests. Barbara explained how it worked: 'One washed, two dried and the rest stood at strategic points between the sink and the cupboard in the dining room where the plates were kept. The plates were thrown from one to the other. Nothing was ever broken but I was always terrified as we had no spare crockery, in fact not nearly enough.'[22]

Bignor Manor was an important link in the chain between London and Tangmere because agents could be held there for hours or days, sometimes even more than a week, until a weather window opened up and made it possible to fly. The airfield was some ten miles from Bignor and the route took the drivers through very few villages, making the movement of agents comfortably inconspicuous.

Barbara would receive a phone call from Tangmere airfield on the evening when her agent-guests were due to fly out. There were two messages: C'est On or C'est Off. That would tell her whether she would be keeping the current group of agents or whether they would be leaving and she could expect a consignment of incoming agents from France. She wrote of this moment when she came back from the phone with the message 'C'est on': 'I hate giving out rum just before they leave, it's so grim, like an execution. At least, I don't really hate it, I feel like an Anglo-Saxon matron, which is nice.' Even if the group at Bignor left it did not mean necessarily that they would actually fly. The weather might change, the situation on the ground become dangerous or the Air Ministry might have some intelligence that would lead to missions being cancelled at the eleventh hour and without warning. Changing sheets in preparation for incomers was left to the very last minute in order to reduce Barbara's workload. On the other hand, if the message was negative she knew they would all be disappointed and on edge:

> It can't be off, it can't be off, it can't be off ... it is, c'est off. I can see by Tony's face. How awful for them. I do hate these last-minute cancels. We shall have to try and be gay tonight. They're amazing how well they take it, it must be an awful strain. Thank goodness I haven't put the rum bottle out, we've only enough for about two ops. This means lunch, dinner and reception pie tomorrow anyway and if c'est off again lunch and dinner perhaps for days. I shall have to go to Chichester.[24]

Barbara wrote: 'In 1940 ... moonlight began to govern our way of life and brought the war, not merely into our lives but into our home.'[25] She knew that from the beginning of the new moon's cycle she was on standby and was ready to receive a phone call from London from a conducting officer to say: 'I'm coming with three.' Or 'I'm coming with nine'.

The outgoing agents with their driver and conducting officer would arrive at about teatime. Barbara was irritated that John Golding was often late whereas Tony was always punctual. She wrote later that she 'kept up an affectionate quarrel' with Golding throughout the war but was careful not to reveal his identity in her memoir. The visitors would be given a cup of tea and then the strict checking would take place. Every pocket had to be gone through, every item of their clothing searched for tell-tale signs of incriminating evidence that might give them away as having been in England – no bus or cinema tickets or a letter with a British stamp could be left in their pockets. The search had to be thorough, but even so an occasional slip was made. Barbara recounted the consequence of an oversight:

> One Frenchman was in the Metro in Paris one morning, standing in the usual squash of passengers, when he found that a copy of the previous day's *Daily Telegraph* was sticking out of his overcoat pocket. He waited until he was nearly at his station then he slipped it out of his own pocket and into the pocket of a German officer standing next to him and quickly got out. This was an oversight easily made as the searching took place in the drawing-room when the coats were hanging up in the hall. I am glad to say that Tony was not the conducting officer in charge that day. It was even thought dangerous for men to go out with hairs from our dog on their trousers, so a clothes brush always had to be handy for them to use at the last minute.[26]

Once the checks had taken place the agents were sent upstairs for their final briefing. There they would be given their fake papers – a fake ID card, a fake ration card and a large amount of French cash – 'Fake for all I knew' Barbara wrote. They were given a small revolver, if they wanted it, a cosh they could hide up their sleeves and a fountain pen-type object that squirted tear gas when the agent pressed a little button. Barbara explained: 'They were all rather sceptical about these. One day, some of them let one off in the bathroom and without telling me what they had done, asked me to fetch something from the bathroom cupboard. My state, when I rejoined them in a fury with my eyes streaming, was enough to convince them that it was very effective.'[27]

Barbara never got to see the handover of material or to hear the briefing instructions. However, she did have a hand in providing some of the other items they were given, such as toothbrushes and razor blades without 'Made in Britain' stamps. Early on her job was to find and buy these precious items. Once she found two dozen unmarked toothbrushes and bought the lot. She was worried lest the shopkeeper, who knew she only had two children, asked her what she needed them for. Fortunately he did not. Then there was the question of soap. Barbara kept all her bars of soap once the name had worn off but British soap was found to lather too well and that would be noticed in French public lavatories. She was not happy taking that risk so in future the War Office supplied all such vital items. Soap with grit arrived at Bignor Manor alongside blank razor blades and toothbrushes. After the war Barbara met a friend who had worked in a company that made and packaged razor blades. She said she had always wondered why, every so often, a consignment of blades without the Made in England stamp was wrapped in different packaging and sent to a different despatch department. Even imitation Gauloises cigarettes had to be supplied by the War Office. 'There was a difficulty about the imitation Gauloises: the gum used on the packet was too good so that it did not disintegrate as soon as opened, as the real ones did. This too was remedied.'[28]

While the agents were being briefed, the driver and Barbara had to go through their luggage to see if they had purchased anything in London that might incriminate them were they caught by the Gestapo. She explained how she dealt with this:

> If they had bought a new suit, the buckle on the back of the waist-coat had to be cut off and the straps sewn together ... Hats were confiscated, they are stamped on the leather band inside and you cannot remove that without making the hat too big. We had nine hats at the end of the war. Gloves had the button wrenched off. Shirts were easy. We rubbed the mark very hard with Milton and it either rubbed out the word, or it rubbed a hole in the shirt.[29]

Generally the agents were happy to let Barbara get on with her erasure but on one occasion she picked up a pair of pink silk pyjamas and was about to give them the Milton treatment when the owner snatched them back with a howl of protest. They were a precious purchase in pre-war Paris and he was not going to have them ruined by bleach.

In addition to vital supplies, the agents were given the exciting tools of their trade that everyone associates with a proper under-cover operation: magnifying glasses, maps printed on fine silk, cards printed in microscopic letters, tiny compasses, knives and pencils. All of these had to be stashed away in the Manor House. The accidental discovery of such a cache by a visitor during the dark moon periods would have been difficult to explain but once again they were fortunate in the old house's idiosyncrasies:

> Luckily there was a secret cupboard over the fireplace which was covered in a plywood board from the pre-war days when books on shelves above the fireplace had become damaged. So when they needed a locked cupboard they simply put a lock on one of the shelves behind the plywood. The dart board was mounted on the ply and the surround made a good background for bad shots.[30]

Besides the spy kits, the agents frequently requested small, everyday items and Barbara prided herself on her growing collection of odds and ends that she picked up whenever she spotted something at a market, in a shop or even on the floor of the village hall that might be of use in future. These could range from safety pins and hair pins to string, nails, scissors, bags and empty tins. They all had to be unmarked, of course, and she was surprised at some of the requests she had for what she regarded as unusual items but she never asked what the agent needed them for. That was their business, not hers. One couple borrowed their typewriter and a pair of metal knitting needles; the typewriter was returned, but the knitting needles disappeared with the agent and were never seen again. She had no idea what they might have been used for – it is possible they were just for knitting.

The agent's baggage consisted of personal cases and sacks of money and the courier messages he or she was carrying back to France. They also had *vivres* – chocolate (imitation French), butter, cigarettes and other little treats that were useful for 'paying' helpers on the ground. Sometimes a sack of *vivres* would be left at Bignor either by mistake or because it would make the luggage too heavy. 'When that happened I always put it in the larder hoping that the conducting officer would forget all about it. The chocolate and butter were especially welcome,'[31] Barbara wrote.

Every ounce of baggage counted and the weight limit was strictly enforced. The first things to be jettisoned when the bags were weighed at the cottage at the airfield were personal belongings such as presents or little luxuries. One agent who was an artist left a nearly new box of oil paints behind. These were entrusted to Barbara personally. The artist was caught and shot in France. The box was a painful reminder of this loss but when a local painter lost his materials in a disastrous fire Barbara gave him the Frenchman's oils believing that he would have approved of supporting a fellow artist in distress.

While the agents were being cared for by Barbara Bertram, the 'Lizzie Boys' at Tangmere were trying to come to terms with their risky job. Mac McCairns described a pep talk he was given by Squadron Leader Guy Lockhart before he became a Lysander pilot:

There is the mental stress to consider. Ops are on, ops are off, Air Ministry can never tell you until the very last minute, so much depends on the final wireless signal from the operator in France. Sometimes you are actually strapped in the plane before news of cancellation comes through. Worse still, it sometimes happens that the message is not decoded in time, and you spend hours stuffed in a turbulent, obstinate aircraft, peering out in the darkness, trying by the light of the moon, if you are lucky enough to fly on a cloudless night, to map-read your way hundreds of miles into France, searching for some miserable plot of land which from the air looks no bigger than a pocket handkerchief. No. It is not a pleasant job, and I would not recommend anyone to try it. Do not be deceived by the glamour.[32]

Glamorous or not, when Commander Hugh Verity arrived at Tangmere to join the Lysander flight in late 1942 he found 'there was an

atmosphere of cinematic stunt-riding about the whole thing'.[33] This
began to change as early lessons had been learned, the resistance networks in France had expanded and the need now was for a safe and
reliable service that could perform methodically and as predictably
as the weather, their main enemy, would permit.

Everything about the operation was secret, dangerous and completely at the mercy of the weather. Unloading of outgoing agents plus
sacks of courier material, and reloading incoming courier and agents
was executed at great speed. On one occasion early in the missions
a bag of courier material was left in France, which was a complete
waste of the risky flight. So thereafter the luggage was always loaded
first and the number of bags marked in chalk on the side of the plane.
The agents had to pile in and find a seat as best they could while
the pilot taxied across the field for take-off. Very occasionally just
a courier bag came back, without agents. One day in 1944 an unaccompanied sack arrived at Bignor Manor. It was heavy and full of
knobbly bits which turned out to contain all the pieces of a V1 rocket.
That was quickly sent up to London for inspection.

There was supposed to be a maximum of two passengers in a
Lysander but this was ignored and three would sit where the rear-
gunner had sat in the back, two on the single seat and one on the
floor with everything piled on top of him. Mac explained:

> The gun had been removed to make way for a small box-seat for
> two and to give additional luggage space. We could take an extra
> 600lbs of luggage: general supplies for the agents and in particular
> delicate radio apparatus which did not survive parachuting. Our
> bomb spats and front-firing Brownings had also been removed to
> lighten the machine's weight so that on all missions we were com-
> pletely unarmed except for a .38 revolver strapped to our waists.[34]

The pilots from No. 161 Squadron were told that they should under
no circumstances ask anything about the mission and ideally they
should not know the names of the agents or even what they looked
like. They referred to them as 'Joes'. However some had become

friends during training at Tempsford. Tony explained how this personal contact 'gave them such an insight into the importance, difficulties and dangers of the agents' work, that they fully realised the responsibility of their own.'[35] The pilots flew in civilian clothing but wore RAF escape boots: 'ordinary black fleece-lined flying boots, with a zipper front; but when the uppers were detached, one was left with a fine sturdy pair of black civilian shoes.'[36] They were told that they were not allowed to be taken alive by the Gestapo.

Mac described life at the picturesque cottage at Tangmere as isolated but smooth. 'We would breakfast about 10am, proceed to do air tests on our individual aircraft and then, if ops were on, the fun would really start ... The afternoon was spent on telephone calls, map-cutting, the study of photographs, flight plans and, most important, the almost hourly consideration of the meteorological information ... Towards evening the tension would increase'[37] If the forecast was fair and all the myriad individual pieces fell into place, the op was on and the moment for the Lysander pilot to complete the final stage of preparation was there. In a ritual that never changed, the pilot would climb up into the cockpit and would be strapped in by his ground crew. Then they would hand him his pistol, thermos and the precious maps which he had so carefully prepared. When he was confident everything was set he would give the 'All Clear' – 'Contact''' and start the engine. 'As the engine was ticking over in its warm-up, the car with the Joes would arrive and after a last hurried farewell they would be bundled in the back, the rear hood fastened and the pilot was given the OK to open the throttle.'[38] Mac wrote:

> I always felt that it was this moment that was the most impressive of all – in fact a perfect picture. The black Lysander, dimly lit by the moon overhead, the ghostly pilot caught by the weak orange rays of the cockpit lights, and the belching exhausts stubs of the motor as each magneto was in turn tested at full throttle. The old Lizzie used to stand there quivering like a horse before the race, waiting for its master to give the word of command. The thought

that in a few hours' time the aircraft would be touching down on some little strip of land in German-held France never failed to thrill me.[39]

It was inevitable that things would not always go as smoothly as Mac would hope. Occasionally missions had to be aborted if the visibility over France was too bad. Sometimes the reception committee was not at the appointed place or the wrong letter was flashed in Morse. The pilots could not risk landing under those circumstances as they might be flying into a German trap. Once or twice the line book at the cottage gives hints of other problems: cows on the field or deep mud. In February 1943 a Lysander was bogged down in a ploughed field. It was dug out by fifty local people with the help of two oxen but had to be torched as it could not take off. Two months later Mac flew his Lysander into a tree but succeeded in landing and returned safely to Tangmere with the damaged plane. Verity wrote in the cottage line book, where pilots put down their thoughts, 'It's not part of the Verity Service to collect firewood.'[40] It was Verity who also quipped: 'Birds and fools fly by day, but only bats and bloody fools by night.'[41]

Once they entered British airspace the pilots on the return flight would be asked by the conducting officers whether the mission had succeeded or not. There was a colour code: red meant they had had a successful round trip, blue meant it had not gone off as planned. When Mac was asked what colour he rated his mission on the night he hit the tree he answered 'pale green'. The Lysanders were not as delicate to handle as a Spitfire, Mac wrote. They reminded him more of a bomber: 'as I dropped the speed before landing, the automatic slats and interlinked flaps burst out with a mighty rush, most terrifying to the novice. Many passengers returning to England have told me that at the moment of landing they thought they were going to be plunged to death after the supposed snapping and breaking-up of a wing.'[42]

On landing at Tangmere the agents would be taken to the cottage where Blaber and Booker would greet them with a drink before sending them onwards to Barbara for reception pie and a good breakfast the following morning. The incoming French would leave Bignor for London the day after their arrival and Barbara would await the next consignment. In what she called the 'dark periods', those weeks between the moons, she would tidy the house and expand her stores so that she was as prepared as she could possibly be for the next moon period. There was time for some relaxation during those weeks. In the quiet periods Squadron Leader John Hunt, who of course knew about the Bertrams' war work, would come to a neighbouring house and perform private concerts for a group of friends. Barbara wrote 'These were lovely interludes in wartime life.'[43]

One of the concerns she had was for her kitchen garden and her animals. The cat was self-contained and could go out mousing whenever he wanted. Duff-the-dog needed walking and that fell to her when Tony was away at RAF Tempsford or in London. The great benefit of having guests staying for several days owing to fog or bad weather was that Tony took them on long walks or horse rides in the countryside and Duff was always included in these excursions. Some of the French came to love Duff and treated him almost as their own. One agent told her when he met her in Paris after the war that as he was being tortured by the Gestapo he tried to visualise where the spots were on Duff's coat to take his mind off what they were doing to him.

The chickens ate dried nettles and scraps from the kitchen, the bees produced honey for the table which was popular with everyone. It was Caroline the goat who was Barbara's biggest concern. She needed milking daily and feeding large quantities of grass. She had to be kept tied up as she could not resist roses or the fruit trees. Her favourite was the peach tree and she would make a beeline for it if she ever had the opportunity to slip her collar. Barbara had to take her to the billy and that involved a long walk down the country lanes, an exhausting exercise with an overexcited, greedy goat on a lead. But Caroline was a great favourite with the men. Barbara wrote:

She became a well-known character. Often the pilots would come over in their Lysanders if an op. was cancelled and swoop down much too low over Bignor, even once or twice flying under the telephone wires. This always alarmed Caroline – but not so much as it did me – so when she was expecting a kid, an order was put up in the Flight's headquarters at Tangmere forbidding any low-flying over Bignor until Caroline was safely delivered.[44]

Later in the war Caroline achieved lasting fame when an operation was named after her. The BBC used to broadcast *Les Messages Personnels* every night to France and among them were coded messages for the resistance workers. One time they introduced Operation Caroline. In order to inform those listening out for news, they would use the word 'blue' in conjunction with the name Caroline to let the Resistance know that a mission was on. So for several nights messages were read out such as:

'Caroline is well.'

'Caroline went for a walk.'

And finally: 'Caroline has a blue dress.' [45]

After the war, when Barbara and Tony were in Paris, some of the former Resistance members would ask her how Caroline was. These were men and women who had never been through Bignor Manor and Tangmere but knew of Operation Caroline. It always amused Barbara that her goat had gained such notoriety in France.

Barbara would get occasional consignments of whisky, gin, tins of butter and 'horrible Grade-3 salmon' from the War Office. Her large vegetable garden and fruit orchards were a great bonus but it was not enough to feed hungry mouths, especially when there were large numbers of guests. The War Office turned her into a catering establishment, like a hotel, so that meant innumerable monthly forms to be returned:

They explained to me that as all my 'visitors' were in the Forces they were entitled to a higher ration than the civilian one, so they told me that if I could not get enough food I could cheat on my

Food Office returns but I was not to let the Food Office know I was cheating. One got rations one month for what one had eaten the month before, so it worked out in the end – but not at the time. My returns were like a fever chart. When the boys were at school and in the dark period it would be one, one, one for every meal, and then suddenly, at the beginning of a moon period, twelve or thirteen for three main meals a day. Very cautiously I would add a few here and a few there and get a little extra but I was terrified of the Food Office who sent someone every month or so to sign the books. I would sit biting my nails, hoping they would not ask awkward questions while they went through the forms. After the war I went to the local Food Office and asked the head woman if she had found my forms very muddled and confused. 'Oh no,' she said, 'I was told never to look at them. I only signed them.' If only I had known . . .[46]

One or two of the agents were keen shots and would go rough shooting on the days they spent waiting for their missions. They would come back with a brace of duck or some rabbits, which were always a welcome addition to the pie. Going shopping for food was difficult because Barbara had to spread her purchases out so that the shopkeepers would not get suspicious, despite her catering licence. When she had a bigger contingent to cater for she would go to Chichester where she could sometimes find food off the ration. After one fruitless trip she was returning empty-handed when she came across a local gamekeeper who was carrying a rack of rabbits. She bought the lot and he never asked her why she wanted so many. He became a useful source of meat when there was insufficient to be had elsewhere.

Barbara had an excellent eye and even agents in disguise could not slip past her unrecognised. One agent who flew out of Tangmere several times was Gilbert Renault-Roulier, known to her at that time only by his code-name, Colonel Rémy. Renault, a film director, escaped to London in 1940 and joined the Free French. His first task had been to collect up-to-date maps of France to send back to Britain but he did more. He built up an impressive spy network called the Confrérie de Notre Dame covering much of occupied France and Belgium. As a result of his outstanding intelligence the British launched successful commando raids on the north-west French port of Bruneval, when they captured the German radar system and its operator, which led to TRE being moved to Malvern in 1942, and the raid on St Nazaire the same year. He was one of General de Gaulle's best secret agents and was decorated after the war by the French, British, Belgians and the Americans. On one visit he arrived with a pot plant for Madame de Gaulle and on another he took the head of a damaged sculpture back to France to have a new body carved. Towards the end of the war he had become well-known to the Germans so he had to disguise himself. 'After his appearance had been altered he walked past his wife and children in the Park, who knew nothing of his plans, and they did not recognize him, so his disguise was considered good enough.'[47] Barbara, however, spotted him immediately when he walked down the path towards the Manor House and greeted him by name. The conducting officer looked horrified and asked if she had been told in advance he was coming. She explained that she had not but that, being partially deaf and needing to lip-read, she looked at a man's mouth more than any other feature of his face. Rémy had changed everything about his face except his teeth, which he refused to have modified, and that was how she recognised him. The two of them agreed that she should keep that to herself for fear he would lose confidence in his disguise.

There were times of intense distress and sadness, such as when an agent was captured. The worst phone call of all was when they heard, often during dinner, that someone had been arrested. A chill settled over the dinner table. 'They could not know if he had talked under torture and had made it unsafe for them to go. Those were terrible evenings.' Barbara wrote: 'All the way through the job the knowledge that those arrested would be tortured was a horrible thought at the back of our minds; seldom mentioned but always present. I was told afterwards that, on the whole, it was the highly intelligent, sensitive ones that withstood torture best, not the "tough guys".[48] She was reminded of the threat of torture and death when the agents asked her to sew a little capsule of poison in the cuffs of their shirts. It always brought her up short, in the same way as when she had to offer them a last drink. She wrote: 'I hope the thought of France won't always make me feel sick and "The Marseillaise" won't always make me cry.'[49]

One evening at dinner, Barbara asked the agent sitting next to her to bring back some French stamps next time he came over, as Tim, her son, had just begun collecting. The man, called Lestanges, promised he would and left on a flight that night. There was an accident. The plane he was in overshot the mark and landed in a ploughed field. It turned over on impact and burst into flames. The pilot was killed and two of the three passengers were thrown clear and unhurt. The reception party rushed to pick them up and dash for safety before the Germans arrived at the scene.

Remarkably, Lestanges managed to crawl out of the burning plane and found himself alone in a ploughed field in a part of France he did not know. Both his arms were badly burned and he knew he needed help. He followed the instructions they all received for such eventualities and made his way to the nearest village and sought out the priest. The priest took him in and realised he needed urgent medical attention. Knowing his local community well the priest was aware that the local doctor was a Nazi sympathiser so that was not an option. He put Lestanges on his bicycle and pushed the injured man five miles to a convent that ran a nursing home. The mother superior immediately took him into her care and locked him in a room for his own safety. She alone nursed him and started a rumour that one of her nuns was having a baby. That was enough to ensure complete secrecy. Meanwhile, the priest got in touch with Lestanges' friends in Paris who in turn notified London. Barbara takes up the story:

We laid on an op. to bring him home three weeks after his accident. He spent those three weeks desperately ill with his burns. We had an ambulance waiting at Tangmere to take him to East

Grinstead hospital. As he got in he handed the Conducting
Officer an envelope to be given to me. In it were the stamps I had
asked for. Of course, I went to see him at East Grinstead and
when I thanked him for the stamps I found he did not remember
anything about them at all. I could not, of course, give them
to the boys until after the war. I am glad that, after the war,
Lestanges returned to the village where the Convent nursing
home was and told people what had really happened in the locked
room.[50]

Other operations had a different outcome. A safe landing did not
of course mean a safe onward passage. On the night of 16/17 June
1943 three female agents, Cecily Lefort, Noor Inayat Khan and
Diana Rowden, and one man, Charles Skepper, were flown into
France from Tangmere. All had been trained by SOE in Britain and
knew what they were due to do on landing. Cecily Lefort was married and had escaped from France with her husband in 1940. She
was in the WAAF and was on her way south with Skepper to meet
Francis Cammaerts. After just three months she was captured and
brutally tortured before being sent to Ravensbrück concentration
camp from where she went to Uckermark and died in the gas chamber sometime in February 1945. Diana Rowden was also a WAAF
officer and was part of the 'Acrobat Network' where she worked
as a courier delivering messages to agents in Marseilles, Lyon and
Paris. She was captured in November 1943 and eventually executed
at Natzweiler-Struthof concentration camp in July 1944 through a
lethal injection of phenol. The third agent was Noor Inayat Khan
who had trained as a corporal wireless operator in the WAAF. She
was a descendant of Tipu Sultan, the eighteenth-century Muslim
ruler of Mysore and became the first woman radio operator in
Paris. Hugh Verity described her brief operational career as 'exceptionally gallant and she was awarded a George Cross and MBE
[posthumously].[51] She too was arrested and interrogated after being
betrayed. Despite interrogation and torture she revealed nothing
but unfortunately had kept copies of all her secret signals which the

Germans used to trick London into sending agents into the waiting hands of Gestapo.' She tried to escape twice, only to be taken to Dachau where she was executed in September 1944. Verity wrote: 'Looking back on the operational supper at Tangmere Cottage with our cheerful passengers just before take-off it was almost impossible to imagine that a group of [three] such as this would all have such terrible fates.'[52]

A great tragedy that touched Barbara and Tony personally was when the son of very close family friends was killed. Barbara had known Stephen Hankey since he was a baby and adored him. The night of the accident, 17 December 1943, she had gone to the airfield for the first and only time in the war. On every other night she stayed at Bignor to prepare for the incoming party but on this occasion there was a new driver who did not know the way from the village to Tangmere so she went with her to give directions. It was a triple operation; three Lysanders each flying three agents and their courier sacks. Stephen was the pilot in one of the planes. 'When they had taken off – three great dragonflies of the night – I was taken back to the cottage for a drink and then driven back to Bignor to prepare reception pie.'[53] Once she had finished cooking and tidied up the kitchen she went to bed in the drawing room and set her alarm clock. The phone didn't ring and the later it got the more anxious Barbara became. Finally, sometime around seven o'clock in the morning Tony rang and she knew at once from his voice that something terrible had happened. He told her he would be coming with two. *Two* from a triple op and why *I'm coming* when there were three officers and three drivers? Barbara wrote. When he arrived he could not tell her anything so they all ate the reception pie in silence and went up to bed. As soon as they were alone Barbara questioned him. He was lying on the camp bed, utterly exhausted. He said: 'Stephen's been killed, and MacBride and Berthel[54] and Cazenave[55]. I'll tell you later.'[56] With that he immediately fell asleep and Barbara was left reeling. She learned later that the weather forecast had been wrong.

Commander Hugh Verity, one of the three pilots that night, had managed to land his Lysander with the help of the controller who brought him safely down from five miles out, though he did not see the landing lights until 300 feet above the ground. He made his way straight to the control tower, anxiously watching as the fog thickened. He wrote: 'Under normal circumstances in a situation such as this I would have had no hesitation in ordering the pilots to bale out, but in this situation it was out of the question as they had passengers on board – agents they had picked up in France – and they didn't have parachutes.'[57] By the time the second Lysander came into land the visibility was down to five hundred yards and the fog was getting thicker and thicker. The pilot made two attempts to land but aborted both at the last minute. On the third attempt he came down too soon and crashed on the run into the airfield. The pilot, McBride, was killed, but miraculously his two passengers survived. The third plane, which Stephen Hankey was flying, was diverted to Ford airfield nearby but the fog was too thick there and the plane crashed, killing Stephen and both passengers.

Tony had had to drive out to Ford to identify the charred bodies before returning to Bignor to face his wife. They had to keep up the appearance that nothing was wrong as there was a French agent at the house who was due to fly out the following night. For Barbara it was her personal low point of the war and she felt Stephen's loss keenly.

Another episode also touched her but in a different way. Pierre Delaye, known to Barbara as Pierre-le-paysan, was a remarkably successful agent who spent an extended period with the Bertrams at Bignor Manor and became a firm favourite with both of them. He came from Marchampt in the Rhone region north of Lyon and was married with a wife and ten year old son. He ran a sawmill and had a few vines. His wife worked as a hairdresser to boost the family's income. Delaye volunteered for the French army but was captured by the Germans near Dunkirk. He was imprisoned first in Poland and later in Russia where he languished in a large prison outside Moscow until 1941. He was freed after the German invasion of Russia and arrived into London Euston several weeks later to be welcomed by Free French officers. He was one of eleven men out of over 700 volunteers who were chosen to be trained as radio operators. He was unusual in that he was already forty-one and most other radio operators were in their twenties. Tony described him as 'A lumbering man, slow to move or think, with a wide sudden smile and large hands that hung clumsily between his knees when they had no work to do. But for the war, I do not imagine he would ever have left his home.'[58] When he completed his signals' training he still wasn't fast enough so he was sent to Bignor to work on it. He installed his transmitting set in the attic and studied hard, practising daily until he improved his speeds. When he had finished his work in the attic he asked Barbara if there was anything he could do in her garden. 'I did not insult him by telling him what needed to be done, I just showed him the tool shed. I have never had my garden so beautifully cared for. When he could do no more he scythed all the long grass he could find and stacked it for Caroline-the-goat and also stinging nettles for both Caroline and the chickens.'[59]

He did not read for pleasure and he was not a great conversationalist so he played out wool for Barbara and told her how to bottle peas and make eau de vie. With time he became a first-class transmitter and was sent to France. He left in a hurry and was miserable that he did not have time to buy Barbara a present, so he gave her ten shillings. He flew out with Squadron Leader Guy Lockhart in August 1942. According to the records, the operator on the ground was drunk and had laid out the flare path in the worst manner possible. The plane crashed into a ditch. Delaye was the only passenger. He and Lockhart were unhurt and Lockhart later said that Delaye had been completely unfazed. While Lockhart burned the plane and escaped back to Britain, Delaye made his way to Macron, near Loyettes, where he carried out four successful operations, providing safe landing sites and impeccable radio messages to London in January, February, March and April 1943. In May the Germans were closing in on him. He managed to relay his message to London while the Gestapo were circling around the house. Knowing he must not be taken prisoner he jumped out of a window and onto his bike. He pedalled just a few metres before he was shot. 'The day he was buried in the little village, not his own ... all the inhabitants stood at their doors holding flowers.'[60] Tony Bertram said of Pierre Delaye later, 'War had not changed him. It had dragged him across Europe and put his hands to the most unlikely work, but he accepted and coped with that situation as he would have accepted and coped with a diseased tree.'

A visitor who came more than once was the successful agent Marie-Madeleine Fourcade. 'She came several times and never looked the same twice running – sometimes red-haired and sometimes black, but always elegant and lovely ... She told me of all the horrors of torture. She became the head of one of the biggest reseaux. Her book *Noah's Ark* is one of the very best of the many books written about the French Resistance.'[61] Marie-Madeleine gave her underground agents animal names hence the title of her book: her nickname was 'hedgehog'. She was caught twice by the Gestapo and imprisoned. The first time she and her staff managed to escape. She somehow got on a plane to London and continued to run the network from there. Later in the war she flew out from Tangmere, via Bignor Manor, and was captured for the second time. This was much more harrowing and she was tortured. Miraculously she managed to escape from her prison cell by stripping naked and squeezing her slim figure through the bars on her window. She joined the Maquis in the last few days before France was liberated. Madame Fourcade survived the war but many members of her Alliance network were captured and executed at Natzweiler-Struthof. Her book, *Noah's Ark*, was dedicated to the 429 men and women who died on service in her Alliance.

There are no exact figures of how many men and women were flown into and out of Tangmere by Lysander, but Hugh Verity estimated that out of 279 operational sorties 186 were successful – that is to say that they landed in France – while others were aborted on account of the weather or other factors. He believed they flew 293 passengers into France and brought out 410. By the time France was liberated in August 1944, Barbara Bertram had had some two hundred

French men and women to stay. They came from all walks of life and from every corner of France. She listed their professions in her memoir: 'priest, seminarian, doctors, nurses, artists, writers and journalists; school masters and mistresses, dressmakers, a perfume manufacturer, a Champagne grower, housewives, peasants, diplomats, members of parliament; lawyers, policemen, motor mechanics and garage owners, soldiers, sailors and airmen, a duke, a princess and a brothel-keeper.'[62]

She cared for them all with equal kindness and was as supportive of them as she possibly could be. In turn they loved and respected her. She represented a beacon of light, hope and comfort in their difficult and often terrifying lives. In the first volume of his memoirs published in 1946, Colonel Rémy – he of the disguise that did not fool Barbara – paid her a rich tribute:

Off we went to spend the night in a charming house nearby, belonging to an English lady, Mrs Barbara Bertram who had volunteered to act as hostess to us birds of passage. Mrs Bertram was to become immensely popular with all the secret agents leaving for France or arriving back ... I didn't envy Mrs Bertram her life. She saw the people arriving from France for only a few hours (oh, how they gazed in amazement at the fried eggs and bacon, the creamy milk, the cakes). The ones who were leaving were mostly there for two or three days; but they were nervous, short-tempered, impatient, and let's face it, scared stiff. Difficult guests, but so good was she with them that I have often heard them say, 'Our best memory of England was the time we had to spend in Mrs Bertram's house'. She won the hearts and the gratitude of all the French who passed through it; and though I am sure that she never said a word about what they were doing – that subject, under her roof, was taboo – many left her with their courage renewed.[63]

*Audley End House, once the court of King Charles II, was used
during the war to train Polish secret agents.*

CHAPTER 11

Station 43: Audley End

Stalin's latest double-cross has been at the expense of the Poles. He promised them arms a short time ago, and now he says that the entry of Great Britain and France into the war has altered the situation and he can no longer supply any armaments at all.

John Colville 11, September 1939

No country in the Second World War suffered as many casualties as Poland, not even close. Out of a population of 35 million in 1939, some 6 million were killed, approximately 17 per cent of the population, compared to Britain, who lost 450,000 men, women and children, representing less than 1 per cent of the population. Of that total figure for Poland, just 240,000 were military deaths, the rest were civilians. The only other nation with a percentage of deaths in double figures, both military and civilian, was the Soviet Union. It is a grim statistic for a country that has suffered more than most, on account of being sandwiched between two powers who fought over its land for 150 years. Between 1795 and 1918, Poland was partitioned three times by Austria-Hungary, the Germans and the Russians. It regained its borders after the First World War, but the twenty years between the wars were not peaceful for the Poles. They were at war with Russia between 1919 and 1921 and then with Germany in a battle of words as Hitler's expansionist ideas led inexorably to the invasion of Poland on 1 September 1939 followed by that of the Soviet Union from the east two-and-a-half weeks later. John Colville, assistant private secretary to Prime Minister Neville Chamberlain, wrote in his diary the following day, 17 September:

> The announcement by which the Soviet Government attempted to justify their act of unequalled greed and immorality is without doubt the most revolting document that modern history has produced. For the first time since the war began I felt really depressed, and frantic at the impossibility of our taking any effective action to prevent this crime.[1]

The Polish population suffered unprecedented brutality from both sides, although the Germans were responsible for the majority of the deaths in their effort to eliminate non-German citizens from the country over the six years of the war.

The Polish resistance movement was more or less in place by the time the German invasion took place. Their underground army was the largest, best organised and most sophisticated resistance army in all of occupied Europe at the time. It was known as the Armia Krajowa (Home Army) and 'it expected all Poles to defy the Germans in every possible way, from non-cooperation to outright sabotage.'[2] They had already laid the groundwork for a resistance army prior to the war with several hundred underground bunkers stashed with weapons and explosives. The Poles were agents in the sense that they were activists and the majority of operatives were drawn from a military background. 'Freedom Fighters' might be a better description, suggested author Ian Valentine, in his book *Station 43*. 'Although many personnel – for instance, the couriers – did operate in civilian clothes, many of the soldiers worked with the Armia Krajowa in Poland in a loosely uniformed, paramilitary and partisan capacity. Their efforts culminated in the Warsaw Uprising in 1944.'[3]

As we have already seen, Gubbins and other members of the security services had the highest respect for the Polish secret services. From 1918 onwards the Poles had 'given top priority to spying and code breaking, specifically aimed at its two chief historic enemies, Germany and Russia. In the words of a former chief of Polish intelligence, "if you live trapped between the two wheels of a grindstone, you have to learn how to keep from being crushed."[4] Lynne Olson, in her book *Last Hope Island*, wrote that a Polish historian estimated years after the war that as many as 16,000 Poles, the majority in the Home Army, were involved in gathering military and economic intelligence within the country. The unstoppable force of the Germans meant that key members of the intelligence services fled into exile but they left behind them a widespread network with whom they kept in close contact from the outset. This was in contrast to other resistance movements that had to be built up over months and years before they could operate effectively and it gave the Poles a special status in the eyes of Gubbins and others in SOE. The great tragedy for him in his efforts to help the Poles was something nobody could change: distance.

The Polish government-in-exile was set up in 1939 in Paris and then Angers until June 1940, when Prime Minister General Władysław Sikorski escaped to England with his ministers. When Sikorski asked Churchill if he would be prepared to help the Polish forces escape France so that they could continue to fight Churchill replied: 'Tell your army in France that we are their comrades in life and in death. We shall conquer together – or we shall die together.'[5] They occupied the Rubens Hotel in London, which also housed their military headquarters. The relationship between the Polish government-in-exile and their British hosts was fraught with difficulties and it often caused headaches in Whitehall as the British tried to balance the Russians on the one hand and the Poles on the other. Sikorski was an impressive leader and a vigorous defender of the Polish cause in diplomatic circles. He had no illusions about Russia's plans for his country in the postwar world and was constantly frustrated that the British and French did not see Russia as the aggressor he knew it to be. Tragically for the Poles, Sikorski was killed in an aeroplane accident on 4 July 1943, just three months after the discovery of the Katyń massacre, when over 4,000 Polish officers were found in a mass grave in the forests of Katyń by the Germans. The Poles demanded an independent enquiry by the Red Cross into the massacre, which Sikorski always believed had been carried out by the Russians. Stalin was furious. He laid the blame firmly at the feet of the Germans and broke off diplomatic relations with the London-based Polish government-in-exile. This and the death of their charismatic and energetic leader left Poland in a weakened state. Thus the work of SOE and the Polish agents became all the more important for morale and to convince the Poles at home that their fight was not being ignored and that they had not been forgotten. It was not until 1990 that the truth of the Katyń massacre emerged. The Russians had indeed carried it out and executed over 22,000 military officers, police officers and intelligentsia.

The Polish section of Special Operations Executive was unusual in two respects. First, the majority of the 520 or so men and women trained by SOE were former soldiers and when they were dropped into Poland they were the responsibility of the Polish underground army, rather than civilian resistance organisations as agents were elsewhere in Nazi-occupied Europe. Secondly, they were kept together and trained by Polish as well as British instructors. In the requisitioned houses where they trained in secret, such as Audley End – home to Station 43 – and Briggens, also in Essex, only Polish was spoken.

The magnificent Jacobean mansion house at Audley End near Saffron Walden survived the Second World War with next to no damage save for one small piece of graffiti on a wall in the coal gallery and a broken stained-glass window that was cracked in storage. The gardens and grounds did not escape so lightly: the presence of Station 43 meant that features such as bridges, walls, streams and trees were perfect props for exercises. Thirty years after the war when the river Cam was dredged evidence of wartime activity was revealed in the very large amount of spent and live ammunition found in the mud. Although the obstacle course, the dummy tank and the aircraft fuselage had long gone and the gardens restored to their current beauty, there are still reminders of the Polish agents' stay, the most obvious of which is the memorial urn at the corner of the Mount Garden. It commemorates the 108 Polish agents who lost their lives during the Second World War.

In June 1939, the elderly seventh Baron Braybrooke offered Audley End to the government as a casualty clearing station, but was piqued when he was told it was of no use as a hospital: 'It was quite unsuitable, having available only two lavatories for the potential two hundred beds, and no electricity... Two bathrooms, even with the splendid brass and mahogany Victorian WC next to the chapel, were quite insufficient for the needs of even a convalescent hospital.' [6] So the house escaped in the first round of requisitioning and the family stayed there throughout the Phoney War.

Life at Audley End had not changed at the outbreak of war, except that non-essential staff were allocated war work and the house was blacked out. Although it did not have as many windows as Blenheim Palace, it was a major feat of sewing to get the hundreds of window frames covered so that not a pin prick of light shone into the darkness. Each turret block has ninety-eight individual panes and the front facade over 250. The first 'guests' at Audley End during the autumn of 1939 were evacuees. They stayed in the service wing but remained for just a few weeks. The biggest change was the ploughing up of the East Park and the lawns to the west of the Cam for planting. The kitchen gardens were turned over to more intensive food production on the instruction of Lord Braybrooke, and his daughter, Caroline, helped to till the land until she joined the First Aid Nursing Yeomanry (FANY) and left home.

Lord Braybrooke died in March 1941 at the age of eighty-five. 'Within a fortnight of his death, and without warning, two civil servants from Cambridge arrived at the house and gave Lady Dorothy notice that she should be out of the house within the week, as it was required for use by the army.' [7] This was a great shock, but fortunately Lady Braybrooke was well-connected and, through the family solicitor, she was able to make contact with someone who reasoned with civil servants in the Office of Works. A longer notice period was negotiated and also a proper contract drawn up with the government which allowed for the taxes owed on the death of Lord Braybrooke to be deferred until after the war. It also gave the family time to ensure that the valuable collection of paintings could be stored securely.

> Wooden screens and panelling were erected to protect the interior of the house from damage. Only one entrance was used, via the north porch by way of an impressive oak door surmounted by, perhaps appropriately, an allegorical carving depicting the rewards of peace. A partition in the Great Hall was erected to close the main Vanbrugh staircase, with access to the other floors by the north stairs. The treads on the stairs and rails were also covered.[8]

The Office of Works was so successful in protecting the walls and covering up the mouldings that former Polish agents who came back to visit after the war did not recognise the interiors, though they immediately felt at home outside and in the grounds. They had no idea they had been surrounded by such opulence during their stay in the house. A photograph of a wartime celebratory dinner shows the Poles and their guests dining in front of Essex board decorated with flags and portraits. Above the board but invisible to the diners stand the arches of Vanbrugh's staircase and the magnificent Jacobean wood panelling around the Great Hall fireplace. Lady Braybrooke's possessions were locked in the Picture Gallery and that was the only room in the house that remained out of bounds for the entire war. The Braybrookes were fortunate that the incumbents who stayed at Audley End the longest, the Poles, were respectful of their wartime home.

By the end of June, just three months after Lord Braybrooke's death, Audley End was handed over to the army. Lady Braybrooke moved into the Old Rectory at Heydon, but that was short-lived as the WAAF requisitioned it in late 1941. From Heydon she moved to Devon but returned to Essex and moved into a property in Littlebury owned by her family. She spent the rest of the war not far from Audley End. Hers was a tragic story. Her younger son George was an ordinary seaman in the Royal Navy, only twenty-one when his ship, HMS *Picotee*, was sunk by a U-Boat on 12 August 1941; all hands were lost. Two years later in 1943, her older son, Richard Neville, the eighth Baron Braybrooke, was killed on active service in Tunisia at the age of 25. He is buried in the Commonwealth War Graves Cemetery at Medjez-el-Bab. The title and house were inherited by the baron's cousin, Henry Seymour Neville.

Audley End was, in a sense, a strange choice of house for one of the most secret organisations in Britain during the war. Roger Kirkpatrick wrote in *Audley End at War*:

> Audley End is built on an Abbey site, with all the characteristics that make it a security nightmare. The site is overlooked from all sides – often from cover or from public roads. It is bounded by a village and a hamlet; both closely integrated with the estate, whose inhabitants, sometimes by right and always by habit, were used to criss-crossing the park. Three roads skirt the park, one a major north–south route. The wall marking the boundary is of very uneven height, and easily scalable at several points, giving on to cover from which the house can be observed ... various retired servants and estate workers continued to live in the grounds throughout the war, even though the family had been evicted from the main house. It was the last place that one would have thought suitable for secret operations of any sort.[9]

The overwhelming advantage of Audley End, however, was its size. It could accommodate over one hundred personnel in the house including thirty to forty agents at any one time. The fact that support personnel were seen running about in uniform probably convinced local people that it was merely another army training establishment.

Special Operations Executive was to occupy Audley End from 1941 until 1944 but it was not the Polish agents who arrived first, rather a contingent of forty-seven soldiers from Bedfordshire, Hertfordshire and Essex. It is believed that these men were either medically unfit for action or had been wounded. Their task was to maintain security at the house and on the estate and to undertake general duties as required. It is unlikely that any of them were briefed about the agents they were about to look after, but they became part of Station 43 and were later proud to have been associated with it. A number of the soldiers left memoirs about their time there. One of these was Sergeant Alfred Fensome, who was injured at Dunkirk and declared unfit for combat as his hearing was impaired following a dive-bombing by a Stuka. He broke his knee in the same attack when hit by flying debris and masonry. He lived at Audley End working as a driver, sharing the so-called transport bedroom above the 1780s laundry with four other drivers. As far as he and the other soldiers were concerned, the house was just a barracks with a fine exterior.

What the army got was a very chilly, very bare shell. Morale was always good in the house but all remembered it as being very cold, even when the fires were lit and the boilers were stoked. The house had no electricity before the army arrived, so they fixed wooden battens across the ceilings for electric lights.

Corporal Peter Howe and Sergeant Alan Watts provided written recollections from when they were stationed at Audley End from 1942 to 1944. As members of the Royal Army Service Corps they were part of the orderly room staff. Watts had previously served at Briggens, known as Station XIV, which housed more Polish agents and the forgery section of SOE. In 1986, he and Howe told English Heritage about the trials and tribulations, along with a great deal of hilarity, about running Audley End day-to-day. 'Stoking the boilers at the back of the Lower Gallery in the house was not a popular job with the British soldiers. Howe said that he felt very vulnerable stoking in the dead of night, particularly as the other boiler to tend to was in the stables away from the main house.'[10]

Even though the risk of invasion was over, there was always an underlying fear of being attacked by German agents working in Britain. In the event, only one German agent who landed in Britain went unnoticed by the security services. The rest were captured and a number agreed to become double-agents. Of course, Watts and Howe couldn't have known this, so the imagined threat of ambush or attack felt real.

The first officer in charge of the military establishment at Audley End was Lieutenant Colonel Arthur Terence 'Terry' Roper-Caldbeck. He had served with the Argyll and Sutherland Highlanders in the Far East between 1926 and 1932, after which he was in Nigeria. At the outbreak of war he was part of the Regular Army Reserve of Officers and was mobilised in 1939, joining SOE in August 1941. He was a fair man who would not tolerate bullying behaviour. When the soldiers first arrived at Audley End, their company sergeant major used to send the men out on long route marches across Essex, get a lift back when he was halfway round and then pretend to run into the house, leaving his men straggling. He was found out. Roper-Caldbeck was livid and gave him his marching orders. The CSM had previously been involved in a fight with Alfred Fensome and everyone was pleased to see him go. His was not the only dismissal. Two quartermasters ended up in jail: the first for stealing rations and the other was caught dipping into mess funds. Roper-Caldbeck was sent temporarily to Canada in December 1941 as the first commandant of STS 103, known as Camp X, a specialist paramilitary and Commando training station on the northwest shore of Lake Ontario. He was liked and respected by the Polish personnel and was helpful when it came to working with the police and Home Guard in Saffron Walden.

One of the things that made for a happy atmosphere at Audley End was the presence of members of the First Aid Nursing Yeomanry, known universally as the FANYs. In 1907 the FANY was the first women's corps to be set up to be at the disposal of the government in the event of hostilities. Members of the corps had to 'qualify in First Aid and Home Nursing, and in addition go through, and pass, a course of Horsemanship, Veterinary Work, Signalling and Camp Cookery.'[11] During the First World War they carried out their work on the continent without complaint and in some of the most gruesome conditions. They ran canteens and hospitals, brought wounded soldiers from the battlefields in their own ambulances purchased with donated funds, and for the first part of the war were the only women driving in France. One sergeant who worked with the FANY drivers said: 'When the cars are full of wounded, no one could be more patient, considerate or gentle than the FANYs, but when the cars are empty they drive like bats out of hell.'[12]

They were a voluntary body largely made up of young women from wealthy backgrounds. FANY historian, Hugh Popham, summed up the special nature of their work:

> That word 'voluntary' is important. The Corps was, and remains to this day, just that ... Far from being paid, members themselves paid a subscription of £1 a year to belong to it, found their own uniforms ... and for all running expenses were dependent on private generosity.[13]

By the beginning of the Second World War the FANYs were in a very strong position to help out. They had Motor Driver Companies scattered from the Highlands of Scotland to Devon and were well connected with friends high up in the military, government and civil service. The government wanted them to be subsumed into the ATS to work as drivers or driving instructors and wear ATS uniform but, as a special concession, they would be allowed to wear their own flash on the shoulder. It was an uncomfortable fit for some of the women, especially those who had been involved in the FANY for years, and a breakaway group formed – the Free-FANYs – which was run by two sisters, Marian and Hope Gamwell, who were called out of retirement in Rhodesia to help organise them. Unlike the other women's services, who were restricted to non-combatant roles, the FANY had no such limitations, meaning that the organisation became an ideal cover for women being trained by SOE. The thinking behind this was that affiliation to a military corps gave wearers of uniform the right to claim prisoner of war status, whereas as civilians they would have had none. In reality, the Gestapo had no time for such niceties and women SOE members affiliated to the FANY who were captured were treated in the same manner as their civilian counterparts.

The Polish forces formed a special association with the FANY which began in the spring of 1940 when a small number of women operated a mobile canteen for the men held in a 'concentrated' camp in Brittany. Although they had only basic necessities on offer, this little gesture of help by three young women meant more to the Poles than they could ever express. One of the women, Pat Waddell, said later: 'People came with all sorts of troubles, and sooner or later the inevitable pocket-case was produced with photos of wife and children, from whom as often as not they had had no news since the war . . . We represented home'.[14]

General Sikorski had refused to accept the German and French decision that the Poles would surrender and promised Churchill they would fight for the Allies. By 1941 there were some 24,000 Poles in Britain and this would gradually grow to 228,000 serving under the high command of the British Army. They formed the fourth largest Allied armed force after the Soviets, the Americans and the British, and fought successfully in the Battle of Britain as well as on the ground at Monte Cassino and Arnhem. Their contribution was vital to the defeat of the Germans in North Africa and Italy. After the war Churchill said: 'His Majesty's Government will never forget the debt they owe to the Polish troops . . . I earnestly hope it will be possible for them to have citizenship and freedom of the British Empire, if they so desire.'[15]

At the peak of their association with the Polish forces, about 250 FANYs worked directly with the Poles in all different roles, from conducting officers for agents to housekeepers and drivers. '"We were supremely happy": those four words . . . epitomise the FANY style and go a long way towards explaining their popularity with those they served. In a regimented world they managed to combine the efficiency of the professional with the enthusiasm of the amateur, and that is a rare and precious thing.'[16]

A big advantage for the FANY as a corps was that they had no specific brief. They acted as 'a reserve of talent when there was work of special delicacy or high responsibility to be done. Thus they tended to turn up in high places, as drivers to very senior officers, or in a variety of posts in the War Cabinet, the Foreign Office, the War Office, and General Headquarters.'[17] These often put them in confidential positions, none more so than with SOE.

The vicarage of St Paul's Church at 31a Wilton Place, Knightsbridge, was made the FANY HQ in October 1940 when the vicar offered it to them rent free. It was a great boon to them because not only was 10 Lower Grosvenor Place, their previous HQ, a drain on their resources but also because they had to race down three flights of stairs to the basement during air raids.

When Brigadier Gubbins needed two women to do confidential work for him within SOE he thought of a family friend, Phyllis Bingham, who worked as secretary to Marian Gamwell in Wilton Place. He approached her and asked her to come and meet him. Although Mrs Bingham was unable to give her boss any reason as to why Gubbins needed to meet her, Gamwell agreed. Mrs Bingham and Peggy Minchin arrived at 64 Baker Street and entered the offices of the Interservices Research Bureau, and with that the murky world of clandestine warfare. Mrs Bingham was asked by Gubbins to see if the FANY could find volunteers for highly secret work. She agreed, and in July 1941 'the Ministry of Labour accepted a proposal that the FANY recruit girls direct from school, often as young as sixteen, and before they were subject to conscription at twenty-one. Thenceforth the FANY provided the backbone of SOE; the drivers, clerks, secretaries, and cooks who kept the organisation going worldwide.'[18] Unwittingly, they had started an extraordinary partnership between the Free-FANYs and SOE that would last for the duration of the war and would be considered a perfect match.

The Free-FANYs unofficial status was key. According to Popham 'they could literally go anywhere and do anything without questions being asked'.[19] SOE, for different reasons, was in a similar position: not answerable to any of the service ministries and independent financially. There is another similarity: while they undoubtedly gave excellent service as drivers and instructors within the ATS, the FANYs most important contribution to the Second World War went unreported during the war. Since then it has been somewhat trumped by the more colourful stories of SOE agents. The FANY kept the service going and SOE could not have operated without the 3,000 women who kept the administrative aspect of SOE's training units and holding houses ticking impeccably.

In *Setting Europe Ablaze,* Douglas Dodds-Parker wrote: They worked on every duty, from parachute packing to top-level staff duties'[20], so that when the agents were going into the field they were relying on the work carried out by the FANYs back home who had packed the parachutes, ensured the explosives that they were carrying worked and had even forged the identity papers that were needed for the cool-headed agent to operate. So the mutual trust had to be there and it was.

Over the course of the war, the Free-FANYs were asked to do so many different types of work that an outsider, or an enemy agent, would have been very pushed to define the exact nature of their work. 'This was an advantage in itself. It was particularly useful for the agents during their training: the FANY uniform gave them both a certain status and a form of protective colouring at a time when half the world was in one kind of uniform or another.'[21] Once they were dropped into France, where most of them operated, or any other occupied country, no amount of uniform would ever protect them from the 'loathsome attentions of the Gestapo if they were caught.'[22]

Probably the most skilled work undertaken by the FANYs was in communications. The women who worked in Signals and Ciphers became expert in Morse code, wireless and decoding. As Gubbins said, wireless was 'the most valuable link in the whole of our chain of operations. Without those links we would have been groping in the dark.'[23] Historian M. R. D. Foot agreed it was the most effective operational work they carried out during the war.

The rapid expansion of SOE in 1942 meant the need for FANY recruits grew. As well as signals work, they were needed to help at the Special Training Schools, such as the one at Audley End. They worked as FANY drivers and dispatch riders, clerks and accountants, cooks and orderlies, wireless operators and instructors, and coders. They were also responsible for the welfare of the agents. These were the women who vanished into 'Bingham's Unit'.

Phyllis Bingham was responsible not only for recruiting the girls into her unit, or 'The Org' as it was known, but also for their physical and mental wellbeing. As the girls could not tell their parents what work they were doing it was doubly important they felt held up by the organisation they had joined. Audrey Swithinbank was just eighteen when she joined the FANY in 1941. She spent four months training in Morse code at Fawley Court near Henley-on-Thames and then had to sign the Official Secrets Act, which meant she was unable to discuss her work with her parents. When she was posted to Grendon Underwood, a country house used as a wireless station, her parents were informed that she was working as an unpaid driver. This confused them as they were not aware that their daughter knew how to drive. It was not until four years later that she was able to tell them a little of what she had been doing.

Mrs Bingham became a legendary character for the girls who were recruited for the unit. Pamela Leach, later Lady Niven, was living with her mother in Folkestone in their house full of billeted soldiers. Pamela was moping around after leaving school at seventeen when one of the army wives told her to pull herself together and go and visit a lady called Mrs Bingham who was starting a new department. She took the train to London and presented herself at the vicarage in Wilton Place for interview. The first question surprised her: 'Did you have a nanny?' Pamela was somewhat taken aback but she said that her younger sister had had one and that she had loved her. 'Good. You'll do what you are told,' came the reply. She was sent to the SOE station for Polish agents at Station XIV at Briggens. She nearly blew her cover in the early days of her stay:

> The drive was about a mile long and I did the awful thing of post-
> ing a letter to my mother from the pillar box at its end – a drama
> because our address was secret (Room 98 the Horse Guards to be
> used for all correspondence). My mother noticed the postmark
> and then naturally wanted to tell some local friends that I was
> nearby.[24]

Pamela was sent from Briggens to Algeria in 1943 and was told that she could not tell her mother where she was being posted or even that she was going abroad. She did not see her mother for two years.

The FANY was a way of life and one most of the girls came to love. For those who started work straight out of school at sixteen it was formative and made a big impact on their later lives and careers. For some of the FANYs it became more than a job. Sue Ryder later gained fame for her charitable work and the homes she founded in Britain and abroad to support people in desperate need. This work was inspired by her experiences of working alongside the Poles during the war. She had joined FANY as a fifteen-year-old, lying about her age to get in, and her life was shaped by her wartime work. She said later: 'I hardly did anything. I just had the honour of being with them. It was remarkable what they did towards the war effort.'[25] She acknowledged her love of Poland and the Polish people when she was created a dame in 1979 and chose for herself the title of Baroness Ryder of Warsaw.

At Audley End the young FANYs were very popular. 'They looked after the SOE agents and gave the place a relaxed atmosphere. The Poles were very proud that there was never a hint of impropriety at Audley End.' Part of their job was to be friendly with the agents and to keep an eye out for them if one of them looked to be under pressure and at risk of cracking. Sue Ryder said:

It was like living with people under a sentence of death. Each group was different, each group had about three or four people in it and the groups were not allowed to talk amongst themselves. We got to know people very well. They talked about things that you would not normally talk about in life, like people who have got a terminal illness. So from that point of view it was extremely memorable. Above all we had <u>enormous</u> affection and admiration for them.[26]

Audley End House was used not only as accommodation for the Polish agents but also as the offices, lecture rooms and mess. The Great Hall doubled as a lecture room and dining hall for the Polish officers while the Bucket Hall became an orderly room and the former Museum Room a mess room for the students. Outside arms and munitions were stored in the stables and in hidden locations throughout the grounds. Only the specialist weapons for use by the agents were stored in the house in a long, narrow room leading to the wine cellar below the Butler's Pantry in the basement of the north wing. The Polish weapons instructor was clear that he wanted these weapons to be used by Polish agents only and for training rather than guarding the house. The weapons included Webley .455s, Smith & Wesson .38s, Colt A .32s, Colt A .22s and Sectional Grenades. There was also a cupboard that contained dummys, oil bottles, pull-throughs for cleaning barrels, eye discs and grouping rings, which were the round paper targets used in firing practice. Years after the war there remained a pungent, oily smell in the room because of lack of ventilation – one of few reminders of the house's activity during those years.

The commanding officers were allocated the guest bedrooms at both ends of the house on the first floor. The majority of the occupants of the house used the second floor where lectures, language training and other courses were held. One room was used as an examination room and another for making, or rather forging, the documents that agents would need in Poland. One of the most interesting rooms was the North Turret Room where authentic Polish clothes were tailored. When SOE was first called into being it had a reasonable supply of foreign clothing from refugees who were given new clothes on arrival in Britain. However, demand outstripped supply and the need for tailors and dressmakers with very high levels of skill were needed. They had to pay meticulous attention to detail to ensure the clothes had European cuts and that every care was taken to avoid using the wrong button or zip fastener which would give away an agent in an instant. 'Other people were employed to "distress" clothes and the brief-cases that contained the radio sets so that they looked old and blended in with the civilian population.'[27] At Audley End, the tailor went to the trouble of ensuring that he had Polish cloth and thread to make the suits and jackets required.

The second floor also served as dormitories for the instructors and agents. They were delighted to discover that they could gain access to the roof from one of the bedrooms and there they could sunbathe undisturbed. The old nursery was used as the orderly room and had an open fire, which was very welcome in the winter as the bedrooms on the second floor were unheated.

All Polish trainees were entitled to extra rations to help build up their strength, including bully beef from the army. Later there were supplies from the Americans, including cigarettes and chocolate. The Poles installed a bread oven in the old kitchen on the ground floor and were allowed to bake their own bread. The kitchen was presided over by Corporal Cottiss, a former Essex policeman, who worked there for two years and provided meals for the canteen. He was popular as he had a stock of chocolate and biscuits which could be bought. There was also a novelty in the canteen, which was a soda fountain. It operated with a gas canister and had flavoured tablets. It was popular but also somewhat unpredictable. One British soldier remembered that it had to be operated with great care otherwise there would be a 'frightful mess' if the glass, gas tablets and water exploded.

In addition to the regular supplies delivered to Audley End House, there were vegetables and fruit from the kitchen garden and the orchards, duck eggs and fish. Pike and carp were fished out of the Cam and kept alive in the disused Victorian fountain where they would swim until they were killed for the plate. Fresh milk was delivered to the stables every other day by a sixteen-year-old girl called Sylvia Thurston. She had no inkling of the real nature of Audley End, believing it to be a regular army camp. Little did she know that there were twenty tons of explosives just feet away from where she and the quartermaster exchanged milk for cash.

Audley End's bathroom facilities were so inadequate that the majority of people on site, whether British or Polish, went to the public baths in Cambridge, some fifteen miles to the north of Audley End. They were driven in a Liberty truck and, if the timing was right, they would visit the local pub for a quick pint before driving home. The trainees were not allowed into Saffron Walden's pubs so these visits were a great treat. However, the instructors of both nationalities were allowed into the town and would meet at the Forces Club.

The majority of the Polish agents came to Audley End from the Highlands where they received instruction at STS 25a, Garramor, five miles from Arisaig. After training in Scotland, they were sent to the headquarters of the Polish Parachute Brigade in the grounds of Largo House in Fife, or to Ringway, outside Manchester. The wood at Largo was full of apparatus that the students used to swing from and between as part of their training. It was variously nicknamed Monkey's Wood, Monkey Grove and even Monkey Paradise. It was far from paradise and there were frequent accidents. Only one in four recruits passed their training and reached the final stage to become agents, which is a reminder of how dangerous their tasks were and of how tough they had to be to complete the course. This is the point at which they were sent to Audley End to await their instructions and papers for their return to Poland.

There was a wide range of training courses on offer at Andley End, including two most important ones: Clandestine (Underground) warfare and the Briefing or Dispatch course. The former required a great degree of physical fitness and expertise, self-reliance and discretion. If candidates characters did not fit the profile they were judged 'unfit for Underground work' on their training sheets and would be returned to their regular military outfits.[28]

The skills listed in Polish of the various specialist instructors reads like a spy novel: invisible inks and photography; shooting, driving and locksmith; partisan sabotage and guerrilla warfare; expert on creating 'legends' for agents and espionage; an artist in various fields including false documents and handwriting; man traps, mine traps and uses of heavy explosives; land mines and booby traps; tailor for special clothing. This 'curriculum for criminals' was as thoroughly followed as the training courses had been at Arisaig. Whereas there the focus had been on physical strength, resilience and expertise, this was engineered to help the agent develop the ability to become a seamless liar.

Some agents stayed at Audley End for up to six months because flights to Poland were only possible when the nights were long enough to make the round trip in darkness. During that time they were constantly undergoing top-up training. This sometimes involved carrying out exercises locally to simulate attacks they would undertake in Poland. Before being accepted as an instructor, Captain Alfons Maćkowiak, known always as Alan Mack, was given the task to take something from Roydon post office and not to get caught by the police. To demonstrate how this could be done effectively, he dressed up as a woman and managed to carry out the raid and get back to Audley End undetected and in broad daylight. Other raids took place at night as this was more realistic for the agents who would usually favour working under the cover of darkness when dropped into Poland. The nocturnal exercises, while an excellent means of final training, were risky.

The police and Home Guard could not tell who was attacking them, and defended themselves for all they were worth. Usually the chasing, uproar and exchange of shots ended with a drink in some local pub, and there was much laughter over the absurd situations that arose, but on other occasions heads were broken and serious fighting took place in which people were maimed. [29]

There were inevitably casualties as there were at other training stations. The only fatality directly linked with training was Captain J. Lemme, who was an instructor in combat fighting. He and Alan Mack were riding motorbikes during an exercise in thick fog. They drove to Lion Gate, Mack turning left and Lemme right. Unfortunately the fog was so dense that Lemme drove straight into a parked lorry and was killed instantly. It was a sad day when the trainees and instructors attended the funeral and laid him to rest in Saffron Walden Cemetery. A British Army corporal, P. Howe, recalled Lemme's death: 'He was blond and Aryan-looking, a big man. Everyone was very upset, as he had been very nice and well liked. The bike was repaired and no one had any qualms about using it.'[30] The other death at Audley End was Major Jan Lipiński who died from a suspected heart attack in April 1944. Injuries were more commonplace, some of which were serious. One man lost his hand when a home-made bomb blew up. Doctors at Addenbrookes tried unsuccessfully to save the damaged limb. Another man sustained serious stomach injuries and a third man almost lost his leg when a bomb he was carrying in his pocket exploded.

Alan Mack became an instructor and was responsible for the outdoor assault course which he designed and had built in the wooded area north-west of the house. The obstacles were made from thick tree branches and there was a deep-water trench in the middle of the wood. He designed a precarious 'bridge' made of two lengths of rope which was strung high above the river between two plane trees close to the Stables Bridge. He did not mind how the trainees got across the river, just so long as they did not fall into the waist-deep and muddy water below. They also built pontoons to cross the river: anything that would better prepare them for natural hazards they might encounter. However, Mack was convinced that the greatest help the trainees could give themselves was to be exceptionally fit. He was able to speak from experience, telling them that being at the peak of fitness had saved his life when he was in Poland. At the outbreak of the war he commanded a light artillery battery but was captured by the Russians. He escaped from captivity and fled to Hungary and then to France where he fought in the Battle of Lagarde as a sniper. After the fall of France, he came to Britain and served with the First Parachute Brigade before joining the Cichociemni, the name given to the Polish agents meaning 'unseen and silent'.

Sergeant Arthur Fensome taught some of the agents to drive. He was surprised to learn that many of the Poles could not ride a bicycle but soon learned that this was a luxury item in pre-war Poland and very expensive. They enjoyed cycling once they had learned and some of them went on to ride motorbikes under Fensome's tuition. He got to know the Polish locksmith, Warrant Officer Gabriel Zając, very well. Even though the British and Poles were kept profession-ally separate and the British were not to speak English with the Polish trainees, they often mixed unofficially. Zając spoke excellent English and made even better coffee. Fensome often gave him lifts into Saffron Walden and the two of them found they had a great deal in common. So did Corporal Cottiss, who became friendly with Private Kazimierz Bilewicz who was in charge of workshops and motorcycles. A love of vehicles of all types proved irresistible to both men and they would spend hours together in the workshop tinkering with the machines.

One of the features of Audley End was explosives. A former trainee told Ian Valentine that 'you couldn't even lift the seat of a toilet with-out a small charge being set off'.[31] Most trainees had already received explosives instruction in Scotland or, later, at Briggens. At Audley End it was expanded. There was a British Valentine tank that the instructors used for anti-tank weapons training, which was situated in the beautifully named Elysian Garden. The tenth Lord Braybrooke, cousin of the eighth Viscount who was killed in Tunisia, visited his 'new' home as an eleven-year-old boy with his parents in 1943. 'I remember how exciting it was to see Lancaster [Halifax] bomber fuselages and the odd tank or two in the grounds, which were blown up on a fairly regular basis.'[32]

The explosives were stored in the stables opposite the 1830s carriage building that was used as a garage and for instruction in the use of arms and for bomb making. 'It is strange to think that this building, built before Audley End House itself, fulfilled such a role when once it had contained royal racehorses.'[33]

Residents in nearby Saffron Walden had an alarming experience when windows in houses close to the estate were blown out because an ammunition, gas and fuel dump exploded. A soldier watching from the stables at Audley End described seeing shells bursting and cart-wheeling through the air in an extraordinary display of fire-power. Most explosions were better contained. Trainees were taught how to burst apart doors of safes, blow up trees to make them fall over to block a road and simulate blowing up trains. The bridges at Audley End were in regular use as props for practising laying mines.

A potentially explosive incident of another kind was averted by Colonel Roper-Caldbeck at the last moment. The recruits received training in the art of silent killing both using the F&S Fighting Knife and by strangulation. They were told that strangling an opponent was tricky and had to be done efficiently and quickly otherwise it would not be silent. One trainee, who wished to remain anonymous, described being sent into the stables in pitch darkness to strangle one of the local cats. Apparently it is difficult to strangle a cat quietly. When Roper-Caldbeck heard that neighbourhood cats, both tame and feral, were being rounded up and taken to Audley End to be used for various purposes to do with training he immediately stamped out the practice, telling the Poles that it was very wrong, as the British were deeply sentimental about animals.

Safety and security were serious considerations at all of the training bases. Officers and other staff were restricted to the areas where they undertook instruction. This was to help with security, so that if one was captured and tortured he could 'divulge only his or her narrow contribution to the training programme and staff.'[34] Local groups such as the Home Guard and other static army formations in the area knew as little as possible. The police were told about the presence of the Poles so that if a member of the public complained about strange goings-on at Audley End there would not be a visit from the local constable. In a further attempt to obfuscate, the Polish trainees at Station 43 wore British Army uniforms, with the Poland flash at the top of the left arm and the Polish White Eagle hat badges.

Another vital aspect of the training for agents was the ever-changing scene on the ground in Poland. They had to know what to expect when they were parachuted into their old country. Major Lipinski, who was the briefing instructor, kept up a permanent intelligence link with Poland in order to stay up to date. For example, agents had to be able to order coffee in a café without attracting attention. They had to know that 'café noir' was no longer the correct expression. It was simply 'café' because milk had been off the menu for many months. They had to learn about the latest bureaucratic changes and understand the uniforms they would encounter. They had to arrive out of the blue and become instantly inconspicuous.

The Poles also had to be taught how to cope with the numbers of Germans they would encounter on their return. Most of them had not seen the German invaders in September 1939 and were alarmed at the prospect of being confronted by one on home ground. In preparation, Audley End was periodically 'visited' by men in Nazi uniforms who would pop out and address a trainee vigorously in German. Sometimes students were hauled out of bed in the middle of the night and interrogated in German.

Once the trainees had learned everything that Lipinski and others could teach them about the Germans in Poland, the intricacies of café culture and the state of the police, they would be given a new identity. This was not just a piece of paper with a new name but a whole background or legend. They had to get used to their new alias and learn to construct the web of logical, perfectly fluent lies that fitted with their new identity. This was followed through to the very last detail: one man, Bronisłlaw Wawrzkowicz, was sent from Audley End to a holding camp at Harrow where he had all the fillings in his teeth removed and replaced by a Polish dentist with the amalgam used in Poland. The forged documents that he took with him had been made in a room on the first floor at Audley End. In order to fade the documents and make them look convincing they were either aged under lamps or taped to the windows in the lower gallery on the first floor above the Great Hall where the sun would do its natural work safely out of view from prying eyes.

Adam Benrad was a Polish officer cadet who had come to England in June 1940 having travelled through Yugoslavia and Italy in 1939. At the beginning of 1943 he was serving with the First Rifle Brigade when he and a small number of other officers were told they were to be interviewed by an unidentified man who might be able to offer them a flight to Poland via a parachute drop. They were asked to consider this proposition and, if they liked it, to meet the man. 'I thought about it and was told not to make a rushed decision. If people were too eager they couldn't go on to become an agent.'[35] Benrad passed muster and took part in parachute training at Ringway where the selection process for him started. He told a story of one young man who was in every way suitable to be an agent but could not be relied upon as he fell unconscious every time he jumped from an aircraft. After Ringway, Benrad was transferred to Audley End where he was first taught sabotage. He learned to blow up bridges, engines and factories. On one occasion, a group of Polish trainees were sent to blow up an unused stretch of railway between Cambridge and London. Unfortunately they misinterpreted their instructions and blew up the main line, causing massive disruption and delays. Engineers had to repair the track as quickly as possible but could not explain how it had been damaged in the first place. The line was out of commission for the best part of a day. After doing a course in basic Morse code, Benrad was taken to London to an area near Victoria station that had been badly damaged by air raids. There he was taught unarmed combat and street fighting 'in an area that resembled bombed-out Warsaw.'[36]

When Benrad was interviewed for the Imperial War Museum Sound Archive in 1983, he talked of how little he knew about the organisation that trained him and others as agents. He said that he never heard the name SOE mentioned during the war and thought it was only in the postwar era that the name of Baker Street was dropped and Special Operations Executive was finally revealed as the overall operation. As far as he was concerned, all he knew was that he was going to Poland to meet up with the Polish underground. He said, 'We never, for a moment, considered ourselves killers. We knew about unarmed combat and we would not hesitate to kill a man if the occasion arose, but we did not consider ourselves killers in cold blood. We saw ourselves as soldiers'.[37]

Benrad enjoyed his time at Audley End, despite his eagerness to get back to his own country. He liked the company of the FANY drivers and he was grateful that they understood the situation in Poland and the danger of the Gestapo. He said later that the one thing that played on his mind was 'this uneasiness at seeing the Germans in the flesh.'[38]

Being confined to Audley End did have its frustrations for some but there were compensations, such as trips to other training establishments for specialised weapons training that required a pistol gallery or some other specific type of range. Agent George Iranek-Osmecki described what happened when they were let out of what he called the 'High School of Falsehood':

We used to leave this course to go to various towns, to mingle with the population and carry out prescribed tasks. Some of the exercises were short, others lasted several days. They were all done in mufti; picking out persons whose descriptions we'd been given, or shaking off the sleuths put on our scent, were among the easiest of the lot. The observation of troop rail-movements at railway junctions, the counting of ships sailing to and from ports, the following of day-to-day events in the docks, making contacts with unknown persons were among the more difficult. All this had to be done discreetly, without attracting the attention of the uniformed police or of security agents. Some, however, were not successful in this and found their way to the nearest police station. When such a thing happened one was not allowed to give the game away, to divulge that these were special exercises. When arrested, one had to lie one's way out of the unpleasant predicament. To show one's cards and own up disqualified one for service with the Underground.[39]

Audley End was also used for training couriers, both men and women, who would carry information to and from Poland for the government-in-exile. They were not flown into Poland as the agents were, or indeed the French couriers going from Tangmere via Mrs Bertram at Bignor Manor, but journeyed overland by train. Sometimes their journeys would take weeks, months and in one case almost a year. Theirs was an equally dangerous task and the length of time taken to complete the journey might mean that their identity papers were out of date by the time they arrived in Poland. There was only one woman agent who landed by parachute. Her name was Elżbieta Zawacka and she had brought reports of the atrocities being committed in the concentration camps in her country. She parachuted into Poland, aged forty-three, on 9 September 1943. She was an exception to the rule because she had worked as an instructor for the Polish Women's Military Training Organisation before the war.

Of the seventy agents trained at Audley End only five were dropped into Poland from Britain. From 1944 it became possible for them to leave for Poland from Brindisi in Italy. One of the reasons why so few were parachuted into Poland was the great distance from Britain. The 2,000-mile round trip took the best part of twelve hours and it was only in winter that they could leave and return in darkness. The flight was cold, exhausting and dangerous, stretching the RAF almost beyond the limits of its capabilities at the time. Both the Poles and Czechs had been keen to form their own national section within the RAF 138 (Special Duties) Squadron, which was

responsible for dropping agents and equipment inside occupied territory, but there was neither the aircraft available nor the political will
to grant such autonomy. The agents therefore had to take their place
in the queue, relying on the RAF and later the USAAF for aeroplanes
and supplies. Naturally this led to conflict, with each nationality
arguing for priority for its own 'most important' mission. Gubbins,
by now an acting major general, was a supporter of the Poles and he
did everything he could to argue for more flights to Poland but it was
never easy and the RAF was always over-extended as it tried to fulfil
the demands of the various governments-in-exile.

One of the Audley End agents who did make it to Poland was
twenty-seven-year-old Major Antoni Nosek, known by his code
name 'Kajtuś'. During his training in Scotland he had shown himself
to be capable of living off the land, snaring rabbits and trapping fish
in the river Morar. He and his fellow trainees were encouraged to
learn breaking and entering by being fined sixpence every time they
went through a door or gate at Garramor. Leaping fences and climbing through windows became second nature. By the time he arrived
at Audley End, Nosek was determined to be one of those who would
be chosen to fly into Poland. He trained hard under Alan Mack,
appreciating the instructor's emphasis on physical strength and fitness. When the two men met again at Audley End in 2002, Nosek
thanked Mack publicly for his excellent tutoring.

To add to the confusion of names, Nosek, or 'Kajtuś' had a new
full name: Antoni Niechrzyński. He spoke about how he had to
forget completely that he had ever been Antoni Nosek and become a
car mechanic who worked in a garage in Chmielna Street in Warsaw.
'When suddenly woken up during the night, I had to reply "I am
Antoni Niechrzyński". Here I also received new German identifica-
tion papers, *Kennkarte* and *Arbeitskarte*.'[40]

Like Nosek, Adam Benrad was also given a new identity which
he once had to use when he was arrested by the Russians. He had
been born in south-east Poland but for his cover he came from a
little village outside Warsaw that had been completely destroyed in
1939, making it almost impossible for the Germans to follow up his

story. He chose a new surname from the pre-war Warsaw telephone directory and he was given a new date of birth. He kept his Christian name because it was a commonly used one. In real life his mother was still alive but he 'killed her off [under] some mysterious circumstances' when his village was bombed in 1939. His father was already dead so he did not have to make that up. Ian Valentine explained what happened when the agents had taken their oath and prepared to depart with their new identities:

> Agents were separated into teams of between three and six ...
> The day before the flight the dispatch of each team took place,
> when each person was told the destination address, safe house
> address and contact addresses, as well as passwords and any spe-
> cial instructions. The parachutists countersigned for money belts
> and post. The leader and deputy leader of the team received two
> copies of lists of equipment that were to be taken by the aircraft.
> At the departure session the document ordering the flight was
> signed by the whole team.[41]

Nosek's flight took him via Brindisi where SOE had an operating station. He remembered seeing the Halifax bomber waiting for him and his fellow parachutists and how they climbed in and sat quietly on the floor. As the plane took off he realised that he was 'cut off from the security of the British Isles, from the comfort of Audley End House, and now exposed to the powerful German security forces such as the Gestapo.'[42] He described in the third person the feelings they had as they sat on the floor of the bomber, unable to speak over the noise and with their heads full of thoughts of the future:

> The flight was long, six or seven hours, sometimes they heard
> strong anti-aircraft fire, but it did not bother them, because they
> were concentrating on adjusting themselves to this new role. They
> were possessed by a strong desire to do well and to accomplish
> everything that was expected of them, but more importantly, not

to disappoint SOE, Audley End House training staff, General Sikorski and the army staff. They were ready to undertake any action, even if there was little chance of survival. When they were in prison, or Gestapo torture chambers, their thoughts went back to Audley End House, the place of birth. Pleasant memories gave them strength and the will to survive. That is why Audley End House is such a dear place for us.[43]

Nosek landed in Poland in May 1944 carrying two pistols, a large money belt strapped around his waist and his various papers and forged documents. Every scrap of material associating him with Britain had been removed, destroyed and replaced by Polish detail. It was an extraordinary transformation. From now onwards he was no longer affiliated to the British but to the Sixth Bureau of the Polish Staff to whom he had been handed over just before he left for Poland. After he jumped and landed, the bomber came round a second time to drop off the containers of courier material and other precious equipment destined for the Armia Krajowa. Nosek remembered looking up and seeing the poignant sight of the bomber retreating in the distance, becoming ever smaller until it was just a dot in the sky and not even a distant rumble of its engines could be heard. He felt very alone.

However, he was not alone. Nosek was taken by a female courier known as an 'Auntie' to a safe house in Warsaw where he stayed with a family while he acclimatised to his new environment. Soon after his arrival he was stopped by a Gestapo official as he crossed a street. He handed over his forged papers expecting the official to arrest him for documents 'made in Britain' but was relieved when they let him go. The *Kennkarte* was the most valuable document for agents but also the one most difficult to forge. There were four different types in Poland denoting racial background: the *Reichsdeutschen* were Germans born in Germany and they had a special card. Then there was one for people who could prove they had third generation German ancestry. Then there were the non-Germans who could prove they had no Jewish blood. They were chillingly referred to as

Nichtdeutschen (not Germans) and Nosek was one of these. Finally there were the Jews who had their own card and had to wear a blue Star of David on a white armband. The *Kennkarte* gave civilians different rights for food coupons; it dictated where they could live and the curfew hours. All this had to be absorbed quickly by Nosek and other agents who landed in Poland.

Nosek spent many of the curfew hours playing bridge in the flat. His partner was the managing director of a civil engineering company who was so impressed that he offered him a job. Shortly after that, Nosek was held up and arrested by the Gestapo on the way to a meeting and taken to Monteluppi prison, a notorious place where underground agents were locked up, interrogated and often tortured. Nosek was released after his papers had been thoroughly checked and the managing director had vouched for him. It was so unusual to be released from this prison that he had difficulty persuading other underground members that he had not cut a deal with the Germans.

He remained active in the Armia Krajowa for the rest of the war, taking part in the Warsaw Uprising in August 1944. Three months later he was sent to Krakow to work with the District AK. When the Russians came in 1945 he was arrested and imprisoned. He was released after six weeks and returned to Britain where he lived in exile until his death in 2007. Many other agents who operated in Poland like Nosek did not survive the war. Working as radio operators or saboteurs there is no doubt that their assignments were among the most dangerous. Out of 316 volunteers from Audley End, Briggens and other Polish stations who were parachuted into Poland over the course of the war 108 lost their lives.

Like Nosek, Benrad flew out of Brindisi to Poland in a Halifax with a Polish crew. He was carrying £2,000 in gold, which was heavy and he worried that he would land too quickly, but in fact the parachute drop went without a hitch and he described it as the easiest thing that ever happened to him. Once he arrived in Warsaw with his appointed 'Auntie' he was put into quarantine for two weeks and given briefings on life in Warsaw under the Germans. He read

German newspapers and gradually built up a picture of the situation in the city which had changed out of all recognition since his last visit in 1939. He joined a partisan guerrilla outfit and felt at home: 'There is a feeling of elation that you are in the midst of something, that something is going to happen here, whether in a few days or a few weeks but you will be fighting again. We understood it was not a normal military fight with guns but that there will be a fight against the occupation.'[44]

The fight was brought to the Germans on 1 August 1944. The aim was to liberate Warsaw from occupation. The Warsaw Uprising was supposed to coincide with the Russian Red Army's approach from the east, but Russians stopped short, allowing the Germans time to regroup and demolish the city, defeating the Polish Resistance who fought for sixty-three days with little support from its Allies. Churchill pleaded with the USA and Russia to help but his requests were stubbornly ignored. He ordered more than 200 low level supply drops without permission from the Russians for air clearance but it was a modicum at best. Without Russian and American assistance it was futile to think that the resistance could stand up to the might of the Germans. The death figures were horrific. Some 16,000 members of the Resistance were killed and several thousand badly injured. The figures for civilian casualties were between 150,000 and 200,000 – the majority of those in mass executions. By January 1945 it was estimated that over 85 per cent of the city of Warsaw had been destroyed. Poland had once again been let down by its allies. The uprising has remained an inspirational story for the Poles and it was the largest single military effort undertaken by any of the SOE-backed resistance movements during the war. It is perhaps one of the most heroic and tragic events in the history of the Polish nation and of Europe in the twentieth century.

As the uprising was entering its second month, Audley End was being wound up. SOE shut down STS 43 and moved its operation to southern Italy. It recorded the successes of the British-trained Polish agents in the field between January 1941 and June 1944: 6,390 locomotives damaged and 800 trains derailed; 19,000 railway wagons and 4,300 army vehicles damaged. In addition, agents had destroyed fuel tanks and depots; they had blocked oil wells and put faulty parts into air-craft engines, condensers and artillery missiles. It is even claimed that they were responsible for the planned assassination of more than 5,700 Germans.[45]

Audley End remained under the control of the Ministry of Works with a small contingent of British soldiers guarding the house and grounds until the end of the war when it was de-requisitioned. Even before the war ended the question of what to do with Audley End had been considered. The architectural historian James Lees-Milne, who was working for the National Trust, was invited to visit the estate with Lord and Lady Braybrooke. He wrote in his diary in May 1944: 'I lunched at the Hyde Park Hotel with Lord Braybrooke who has recently succeeded two cousins (killed on active service), inheriting the title and Audley End. He is a bald, common-sensical, very nice business man of 45, embarrassed by his inheritance. At his wits' end what to do with Audley End. Who wouldn't be?'[46] In January 1945 Lees-Milne endured a freezing cold picnic lunch in the house with Lord Braybrooke and became con-vinced that it was a house that had to be saved for the nation – but there was no suggestion as to how. The house and grounds were in need of work and the cost of two lots of death duties and running Audley End was too much for the family. They considered living in a small part of the house but this would have condemned the rest of the magnificent building slowly to rot away. The family took the heart-breaking decision to sell it. The tenth Lord Braybrooke, then sixteen years old, recalled a visit from Hugh Dalton, Chancellor of the Exchequer: 'The future of the house was settled over lunch, when a deal was brokered that the family could keep the contents of the house and be paid £30,000 for the property.'[47] The house and estate were put into the care of the Ministry of Public Buildings and Works and transferred to English Heritage in 1984. It is visited by thousands of people every year, including a small and sadly dwindling number of former Polish agents to whom the house and grounds will forever be part of their country's history. At the 2002 reunion, Antoni Nosek spoke of the training at Audley End and of the great emphasis placed on fitness. Alan Mack's assault course in the wooded area north-west of the house was remembered by all. 'Collapsed culverts have been blamed for marked undulations in this area in recent years, but perhaps SOE and Alan Mack were responsible for certain amendments to Capability Brown's schemes.'[48]

Melford Hall was regarded as one of the finest examples of a Tudor mansion in England. During the war it was used as an army training camp.

CHAPTER 12

The Army at Home

Starting at the top of the scale of destruction, a not insubstantial number of houses were either burnt down entirely, or at least partly gutted by fire.[1]

John Martin Robinson

All the houses featured so far, with the exception of Inverailort Castle in the Highlands, sustained little or no substantial damage during their period of occupancy in the war. However, not all homeowners were as fortunate as the Actons at Aldenham or the Mortons at Aston Abbotts. Many houses suffered lasting damage during the five or six years they were requisitioned and some had to be demolished, although this was not always through wanton destruction but rather neglect. The group of people who caused most damage to the English country houses in the Second World War were the military. Melford Hall, the subject of this chapter, was badly damaged by fire in 1942 as were other houses used by the armed forces.

In 1938 the Treasury asked the armed services and other major government bodies to stake their claim on properties in the event of war. Most were stabbing in the dark and a survey of estimates versus actual usage conducted in 1941 showed how difficult it had been to guess what would be needed. For example, the air force had put in a bid for 5,000 premises but in the event they occupied over 20,000. The army needed large establishments for training and housing troops and that need grew as the build-up towards D-Day saw a high point of over 1.5 million American servicemen and women. All these, plus 350,000 Canadians who passed through Britain over the course of the war, not to speak of the Czechs, Poles and others who fought alongside the Allies, needed to be accommodated.

They arrived in large numbers and took over houses, outbuildings, gardens and fields wholesale, setting up cookhouses, latrines, tent cities and hospital huts. It was not just British units that took over country houses. Many were occupied by successive waves of military organisations and by fighting men of different nationalities. The first wave of incoming servicemen came from Canada, Norway, Poland and Czechoslovakia. This was a major change for many areas where outsiders were viewed either with suspicion or as a novelty. Towns where foreigners were almost completely unknown before the war, villages where a visitor from a neighbouring county were considered strangers suddenly became multi-cultural. Unfamiliar languages were heard on the streets and accents that belonged in the cinema held conversations in local pubs. One girl in Ayrshire told historian Norman Longmate that by the end of the war she had met French Canadians who played ice hockey but 'would fight at the drop of a hockey stick and threw the puck at the spectators'.[2] She had also seen Indians, Dutchmen and black Americans. She was once warned not to get too close to the Poles as they were rumoured to sleep in hairnets. All these men had to be accommodated and it was inevitable that large houses in the countryside would be needed.

In his *Problems of Social Policy*, Richard Titmuss explained that 'the Army . . . had a habit of requisitioning just the type of house fit for use as a hostel or nursery. In many areas it had taken over by the end of 1940 all large houses, village halls and empty buildings, even after some had been inspected and earmarked for the reception of evacuated mothers and children.'[3] It was natural that rival groups would be fighting for accommodation in the safer parts of the country. The armed forces needed to be able to train in areas undisturbed by the enemy, but equally, companies manufacturing vital war goods wanted factories away from target areas and civilians needed some respite from the bombardment in the cities. Usually the army won the battle for houses.

During 1940, the War Office greatly expanded the number of houses it requisitioned in all parts of the country. By 1941 there were over 2 million British and colonial troops based in England, Scotland and Northern Ireland. The West Country was much favoured after the evacuation of Dunkirk and the fall of France. Far from the continent and sparsely inhabited, it also had ideal countryside for training. Furthermore, there were plenty of large properties that could be taken over. Usually only the officers and battalion HQ occupied the main house. The rest of the regiment was billeted in stables, outbuildings, cottages and tents, and later Nissen huts which provided more permanent accommodation.

Jeffrey Morrell was an eight-year-old boy living at home with his parents near Doncaster when the army arrived, shortly after Dunkirk. The local grand house, Brodsworth Hall, was taken over and tents planted in the grounds while the woods were used for bomb practice. One day, not long after the army had arrived, an officer came to the front door and said to his father: 'We are taking your farm building and house over, Mr Morrell.' Somewhat taken aback, Jeffrey's father enquired when. 'Now!' came the reply. With that the army took over five bedrooms, the dining room and the back kitchen, where they installed a new range. The house became the officers' mess feeding about twenty-five for lunch and supper. The batmen to the officers, about eight of them, lived in a back bedroom on bunk beds. Jeffrey's mother was astonished to discover the cook had previously been the pastry chef at the Savoy Hotel in London.

For Jeffrey this was a thrilling time. Corporal Kay, who was in charge of the officers' mess, used to take him shopping in an army vehicle. They shopped at the local market and the local wine merchants, but the village shops did not benefit from the army's presence as the soldiers had a NAAFI and bought their cigarettes, chocolate and other bits and bobs there. Jeffrey said: 'The village folk didn't come into contact that much with the soldiers and we boys were forbidden from going into the woods to collect souvenirs from the bombs. Didn't always stop us though!'[4] When the 45th Division left for Africa, the 44th Division arrived and took over the set-up. Although Jeffrey found it exciting having the army in the village, his parents were not so amused. 'The army knocked hell out of the furniture and Mum's kitchen. My parents got very little in the way of compensation.'[5]

Sometimes whole villages were taken over, as was the case of Tyneham and Worbarrow in Dorset, which were evacuated in December 1943 and have remained deserted ever since. Poignantly, the villagers of Tyneham left a note on the church door as they evacuated. It read: 'Please treat the church and houses with care; we have given up our homes where many of us lived for generations to help win the war to keep men free. We shall return one day and thank you for treating the village kindly.'[6]

However, they never did return. The villagers felt it was a very heavy price to pay for supporting the war effort, and there have been periodic attempts to fight for Tyneham but none has been successful and it remains a ghost village. Tyneham, Worbarrow and 7,500 acres of land and Jurassic coastline are now managed by the Ministry of Defence and access to the area is still limited as it is part of the Lulworth Ranges, used by the army for training. An unexpected consequence of the occupation is that wildlife has flourished in the area as no modern farming methods have been introduced.

That the army was guilty of vandalism and wanton destruction cannot be denied. John Martin Robinson wrote, 'Some ... treated the buildings better than others, but from the point of view of the owners, occupation of their houses by the armed forces, especially by the army, was the worst fate that could befall them.'[7] There are stories of Van Dycks being used as dartboards and staircases chopped up for firewood, jeeps were driven into carved gates or into lakes where they were found years later. Some houses, such as Warnford Park in Hampshire, were so badly damaged that they had to be demolished. Lowther Castle in Cumbria had to be abandoned and today stands as a carefully restored ruin.

Author Caroline Seebohm was more generous in her summary of the impact of the army on country houses. She looked at the situation from the other side of the story:

> If soldiers were the main culprits in causing damage to houses, it must be remembered that in many cases these were young, inexperienced men, far from home, waiting to be called to action from which they might never return. If they looked around them at all, they saw, not beautiful antique banisters or glorious eighteenth-century mouldings, but grim dormitories, the precincts of death.[9]

However, more often than not it was either neglect or frustration at the inadequate accommodation that was the cause of the greatest damage. For six years no routine maintenance was carried out on properties that were centuries old and in need of constant attention. Roofs remained unrepaired, window frames unpainted and rot untreated, leading to serious problems in Britain's damp climate. These great houses, with their scores of bedrooms and vast entertaining rooms, were not heated. Most had been run by armies of servants who tended fires, carried hot water up and down stairs year in year out, and kept the places warm and cared for a tiny number of pampered inhabitants. It was not unusual for a family of four to be attended by upwards of thirty indoor maids, butlers, housekeepers, cooks and cleaners with a similar number working in the grounds and stables. Without the staff to keep the houses going there were few comforts, not nearly enough bathrooms and sometimes the houses were less attractive or comfortable for their new occupants than a Victorian barracks built for mass accommodation. Evelyn Waugh was unimpressed when he was billeted in Kingsdown House in Kent in January 1940.

The house was derelict and surrounded by little asbestos huts . . .
one bath for sixty men, one wash basin, the WCs all frozen up and
those inside the house without seats. Carpetless, noisy and cold. A
ping-pong table makes one room uninhabitable, a radio the other.
We are five in a bedroom without a coat peg between us.[10]

A fresh wave of requisitioning began when over a million more
American GIs arrived to prepare for the invasion of Europe. Few
of them had left America before and by the time they arrived in
unfamiliar Britain they had suffered a debilitating troopship crossing of the Atlantic in their convoys, dodging submarines, often
landing in Northern Ireland before being billeted who only knew
where. They were put up in remote country villages where no restaurant had even heard of – let alone served – a hamburger. The
lack of showers, central heating and lager led many to feel homesick initially, but some grew to love the pretty countryside and the
quirky English ways. By and large they were welcome guests and
had a good reputation among local communities for putting things
right if they went wrong. A schoolboy in Dorset said that a neigh-
bour had been delighted when his farm, damaged by American
tanks on manoeuvres, was restored within a week. They repaired
all the hedges and even helped out with the harvest, towing the
old-fashioned binding machines with their jeeps. Another group
damaged an ancient gateway leading to a fine manor house but
restored it to its former glory in two days. The owners of Peover
Hall in Cheshire were not so enthusiastic as the farmer in Devon.
The US Third Army was based there and General Patton had his
headquarters in the large Georgian wing in the build-up to D-Day.
In 1944 a fire was started by a soldier and the house was so badly
damaged that the wing was demolished after the war and the
house returned to its pre-Georgian dimensions.

The arrival of Americans in such vast numbers had a major
impact on life in certain areas of Britain. Not only were even more
properties taken over but tented cities sprang up on the edge of
villages or in the grounds of large country houses. The village of

Fowey in Cornwall had the magnificently named USN AATSB, or the United States Naval Advanced Amphibious Training Sub Base, which trained at Pentewan Beach twelve miles to the west. The officers were billeted at Heligan House and 850 men lived in tents. It was said that in the build-up to D-Day it was possible to walk across the river from Fowey to Polruan on American boats and landing craft, a distance of over 400 metres at high tide. Soldiers charged around the tiny narrow lanes in convoys of jeeps, while the village halls shook to jitter-bugging and children crowded around for sweets and chewing gum, which the Americans seemed to have in unlimited quantities. The US military took great trouble to help their men fit into wartime Britain and gave them advice on what to expect from the reserved Englishman or woman. 'If Britons sit in trains or buses without striking up conversation with you, it doesn't mean they are being haughty or unfriendly.'[11] The citizens of Fowey quickly became used to their new guests with their enthusiasm and energetic attitude towards life. Then one day they woke to find the harbour empty and the Americans gone. They, like all the other GIs spread across the south-west, had left the shores for the beaches of Normandy.

The US 333rd Field Artillery Battalion (FAB) arrived in Britain in February 1944 in preparation for the Ardennes offensive, or the Battle of the Bulge. The soldiers were a black battalion from Alabama, a small number of the 130,000 black soldiers billeted in Britain from 1942 onwards. For many inhabitants of the small Cheshire village of Tattenhall, where the US 333rd FAB were housed, it was the first time they had encountered a black man. Equally, the Cheshire countryside provided a novelty for the southern American soldiers: it was the first time they had ever seen snow. They were billeted in and around a house called the Rookery, hunkered under the commanding ruin of Beeston Castle which is situated on a magnificent rock towering over the Cheshire plain and leading the eye westward to north Wales.

Alabama in 1944 was still a segregated state, but that was unknown in Britain and the local community extended warm hospitality and friendship. The soldiers had to be reassured that it was permissible for them to walk on pavements or go into the same pubs, shops and restaurants as their British hosts. Unsurprisingly, this caused a problem and the US Army had to warn its white soldiers that it was acceptable in Britain for people to socialise together regardless of the colour of their skin. Longmate wrote: 'Relations between the coloured GIs and British civilians were always excellent, but some serious disorders occurred between white and coloured Americans.'[12] There were one or two well-publicised incidents where fights ended with fatalities. In Kingsclere near Newbury in Hampshire a group of black soldiers took exception to being shut out of a pub and attacked the premises with rifle fire. Several people died including the wife of the publican. Tragic though these few incidents were, they were not the experience of the majority. When the 333rd Field Artillery Battalion left Tattenhall in summer sunshine six months after they had arrived in snow, one of the soldiers, Private George Davis, wrote, 'We have found Paradise'. Wretchedly, many of them were killed or captured near Antwerp. Davis was one of eleven soldiers who became separated from the rest and was hidden by a sympathetic Dutch farmer, only to be betrayed by a Nazi sympathiser and brutally murdered by the Germans at Wereth.

Wollaton Hall in Nottinghamshire played host to the 508th Parachute Regiment from Camp Blanding in Florida. They arrived in Belfast in early January 1944 and spent a bitterly cold month at Portstewart before transferring to Wollaton Hall to take over one of the more unusual of Britain's requisitioned properties. The men were housed in tents in the grounds below the house and were catered for by field kitchens, but the officers used the hall itself as a mess. Wollaton Hall is a spectacular Elizabethan mansion that stands at the top of a low hill, dominating the park and countryside around it. It had belonged to the Willoughby family between 1580 and 1925, when the eleventh Baron Middleton, Michael Willoughby, sold it to Nottingham Council who converted it into a natural history museum. When the officers of the 508th arrived at their new home they found a large collection of stuffed animals and birds, including an ostrich, a giraffe, a puma, a silver-back gorilla, kangaroos, turtles, a magnificent albatross and a shark as well as thousands of insects, geology and botany specimens.

One of the officers in the regiment was Captain William 'Bill' Nation, from Texas. He made three short films on an eight-millimetre cine camera of the regiment's stay at Wollaton Hall which he sent back, unprocessed, to his parents before he left the hall in December 1944. The film was silent and initially there was no indication as to the location of the 508th regiment, but Nation's parents worked out where their son had been by piecing together clues, such as one of the men posing as Robin Hood next to a tree. A commentary was added after the war and is an enchanting insight into the lives of the young American parachutists prior to their introduction into occupied Europe: 'We loved it there, the people, the quaint pubs and inns, the girls. Friendly pubs and families took us in and made us feel part of home life.'[13]

The narrative goes on: 'I enjoyed visiting Nottingham Palladium where they had big band music and dancing and many, many girls who wanted to dance with the soldiers. We busted our butts during the daylight hours getting the camp ready but once the sun set we busted those same butts in town . . .'[14]

It is hard to remember the training in the lovely Nottinghamshire countryside was setting them up for the terrifying prospect of jumping out of an aeroplane in the dark into enemy territory, with trees and swamps and other unseen hazards between the sky and the ground, before they met a single German. By June the 508th were ready to be included in the D-Day attacks. They left Folkingham on the night of 5 June and fought bravely over the next thirty-three days, sustaining over 300 casualties. In September, the 508th took part in Operation Market Garden at Arnhem with a further 681 casualties. By November they had regrouped in France and on 31 January 1945 Bill Nation was killed when his command post was hit by shells. He never saw the film footage he shot the previous summer and his parents would only piece together the last months of their son's life much later. He was one of the half of his regiment who would not return to the United States. Wollaton Hall was vacated by September 1944 and the stuffed animals, birds and fish remained undisturbed for the rest of the war.

In the south and the east, the coastal counties of Britain were under threat of attack for most of the war. Melford Hall, Holy Trinity Church and Kentwell Hall form a striking triangle of buildings in the Suffolk village of Long Melford. So striking, according to recent research, that Luftwaffe pilots and navigators were ordered not to bomb them. They used them as a landmark with which to orientate themselves as they flew over the coast at Felixstowe, some thirty miles east as the crow flies. The prosperous market town of Long Melford was on the second line of defence during the Second World War. The first line of defence ran from Colchester to Beccles and was designed as forward boundaries for reserves moving up to confront an invader. If the first line fell, the second line would become critical as a defensive line.

Colchester, a garrison town just eighteen miles south and home of the 4th Infantry Division, was swollen by 1st Battalion East Surrey Regiment, 1st Battalion Oxfordshire and Buckinghamshire Light Infantry as well as other field and anti-tank regiments. The port of Ipswich is twenty-three miles to the east of the town. The Germans targeted Ipswich docks and the surrounding areas where a large munitions factory was placed. It was clear that Long Melford would be involved in one way or another; the question was not if but who would occupy the main buildings and when. Kentwell Hall was requisitioned as a major army transit camp throughout the war and as an assembly point for troops preparing for the D-Day landings in 1944.

A succession of regiments used Melford Hall and its extensive grounds for training; each regiment staying some four to six months and then moving on. In 1937, Arthur Oswald, writing in *Country Life*, described Melford Hall externally as 'one of the most perfect Tudor houses that have come down to us. Its beautifully balanced design and picturesquely varied outline alike reflected the ideals of the age in which it was built. Order and symmetry on one hand, lavishness and variety on the other were equally delightful to the Elizabethans.'[15] James Lees-Milne was also enchanted by the house when he visited, writing: 'The motorist arriving from the south has a most tantalising glimpse over the wall of towers, cupolas, twisted chimneys and tufted trees. A turreted gatehouse in the style of, but much later than the house is a prelude of what is to come. It is the entrance to the short drive, which leads to a circular gravel sweep before the Hall.'[16]

Melford Hall was nearly five hundred years old and parts of it were even older, dating back to the eleventh century, when it had been used by the abbots of Bury St Edmunds. The Hyde Parker family had owned the hall since 1786. Sir William Hyde Parker, who had fought in the South African War and the First World War, offered Melford Hall to the War Office at the beginning of the war and it was accepted, though it would have been requisitioned had he not offered it. It was used initially as a training camp and then as a starting off point for soldiers heading into occupied Europe, including American troops in the build-up to D-Day. In 1939, the Hyde Parker family consisted of Sir William and Lady Ulla, an artist of Danish descent, who had met her English baronet when she accompanied her father, the Old Testament scholar Christian Ditlef-Nielsen, to London. She had been studying art in Copenhagen but gave it up to marry in 1931. Their first child, a son, Richard, was born in 1937; two years later, Lady Ulla was expecting their second child. She wrote in a memoir: 'On 3 September 1939 war was declared, and that same day our little daughter Beth was born. While I was still in bed after her birth, the army took over the house as the second defence line ran through the park. 105 officers and 100 men moved into Melford Hall, and subsequently hundreds more men were billeted in Nissen huts in the park and grounds.'[17]

Sir William was waiting to join his old regiment, though at forty-seven years of age he knew he would not see active service abroad. Meanwhile he joined the Home Guard, but was badly injured in the blackout when his car was involved in a crash with an army lorry. His injuries were so severe that he had to be sent to London where 'Sir Harold Giles performed the operation and subsequent plastic surgery to save his face from being completely disfigured for life.'[18] Sir Harold told Lady Hyde Parker that Sir William would need complete rest and total quiet for several months in order to recover his strength. Long Melford was bristling with soldiers in training and was far from quiet so was clearly unsuitable for a convalescent. Eventually Lady Ulla had the idea to ring Sir William's cousin Beatie, who she had met on several visits to the Lake District. This was Beatrix Potter, now in her seventies. She had spent a great deal of time at Melford Hall at the end of the nineteenth century sketching architectural details, the garden and the servants' quarters for her children's books. Jeremy Fisher's pond is the ancient fish pond at Melford Hall; the fireplace in *The Tailor of Gloucester* is a perfect copy of the one in the servants' kitchen, and both Jemima Puddle-Duck and the Foxy Whiskered Gentleman were sketched in the family visitors' book.

When Ulla rang, Beatie's immediate response was warm and generous: 'Come here; bring him and the little ones. I will find somewhere for you to stay.' [19] So off they went. Lady Ulla and the nanny, a local girl called Sibyl May Kitchen, packed up the pram, cots, baby bath and baggage onto a trailer behind a large hired car. 'Willie and I sat on the back seat with little Beth in a carry cot at our feet. Richard sat on Nanny's knee in front, and Mr Young, the owner of the car and the garage in Melford, drove us.'[20]

Sir William was weak and very ill so it took the party two days to reach Castle Cottage. Beatrix Potter gasped when she saw the state of her cousin, greeting him and Lady Ulla with 'Oh my dears!' She had arranged for them to say at the local inn but the landlady was also horrified by Willie's condition and told them that she could not take responsibility for such a sick man. Beatrix offered them Hill Top. This was her own home and the place where she went to be quiet when she needed peace. When she had married, she'd shut the door and turned the key in the lock. She and William Heelis would never live there. Beatrix said to Ulla: 'You know and understand what Hill Top means to me, therefore I shall let you all live there. No one has slept there since I left.'[21] That had been twenty-six years earlier, in 1913.

> Soon we were installed at Hill Top Farm. I do hope Cousin Beatie realised how grateful I was. Willie improved greatly there. He and Cousin Willie [Heelis] spent much time together, mostly fishing when Cousin Willie was free to do so. The children, the house and the cooking kept Nanny and me very busy, especially as the house did not have the same conveniences as Melford. Coal was kept in the old pigsty, and we collected kindling and wood in the little spinney nearby. We used an oil stove for cooking. The peace and simplicity of lovely Hill Top farm did us all a great deal of good. The horrors of war and of the Gestapo in occupied countries, like my native Denmark, seemed further off. [22]

The family spent a year living in the Lake District. Sir William's health improved and everyone benefitted from the outdoor life in that beautiful corner of Cumbria. In 1941, they returned to a house called the Grange on the village green in Long Melford and observed with some alarm the transformations that had taken place in the village and, most of all, at the hall. Regiments spent up to six months at the hall and each introduced their own changes. The herbaceous borders had been removed and the land around the hall was littered with Nissen huts for up to 1,000 men. The cookhouse was close to the entrance gates and the army had constructed a sewerage pit in the gardens. The hall already had gas in each room but the army introduced wiring for electricity and brought huge water tanks into the attics.

A recent find under floorboards in Melford Hall revealed some delightful everyday details about life there during the war. Private R. H. Bell of the Berkshire Regiment used the Clacton Steam Laundry Ltd to service one shirt, two vests, one pair of pants, one pair of socks and a towel per week. The finds also show that Mars

bars have barely changed their logo in almost a century and that soldiers had been entitled to Cadbury's Ration Chocolate, presumably
supplied through the NAAFI. Other items found include darts, leave
passes and a battered copy of Norman Lindsay's uproariously funny
novel *The Cautious Amorist* from 1932.

Richard and Beth Hyde Parker were now old enough to understand some of what was going on in the village around them. They
lived opposite the entrance to the hall and would lean out of the
windows to watch the comings and goings. Beth remembered
riding on the back of her mother's Great Dane who ambled up to
the guard on the gate who took hold of the dog's collar, turned it
around and patting it on the bottom sent it back across the green
to where it had come from. Richard described the war as 'fun
and hell all mixed up'. Another boy of a similar age described his
memories of Long Melford during the war years. 'It saw change
overnight, it was no longer safe for young children to cross the
road alone. There were military vehicles, dispatch riders and tanks
along with the familiar sight of horses pulling farm carts. There
were also squads of soldiers being drilled up and down the road,
but even they had to give way occasionally to animals being driven
to market in Sudbury or to a change of pasture.'[23] There were men
charging around on foot, carrying out manoeuvres; there were
army vehicles of all shapes and sizes coming in and out of the
entrance to the hall and Richard recalled how astonished he was by
the size of the American lorries that thundered down the long high
street in the build-up to D-Day. Beth agreed with the memory: 'I
leant out of the nursery window as the Yanks arrived. They were
the biggest trucks I had ever seen, driven by black men with hats
askew. They sometimes kicked one foot out of the cab door and
they chewed on cigars rather than smoking them.'[24] Above them,
the skies were full of B24 and B17 aircraft that flew from two large
bomber stations, RAF Lavenham and RAF Sudbury nearby. This
peaceful corner of the country had come alive with round-the-
clock activity and preparations.

One of Richard's strongest recollections was of the Grange's cellar during the air raids in 1944. 'If the sirens went off we went into the cellar, which smelled of white wash and egg preserving liquid.' Being physically close to his parents, nanny and the evacuees made a great impression on him. He loved the smell of the blankets and the warmth of human bodies so close together. V2 rockets came from Norway and landed in the pond, in a hay stack and further away in the woods. The hall was never hit, either by a V2 or by German bombers earlier in the war, but the surrounding area came under attack because of the airfields close by. Once, three schoolboys found an unexploded bomb after an air raid. It had fallen in Stanstead Great Wood a couple of miles to the north of the village. The woods were cordoned off but the boys could not resist the temptation. Arthur Kemp, then ten years old, described seeing a bomb flight sticking out of the ground. It was about three inches long and the whole bomb was eight inches in diameter. It had German writing on it and a button. They picked up the bomb and gingerly carried it back through the village to the primary school, taking turns to carry it in twos as it was very heavy. They laid it carefully out on the grass about three metres from the school buildings and rang the doorbell of the headmaster's house. His wife opened the door, saw the bomb and fainted. Her husband took charge, sending the boys through to the school yard where they were told to stand with their hands against the wall until the bomb had been made safe. They were given a severe ticking off by the army disposal squad, who took the bomb away and blew it up in the park beyond Melford Hall. The following day they were caned for their dangerous actions but it did not stop Arthur Kemp looking out for other war booty over the next few years of the war.

The army's occupation of Melford Hall resulted in several disasters for the house, the most catastrophic of which happened in February 1942 when the Berkshire Regiment held a fundraising ball at Melford Hall for war savings week. Sir William and Lady Hyde Parker were invited. Lady Hyde Parker was somewhat shocked to see a bar set up in the library but the ball was a success and raised enough money to buy two Bren gun carriers. Late in the evening a small group of junior officers broke into the north wing, which was strictly out of bounds as it housed the family's stored treasures, including a bed that had been slept in by Queen Elizabeth in 1578 when she was on a visit to Suffolk. In one of the bedrooms they set up a roulette table, something the local girls who were invited to the ball had never seen before. They played roulette and cards and drank heavily. It was a bitterly cold night so one of the soldiers set a fire in the hearth to warm the room. In the early hours they crept back into the main hall and thence to their village billets.

The following morning was cold and frosty. A gardener, up at an early hour spotted smoke billowing out of the chimney in the north wing, then saw flames leaping from the roof. He immediately called Sir William who rushed out of the Grange in his pyjamas and gave orders to summon the fire brigade. They received the call at 8.03am according to the *Lavenham Press* from the report written up in *Firefighting in Suffolk,* but struggled with their thirteen pumps and hoses which had frozen. The pond was frozen too and Sir William had trouble breaking the ice.

The *East Anglian Daily Times* reported the fire a week later:

> Long Melford, Hadleigh, Ipswich, Clare and Sudbury Brigades were all engaged with a dozen pumps working at full pressure and a network of hoses running through the grounds from the river whose water was incessantly poured upon the flames from many jets. The roof of the north wing soon collapsed while parts of the walls also came crashing down, leaving the interior a raging inferno. The flames were making headway through the middle section which connects the south wing, and, for a time, it seems as if the whole of the mansion would be involved . . .[25]

Over the course of the day the fire brigade worked tirelessly to contain the fire, fighting it and eventually cutting it off in the roof of the Long Gallery in the west wing. When it was finally extinguished the damage could be assessed. The north wing was completely gutted and stood as an empty, smouldering shell. The west wing had lost its roof to the flames, though later it was the damage caused by the water that was the biggest blight. The wing was beset with dry rot.

Mercifully none of the fire-fighters lost their lives but one man suffered a broken leg. Meanwhile, Lady Ulla was busy at the scene, trying to persuade the officers housed in the hall to help clear out the precious works of art and other treasures stored in the north wing. The colonel refused to oblige so she ran to the Nissen huts and urged the men to help, which they did willingly, forming a human chain to rescue as much as they could from the wing. Lady Ulla was at the head of the chain, selecting the most vital and important works. All this time the fire was raging in the roof above and the north wing was becoming ever more dangerous. One of the men in the chain realised they had moved everything they safely could and pulled Lady Ulla out of the burning building just as a huge chandelier came crashing down behind her. His actions almost certainly saved her life. Left behind in the blaze was a large painting by George Stubbs, a Titian and the Elizabethan four-poster bed.

Photographs from the immediate aftermath of the fire show the smouldering ruins of the north wing and the almost completely destroyed roof of the west wing. The frozen ground in front of the hall was littered with tables, chairs, pictures, ornaments. There was great sympathy locally for Sir William and Lady Hyde Parker, who had lost so many of their treasures. A contemporary, anonymous account said: 'It was a strange sight to see furniture, paintings, silver, armaments and carpets and curtains laying on the lawns while the descending snow quickly covered them all with its white blanket and long icicles hung from the black charred walls of the burnt-out wing.'

While no one ever admitted responsibility for the blaze, the cause was never in doubt. The officers who had sneaked into the north wing had lit a fire on the hearth in the absence of a grate and this had burned into a beam which smouldered all night and eventually caught fire. No one understood why the colonel had refused to help Lady Ulla to rescue her possessions from the north wing until it transpired, in a court martial, that there was an illegal stash of ammunition in the cellar of the wing. One can only imagine what might have happened if that stash had ignited.

After the fire was extinguished Sir William was nowhere to be seen. A search party was sent out, anxious that he might have been overwhelmed by the disaster that had befallen his home, but he was found on horseback in the woods marking oak trees. He was determined from the moment he saw the damage that he would rebuild the hall and that he would devote all his resources and energy to the restoration, as well as a great quantity of seasoned oak.

The last regiment to use Melford Hall as a training base was the Royal Hampshire in 1944. They remained there for almost six months in the build-up to D-Day and were visited by the King in late June. The local newspaper reported that George VI went to Long Melford to inspect spearhead troops assembled for the Normandy invasion. A local girl called Mary Young remembered the visit clearly as her father, Harold Young, was a special constable involved in organising security for the King. He arranged for Mary to stand on the bridge parapet in order to get a good view of him as he passed by in his car: 'He looked very small with a yellow face. I think he was accompanied by General Alexander. I could see my father in the distance, forming a cordon across the road with other special constables, to allow the King to pass through the Hall gates.'[26]

Sir William Hyde Parker would never again live in his family home, Melford Hall. He died before the restoration on the great building had been completed. Like other properties that were sadly abused through occupation by the armed forces, it was remarkable that the short but ferocious period of war activity could undo centuries of architectural heritage through carelessness and neglect.

CONCLUSION

Restoration and Reintegration

It isn't always to the advantage of a property to be swallowed up by our capacious if benevolent maw. These pious reflections came to me in the bath this morning.

James Lees-Milne, 1 June 1945

On the night of 2 September 1939, the last night of peace, there had been a tremendous thunderstorm. 'As if nature were determined to round the war off tidily, there was also a torrential downpour during the early hours of VE Day, Tuesday 8th May 1945, but this time people woken by the noise went peacefully to sleep again, free at last from the fear of bombs.'[1] This was Norman Longmate's attempt to book-end his remarkable survey of life on the home front in the Second World War with a tidy flourish. As I wrote at the beginning, history is messy and no more so when there has been a world war raging for six years. The weather might have tidy but the country was in a state of extreme untidiness. However, before people began to take stock there were celebrations.

All over the country street parties were held to mark the end of the war in Europe and communities made a special effort to entertain the children, especially those who had known nothing but war in their short lives. Grocers handed over their sweet and jelly stocks to the organisers; mothers and older siblings gave up their sweet rations to provide a feast the like of which most of the children had never seen or tasted in their lives. Some had their first taste of ice cream; one little boy in Burnley ate thirteen jam tarts. Yet for others, older and bruised by the war, there was less celebrating and more contemplation. The prolific novelist Dame Barbara Cartland wrote in her autobiography:

> We were glad, but still our hearts refused to sing, the shadow of war still lay over us in a restriction of freedom, in controls and coupons. We had only to look at our empty larders, empty store cupboards and half-empty coal cellars to know war had not receded very far from our daily lives. To practically everyone in Great Britain the war had brought the loss of someone they loved – either man, woman or child – and for many there were crippled bodies or blinded eyes as a legacy from the nights of terror and fire.[2]

VE Day marked the beginning of the end of the most destructive war in history. Unlike the First World War which ended when the fighting ceased, the Second World War was drawn out by the continued fighting in the Far East. It was only brought to its conclusion by the dropping of two atomic bombs on the Japanese cities of Hiroshima and Nagasaki, an act of war which polarised society but led to the release of tens of thousands of prisoners of the Japanese, both civilian and POW, my grandfather included.

At home, Britain had changed out of all recognition. A day before VJ Day, 14 August 1945, a minute for the cabinet came from the Treasury's economist, J. Maynard Keynes. It summed up a grim situation for the country which was now faced with 'a financial Dunkirk'.

> Lend-lease, sure enough, was terminated abruptly. With external deinvestment amounting to four thousand million pounds; with her shipping, an important source of invisible exports, reduced

by thirty per cent; with her civilian industries severely run down after six years of war and her visible exports running at no more than four-tenths of her pre-war level; with 355,000 of her citizens dead by enemy action at home or abroad; with bread rationing looming ahead and spirit and flesh rebelling against further effort, the nation could consider only wanly the good fortune which had spared her the destiny of Germany, or Russia, or Japan.[3]

Physically the country had changed too: criss-crossed by corps lines, dotted with pill boxes, observation posts and surrounded by barbed wire, it would take years to dismantle the hardware constructed to protect Britain. The great cities and many towns had suffered serious damage from the years of aerial bombardment. Two million homes had been damaged or destroyed and over 2.25 million people had been made homeless. For those returning from the countryside to the cities the future looked bleak, with little temporary housing in situ and a shortage of building materials to hand. The government set a restriction of £25 per household for building and repair works, hardly sufficient to turn a bomb-damaged house into a habitable home. Then there were the returning servicemen and women. A lucky few were welcomed back to a familiar house by their own family with a warm embrace, but for many, too many, life had changed so dramatically that it took weeks, months, sometimes years to adjust. Children born in the late 1930s were now six years older and more independent. Spouses had grown apart through circumstance and marriages were severely strained. The divorce rate in England and Wales reached an all-time high in November 1947.

Yet people are resilient, especially the young, and there was, amongst austerity and continued rationing, a determination to move forwards. In June 1945 Britain voted in a new government. There was a young and universally popular health service on the horizon and social mobility had given a generation the confidence that class barriers could be crossed in the future. Help for housing came in the form of the prefabricated house, or 'prefab', a triumph of space planning and mod cons. Each house had two bedrooms, a living room, fitted kitchen with both hot and cold running water, a cooker and built-in refrigerator and a fitted bathroom with a heated towel rail. For those who had been homeless or living in Victorian tenements, these little houses spelled luxury. By 1949 more than 156,600 were helping to plug the gap in housing while more permanent houses were constructed.

For the land and country house owners at the other end of the social spectrum, the end of the Second World War ushered in a new era of great change. In Britain as a whole almost a thousand country houses were lost in the decade after the war, nearly all of them as a result of damage caused by wartime occupancy or by neglect for their upkeep, some wilful but often just because there was no one in charge to maintain them. 'While not as thoroughgoing as the dissolution of the monasteries in the sixteenth century, [this] can only be paralleled in English cultural history by the architectural losses of the Reformation,'[4] wrote John Martin Robinson. In that respect the climate, rather than the occupants, was the greatest adversary with damp the number one enemy for wooden window frames, doors and roof beams. In an era when almost everyone smoked the risk of fire was immense. 'Casually discarded cigarettes were lethal when combined with the ancient dust, dry woodwork and straw insulation of old houses'[5]. Several burned down as a result of fire caused by carelessness, such as smoking or over-stacked fires that caused chimney conflagrations. Another reason for the loss of the great houses was financial. The Labour government set the top rate of tax at 98 per cent in 1945 and death duties were ratcheted up twice in four years, meaning crippling payments for cash-poor owners.

Coleshill House, home of the Auxiliary Units from 1940 to 1944, was returned to the Pleydell-Bouverie family in early 1945. Although it had sustained a fair degree of wear and tear as a result of its wartime occupation, the destruction of one of the magnificent seventeenth-century gate piers and the wall of the service court in an accidental explosion were the only serious architectural casualties. The grounds were gradually cleared of the military hardware but the woods still had traces of concrete footings. The estate had suffered three lots of death duties since the beginning of the century, so after consultation with the family, the sisters decided to hand it over to the National Trust. 'This could not be done without a considerable endowment for which funds were not available, so it was sold to Ernest Cook at considerably below market price, on condition that he, the millionaire behind Thomas Cook, the travel agents, passed it on sufficiently endowed, at his death, to the NT.'[6] Cook was a preservationist with a keen interest in English country houses and their estates. He sometimes purchased them for their architectural merit but at other times because they were famous hunting estates. By the time he bought Coleshill he already owned Montacute, the Bath Assembly Rooms, Hartwell and a dozen other properties. Katharine Pleydell-Bouverie moved to Kilmington Manor in Wiltshire where she built another kiln, this time an oil-fired one. She returned to her pottery and continued to work until her death in 1985. Mollie moved to Elcombe near Swindon.

In September 1952, builders were completing the final restoration touches at Coleshill when a fire broke out. Farmers, estate workers, villagers and those who had been working on the house rushed to help remove as many valuables as they could carry. 'Only when the molten lead cascaded from the roof did we give up,' said Mr Williams, a local farmer. Everything but a few heavier pieces of furniture was removed and then the rescuers could only stand back and watch in horror: 'Suddenly a wave of heat swept over the spectators and a mushroom of yellow smoke rose skywards as the second floor caved in, whilst firemen continued in vain to play water on the flames from a turntable ladder.' They took water from the river Cole, pumped via the goldfish pond in front of the house. 'Even this was inadequate to meet demand and the goldfish were soon left floundering in the mud.'[7]

The fire started in the roof by a builder leaving a blowtorch lit. Despite the valiant efforts of firemen from three counties the water supply was so inadequate that they could not even contain the fire, much less put it out. It burned fiercely for ten hours by which time the damage was so complete that the house had to be pulled down.

Ernest Cook was said to be too distraught to make any comment in the immediate aftermath of the blaze.

Only the ground plan of the house survives today, marked out by little box hedges. The outbuildings and stables are still standing and guided trips around the grounds and into the woods show the visitor where the Auxiliary Units were trained. The property is owned and managed by the National Trust and the memory of the Auxiliary Units at Coleshill is kept alive by an active group called CART (Coleshill Auxiliary Research Team), which runs the British Resistance Archive.

In the summer of 1944 the army left Melford Hall and the Hyde Parker family were able to survey the ruins of their former home. Apart from the devastating fire of 1942 and the general demolition of the garden and the herbaceous borders, the most aggravating thing the army did was to raid Sir William's excellent wine cellar. What piqued him more than anything else was the discovery that someone had taken the trouble to refill the empty bottles with water and replace the corks to look as if nothing had happened. As there were a dozen regiments that used the hall over the five years it was occupied it was impossible to establish who was guilty of this theft and deceit.

Sir William had, from the moment the fire was under control, sworn that he would rebuild the hall to its former glory. Lady Hyde Parker was determined to find an architect who could do the work sympathetically, although most professional advice was to pull the north wing down as it was so badly damaged. She approached Sir Albert Edward Richardson, who was regarded as one of the leading architects of the era and who had already established a reputation for pioneering work in bombed-out London. He was responsible for the conservation and restoration of many London landmarks, including Nelson's stairs at Somerset House, also known as the Navy Stairs; St James Church, Piccadilly and Trinity House in the City of London. To her delight, Sir Albert agreed to take on the restoration of Melford Hall and he succeeded in blending modern construction techniques with the Tudor design that matched the rest of the house. He designed a concrete frame within the burnt-out brick shell to support the new floors and roof. The layout of the wing was influenced by Lady Hyde Parker who chose to replace the former dark interiors and heavy oak furnishings with a Danish-inspired design of bright, light walls and floors. Between them, Sir Albert and Lady Hyde Parker took great trouble to find suitable older materials from other houses that were not to be saved in order to restore features such as staircases.

The painstaking work to reconstruct Melford Hall took six years and the family reoccupied the house in 1951, twelve years after they had moved out. Tragically, Sir William died just months before the family was due to move back in. He was only fifty-nine and his children thought the combination of his war service in South Africa and during the First World War, the horrific car crash at the beginning of this war and the distress over the fire of 1942 contributed to his early demise. Crippling death duties resulted in Lady Ulla offering the hall and its land to the National Trust. This was turned down as the hall was thought to be uneconomical. However, Lady Hyde Parker would not give up. She resolved to save the Hall and prove to the Trust it could be made to pay its way. She wrote: 'Houses like Melford are not just bricks and mortar – surely they are like all other beautiful things, manifestations of what takes place when spirit and matter meet. Melford is an expression of our deep desire for beauty and perfection, which is something very vital to us all. It must go on living – which means giving, contributing to life and life as we know it today.'[8]

She arranged various rooms to be set up as 'show rooms' and to be opened to the public for a fee and wrote a guidebook for the hall. On open days Nanny would sit by the front door and collect the admission fees. Eventually, in 1960, the National Trust was convinced of the economic argument for Melford Hall being open to the public and they agreed to take it into their care. Lady Ulla was to act as the administrator and lived as a tenant in the north wing that she had redesigned.

In the 1970s, Lady Ulla's son, Sir Richard, returned to live at Melford Hall with his wife, Jeanie. They made further improvements, including a full-scale renovation of the south wing, which had barely been touched since the army left in 1944. This allowed bedrooms in the west wing to be opened to the public, and in time they also created a museum room which was dedicated to the Beatrix Potter connection with Melford.

The hall survived because of the passion and tenacity of Sir William and Lady Hyde Parker. In all, some forty country houses were lost in Suffolk over the course of the twentieth century. After the war the severe lack of building material and builders added to house owners' woes while high death duties and low compensation from the government made many financially unviable. Yet despite this gloomy assessment, a large number of country houses did survive, especially those in the hands of owners who were flexible enough to look into the future and imagine life without armies of servants. There is no doubt that the National Trust played a major role in rescuing a number of houses for the nation when their owners had no way of keeping them going. Sometimes the houses taken over by the Trust received donations of art collections from other houses. Montacute House in Somerset was the recipient of a magnificent collection of twenty-five old masters from the collection of Lord Crawford of Haigh Hall. James Lees-Milne wrote: 'He is packing up and leaving the place for good. I said how sad it must be for him. He looked desperately unhappy for a moment and replied, "Really, it is just terrible how much I mind".'[8]

Sounding an optimistic note, John Martin Robinson wrote in *The Country House at War*: 'The amazing thing after 1945 is not that so many country houses were given up and demolished in the aftermath of the Second World War as that the majority were restored and revived ... The younger generation was more energetic and determined to make a go of it. Having won the war, they were not going to be daunted by dry rot and collapsing ceilings.'[9]

Blenheim Palace had suffered badly from general neglect and lack of maintenance over the six years of the war. The Ministry of Works was responsible for the restoration of the palace and was dismayed to discover the extent of the damage: 'The roof was defective in many areas, with rain pouring into the attics. The ministry discovered that the south-east tower was leaning so badly that it needed to be rebuilt from the ground up. The Duke of Marlborough decided to make the structural repairs and the reinstatement of the state rooms his priorities. The upper floors were left empty, and the family continued to live in the east wing as they had done during the war.'[10]

The enormous cost of the restoration focused the duke's mind on the future of the palace. It had been open as a tourist attraction before the war and in 1950 it was reopened to the public, not as John Martin Robinson wrote, 'as a *noblesse oblige* gesture but as a money-making business, just as several other of the largest houses in England were doing at that time. In retrospect, it was the houses which opened to the public in the aftermath of the war that secured their own long-term future.'[11] Today, Blenheim Palace remains one of the country's most spectacular visitor attractions and has World Heritage status, with the upkeep paid for by the annual visitor fees.

The duke wrote to the headmaster of Malvern College, Canon Gaunt, after the war to say that the boys had done less damage to the palace than any of the subsequent occupants. However, two boys had stolen the two smallest pipes from the magnificent Willis Organ – the largest organ in a private house in Europe with over 2,300 pipes. They were never found and the school paid for replacements after the war. Decades later, the widow of one of the two thieves sent the pipes back to Malvern College after his death. It had been a silly prank and he always felt that the pipes should be returned but never quite got around to plucking up the courage to do it. The school has never revealed the identity of the boy out of respect for his widow but Blenheim now has the original pipes in the Willis Organ.

Malvern College was back in its own surroundings by the beginning of the autumn term in 1946. Relief at being safely home was tempered by frustration that the government resolutely refused to compensate the college for the large loss of earnings resulting from the second evacuation to Harrow in 1942 which had taken place at such short notice. The headmaster and governors felt they could not reasonably charge the parents more than two thirds of the term's fees but they were obliged to pay their staff and all other school expenses. This left them with a shortfall of £4,500 – worth approximately £180,000 now. The chairman of governors, Lord Cobham, began a lengthy correspondence with the Ministry of Education trying to right this wrong. For two years he was fobbed off with excuses that the responsibility for his request fell between the Department of Education, the Ministry of Works and the War Office. In the end nothing was paid and the reasons hinted at, though never made explicit, was the government feared that if they reimbursed Malvern for a legitimate claim there would be a slew of claims from other institutions with grievances and that was something they were keen to avoid.

There is a sad footnote to the Malvern College story that provides a reminder of the enormous sacrifice made during the war by those who left their countries of occupied Europe to train in Britain and return to fight. Of the sixty-three Free French boys who were trained at Malvern, 'thirty-five died when they returned to France with the Army of Liberation and led the newly-raised, enthusiastic, but untrained militia into battle.'[12] There is a memorial bench outside number 5 house at Malvern which commemorates their stay.

Getting compensation from the Ministry of Works to pay for damage to properties was a convoluted and often drawn out procedure. From the outset it had been clear that regular insurance companies could not be responsible for paying war damage claims and the War Damages Act, updated several times during the war, was introduced to deal with property owners. Lord Rothschild had multiple claims for damages to Waddesdon Manor, the majority of which arose from the presence of the petrol depot in the grounds and troop activity and manoeuvres in the park. The Ministry of Works and Planning, the War Office and the RAF had between them taken over 136 acres of land at Waddesdon and a further thirty-four acres at the Rothschild's farm, Eythrope, plus six miles of metalled road, all of which had been thoroughly wrecked. Road repairs, replacement fencing, the removal of corrugated iron and brick shelters, ammunition huts, concrete standings and so on came to £19,836 (a project cost today over £1.6 million). The arguments over which department should pay for what part of each claim rumbled on well into the 1950s, but in the end it would seem that Lord Rothschild's claims for the estate were settled.

James and Dorothy oversaw and paid for the restoration of the interior of Waddesdon Manor personally, returning it to its former glory. The house survived the war despite a flood on the very last morning when someone left a bath tap running and the water cascaded into rooms falling 'plumb onto the pictorial marquetry of the writing table given by his friends to Beaumarchais in 1781, and spread from there to a pile of books which were also stored in the Baron's room.'[13] Once the children's cots and tables were cleared the scars of war showed through, mostly below adult waist level. The silk wallpaper in the Red Drawing Room was damaged by sticky finger marks and chalk but the worst damage was to the red damask curtains which had rotted beyond repair in the sunlight that had been allowed to stream into the rooms. Dorothy wrote:

> Following the departure of the children we were confronted with the problem of what to do with the house. Shortages of every sort in the post-war period included a shortage of personnel and the idea of re-instating Waddesdon for us two old people seemed out of the question. But something had to be done: we could not leave all the contents of the house in a few rooms, stacked up to the ceiling . . . It was then that the solution of the National Trust began to germinate in my husband's mind and I cannot say how thankful I am that it did.[14]

With a great deal of effort and dedication, the Rothschilds refurbished the damaged walls and reinstated the furniture, paintings and porcelain so that they had something to offer to the National Trust rather than just a shell of a house full of stored art. After initial misgivings, the Trust agreed to take over the house. Lord Esher, an influential member, had told the trustees that he hated French furniture. Others on the board were concerned that the house was too modern but Lord Crawford, the Trust's chairman, persuaded his colleagues of the value of the outstanding collections. James Lees-Milne was despatched to Waddesdon in May 1946 to give his opinion. He was impressed: 'What a house! An 1880 pastiche of a French Premier château. Yet it is impressive because it is on a grand scale. There is symmetry, and craftsmanship and finish. I suppose most people today would pronounce it hideous. I find it compelling ... In all a better Cliveden. I have written a report, which is by no means contemptuous, upon it.'[15]

It was decided that a management committee should be established, to be chaired by a family member, and a large endowment ensured the family's continued financing of operations. The endowment was intended to be large enough to ensure that the maintenance of Waddesdon would not cost the National Trust a penny. The Treasury initially argued that the endowment was too generous and ought to be taxed but eventually it was agreed and Dorothy wrote later: 'experience has shown very clearly that the amount needed to maintain Waddesdon had been correctly gauged by its donor, but only thanks to wise subsequent investment.'[16] James de Rothschild died in May 1957, the year before the manor was handed over to the National Trust. Dorothy moved out of Waddesdon and into Ethyrope, the farm that her husband had inherited from Miss Alice at the same time as the manor. She lived there until her death in 1988, remaining constantly active and involved in her former home and its history.

The Cedars operated as a children's home until 1952 when the youngest boy left school and went to university. All that time Dorothy and James continued to take a lively interest in the children, their wellbeing and their development. When one of the boys developed severe emotional problems the psychiatrist called in to examine him liaised with Dorothy, presumably because she and James were paying for the treatment. The boy was eventually sent to a boarding school in Chichester from where he wrote to her in

December 1945 to thank her for the book token she sent him for Christmas and to tell her he was still playing chess with the set they had given him when he left Waddesdon. Most of the Cedar Boys kept in touch and Dorothy received letters over the years from all corners of the world, telling her of their various activities. She wrote: 'Their careers are diverse; one is the Assistant Agent to a big estate in England; another, also in England, is a Master baker. One is the head green-keeper at the Caesarea golf course in Israel and others are lawyers, writers and industrialists in a variety of countries.'[17] At the end of the war Mrs Steinhardt listed the parents of the boys who had been murdered in German concentration camps: Hans and Georg Bodenheimer had lost both parents; Irwin Freilich's mother was dead and his father missing, and a further twelve boys had lost parents and siblings. That represents almost half of the boys and the combined loss of family members was thirty-two. One of the boys told a journalist from the *New York Times* years later: 'Without [the Rothschilds] all of us here would have been just a statistic of the Nazi death camps'[18]. Another boy, Otto Decker said: 'I think our experience made us more determined and more ambitious to succeed in life, to justify why we had survived when so many died.'[19]

And succeed they did. Otto Decker owned an engineering company in Puerto Rico. Gert Heuman, who changed his name to Gerard Hartman, left Aylesbury Grammar School with six distinctions and five credits in his School Certificate, coming top out of seventy-two boys in the year. He left the Cedars that summer and sailed for New York. His mother wrote to the Rothschilds the following year thanking them from the bottom of her heart for looking after her son who she finally set eyes on after seven-and-a-half years: 'I do not know how to express my gratitude to you, who have made it possible for the child to escape the Nazi terror and be such a wonderful and nice boy today.'[20] Gerard went on became a professor at Harvard. Ulrich Stobiecka, who also changed his name, joined the Israel Foreign Office and was twice posted to the Israeli Embassy in London as Uri Sella. He joined fifteen former boys from the home for a reunion at Waddesdon in 1983 when Dorothy, then eighty-eight, planted a Cedar of Lebanon given to Waddesdon by the Cedar Boys to commemorate life there between 1939 and 1952. Henry Black said, 'Trees are planted to give pleasure and shelter to future generations. May this tree grow to fulfil its purpose.' It was a very emotional day and the boys were delighted to see Julian Layton, who had facilitated their departure from Frankfurt forty-four years earlier and to hear Dorothy, with tears in her eyes, tell them: 'Although you are very much grown up you will always remain boys to me. It's been such a very long time since you've been here with me.'[21] Peter Gortatowsky spent seven years at the Cedars before moving to New York to join his parents who had managed to escape from Germany. In 1946, he wrote a letter to the Rothschilds thanking them 'for the great kindness that you have shown me during my stay in this country ... I will endeavour to lead the kind of life which your interest in me has taught me to lead, and I feel confident that I shall live up to your expectations.'[22] Thirty-seven years later he was invited to the reunion but decided not to attend. He explained to Dorothy his reason:

As you must know, prior to our arrival in England there was not much of a childhood for any of us ... My only real happiness as a child was under your auspices. The whole truth is that I do not wish to lose my illusions and happy memories of Waddesdon and England. I know of course that during the past forty or so years things have changed, as they must. I however want to remember things as they were and live with my memories.[23]

Lord Bearsted was falling ill and retired from Shell in 1946 at the age of sixty-four. He was anxious to ensure the donation of Upton House in Warwickshire with its magnificent collections of paintings and porcelain, along with a generous endowment for its upkeep. Lees-Milne was there in March 1946 to be shown around the house. He stayed the night and wrote of his hosts 'both charming, with the unassuming manners of the well-bred'. Lord Bearsted gave him a tour of the house:

Inside there is nothing of consequence architecturally save a few early eighteenth-century chimneypieces and a beautiful Coleshill-style staircase, rearranged by Lord B. and extended. But heavens, the contents! There is a lot of Chippendale-style furniture and some marvellous Chelsea china of the very best quality. The picture collection superb, as fine as any private collection in England.[24]

Lord Bearsted died in November 1948 and the house and gardens passed into National Trust ownership with a generous endowment. Lady Bearsted's beautiful aluminium-leaf covered bathroom is one of the house's most intricate features and the art collection is indeed outstanding but the gardens, designed in the late 1920s, are a real glory of Upton House and the three cedars, which Peter Samuel had written to his mother about from the desert, still stand.

Brocket Hall in Hertfordshire continued to function as a maternity home until 1949 when the City Road Maternity Hospital reopened in East London. Lord Brocket outlived his son and as a result the estate passed on his death to his fifteen-year-old grandson, Charles Ronald Nall-Cain, known as Charlie Brocket. He became famous as a playboy and once owned forty-two Ferraris. In 1996 he was convicted of insurance fraud and sentenced to five years in prison, of which he served two-and-a-half. In 2004 he took part as a contestant in the third series of *I'm a Celebrity ... Get Me Out of Here!* As a result of Lord Brocket's insurance problems the trustees of the estate decided to sell a sixty-year leasehold interest to a German company. At the time of writing Brocket Hall is advertised as 'an exclusive venue for corporate events, weddings and parties and is fully staffed with butlers discretely anticipating your every whim.'[25] The Brocket Babies continue to meet at the hall and celebrate their shared birth place with its deliciously sumptuous if at times scandalous history.

At Aldenham Park everything changed. The day the school left Lord Acton uncorked a bottle of champagne to celebrate the departure of their wartime guests. The house was quieter without the girls of the Assumption, but more messy as the Acton children did not clear up after themselves, Ronald Knox complained. Lord Acton's sister, Princess Rospigliosi and her three children came to live in the house, which meant a lively companion for Lady Acton, but just increased Ronald's feeling of isolation. Lord Acton returned to the park in September 1945 and in December he received the MBE for his 'gallant and distinguished services in Italy'. He never spoke about the war but he did tell the *Assumption Chronicle* about his visit to Rome in 1944 after the city fell. He succeeded in gaining a private audience with the Pope. 'I sat on a red cushion and we talked in French. I told him about Ronnie's translation of the Bible. He was very interested ... There were two telephones on his table: a white one and a gold one. The telephone rang and he spoke a few words in German down the golden instrument.'[26]

On his return to Aldenham, Lord Acton tried to make a success of farming the estate but it did not work out. The house was in need of significant repairs and even if those were carried out, there was the upkeep of a large house in constant need of attention and money. Eventually he decided to emigrate and bought a property in southern Rhodesia next door to a friend from the Shropshire Yeomanry. He moved abroad in early 1947 but Lady Acton was pregnant again so had to wait for the birth of her next baby in June. Daphne's step-mother, Kathleen Lady Rayleigh, bought Aldenham Park in August of that year for her and her son, Daphne's half-brother, Guy Strutt, thus giving the Acton family a welcome injection of cash as they left Britain for Rhodesia. Ronald Knox wrote in a letter to a friend that Daphne would be taking 'the Rospigliosis, the pigs and the family portraits'.

There was a steady stream of visitors to the Actons in Rhodesia including Evelyn Waugh, who made two extended visits. In a letter to Ann Fleming in 1958, he described life at M'bebi, the Actons' farm: 'Children were everywhere, no semblance of a nursery or a nanny, the spectacle at meals gruesome, a party-line telephone ring-ing all day, dreadful food ... ants in the bed, totally untrained black servants (all converted by Daphne to Christianity, taught to serve

Mass but not to empty ashtrays). In fact, everything that normally makes Hell, but Daphne's serene sanctity radiating supernatural peace. She is the most remarkable woman I know.'[27]

As the Actons settled to their new life in Rhodesia, Ronald Knox was in his sixtieth year and feeling cold, underfed and impoverished. He had lived as a recluse for the best part of eight years while he was working on the Bible and with the sale of Aldenham he was homeless. Fortunately Katharine Asquith heard of his plight and invited him to Mells in Somerset as a paying guest for the summer of 1947. She was the sister of his friend from prep school, Edward Horner, and a friend of Daphne Acton. He accepted the invitation to become the house's chaplain and wrote to Claudia Macaskie that autumn: 'It's rather beastly to feel that on Tuesday I shut up the chapel for (as far as I know) good and all.'[28]

He enjoyed the quiet life at Mells, joking with Claudia's sister, Nicola: 'One curious effect of my present move is that for the first time in nearly forty years I am not living with people noticeably younger than myself. In fact, believe it or not, I am *under* the average age at the Manor House.'[29] He found that he missed the hubbub of the school and the noise of young people rushing about so he made every effort to keep in touch with them. He was a regular guest at the Macaskie's home in Kensington and attended many of the former pupils' weddings, giving memorable and personal addresses which he published, preserving the girls' anonymity, in a book entitled *Bridegroom and Bride*. He was a constant in their lives and a much-loved presence, so that even after his death they spoke about him as if he were still alive but just no longer in the room.

In 1954 he made his one and only visit to Rhodesia, which coincided with the birth of the eleventh of Daphne's children, a little girl called Jane. Daphne had been slowly repaying the loans he had made to her during the war, but in 1957 he wrote to tell her that he was terminally ill and instead of paying the £1,200 outstanding she should offer it to the archbishop to help fund a church or build one herself. She did the latter. There was a moving link to Aldenham in the new church. Lord Acton had commissioned a stained-glass window in 1946 for the chapel at Aldenham as a memorial for his brother Peter and his wife, killed in an air crash that year. The tragedy was a factor in their decision to emigrate the following year and the window had remained in its packing cases. Nearly twenty years later it was installed in the new church in Rhodesia, which was consecrated in 1964.

Ronald Knox died quietly at Mells in August 1957. Mourned by everyone who had known him but still criticised by some in the Church for his translation of the Bible, he has disappeared to some extent from history but his influence is felt by the former pupils of the Assumption even today. The Knox Bible is no longer in print but every one of the girls I spoke to has their own signed copy. Aldenham Park was purchased from the Strutt family in 1959 by Mr and Mrs Thompson who demolished the library wing, which was beyond repair, and the chapel, but they restored the remainder of the house. At the time of writing it is the family home of their granddaughter, Hettie Fenwick.

Howick Hall in Northumberland is now the family home of Lord and Lady Howick. On the death of the fifth Earl Grey the house passed to his daughter, Lady Mary. She was married to Evelyn Baring of the wealthy banking family. He was governor of Southern Rhodesia from 1942–44, high commissioner for Southern Africa from 1944–51 and governor of Kenya from 1952–59. He was created first Baron Howick of Glendale in 1960, taking the name from his wife's home. Howick Hall fell into partial disrepair after the war and most of the upstairs rooms are now uninhabitable. A new visitor centre has been opened in the restored entrance hall but the main attractions today are the gardens, which were laid out by Lord Grey and his wife Mabel in 1920. The gardens are best known for their spring bulbs. Lady Grey had started a tradition of planting tulips in long grass which the family continues to foster. The present Lord Howick began to plant an arboretum in the mid-1980s to surround the gardens, which had for years been open to the public. He wrote: 'I decided that it would be more useful and more fun to start an arboretum grown from seed collected in the wild and planted in geographic rather than generic groups.'[30] Decades on, the trees have grown and matured, giving visitors and the family great pleasure. Lord Howick likes to walk around the arboretum and recall where he collected the seeds from. 'A private pleasure but none the worse for that.'[31]

Of the five properties in this book that had secret organisations billeted in their houses and grounds, only Audley End is open to the public. It was sold to the nation for £30,000 and is today cared for by English Heritage who describe it on their website as a 'decadent Jacobean mansion' – not a description that would have fitted the house during the war. Statistics show that Britain made 485 air drops into Poland between 1942 and 1944, despite the limiting factors of weather and distance. They delivered 600 tons of material, 40 per cent of it to the Warsaw uprising, at considerable cost for the RAF who were unaided by either Russia or the USA. Three hundred and eighteen agents were dropped into Poland by parachute. They had all been trained by SOE.

The Polish wartime occupants of Audley End are now few in number and elderly. After the war some returned to Poland but others chose to live in exile for the rest of their lives. For the Poles, the war did not end on 8 May 1945. Theirs was a country that had been broken by the brutality of the occupation. Of the six million Polish men, women and children who lost their lives the vast majority – over 90 per cent – were civilians who died of starvation, brutality and mass murder. As a result of the Yalta Conference of February 1945, Poland was to be left under the control of the Soviet Union, leaving the majority of the country and its leaders feeling it had once again been betrayed by the Allies. 'Under Stalin no Polish servicemen were allowed to take part in the victory parade in 1946. No Poles took part in the victory parade in London ... The RAF protested, and an exception was made for the Polish pilots. However, they were not prepared to march without their compatriots, so no Poles were represented on VE Day in London. This affected over a quarter of a million servicemen in Britain.'[32] If servicemen returned to Poland they risked being arrested and tried for war crimes because they had fought against the Red Army. In the space of just two years more than 30,000 Poles died at the hands of the Soviets. The Polish government-in-exile remained in London until 1990 in opposition to Communist rule.

Like the Poles, the Czechs would soon find their country under rule from Moscow but, initially, this was not something that troubled the returning regime. President and Mrs Beneš left Aston Abbotts in March 1945. They were sorry to leave their beautiful temporary home but the free Czechoslovakia for which Dr Beneš had worked tirelessly, and never doubted would be restored, was waiting for him. His parting gift to the community of Aston Abbotts and Wingrave was £150 to Wingrave Parish Council for the construction of a bus shelter, which still stands. He and his staff had noticed schoolchildren waiting at the bus stop on the busy Leighton Buzzard to Aylesbury road in all weathers and thought that they, like their counterparts in the villages of Czechoslovakia, deserved protection from the weather. Its inscription reads: 'This bus shelter was donated by President Beneš of Czechoslovakia to thank the people of Aston Abbotts & Wingrave whilst he and his cabinet were in exile here during World War II.'

Back in Prague for the first time in six years, Beneš was triumphant. He spoke of 'looking across to shattered Berlin and Munich and to the ruins of the Third Reich, our heads high, our conscience clear, in the knowledge of a great historic victory and in the knowledge that our great democratic national truth has prevailed, conscious of the unity of our national State and with great moral and political satisfaction for all that happened at Munich and afterwards.'[33]

President Beneš could not know that while he was looking across to the west and shattered Berlin, the Communists in the east had designs on his country. Moravec had warned him while he was still in London but the president was an optimist and remained defiantly trusting of Stalin. The Communists moved forwards inexorably with their plan to remove the democratic government and this finally took place in February 1948. Beneš warned Moravec that he was persona non grata with the Communists so the former master of spies prepared for a second time in less than a decade to flee for his life. He and his wife left the next day and reached America, where they spent the rest of their lives living as exiles. The foreign minister, Jan Masaryk, was not so fortunate. He was found dead on the ground below his official flat on 10 March 1948 having purportedly committed suicide. An investigation in the early 1990s concluded that he had been murdered, something most Czechs had always supposed. Beneš had been ill since the end of the war and was suffering from spinal tuberculosis. He suffered two strokes in 1947 and died in September 1948. His wife outlived him, dying in 1974.

Like the Poles, the Czechoslovak servicemen who returned to their country met hostility. Moravec wrote that in taking over Czechoslovakia the Kremlin had just taken another 13 million prisoners. In 1945 there were about 600 British war brides in Czechoslovakia, including several from Buckinghamshire. From 1948 onwards, Czechoslovak soldiers who had been in Britain were either imprisoned by the Communist authorities or escaped into exile again. Contact between people in Aston Abbotts and their friends in Czechoslovakia became difficult and it was only with the Velvet Revolution of 1989 that free movement between the two countries became possible. As soon as they could, Czech and Slovak veterans made contact with Cholmondeley and arranged a reunion with a service held at the memorial in 1990. The sculpture by František Bělský, which had originally been unveiled by Jan Masaryk on 28 September 1940 for the St Wenceslas Day celebrations, was rededicated. Franz Kaplan wrote in 2000: 'When you mention Cholmondeley to your comrades in what was, not so long ago, still Czechoslovakia, their faces light up at the recollection of what the place meant, and still means, to them.'[34]

Colonel Karel Trojanek was the highest-ranking judiciary officer of the Czechoslovak forces in Britain during the Second World War. He died in 1987 in the USA and in his will he requested permission to return to Cheshire: 'to rest amongst the kindest and friendliest people he ever encountered in his life.'[35] After his death his ashes were brought to Britain and interred in Bickley churchyard. His memorial is still cared for by local parishioners.

In Aston Abbotts, two more lime trees were added to the one planted by President Beneš in the Abbey gardens. The first was planted in 1990 to mark the official visit of President Václav Havel to Britain. He made a point of asking to be shown the site of the Czechoslovak president-in-exile's Buckinghamshire home but so little was known in the Czech Republic about the wartime details that he visited Wingrave instead of Aston Abbotts, donating a wooden bench. It was only when Buckinghamshire local historian Neil Rees began to do in-depth research into the Czechs in the county that he was able to paint a full picture of who had lived where. The third lime tree was planted on a triangle of land close to the church in Aston Abbotts, near to the abbey gate to mark the six-tieth anniversary of D-Day and the contribution made by the Czech armed forces. The churchyard has two commemorative roses to the heroes of Operation Anthropoid, Gabčík and Kubiš.

Bignor Manor, host to so many men and women of the Free French remained in private hands. Mrs Bertram was considered a heroine by those men and women in the French Resistance who had known of her activities during the war in support of the couriers. In 1945 Tony Bertram secured a job with the British Council and the family moved to Paris for a year before returning to Bignor Manor in the autumn of 1946. The following summer there was a family trag-edy, 'the only tragedy of my life so far' Barbara said in her memoir. Her younger son, Nicky, had been exploring a haystack in a Dutch barn and had fallen into a hole in the hay and died. Barbara found solace in her husband's faith and converted to Catholicism. In 1950 they had another son, Jerome. Tony's career took them abroad to the United States and eventually back to Britain. Barbara Bertram died in Oxford in 2000 at the age of eighty-four. The war years were a mere six of her long life but they had a lasting impact on the men and women who passed through her home.

And finally, to northern Scotland and the houses occupied by Major General Sir Colin Gubbins' Special Operations Executive. 'In total, SOE schools trained at least 6,810 students, of whom over 480 were British SOE agents. The rest came from sixteen foreign nations, as well as 872 students from Britain's SIS and 172 students from the SAS (Special Air Service).'[36] The dozen or so SOE special training schools were handed back to their owners and are still standing. Arisaig House is a small hotel and the wartime activities of this top-secret area of Scotland are commemorated in a little museum in the village of Arisaig where there is a memorial to the Czech and Slovak agents who were trained there with a list of the forty-eight missions carried out by them including, top of the alphabetical list, Anthropoid.

I have tried to keep the personal out of this book as I wanted you, the reader, to be able to make up your own mind about the men and women whose stories are told here. But with Gubbins I cannot be impartial. To me he stands out as one of the most interesting, impressive, energetic, devoted, patriotic and delightful men I have ever written about. Gubbins was an authentic hero. He possessed what E. M. Forster called the three heroic virtues: courage, generosity and compassion.

In Britain Gubbins is little known but in the countries of former occupied Europe he was considered to be a great man. The explanation offered by his biographer, Joan Bright Astley, was that:

> Britain was spared the shame and misery of enemy occupation; without this experience it is difficult to appreciate the part played by clandestine resistance both in restoring national self-respect and in permitting courageous individuals to escape from the ignominy of their situation ... It was as a resistance leader that he came to fashion Special Operations Executive, and to write his own page in the history of almost every country occupied by the enemy in the Second World War.[37]

In April 1944, the question of what would happen to SOE in a postwar world was eagerly considered by those at the top of the organisation. Lord Selborne, who had taken over from Hugh Dalton as Minister of Economic Warfare in 1942, and was therefore in charge of SOE, agreed with Gubbins that there was a case for keeping the organisation going for the future. Selborne, who was close friends with Churchill and who had on more than one occasion used the prime minister's influence to get SOE out of a scrape with its domestic rivals, had put the case firmly for its continuation. Churchill replied to his letter four days later: 'My dear Top, the part which your naughty deeds in war play, in peace cannot at all be considered at the present time.'[38]

This disappointment came on top of a personal tragedy. Gubbins' older son, Michael, had been killed in Italy two months earlier when he was on the way to establish a rendezvous point with a new SOE courier. He was twenty-two years old. His body was never recovered and the tragedy of his death was a reminder of how randomly war destroys lives. Gubbins went out to Italy in May 1944 to look for Michael's grave but there was no trace of him. One of the FANY who was there at the time remembers him walking around the sand dunes shaking his head and muttering 'so useless, so useless'.

Despite Lord Selborne's vigorous efforts to badger the Foreign Office to find a role for SOE postwar, Gubbins received notification from the War Office in October 1945 that his present appointment was to end and he would not be given further employment. It was a bitter time but he took some solace in the dazzling array of foreign orders and decorations he received. He was advanced to KCMG in the New Year's Honours of 1946 and the rule restricting officers to just four foreign honours for services during the Second World War was waived for Gubbins. He already held the Order of St Stanislas, II Class, from his tour of duty in Archangel in 1918 and the Polish Cross of Valour for his work on behalf of Poland. The prime minister, Clement Attlee, informed Lord Selborne that Gubbins 'would be permitted to accept for service in the war not only Polish, French and Belgian Honours, but also Czechoslovak, United States and Norwegian decorations ... also Netherlands, Danish and Greek awards ... He may then have, as a minimum, for service in both wars, some twenty awards in all, British and foreign.'[39] For the record, he received the Légion d'Honneur and Croix de Guerre from France, the Order of Leopold and Croix de Guerre from Belgium, the Royal Order of Saint Olaf from Norway, the Order of Merit from the USA, the Order of the White Lion from Czechoslovakia, Order of the Dannebrog from Denmark, the Order of Orange-Nassau from the Netherlands, as well as Greek and Italian awards.[40]

After the war, Gubbins remarried, this time to a widow of a Norwegian pilot who had died flying for the RAF. They applied for British citizenship for her, but this was turned down on the grounds that Gubbins had been born in Japan and was therefore a British subject, not a British citizen. So he had to apply for British citizenship himself so that his new bride could do the same. That must have seemed to him particularly bureaucratic.

Lord Selborne had tried to get the military to agree to allow Gubbins to be raised to substantive major general in order to give him a proper pension. This was refused and he was forced to retire on a substantive colonel's pay which meant he urgently needed a civilian job. He was given a role as managing director of a large textile and carpeting firm, W. Gray & Co. which had premises in London, Yorkshire, Scotland and Northern Ireland. His work meant that he travelled widely and although he had no official role in foreign affairs, he was frequently invited to attend celebrations and anniversaries of resistance groups throughout Europe. His heart remained with SOE and he was instrumental in setting up the Special Forces Club in London with the primary objective of perpetuating 'the comradeship which had been such a marked feature of the Resistance and as a means of dispensing financial support to its victims.'[41]

Gubbins also became deeply involved in the promotion of European unity. In 1946 an old Polish friend of his, Josef Retinger, gave an important lecture at Chatham House about the European continent which led to the setting up in Brussels of the Independent League for Economic Cooperation. This was one of many similar organisations devoted to European unity postwar and they all merged in 1947 into an International Committee of the Movement for European Unity, of which Churchill's son-in-law Duncan Sandys became the chairman. In 1954, Gubbins and Hugh Gaitskell, as representatives for Britain, became founder members of the Bilderberg Group, an organisation set up to promote a strengthening of US–European relations and prevent another world war.

Gubbins told his biographer that he was certain a happy life was 'to know everything about something, to know something about everything and to play a musical instrument.'[42] At the age of sixty-five he started learning to play the concertina. In his retirement he became an avid gardener, though his wife joked that he planted everything in regimented straight lines. He lived life to the full almost to the end, dying a week after suffering a heart attack in Scotland on 11 February 1976. At the memorial service held in St Martin-in-the-Fields, London, the congregation was as rich a mixture of people as he had known in SOE. The Prince of Wales, the King of Norway and the president of the United States of America sent their representatives. Prince Georg of Denmark attended with the Danish ambassador, Colin Mackenzie represented Earl Mountbatten and there were friends from Belgium, Denmark, France, Norway, the Netherlands, wartime Polish GHQ and contingents of resistance fighters. In his address Peter Wilkinson said of Gubbins:

... of the decisive importance of Colin Gubbins' personal contribution to the allied victory there can be no question. His name is honoured officially in many lands. For in the dark hours it was *his* duty to fan the spark and keep alive the flame of freedom. It was *his* exertions that gave hope to thousands of patriots in occupied countries all over the world. These men and women are unlikely to forget him. Nor will he ever been forgotten by his countless personal friends. They will always remember him with great respect, with the warmest affection and, above all, with gratitude. For whatever Colin Gubbins was called on to do in his long life, he not only did it extremely well, but he contrived in the process to make life extraordinarily rewarding and agreeable for anyone who had the good fortune to be with him.[43]

To the man who set Europe ablaze it seems to me particularly fitting that Gubbins considered it perhaps the greatest honour of his life to have been chosen to be a founder member of a group to promote EU–US understanding and to prevent a future war. In a way, his story sums up the dichotomy I proposed at the beginning of this book, which is that a government has two responsibilities in war: to prosecute the war as vigorously as possible so as to defeat the enemy, and to protect its citizens as far as possible from the dangers posed by that enemy.

The stories in *Our Uninvited Guests* were inevitably going to focus more on the people who occupied the houses rather than on the buildings themselves. But without the houses there would have been no backdrop for the stories of the people who were their temporary uninvited guests.

BIBLIOGRAPHY

Books

Allan, Stuart, *Commando Country* (Edinburgh: NMS Enterprises Ltd 2007)

Atkin, Malcolm, *Fighting Nazi Occupation: British Resistance 1939–1945* (Barnsley: Pen & Sword Military 2015)

Bailey, Roderick, *Forgotten Voices of the Secret War: An Inside History of Special Operations in the Second World War* (Great Britain: Ebury Press 2009)

Bell, The Right Reverend G. K., Bishop of Chichester, *Humanity and the Refugees* (Oxford: Oxford University Press 1939)

Bertram, Anthony and Barbara, *The Secret of Bignor Manor* (Lulu. com 2014)

Bertram, Barbara, *French Resistance in Sussex* (Launceston: Barnworks Publishing 1998)

Bertram, Barbara, *Memoirs* (Oxford: Jerome and Tim Bertram 2001)

Blumenau, Ralph, *A History of Malvern College 1865–1965* (London: Macmillan & Co. 1965)

Botting, Douglas, *Gavin Maxwell, A Life* (London: HarperCollins 1994)

Buckmaster, Maurice, *They Fought Alone: The True Story of SOE's Secret Agents in Wartime France* (London: Biteback Publishing Ltd 2014 (first published 1958 by Odhams (Watford) Ltd))

Bull, Dr Stephen (ed.), *The Secret Agent's Pocket Manual 1939–1945* (London: Conway 2009)

Calder, Angus, *The People's War: Britain 1939–1945* (London: Pimlico 2008 (first published 1969 by Jonathan Cape Ltd))

Cartland, Dame Barbara, *The Years of Opportunity 1939–1945* (London: Hutchinson 1948)

Channon, Sir Henry, *'Chips': The Diaries of Sir Henry Channon* (London: Phoenix, new edition 1996)

Colville, John, *The Fringes of Power: Downing Street Diaries 1939–1955* (London: Hodder and Stoughton 1985)

Corbishley, Thomas, *Ronald Knox The Priest* (London: Sheed & Ward 1964)

Dalton, Hugh, *The Second World War Diary, 1940–45* ed. Ben Pimlott (London: Jonathan Cape 1986)

Dodds-Parker, Douglas, *Setting Europe Ablaze* (London: Springwood Books Ltd 1983)

Dorril, Stephen, *M16: Inside the Covert World of Her Majesty's Secret Intelligence Service* (London: Fourth Estate Limited 2000)

Dourlein, Pieter, *Inside North Pole: A Secret Agent's Story* (London: Kimber 1953)

Dow, George, *The Story of The West Highland* (Northern Books 2009 (first published 1944 by the London & North Eastern Railway))

Enright, Dominique, *The Wicked Wit of Winston Churchill* (London: Michael O'Mara Books 2001)

Escott, Beryl E., *The Heroines of SOE: Britain's Secret Women in France F Section* (Stroud: The History Press 2010)

Fairbairn, W. E., *All-In Fighting*, (London: Faber & Faber 1942)

Fenby, Jonathan, *The General: Charles de Gaulle and the France He Saved* (London: Simon & Schuster UK 2010)

Ferguson, Aldon, *Cheshire Airfields in the Second World War* (Newbury: Countryside Books 2014)

Foot, M. R. D., *SOE: The Special Operations Executive 1940–46* (London: British Broadcasting Corporation 1984)

Foot, M. R. D., *SOE in France: Account of the Work of the British Special Operations Executive in France 1940–44* (London: HMSO 1966)

Freethy, Ron, *Cheshire: The Secret War 1939–1945* (Newbury: Countryside Books 2012)

Gardiner, Juliet, *Over Here: The GIs in Wartime Britain* (London: Collins & Brown Ltd 1992)

Garrett, Bradley L. (compiled by), *Subterranean London: Cracking the Capital* (Munich: Prestel Verlag 2015)

Gaunt, H. C. A., *Two Exiles: A School in Wartime* (London: Sampson Low, Marston & Co., Ltd 1946)

Gilchrist, Donald, *Castle Commando* (Inverness: West Highland Museum 2005 (first published 1960))

Gildea, Robert, *Fighters in the Shadows* (London: Faber & Faber Ltd 2015)

Gubbins, Colin McVean, *The Art of Guerrilla Warfare* (CreateSpace Publishing Independent Publishing Platform 2016 (first published SOE 1939))

Gurney, Ivor and Carr, Norman, *Waddesdon Through the Ages* (The Alice Trust: Waddesdon Manor 2004)

Harford, Tim, *Messy: How to be Creative and Resilient in a Tidy-Minded World* (London: Little, Brown 2016)

Hargreaves, E. L. and Gowing, M. M., *Civil Industry and Trade* (London: Her Majesty's Stationery Office and Longmans, Green & Co. 1952)

Harrison, David M., *Special Operations Executives: Para-military training in Scotland during World War 2* (Clitheroe: D. M. Harrison 2001)

Hartley, Dorothy, *The Land of England: English Country Customs Through the Ages* (Macdonald General Books 1979)

Hastings, Max, *The Secret War: Spies, Codes and Guerrillas 1939–1945* (London: William Collins 2015)

Helm, Sarah, *A Life in Secrets: The Story of Vera Atkins and the Lost Agents of SOE* (London: Abacus 2006)

Henriques, Robert, *Marcus Samuel First Viscount Bearsted and*

*Founder of the 'Shell' Transport and Trading Company
1853–1927* (London: Barrie and Rockliff 1960)

Henriques, Robert, *The Commander: An Autobiographical Novel
of 1940–41* (London: Secker and Warburg 1967)

Hodgson, Vere, *Few Eggs and No Oranges: Vere Hodgson's Diary
1940–45* (London: Dobson Books, 1976)

Household, Geoffrey, *Rogue Male* (London: Heinemann
Educational Books Ltd 1982 (first published by Chatto &
Windus 1939))

Howarth, Stephen, *A Century in Oil: The 'Shell' Transport
and Trading Company 1897-1997* (London: Weidenfeld &
Nicolson 1997)

Hyde Parker, Ulla, *Cousin Beatie: A Memory of Beatrix Potter*
(London: Frederick Warne & Co. Ltd 1981)

Iranek-Osmecki, George, *The Unseen and Silent* (London: Sheed
& Ward 1954)

Jackson, Sophie, *British Interrogation Techniques in the Second
World War* (Stroud: The History Press 2012)

Jones, R V, *Most Secret War: British Scientific Intelligence 1939–
1945* (London: Coronet 1979 (first published 1978 by Hamish
Hamilton Ltd))

Kemp, Peter, *No Colours or Crest* (London: Cassell 1958)

Knox, Ronald, *A Spiritual Aeneid* (London: Longmans, Green and
Co. 1918)

Knox, Ronald, *The Mass in Slow Motion* (London: Sheed & Ward
1948)

Knox, Ronald, *Literary Distractions* (London: Sheed & Ward 1958)

Knox, Ronald, *The Creed in Slow Motion* (London: Sheed & Ward
1959)

Lampe, David, *The Last Ditch, Britain's Secret Resistance and the
Nazi Invasion Plan* (Barnsley: Frontline Books 2013)

Langelaan, George, *Knights of the Floating Silk* (London:
Hutchinson 1959)

Lees-Milne, James, *Diaries, 1942–1954* (London: John Murray
Publishers 2007)

Lett, Brian, *SOE's Mastermind: The Authorised Biography of Major General Sir Colin Gubbins KCMG, DSO, MC* (Barnsley: Pen & Sword Military 2016)

Linderman, A. R., *Rediscovering Irregular Warfare: Colin Gubbins and the Origins of Britain's Special Operations Executive* (USA: University of Oklahoma Press 2016)

Longmate, Norman, *The G.I.'s: The Americans in Britain, 1942–1945* (London: Hutchinson 1975)

Longmate, Norman, *How We Lived Then: A History of Everyday Life During the Second World War* (London: Arrow Books 1973)

MacDonald, Callum, *The Assassination of Reinhard Heydrich* (Edinburgh: Birlinn 2007)

Mackenzie, Compton, *Dr Beneš* (London: George G. Harrap 1946)

Mackenzie, William, *The Secret History of SOE: The Special Operations Executive 1940–45* (London: St Ermin's Press 2000)

McCairns, James Atterby, *Lysander Pilot: Secret Operations with 161 Squadron* (Tangmere Military Aviation Museum 2016)

McCamley, N. J., *Saving Britain's Art Treasures* (Barnsley: Leo Cooper 2003)

McKay, Sinclair, introduction by *The British Spy Manual Volumes I & II* (London: Aurum Press Ltd 2014)

May, Elizabeth, *Wollaton Hall: Family House and Natural History Museum* (Derby: Hall 1989)

Meakin, Avril, *Howick's Seven Tales of the Unexpected* (Alnwick: The Howick Heritage Group 2014)

Milton, Giles, *The Ministry of Ungentlemanly Warfare: Churchill's Mavericks Plotting Hitler's Defeat* (London: John Murray 2016)

Moravec, Frantisek, *Master of Spies: The Memoirs of General Frantisek Moravec* (Great Britain: Sphere Books 1981)

Norman, Andrew, *Tyneham: A Tribute* (Wellington: Halsgrove 2007)

O'Connor, Bernard, *Churchill's School for Saboteurs: Station 17* (Stroud: Amberley Publishing 2014)

Olson, Lynne, *Last Hope Island: Britain, Occupied Europe, and the Brotherhood that Helped Turn the Tide of War* (London: Scribe UK 2017)

Pidgeon, Geoffrey, *The Secret Wireless War: The Story of MI6 Communications 1939–1945* (St Leonards-on-Sea: UPSO Ltd 2007)

Popham, Hugh, *The FANY in Peace & War* (Barnsley: Leo Cooper 2003 (first published by Leo Cooper 1984))

Robinson, John Martin, *The Country House at War* (London: The Bodley Head 1989)

Roscoe, Barley (ed.), *Katharine Pleydell-Bouverie: A Potter's Life 1895–1985* (London: Crafts Council 1986)

Rothschild, Mrs James de, *The Rothschilds at Waddesdon Manor* (London: William Collins Sons & Company 1979)

Rowe, Albert Percival, *One Story of Radar* (Cambridge: University Press 1948)

Ryder, Sue, *Child of My Love* (London: Harvill 1997)

Seaman, Mark (ed.), *Special Operations Executive: A new instrument of war* (London: Routledge 2006)

Seebohm, Caroline, *The Country House: A Wartime History 1939–45* (London: Weidenfeld & Nicolson 1989)

Stafford, David, *Secret Agent: The True Story of the Special Operations Executive* (London: BBC Worldwide Ltd 2000)

Sweet-Escott, Bickham, *Baker Street Irregular* (London: Methuen 1965)

Tinniswood, Adrian, *The Long Weekend: Life in the English Country House Between the Wars* (London: Jonathan Cape 2016)

Titmuss, Richard M, *Problems of Social Policy* (London: HMSO and Longmans, Green & Co 1950)

Tyerman, Christopher, *A History of Harrow School 1324–1991* (Oxford: Oxford University Press 2000)

Valentine, Ian, *Station 43: Audley End House and SOE's Polish*

Section (Stroud: Sutton Publishing 2004)

Verity, Hugh, *We Landed by Moonlight* (Manchester: Crécy
  Publishing Limited 2013 (first published 1978 by Ian Allan
  Limited))

Walters, Anne-Marie, *Moondrop to Gascony* (Wiltshire: Moho
  Books 2009 (first published 1946 Macmillan & Co. Ltd))

Warwicker, John, *Churchill's Underground Army* (Barnsley:
  Frontline Books 2013)

Waugh, Evelyn, *Put Out More Flags* (London: Penguin Books 1943)

Waugh, Evelyn, *Men at Arms* (London: Penguin Books 1964 (first
  published Chapman & Hall 1952))

Waugh, Evelyn, *Officers and Gentlemen* (London: Penguin Books
  1964 (first published Chapman & Hall 1955))

Waugh, Evelyn, *Unconditional Surrender* (London: Penguin Books
  1964 (first published Chapman & Hall 1961))

Waugh, Evelyn, *The Life of the Right Reverend Ronald Knox*
  (London: Penguin Classics 2011)

Wilkinson, Peter and Bright Astley, Joan, *Gubbins & SOE*
  (London: Leo Cooper 2010 (first published 1993))

Woodward, Antony and Penn, Robert, *The Wrong Kind of Snow:
  the Complete Daily Companion to the British Weather*
  (London: Hodder & Stoughton 2007)

Wylie, Neville (ed.), *The Politics and Strategy of Clandestine War:
  Special Operations Executive 1940–1946* (London: Routledge
  2006)

Young, Gordon, *In Trust and Treason: The Strange Story of
  Suzanne Warren* (London: Edward Hulton 1959)

Periodicals, Reports and Leaflets

The Assumption Chronicle (War Issue No. 1) April 1942

The Assumption Chronicle (War Issue No. 2) January 1943

The Assumption Chronicle (War Issue No. 3) October 1943

The Assumption Chronicle (War Issue No. 4) October 1944

The Assumption Chronicle (War Issue No. 5) October 1945

Bignor Roman Villa Guide Book
Bugle & Sabre VIII, ed. Jenkins, Stanley, 2015
Country Life February 1940
East Anglian Daily Times February 1942
The Malvernian 1939
Melford Hall, Suffolk (A property of the National Trust by James
     Lees-Milne, London Country Life Limited for The National
     Trust 1961)
Melford Hall (The National Trust 1990)
Ministry of Health advice leaflet, HMSO, 1939
Monthly Report of the Meteorological Office, Vol. 57, No. 1 MO
     454
Pittsburgh Post-Gazette March 1945
The Spectator 8 July 1966
Scott, Hamish 'Inside Story: Garramore House', *Daily Telegraph*
     11 November 2000
Wollaton Hall and Park: official descriptive and illustrated
     brochure (Wollaton, Nottingham 1944)

Films

The Secrets of Underground Britain: Wartime Secrets Peach TV
     2008
The Silent Village 1943
Hitler's Britain: What Hitler Had in Store for Occupied Britain
     2008

Audio Recordings

Adam Benrad © IWM Sound Archive, 8683
Baroness Ryder © IWM Sound Archive, 10057
Barbara Bertram © IWM Sound Archive, 16367

Unpublished Material

Adler, Barney, *Wartime Experiences 1940–1946*

Ashby, Bill, *GHQ Auxiliary Units*

Cameron-Head papers, Highland Council Archive, D271/B/11

Hall, Major R. F., MC, *The Big House* (unpublished transcript of a lecture to the Moidart History Group) 13 August 2001

IWM 6428 94/34/1 Mrs B. Bertram

IWM 8227 99/37/1 Miss M. E. B. Cook

IWM 12618 Private Papers of Major General Sir Colin M. Gubbins KCMG DSO MC

IWM D 9027 Ministry of Information Second World War Official Collection

IWM 13337 05/76/1 Lady Pamela Niven

IWM 15704 07/36/1 Captain J. H. B. Roy

Kaplan, Franz, *Czechoslovak Forces – Cholmondeley Park* 25 May 2000

Kirkpatrick, Roger, *Audley End at War* (Saffron Walden Library Archive V4949, 1992)

Locock, Malcolm, *Wartime Memoirs* 2000

Meakin, Arthur, *Inconsequential Jottings, Memory Meanderings and Tales I Wos Told*

NA HS 9/109/3 Lord Walter Harold Bearsted

NA CAB 21/2564 Lord President's Committee, sub-committee on accommodation. Memorandum to the War Cabinet 28 April 1942 by the president of the Board of Education

NAKV 5/3 The Anglo-German Fellowship

NA PREM 4 34/4 Correspondence with Churchill regarding requisitioning

NA WO 260/8, War Office Records

NA WORK 50/23 (A-B)

Temple, Beatrice, personal diary

Websites

www.bbc.co.uk/history/ww2peopleswar/stories/73/a4453373.shtml
www.brocketbabies.org.uk
www.coleshillhouse.com
www.Holdsworthtrust.org
www.holocaustresearchproject.org
www.Howickhallgardens.org
Monthly Report of the Meteorological Office: www.metoffice.
gov.uk/learning/library/archive-hidden-treasures/
monthly-weather-report
www.mi5.gov.uk/mi5-in-world-war-ii
www.nigelperrin.com
www.oxforddnb.com

ACKNOWLEDGEMENTS

This book has been one of the most ambitious projects I have undertaken and I could not have completed it without the help, support, advice and good humour of a very large number of people. I have chosen to mention them in connection with the house they were concerned with, though several were of course involved right across the book. Any errors are my responsibility.

Jim Crace, the novelist, inspired me to research the story of Brocket Hall during the war as he was born in the Ribbentrop bedroom in 1947, something that made an indelible impression on him. The full story could not have been told without the brilliant website for the Brocket Babies, managed by David Green. Of those whose stories have contributed to the chapter I thank warmly Alan Brocket Lowe, Janice Hawker, Julie Bloomfield, Les Cook, June Godby, Mo Neate, Barbara Perry and Timothy Reeves. Terry Morris, Mary de Soyres and Andy Chapman of the Lemsford Local History Group were very generous with their research and support.

Waddesdon Manor is run by the National Trust and the archives are outstanding. The archivist, Catherine Taylor, could not have been more generous or welcoming and I spent many hours in the magnificent Rothschild archive building. Thanks are also due to Pippa Shirley, head of collections and gardens and Nicola Tinsley, Waddesdon's photo librarian.

I first visited Aldenham Park in 2015 and met the present owner, Hettie Fenwick. Since then I have met members of the Acton family who have read and made tweaks to the story of their ancestral home, sharing their memories of their parents and Father Ronald

Knox. My warm thanks go to Edward Acton, Pelline Marffy and Jane Smiley. The nuns of the Assumption live in St James's Square and Sister John-Mary made me welcome when she showed me the archive and introduced me to a number of old girls: Alannah Dowling, Nicola McCaskie, and Faine Meynell kindly shared their memories.

Malvern College's retired archivist, Ian Quickfall, has an encyclopaedic memory and knack of bringing the best stories to my attention, for which I am most grateful. Paul Godsland and Syd Hill have also been helpful in tracking down statistics and photographs. Tace Fox at Harrow gave me material from the archives there and Sir Stephen Brown talked to me about life at Malvern and Harrow in the 1940s. Louise Locock kindly let me use her father's memoir written for his grandson in 2000. She said he would be amused to appear on the same page as Winston Churchill.

Lord and Lady Howick were hospitable and generous in letting me stay at Howick Hall and rummage through their photograph albums at leisure. Anne Dawnay remembered the hall during the war and told me some amusing stories. A thank you is extended to Avril and Arthur Meakin who were helpful to me at every turn whether sharing their own research, helping me to get photographs taken or rescuing me from Alnwick station in the pouring rain. Extracts from the diaries of Lady Sybil Middleton are reproduced in the book with kind permission from Simon Boyd, Caroline Boyd, James Boyd and Diana Braithwaite from the estate of Lady Sybil Middleton.

Upton House in Warwickshire was gifted to the National Trust by Lord and Lady Bearsted. NT volunteer Charlie Cox was particularly kind to me on my visit. My thanks also to Michelle Leake and Jane Roughley of the National Trust and to Robert Whaley Cohen, who was able to give me a little insight into the most private of men, Lord Bearsted. Family members of wartime banking staff kindly spoke to me about their parents: Patrick Hope Falkner, Philippa Munday, Charles Tubbs and Ruth Liss. Mark Summers explained the workings of a merchant bank, for which I am very grateful.

I first visited Coleshill House in 2013 with Dr John Forster. I have been in contact Bill Ashby, Nina Hannaford and Tom Sykes, all members of CART (Coleshill Auxiliary Research Team), who help to run the British Resistance Archive. Thank you all.

My visit to northern Scotland remains one of the highlights of my research for this book. I am grateful to Sarah Winnington-Ingram at Arisaig House who looked after us and let us look through the map chest that contained plans of the house with wartime annotations including the pistol gallery in the servants' quarters. I was fortunate to meet Donald Cameron of Lochiel in his ancestral home of Achnacarry Castle and also Christine Falconer at Achdalieu who were both very generous with their time. My thanks to Michael Gubbins who gave permission for me to quote from his grandfather, Sir Colin McVean Gubbins' papers at Imperial War Museum, London.

My interest in the Czechoslovak forces in the UK and subsequently the whole story of the Czech government in exile was piqued by a conversation in 2015 with the manager of the Cholmondeley Estate, James Hall. I met Neil Rees, who shared the history of the Czechs in exile. My dear friend, Ingram Murray, shared his vast knowledge of the Second World War and kindly read this and other chapters.

Bignor Manor is a private house in Sussex. I thank the current owner for letting me visit in 2016. The team at RAF Tangmere have been helpful and I thank Dudley Hooley for sourcing images for me. I also wish to thank Father Jerome Bertram for permission to use excerpts from his parent's papers.

Ian Valentine's book on the war years at Audley House is outstanding and I am grateful to him for letting me use excerpts from it. I also thank Chris Bozejewicz from the Polish Underground Movement Study Trust and Sarah Turpin at Saffron Walden Library.

Melford Hall is owned by the National Trust. My thanks to Sir Richard and Jeanie Hyde Parker for allowing me to interview them along with Sir Richard's sister, Lady Camoys. Trudi Jefferis of the

National Trust showed me wartime memorabilia that had been found beneath the floorboards and John Toosey, my cousin, was a very entertaining host when I was weary of research.

Others who have helped with their time and expertise are Justine Hobson, Melanie Bryan and Toby Keel of *Country Life*; Simon Offord, Richard Hughes and members of the Department of Documents at Imperial War Museum, London; Rachael Merrison at Cheltenham College.

Friends and family have answered endless queries over the last four years: Jane Summers and Leonoragh Teak helped me with Gaelic translations; Martin Poole showed me how a Sten gun works or indeed fails to work; Paul and Brenda Carden, Roger Barrington, Graham Ives, Andy Ballingall, Naomi Sharma and Owen Whittaker cheered me along and my great friend and fellow author, Diane Setterfield, offered an expert ear and a kind hug when the book felt unwieldy. There can be no substitute for someone who understands, truly, what writers go through.

Alex Harrison helped me for several months working in the Red Cross archives and at the National Archives. He has an excellent nose for a good story and I really appreciated his skill. Stephen Rockcliffe also helped to dig out extra details as did Florence Smith. Francine Fletcher told me the story of Tyneham. Kate Ogilvy read an early draft and my father Peter helped with proof reading.

The team at Simon & Schuster have been exceptionally support-ive. Iain MacGregor, my editor, challenged me with great tact and lots of enthusiasm which I appreciate immensely. Suzanne Baboneau has been a good friend and support throughout. Liz Marvin copy-edited with patience. Catherine Clarke, my literary agent, is so positive and encouraging: I cannot thank her enough. And thanks also go to Michele Topham and Jackie Head at Felicity Bryan Agency who were sane voices when I needed them.

The book is dedicated to the memory of Helena Pozniak, known to us all our childhood as Mrs P. She was a refugee from Poland who came to Britain with her four sons, one of them a babe in arms, during the war. A true lady, a deeply wonderful human being and an eternal optimist, she represented for me everything that I admire about Poland and its people.

Finally, none of this could have been achieved without the emotional support and wicked humour of my family. Simon, Richard and Sandy are wonderfully encouraging and my husband Chris, who puts up with hours of pillow talk, will finally get to read this book when it appears in hardback. Thanks boys. You're fantastic.

NOTES

Introduction: An Invasion of Privacy

1   Mrs Cameron-Head to Lochiel, May 1940, Cameron-Head papers, Highland Council Archive, D271/B/III/1
2   Emergency Powers (Defence) Act 1939
3   Titmuss, Richard, *Problems of Social Policy*, p. 54
4   Robinson, J. M .,*The Country House at War* p. 12
5   Robinson, J. M ., *The Country House at War* p. 44
6   Lady Desborough to Winston Churchill, 5 November 1942
7   Lady Desborough to Winston Churchill, 5 November 1942
8   Telegram from Winston Churchill to Lady Desborough 6 November 1942
9   Olson, Lynne, *Last Hope Island*, p. 65
10 Hodgson, Vere, *Few Eggs and No Oranges* 18 April 1943

Chapter 1: Brocket's Babies

1   www.brocketbabies.org.uk
2   www.brocketbabies.org.uk
3   www.brocketbabies.org.uk
4   Lily Lowe to her mother 5 September 1939 www.brocketbabies.org.uk/
5   Lily Lowe to her mother 12 September 1939 www.brocketbabies.org.uk/
6   Lily Lowe to her mother 12 September 1939 www.brocketbabies.org.uk/
7   www.brocket-hall.co.uk/brocket-hall/history
8   The Anglo-German Fellowship, National Archives KV 5/3
9   The Anglo-German Fellowship, National Archives KV 5/3
10 From Dorothy Louisa Beasley www.brocketbabies.org.uk
11 From Dorothy Louisa Beasley www.brocketbabies.org.uk
12 www.brocket-hall.co.uk/brocket-hall/history/
13 Peter Mandler, 'Lamb, William, second Viscount Melbourne (1779–1848)', *Oxford Dictionary of National Biography*, Oxford University Press, 2004; online edn, Jan 2008

14   Ministry of Information Second World War Official Collection IWM D 9027
15   Irene Grainger to her husband, February 1943, www.brocketbabies.org.uk/
16   Irene Grainger to her husband, February 1943, www.brocketbabies.org.uk/
17   Doreen Glover www.brocketbabies.org.uk
18   Doreen Glover www.brocketbabies.org.uk
19   June Godby 15 March 2013, www.brocketbabies.org.uk
20   www.brocketbabies.org.uk
21   www.brocketbabies.org.uk
22   www.brocketbabies.org.uk
23   www.brocketbabies.org.uk
24   www.brocketbabies.org.uk
25   www.brocketbabies.org.uk
26   www.brocketbabies.org.uk
27   www.brocketbabies.org.uk
28   Norah Hearn www.brocketbabies.org.uk
29   Norah Hearn www.brocketbabies.org.uk
30   Julie Bloomfield www.brocketbabies.org.uk
31   Mo Neate www.brocketbabies.org.uk
32   Mo Neate www.brocketbabies.org.uk
33   Mo Neate www.brocketbabies.org.uk
34   Les Cook www.brocketbabies.org.uk

Chapter 2: Waddesdon at War

1   Bell, G. K. A., *Humanity and the Refugees*. The Fifth Lucien Wolf Memorial Lecture 1 February 1939 to the Jewish Historical Society of England
2   Ministry of Health advice leaflet, HMSO, 1939
3   Ministry of Health advice leaflet, HMSO, 1939
4   Rothschild, Mrs James de, *The Rothschilds at Waddesdon Manor*, p. 118
5   Gurney, Ivor and Carr, Norman, *Waddesdon Through the Ages* p. 53
6   Rothschild, Mrs James de, *The Rothschilds at Waddesdon Manor* p. 19
7   Rothschild, Mrs James de, *The Rothschilds at Waddesdon Manor* p. 20
8   Rothschild, Mrs James de, *The Rothschilds at Waddesdon Manor* p. 81
9   Catherine Taylor in conversation with JS 7 January 2016
10   Unpublished, undated speech to an audience in Glasgow probably March 1939 © Waddesdon Manor Archive
11   Rothschild, Mrs James de, *The Rothschilds at Waddesdon Manor* p. 122
12   *New York Times*, 28 July 1983
13   Guenter Gruenebaum to Dorothy and James de Rothschild 12 March 1946 © Waddesdon Manor Archive
14   *'Chips': The Diaries of Sir Henry Channon*, 17 December 1942
15   Rothschild, Dorothy de, Diary 25 August 1939 © Waddesdon Manor Archive
16   Colville, John, *The Fringes of Power: Downing Street Diaries 1939–1955*,

23 September 1939

17 Titmuss, Richard, *Problems of Social Policy*, p. 372

18 Rothschild, Mrs James de, *The Rothschilds at Waddesdon Manor* p. 122

19 Unpublished memoir © Waddesdon Manor Archive

20 Unpublished memoir © Waddesdon Manor Archive

21 Gurney, Ivor and Carr, Norman, *Waddesdon Through the Ages* p. 54

22 Rothschild, Mrs James de, *The Rothschilds at Waddesdon Manor* p. 126

23 Rothschild, Mrs James de, *The Rothschilds at Waddesdon Manor* p. 126

24 Unpublished memoir © Waddesdon Manor Archive

25 Unpublished memoir © Waddesdon Manor Archive

26 Unpublished memoir © Waddesdon Manor Archive

27 Rothschild, Mrs James de, *The Rothschilds at Waddesdon Manor* p. 128

28 Rothschild, Mrs James de, *The Rothschilds at Waddesdon Manor* p. 122

29 Christine Bride to Dorothy de Rothschild August 1941 © Waddesdon Manor Archive

30 Christine Bride to Dorothy de Rothschild 7 January 1942 © Waddesdon Manor Archive

31 Unpublished memoir © Waddesdon Manor Archive

32 Miss Mabel Hill to Dorothy de Rothschild 12 October 1939 © Waddesdon Manor Archive

33 Helen Crosfield to Dorothy de Rothschild 11 September 1939 © Waddesdon Manor Archive

34 Christine Bride to Dorothy de Rothschild 7 January 1942© Waddesdon Manor Archive

35 Helen Crosfield to Dorothy de Rothschild 19 November 1939 © Waddesdon Manor Archive

36 Helen Crosfield to Dorothy de Rothschild 19 November 1939 © Waddesdon Manor Archive

37 Miss Mabel Hill to Dorothy de Rothschild 12 October 1939 © Waddesdon Manor Archive

38 Mrs Fillingham to Christine Bride, 25 November 1939 © Waddesdon Manor Archive

39 Mrs Noakes to Mr & Mrs de Rothschild 18 October 1939 © Waddesdon Manor Archive

40 Mrs Noakes to Mr & Mrs de Rothschild 18 October 1939 © Waddesdon Manor Archive

41 Unpublished memoir © Waddesdon Manor Archive

42 Unpublished memoir © Waddesdon Manor Archive

43 Report from Under-Matron on Christmas 1939, undated © Waddesdon Archive

44 Report from Under-Matron on Christmas 1939, undated © Waddesdon Archive

45 Conversation between Mrs Beatrice Whitehouse, Catherine Taylor and Pippa

Shirley 21-7-2010 © Waddesdon Archive
46 GP Milson to Philip Sydney Woolf 29 September 1940© Waddesdon Archive
47 Rothschild, Mrs James de, *The Rothschilds at Waddesdon Manor*, p. 124
48 Gurney, Ivor and Carr, Norman, *Waddesdon Through the Ages* p. 149
49 Gurney, Ivor and Carr, Norman, *Waddesdon Through the Ages* p. 150
50 Rothschild, Mrs James de, *The Rothschilds at Waddesdon Manor* pp. 124–5

Chapter 3: Girls, Ghosts and Godliness

1   *Daily Telegraph* 22 March 2003 Daphne Lady Acton Obituary
2   Waugh, Evelyn, *The Life of Right Reverend Ronald Knox* pp. 34–5
3   Waugh, Evelyn, *The Life of Right Reverend Ronald Knox* p. 82
4   Knox, Ronald, *A Spiritual Aeneid* p. 48
5   Waugh, Evelyn, *The Life of Right Reverend Ronald Knox* p. 115
6   Waugh, Evelyn, *The Life of Right Reverend Ronald Knox* p. 67
7   Waugh, Evelyn, *The Life of Right Reverend Ronald Knox* p. 179
8   Snoddy, Raymond, *NewsWatch* 16 June 2005
9   Knox, Ronald, *Essays in Satire* A Forgotten Interlude
10 Bourne, Cardinal, *The Tablet* January 1926
11 Waugh, Evelyn, *The Life of Right Reverend Ronald Knox* p. 239
12 Waugh, Evelyn, *The Life of Right Reverend Ronald Knox* p. 240
13 Waugh, Evelyn, *The Life of Right Reverend Ronald Knox* p. 241
14 The Annals of Kensington 1 September 1939
15 The Annals of Kensington 13, 14, 16 September 1939
16 The Annals of Kensington 21 September 1939
17 The Annals of Kensington 17 October 1939
18 The Annals of Kensington 22 September 1939
19 The Annals of Kensington 23 September 1939
20 Waugh, Evelyn, *The Life of Right Reverend Ronald Knox* p. 268
21 The Annals of Kensington 25 September 1939
22 The Annals of Kensington 25 September 1939
23 The Annals of Kensington 9 September 1939
24 The Annals of Kensington 17 December 1939
25 Alannah Dowling email to JS 2 November 2016
26 Alannah Dowling email to JS 9 November 2016
27 Nicola Macaskie in conversation with JS April 2016
28 *The Assumption Chronicle* (War Issue No 2), 1943
29 Nicola Macaskie in conversation with JS May 2016
30 Pelline Marffy née Acton in conversation with JS 14 May 2017
31 Knox, Ronald, *Literary Distractions* pp. 225–6
32 Knox, Ronald, *Literary Distractions* pp. 226–7
33 Waugh, Evelyn, *The Life of Right Reverend Ronald Knox* p. 272
34 Alannah Dowling in conversation with JS April 2016

35   Faine Meynell in conversation with JS August 2015

36   *The Assumption Chronicle* (War Issue No. 1) 1942 p. 6

37   *The Assumption Chronicle* (War Issue No. 2) 1943 p. 14

38   Knox, Ronald, *The Mass in Slow Motion: At the Foot of the Altar* p. 3

39   Knox, Ronald, *The Mass in Slow Motion: At the Foot of the Altar* p. 3

40   *The Assumption Chronicle* (War Issue No. 5) 1945 p. 32

41   *The Assumption Chronicle* (War Issue No. 1) 1942 p. 24

42   *Assumption Chronicle* (War Issue No. 1) 1942 p. 37

43   Knox, Ronald, *The Mass in Slow Motion* p. 104

44   *The Assumption Chronicle* (War Issue No. 3) 1944

45   *The Assumption Chronicle* (War Issue No. 1) 1942 p. 18

46   *The Assumption Chronicle* (War Issue No. 1) 1942 p. 21

47   *The Assumption Chronicle* (War Issue No. 1) 1942 p. 38

48   *The Assumption Chronicle* (War Issue No. 2) 1943 p. 21

49   *The Assumption Chronicle* (War Issue No. 1) p. 21

50   *The Assumption Chronicle* 1945 (War Issue No. 5) p.22

51   *The Assumption Chronicle* (War Issue No. 1) 1942 p. 12

52   Pelline Marffy née Acton in conversation with JS 14 May 2017

53   Nicola Macaskie in conversation with JS April 2016

54   Alannah Dowling in email to JS 8 November 2016

55   Alannah Dowling in conversation with JS August 2016

56   Nicola McKaskie in conversation with JS August 2016

57   Woodward, Antony and Penn, Robert, *The Wrong Kind of Snow, the Complete Daily Companion to the British Weather* 28 January

58   The Annals of Kensington 1 February 1940

59   *The Assumption Chronicle* (War Issue No. 1) 1942 p. 12

60   *The Assumption Chronicle* (War Issue No. 4) October 1944

61   *The Assumption Chronicle* (War Issue No. 5) October 1945

62   Pelline Marffy née Acton in conversation with JS 14 May 2017

Chapter 4: Twice Removed

1   Gaunt, H. C. A., *Two Exiles: A School in Wartime* p. 3

2   Gaunt, H. C. A., *Two Exiles: A School in Wartime* p. 3

3   Longmate, Norman, *How We Lived Then* p. 65

4   Gaunt, H. C. A., *Two Exiles: A School in Wartime* p. 4

5   Gaunt, H. C. A., *Two Exiles: A School in Wartime* p. 6

6   Gaunt, H. C. A., *Two Exiles: A School in Wartime* p. 6

7   Gaunt, H. C. A., *Two Exiles: A School in Wartime* p. 7

8   Gaunt, H. C. A., *Two Exiles: A School in Wartime* p. 7

9   Gaunt, H. C. A., *Two Exiles: A School in Wartime* p. 5

10   Gaunt, H. C. A., *Two Exiles: A School in Wartime* p. 8

11   Gaunt, H. C. A., *Two Exiles: A School in Wartime* p. 12

12   Gaunt, H. C. A., *Two Exiles: A School in Wartime* p. 13
13   Tom Gaunt's letter to parents of Malvern College boys dd. 9 September 1939
14   Robinson, John Martin, *Requisitioned* p. 48
15   Hussey, Christopher, *Country Life* 3 February 1940 pp. 121–2
16   Gaunt, H. C. A., *Two Exiles: A School in Wartime* p. 15
17   Gaunt, H. C. A., *Two Exiles: A School in Wartime* p. 33
18   Captain James Roy to his mother 7 October 1939
19   Captain James Roy to his mother 14 October 1939
20   Hussey, Christopher, *Country Life* 3 February 1940 pp. 121–2
21   Email from Karen Wiseman at the Blenheim Education Team 13 October 2016
22   Gaunt, H. C. A., *Two Exiles: A School in Wartime* p. 20
23   Hussey, Christopher, *Country Life* 3 February 1940 pp. 121–2
24   Gaunt, H. C. A., *Two Exiles: A School in Wartime* p. 34
25   James Roy to his mother 22 October 1939
26   *The Malvernian* December 1939
27   James Roy to his mother 21 January 1940
28   James Roy to his mother 28 January 1940
29   Blumeneau, Ralph, *A History of Malvern College* p. 129
30   James Roy to his mother 26 May 1940
31   James Roy to his mother 30 June 1940
32   Sir Stephen Brown in conversation with JS 6 April 2017
33   Gaunt, H. C. A., *Two Exiles: A School in Wartime* pp. 40–41
34   Monthly Weather Report of the Meteorological Office, Vol 57. No. 6 MO 454
35   Roy, James *Memoirs* pp. 38–9 IWM 07/36/1
36   Blumenau, Ralph, *A History of Malvern College 1865–1965* p. 130
37   Gaunt, H. C. A., *Two Exiles: A School in Wartime* p. 41
38   Gaunt, H. C. A., *Two Exiles: A School in Wartime* p. 41 .
39   Sir Stephen Brown in conversation with JS 6 April 2017
40   Tom Gaunt to parents June 1940
41   www.mi5.gov.uk/mi5-in-world-war-ii
42   BBC.co.uk The People's War Helen Quin, Article A4427084 11 July 2005
43   Robinson, J. M., *The Country House at War* p. 112
44   Gaunt, H. C. A., *Two Exiles: A School in Wartime* p. 47
45   Gaunt, H. C. A., *Two Exiles: A School in Wartime* p. 50
46   Lord Presidents Committee, sub-committee on accommodation. Memorandum to the War Cabinet 28 April 1942 by the President of the Board of Education NA CAB 21/2564
47   Lord Presidents Committee, sub-committee on accommodation. Memorandum to the War Cabinet 28 April 1942 NA Cab 21/2564
48   Lord Presidents Committee, sub-committee on accommodation. Memorandum to the War Cabinet 28 April 1942 by the President of the Board of Education NA CAB 21/2564

49   Gaunt, H. C. A., *Two Exiles: A School in Wartime* p. 52
50   Gaunt, H. C. A., *Two Exiles: A School in Wartime* p. 61
51   Blumenau, Ralph, *A History of Malvern College 1865–1965* p. 140
52   Malvern College Exhibition on RADAR 2016-17
53   Gaunt, H. C. A., *Two Exiles: A School in Wartime* pp. 73–4
54   Gaunt, H. C. A., *Two Exiles: A School in Wartime* p. 64
55   Gaunt, H. C. A., *Two Exiles: A School in Wartime* p. 67
56   Blumenau, Ralph, *A History of Malvern College 1865–1965* p. 143
57   Blumenau, Ralph, *A History of Malvern College 1865–1965* p. 142
58   Gaunt, H. C. A., *Two Exiles: A School in Wartime* p. 81
59   Blumenau, Ralph, *A History of Malvern College 1865–1965* p. 143
60   Blumenau, Ralph, *A History of Malvern College 1865–1965* p. 144
61   *Daily Telegraph* 23 February 1944
62   *Daily Telegraph* 23 February 1944
63   Sir Stephen Brown in conversation with JS 6 April 17
64   Locock, Malcolm, unpublished memoir
65   Locock, Malcolm, unpublished memoir
66   Locock, Malcolm, unpublished memoir
67   Blumenau, Ralph, *A History of Malvern College 1865–1965* pp. 144–5
68   Gaunt, H. C. A., *Two Exiles: A School in Wartime* p. 83
69   Blumenau, Ralph, *A History of Malvern College 1865–1965* p. 150
70   Blumenau, Ralph, *A History of Malvern College 1865–1965* p. 150
71   Malvern College Exhibition 2016–17
72   Blumenau, Ralph, *A History of Malvern College 1865–1965* p. 152
73   Rowe, A. P., *One Story of Radar* p. 161
74   Malvern History Flipbook www.qinetiq.com
75   Gaunt, H. C. A., *Two Exiles: A School in Wartime* p. 77

Chapter 5: Lady Grey's Guests

1   Meakin, Avril, *Howick's Seven Tales of the Unexpected* p. 18
2   www.metoffice.gov.uk/binaries/content/assets/mohippo/pdf/t/5/feb1941.pdf
3   Medical Services General History Vol 1 by Major General Sir W. G.
      Macpherson, KCMG CB LLD p. 85
4   Titmuss, Richard, *Problems of Social Policy* p. 460
5   Titmuss, Richard, *Problems of Social Policy* p. 54
6   Titmuss, Richard, *Problems of Social Policy* pp. 54–5
7   Maurice Patterman to Lady Sybil Grey 4 February 1915
8   Private H. Heroies to Lady Sybil Grey 7 January 1915
9   Howickhallgardens.com/history-of-howick-hall-and-gardens/
10   Howickhallgardens.com/history-of-howick-hall-and-gardens/earl-grey-an
      d-the-earl-grey-family
11   Lord Howick in conversation with JS 23 June 2016

12 Miss M. E. B., Cook IWM 99/37/1
13 Meakin, Avril, *Howick's Seven Tales of the Unexpected* p. 16
14 Meakin, Arthur, *Inconsequential Jottings, Memory Meanderings and Tales I wos Told* (unpublished) p. 1
15 Meakin, Arthur, *Inconsequential Jottings, Memory Meanderings and Tales I wos Told* (unpublished) p. 5
16 Miss M. E. B., Cook IWM 99/37/1
17 Miss M. E. B., Cook IWM 99/37/1
18 Miss M. E. B., Cook IWM 99/37/1
19 Miss M. E. B., Cook IWM 99/37/1
20 RCB/2/49/1/8 to 13 – *British Red Cross Society Northumberland Country Branch reports*, 1939 to 1947
21 Miss M. E. B., Cook IWM 99/37/1
22 Miss M. E. B., Cook IWM 99/37/1
23 Meakin, Avril, *Howick's Seven Tales of the Unexpected* p. 17
24 Miss M. E. B., Cook IWM 99/37/1
25 Meakin, Avril, *Howick's Seven Tales of the Unexpected* unnumbered page (introduction)
26 Miss M. E. B., Cook IWM 99/37/1
27 Miss M. E. B., Cook IWM 99/37/1
28 Miss M. E. B., Cook IWM 99/37/1
29 Miss M. E. B., Cook IWM 99/37/1
30 Meakin, Avril, *Howick's Seven Tales of the Unexpected* p. 18
31 Ann Dawnay in conversation with JS 24 June 2016
32 Lorna Granlund in conversation with JS 18-11-2015
33 Lorna Granlund in conversation with JS 18-11-2015
34 Lorna Granlund in conversation with JS 18-11-2015
35 Miss M. E. B., Cook IWM 99/37/1
36 Meakin, Avril, *Howick's Seven Tales of the Unexpected* pp. 15–16
37 Diary of Lady Sybil Middleton, 5 September 1940
38 Diary of Lady Sybil Middleton 4 January 1943
39 RCB/2/49/1/8 to 13 – *British Red Cross Society Northumberland Country Branch reports*, 1939 to 1947
40 Meakin, Arthur *Inconsequential Jottings, Memory Meanderings and Tales I wos Told* (unpublished and unnumbered) p. 7
41 Miss M. E. B., Cook IWM 99/37/1

Chapter 6: Dear 'K'

1 Henriques, Robert, *Marcus Samuel First Viscount Bearsted and founder of The 'Shell' Transport and Trading Company 1853–1927* p. 636
2 Henriques, Robert, *Marcus Samuel First Viscount Bearsted and founder of The 'Shell' Transport and Trading Company 1853–1927* p. 640

3   *New York Times* 10 November 1948
4   Peter Samuel to his parents 15 June 1943
5   Adler, Barney, *War time experiences 1940–1946* unpublished MS p. 1
6   Adler, Barney, *War time experiences 1940–1946* unpublished MS p. 2
7   Adler, Barney, *War time experiences 1940–1946* unpublished MS p. 3
8   Howarth, Stephen, *A Century in Oil* p. 192
9   Howarth, Stephen, *A Century in Oil* p. 192-3
10   Howarth, Stephen, *A Century in Oil* pp. 197-8
11   Howarth, Stephen, *A Century in Oil* p. 192
12   Howarth, Stephen, *A Century in Oil* p. 168
13   Howarth, Stephen, *A Century in Oil* p. 168
14   Howarth, Stephen, *A Century in Oil* p. 205
15   Howarth, Stephen, *A Century in Oil* p. 206
16   Howarth, Stephen, *A Century in Oil* p. 207
17   Howarth, Stephen, *A Century in Oil* p. 209
18   From notebooks in Upton House display by National Trust
19   Lord Bearsted to W. Gibson 1941
20   Lord Bearsted to W. Gibson 18 March 1942
21   Foot, M. R. D., *The Special Operations Executive 1940–46* p. 10
22   Foot, M. R. D., *SOE The Special Operations Executive 1940–46* p. 2
23   Foot, M. R. D., 'SOE in France p. 2
24   Bickham Sweet-Escott, *Baker Street Irregular* pp. 20-1
25   Warwicker, John, *Churchill's Underground Army* p. 178
26   Warwicker, John, *Churchill's Underground Army* p. 179
27   Lord Bearsted report January 1943 NA HS 9/109/3
28   DCR/OR/9379 from D/CR to AQ/M 18 October 1943

Chapter 7: Secret Saboteurs on the Home Front

1   www.warlinks.com/pages/auxiliary.php#special
2   CART website www.coleshillhouse.com/auxiliers.php
3   Churchill, 4 June 1940 in the House of Commons quoted in Enright,
     Dominique, *The Wicked Wit of Winston Churchill* p. 45
4   Atkin, Malcolm, *Fighting Nazi Occupation: British Resistance 1939–1945*
     p. 2
5   Allan, Stuart, *Commando Country* p. 23
6   Foot, M. R. D., 'Holland, John Charles Francis (1897–1956)', rev. *Oxford
     Dictionary of National Biography*, Oxford University Press, 2004; online edn,
     May 2008
7   Mackenzie, William, *The Secret History of SOE: The Special Operations
     Executive 1940–45* p. 8
8   Foot, M. R. D., *The Special Operations Executive 1940-46* p. 12
9   Wilkinson, Peter and Bright Astley, Joan, *Gubbins & SOE* p. 9

10 Linderman, A.R.B. *Rediscovering Irregular Warfare: Colin Gubbins and the Origins of Britain's Special Operations Executive* p. 40

11 Wilkinson, Peter and Bright Astley, Joan, *Gubbins & SOE* pp. 15–16

12 Wilkinson, Peter and Bright Astley, Joan, *Gubbins & SOE* p. 34

13 Wilkinson, Peter and Bright Astley, Joan, *Gubbins & SOE* pp. 34-5

14 Gubbins, MG Colin, *The Art of Guerrilla Warfare* p. 1

15 Dodds-Parker, Douglas, *Setting Europe Ablaze*, p. 182

16 Olson, Lynne, *Last Hope Island*, p. 163

17 Gubbins papers IWM 3/2/57, CG's comments on MRF Foot's book, undated

18 Gubbins address to the Anglo-Polish Society, 18 November 1972 IWM 4/1/41

19 Private Papers of Major General Sir Colin M Gubbins KCMG DSO MC IWM 12618

20 Wilkinson, Peter and Bright Astley, Joan, *Gubbins & SOE* p. 69

21 Wilkinson, Peter and Bright Astley, Joan, *Gubbins & SOE* p. 69

22 Foot, M. R. D., 'Grand, Lawrence Douglas (1898–1975)', *Oxford Dictionary of National Biography*, Oxford University Press, 2004; online edn, Jan 2008

23 Warwicker, John, *Churchill's Underground Army* p. 181

24 Warwicker, John, *Churchill's Underground Army* p. 181

25 Warwicker, John, *Churchill's Underground Army* p. 181

26 www.coleshillhouse.com/auxiliers.php

27 www.coleshillhouse.com/auxiliers.php

28 Warwicker, John, *Churchill's Underground Army* p. 4

29 Hitler's directive No. 16 quoted in Warwicker, John, *Churchill's Underground Army* p.35

30 Warwicker, John, *Churchill's Underground Army* p. 3

31 www.coleshillhouse.com/auxiliers.php

32 Lampe, David ,*The Last Ditch: Britain's Secret Resistance and the Nazi Invasion Plans* p. 74

33 www.coleshillhouse.com/auxiliers.php

34 www.coleshillhouse.com/auxiliers.php

35 www.coleshillhouse.com/auxiliers.php

36 Warwicker, John, *Churchill's Underground Army* p. 87

37 www.coleshillhouse.com/capt-ian-benson.php

38 Warwicker, John, *Churchill's Underground Army* p. 146

39 Lampe, David, *The Last Ditch* p. 79

40 Fleming, Peter, *The Spectator* 8 July 1966

41 *Hitler's Britain: What Hitler Had in Store for Occupied Britain* DVD

42 Captain Ian Benson interviewed www.coleshillhouse.com

43 Beatrice Temple personal diary 24 November 1941

44 www.coleshillhouse.com/

45 www.coleshillhouse.com/specialdutiesbranch/beatrice-temple.php

46 www.coleshillhouse.com/specialdutiesbranch/beatrice-temple.php

47 www.coleshillhouse.com/specialdutiesbranch/beatrice-temple.php

48   Bines, Graham, former curator of the Museum of the British Resistance
      Organisation quoted in Warwicker, John, *Churchill's Secret Army* p. 126
49   Warwicker, John, *Churchill's Secret Army* p. 93
50   Warwicker, John, *Churchill's Secret Army* p. 93
51   *The Secrets of Underground Britain: WARTIME SECRETS* (film)
52   Britain's Secret 'Underground', *Times* [London, England] 14 Apr. 1945
53   Atkin, Malcolm, *Fighting Nazi Occupation: British Resistance 1939–45*
      p. 87
54   Warwicker, John, *Churchill's Secret Army* p. 83
55   Atkin, Malcolm, *Fighting Nazi Occupation: British Resistance 1939–45*
      p. 87
56   Atkin, Malcolm, *Fighting Nazi Occupation: British Resistance 1939–1945*
      p. xii

Chapter 8: Guerrillas in the Mist

1   Mackenzie, William, *The Secret History of SOE: The Special Operations
      Executive 1940-45* p. 746
2   Kemp, Peter, *No Colours or Crest* p.25
3   Dourlein, Pieter, *Inside North Pole* p. 81
4   Pimlott, Ben ed., *The Second World War Diary of Hugh Dalton* pp. 57–59
5   Pimlott, Ben ed., *The Second World War Diary of Hugh Dalton* p. 62
6   Ingram Murray in email to JS 26 February 2017
7   Ingram Murray in email to JS 26 February 2017
8   Wilkinson, Peter & Bright Astley, Joan, *Gubbins and SOE* p.101
9   Pimlott, Ben ed. *The Second World War Diary of Hugh Dalton* p. 97,
      8 November 1940
10   Pimlott, Ben ed. *The Second World War Diary of Hugh Dalton* p. 115
      5 December 1940
11   Wilkinson, Peter, 'Gubbins, Sir Colin McVean (1896–1976)', rev. *Oxford
      Dictionary of National Biography*, Oxford University Press, 2004
12   Ingram Murray to JS email 26 February 2017
13   Foot, M. R. D., *SOE: The Special Operations Executive 1940–46* p. 22
14   Allan, Stuart, *Commando Country* p. 16
15   Allan, Stuart, *Commando Country* p. 21
16   Allan, Stuart, *Commando Country* p. 22
17   War Office Records, National Archives WO 260/8
18   Allan, Stuart, *Commando Country* p. 40 quoting speech by Major R. F. Hall
      MC 'The Big House' 31 August 2001 to the Moidart Local History Society
19   Longland, Jack, 'Chapman, Frederick Spencer (1907–1971)', rev. *Oxford
      Dictionary of National Biography*, Oxford University Press, 2004; online
      edn, Jan 2011
20   Kemp, Peter, *No Colours or Crest* p. 19

21   Buckmaster, Maurice, *They Fought Alone* p. 249

22   Foot, M.R.D. *SOE: The Special Operations Executive 1940–46* p. 63

23   Pimlott, Ben ed., *The Second World War Diary of Hugh Dalton* p. 133

24   Linderman, A. R. B., *Rediscovering Irregular Warfare: Colin Gubbins and the Origins of Britain's Special Operations Executive* p. 40

25   Dalton's letter to George Wicks MP, 30 December 1941, in file 'Organisation & Administration. Property, SOE records, National Archives H 8/337

26   Allan, Stuart, *Commando Country* p. 170

27   Allan, Stuart, *Commando Country* pp. 53–4

28   Botting, Douglas, *Gavin Maxwell* p. 56

29   www.coleshillhouse.com/eric-anthony-sykes-the-forgotten-hero-of-combatives.php

30   Hall, Major R F MC, *The Big House* (unpublished transcript of a lecture to the Moidart History Society) 13 August 2001

31   Allan, Stuart, *Commando Country* p. 57

32   Fairbairn, W., *All-In Fighting* pp. 7–8

33   Allan, Stuart, *Commando Country* p. 56

34   Langelaan, George, *Knights of Floating Silk* p. 68

35   Botting, Douglas, *Gavin Maxwell* p. 49

36   Botting, Douglas, *Gavin Maxwell* p. 11

37   Botting, Douglas, *Gavin Maxwell* p. 29

38   Botting, Douglas, *Gavin Maxwell* p. 56

39   Botting, Douglas, *Gavin Maxwell* p. xxxii

40   Botting, Douglas, *Gavin Maxwell* p. 57

41   Botting, Douglas, *Gavin Maxwell* p. 58

42   Botting, Douglas, *Gavin Maxwell* p. 64

43   Botting, Douglas, *Gavin Maxwell* p. 64

44   Botting, Douglas, *Gavin Maxwell* p. 64

45   Botting, Douglas, *Gavin Maxwell* p. 61

46   Scott, Hamish, 'Inside Story: Garramore House', *Daily Telegraph* 11 November 2000

47   Botting, Douglas, *Gavin Maxwell* p. 65

48   Harrison, David M, *Special Operations Executives: Para-Military Training in Scotland during World War 2* p. 51

49   Harrison, David M, *Special Operations Executives: Para-Military Training in Scotland during World War 2* p. 52

50   Harrison, David M, *Special Operations Executives: Para-Military Training in Scotland during World War 2* p. 54

51   Harrison, David M, *Special Operations Executives: Para-Military Training in Scotland during World War 2* p. 53

52   Harrison, David M, *Special Operations Executives: Para-Military Training in Scotland during World War 2* p. 54

53   *Daily Telegraph Obituaries* 9 August 2011

54   *Daily Telegraph Obituaries* 9 August 2011
55   *Daily Telegraph Obituaries* 9 August 2011
56   *Daily Telegraph Obituaries* 9 August 2011
57   *Daily Telegraph Obituaries* 9 August 2011
58   Foot, M. R. D., SOE: *The Special Operations Executive 1940–46* p. 205
59   Botting, Douglas, *Gavin Maxwell* p. 72
60   Botting, Douglas, *Gavin Maxwell* p. 72
61   Allan, Stuart, *Commando Country* p. 22

Chapter 9: Three Lime Trees

1   Mackenzie, Compton, *Dr Beneš* p. 18
2   Mackenzie, Compton, *Dr Beneš* p. 177
3   Moravec, František, *Master of Spies* pp. 22–3
4   MacDonald, Callum, *The Assassination of Reinhard Heydrich* p. 67
5   Quoted by Alexander Werth in *France and Munich* (H. Hamilton, 1939), p. 120
6   Adolf Hitler in a speech in Munich, September 1938 reproduced in *Dr Beneš* by Compton Mackenzie p. 13
7   Mackenzie, Compton, *Dr Beneš* p. 15
8   Mackenzie, Compton, *Dr Beneš* p. 190
9   Mackenzie, Compton, *Dr Beneš* p. 197
10   Mackenzie, Compton, *Dr Beneš* p. 208
11   Mackenzie, Compton, *Dr Beneš* p. 215
12   Winston Churchill, 21 September 1939
13   Mackenzie, Compton, *Dr Beneš* pp. 236–7
14   Churchill, Winston, *A Total and Unmitigated Defeat. Speech in the House of Commons* 5 October 1938
15   Mackenzie, Compton, *Dr Beneš* p. 239
16   MacDonald, Callum, *The Assassination of Reinhard Heydrich* p. 67
17   Moravec, František, *Master of Spies* p. 39
18   Moravec, František, *Master of Spies* pp. 39-40
19   Moravec, František, *Master of Spies* p. 133
20   Moravec, František, *Master of Spies* p. 137
21   MacDonald, Callum, *The Assassination of Reinhard Heydrich* p. 23
22   Mackenzie, Compton, *Dr Beneš* p. 252
23   MacDonald, Callum, *The Assassination of Reinhard Heydrich* p. 85
24   MacDonald, Callum, *The Assassination of Reinhard Heydrich* p. 81
25   Franz Kaplan, *Czechoslovak Forces – Cholmondeley Park* 25 May 2000
26   Franz Kaplan, *Czechoslovak Forces – Cholmondeley Park* 25 May 2000
27   Franz Kaplan, *Czechoslovak Forces – Cholmondeley Park* 25 May 2000
28   Franz Kaplan, *Czechoslovak Forces – Cholmondeley Park* 25 May 2000
29   Franz Kaplan, *Czechoslovak Forces – Cholmondeley Park* 25 May 2000

30   Beith, Richard, *The Postal History of the Free Czechoslovak Forces in Great Britain 1940–1945* p iii
31   Franz Kaplan, *Czechoslovak Forces – Cholmondeley Park* 25 May 2000
32   Franz Kaplan, *Czechoslovak Forces – Cholmondeley Park* 25 May 2000
33   Beith, Richard, *The Postal History of the Free Czechoslovak Forces in Great Britain 1940–1945* p. 3
34   Mackenzie, Compton, *Dr Beneš* p. 262
35   Mackenzie, Compto,n *Dr Beneš* p. 262
36   Mackenzie, Compton, *Dr Beneš* p. 273
37   MacDonald, Callum, *The Assassination of Reinhard Heydrich* p. 165
38   Moravec, František, *Master of Spies* p. 193
39   Linderman, ARB *Rediscovering Irregular Warfare: Colin Gubbins and the Origins of Britain's Special Operations Executive* pp. 154–5
40   Wilkinson, Peter and Bright Astley, Joan, *Gubbins & SOE* p. 107
41   Moravec, František, *Master of Spies* p. 195
42   Moravec, František, *Master of Spies* p. 196
43   www.holocaustresearchproject.org/nazioccupation/heydrichkilling.html
44   MacDonald, Callum, *The Assassination of Reinhard Heydrich* p. 188
45   MacDonald, Callum, *The Assassination of Reinhard Heydrich* p. 188
46   www.holocaustresearchproject.org/nazioccupation/heydrichkilling.html
47   Mackenzie, Compton *Dr Beneš* p. 256

Chapter 10: Birds of Passage

1   Quoted in Fenby, Jonathan, *The General: Charles de Gaulle and the France He Saved* p. 132
2   Bertram, Mrs B., IWM 6428 p. 2
3   Barbara Bertram, IWM Interview 22 March 1999 catalogue 18783
4   Bertram, Anthony & Barbara, The Secret of Bignor Manor p. p. 181
5   Bertram, Barbara, *French Resistance in Sussex* p. 4
6   Barbara Bertram, IWM Interview 22 March 1999 catalogue 18783
7   Bertram, Mrs B., IWM 6428 p. 1
8   Bertram, Barbara, *French Resistance in Sussex* p. 4
9   Bertram, Barbara, *French Resistance in Sussex* p. 8
10   Bertram, Barbara, *French Resistance in Sussex* p. 6
11   Bertram, Mrs B., IWM 6428 p. 1
12   Bertram, Barbara *French Resistance in Sussex* p. 21
13   Bertram, Barbara, *French Resistance in Sussex* pp. 22–3
14   McCairns, James Atterby, *Lysander Pilot: Secret Operations with 161 Squadron* p. 25
15   Verity, Hugh, *We Landed by Moonlight* p. 21
16   Verity, Hugh, *We Landed by Moonlight* p. 21
17   McCairns, James Atterby, *Lysander Pilot: Secret Operations with 161*

Squadron p. 1

18 Verity, Hugh, *We Landed by Moonlight* pp. 108-9

19 McCairns, James Atterby, *Lysander Pilot: Secret Operations with 161 Squadron* p. 17

20 Bertram, Barbara, *French Resistance in Sussex* p. 25

21 Bertram, Barbara, *French Resistance in Sussex* p. 23

22 Bertram, Barbara, *French Resistance in Sussex* p. 28

23 Bertram, Barbara, *French Resistance in Sussex* pp. 4–5

24 Bertram, Mrs B., IWM 6428 p. 5

25 Bertram, Barbara, *French Resistance in Sussex* p. 1

26 Bertram, Barbara, *French Resistance in Sussex* pp. 10–11

27 Bertram, Barbara, *French Resistance in Sussex* p. 11

28 Bertram, Barbara, *French Resistance in Sussex* p. 12

29 Bertram, Barbara, *French Resistance in Sussex* p. 13

30 Bertram, Barbara, *French Resistance in Sussex* p. x

31 Bertram, Barbara, *French Resistance in Sussex* p. 20

32 McCairns, James Atterby, *Lysander Pilot: Secret Operations with 161 Squadron* p. 16–17

33 Verity, Hugh, *We Landed by Moonlight* p. 66

34 McCairns, James Atterby, *Lysander Pilot: Secret Operations with 161 Squadron* pp. 24-5

35 Bertram, Anthony & Barbara, *The Secret of Bignor Manor* p. 96

36 McCairns, James Atterby, *Lysander Pilot: Secret Operations with 161 Squadron* p. 39

37 McCairns, James Atterby, *Lysander Pilot: Secret Operations with 161 Squadron* p. 25

38 McCairns, James Atterby, *Lysander Pilot: Secret Operations with 161 Squadron* p. 28

39 McCairns, James Atterby, *Lysander Pilot: Secret Operations with 161 Squadron* p. 28

40 Verity, Hugh, *We Landed by Moonlight* p. 231

41 McCairns, James Atterby, *Lysander Pilot: Secret Operations with 161 Squadron* p. 20

42 McCairns, James Atterby, *Lysander Pilot: Secret Operations with 161 Squadron* p. 19

43 Bertram, Barbara, *French Resistance in Sussex* p. 61

44 Bertram, Barbara, *French Resistance in Sussex* p. 61

45 Bertram, Barbara, *French Resistance in Sussex* pp. 61–2

46 Bertram, Barbara, *French Resistance in Sussex* pp. 59–60

47 Bertram, Barbara, *French Resistance in Sussex* p. 45

48 Bertram, Barbara, *French Resistance in Sussex* p. 30

49 Bertram, Mrs B., IWM 6428 p. 16

50 Bertram, Barbara *French Resistance in Sussex* p. 34

51   Verity, Hugh, *We Landed by Moonlight* p. 100
52   Verity, Hugh, *We Landed by Moonlight* p. 100
53   Bertram, Barbara, *French Resistance in Sussex* p. 35
54   Albert Kohan codename 'Berthel' Might be better to asterisk them in the final version
55   Jacques Taylor code name 'Cazenave'
56   Bertram, Barbara, *French Resistance in Sussex* p. 36
57   Verity, Hugh, *We Landed in Moonlight* p. 157
58   Bertram, Anthony and Barbara, *The Secret of Bignor Manor* p. 127
59   Bertram, Barbara, *French Resistance in Sussex* p. 42
60   Bertram, Barbara, *French Resistance in Sussex* pp. 85–6
61   Bertram, Anthony and Barbara, *The Secret of Bignor Manor* p 129
62   Bertram, Barbara, *French Resistance in Sussex* p 38
63   First published in *Le Livre due Courage et de la Peur* (Edition aux Trois Couleurs, Paris 1946) and reproduced with permission in Bertram, Barbara, *French Resistance in Sussex* pp. xii–xiv

Chapter 11: Station 43: Audley End

1   Colville, John, *The Fringes of Power: Downing Street Diaries 1939–1945* 17 September 1939
2   Olson, Lynne, *Last Hope Island*, p. 168
3   Valentine, Ian, *Station 43: Audley End House and SOE's Polish Section* p. xiv
4   Olson, Lynne, *Last Hope Island*, p. 156
5   Olson, Lynne, *Last Hope Island*, p. 61
6   Kirkpatrick, Roger, *Audley End at War* p. 7
7   Kirkpatrick, Roger, *Audley End at War* p. 7
8   Valentine, Ian, *Station 43* p. 58
9   Kirkpatrick, Roger *Audley End at War* p. 9
10   Valentine, Ian, *Station 43* p. 60
11   Popham, Hugh, *The FANY in Peace and War* p.4
12   Popham, Hugh *The FANY in Peace and War* p. 27
13   Popham, Hugh, *The FANY in Peace and War* p. 32
14   Popham, Hugh, *The FANY in Peace and War* p. 75
15   Thompson, Dorothy (2 March 1945) *Major Questions Unanswered* Pittsburgh Post-Gazette p. 8
16   Popham, Hugh, *The FANY in Peace and War* p. 78
17   Popham, Hugh, *The FANY in Peace and War* p. 84
18   Murray, Ingram, *Secret Communications in World War II Mrs Bingham's Unit – the Free FANYs and 'the Org'* published in Bugle & Sabre 2015 p. 28
19   Popham, Hugh, *The FANY in Peace and War* p. 87
20   Dodds-Parker, Douglas, *Setting Europe Ablaze* p. 120

21   Popham, Hugh, *The FANY in Peace and War* p. 89
22   Popham, Hugh, *The FANY in Peace and War* p. 89
23   Popham, Hugh, *The FANY in Peace and War* pp. 89–90
24   Niven, Lady Pamela, unpublished MS IWM 05/76/1 p. 2
25   Lady Sue Ryder IWM Oral History 10057
26   Lady Sue Ryder IWM Oral History 10057
27   Valentine, Ian, *Station 43* pp. 40–41
28   Valentine, Ian, *Station 43* p. 77
29   Valentine, Ian, *Station 43* p. 93
30   English Heritage *Recollection of Corporal P Howe*
31   Valentine, Ian, *Station 43* p. 100
32   Valentine, Ian, *Station 43* p. 101
33   Valentine, Ian, *Station 43* p. 100
34   Valentine, Ian, *Station 43* p. 116
35   Adam Benrad IWM Oral History 8683
36   Adam Benrad IWM Oral History 8683
37   Adam Benrad IWM Oral History 8683
38   Adam Benrad IWM Oral History 8683
39   Iranek-Osmecki, *Silent* pp. 11–12
40   Valentine, Ian, *Station 43* p. 109
41   Valentine, Ian, *Station 43* pp. 47–8
42   Valentine, Ian, *Station 43* p. 135
43   Valentine, Ian, *Station 43* p. 135
44   Adam Benrad IWM Oral History 8683
45   Valentine, Ian, *Station 43* p. 186
46   Lees-Milne, James, *Diaries 1942–1954* p. 152
47   Valentine, Ian, *Station 43* p. 171
48   Valentine, Ian, *Station 43* p. 97

Chapter 12: The Army at Home

1   Robinson, John Martin, *The Country House at War* p. 161
2   Longmate, Norman, *How We Lived Then* p. 470
3   Titmuss, Richard, *Problems of Social Policy* pp. 371–372
4   Jeffrey Morrell in conversation with JS 30 November 2014
5   Jeffrey Morrell in conversation with JS 30 November 2014
6   Robinson, John Martin, *The Country House at War* p. 169
7   Robinson, John Martin, *Requisitioned* p. 131
8   Hyde-Parker, Lady Ulla, *National Trust Guide to Melford Hall* 1960, introduction
9   Seebohm, Caroline, *The Country House: A Wartime History 1939–45* p. 58
10   Robinson, J. M., *The Country House at War* p. 132
11   Instructions for American Servicemen in Britain 1942

12   Longmate, Norman, *How We Lived Then* p. 479
13   Captain Nation's film narrated by US colleague
14   Captain Nation's film narrated by US colleague
15   *Country Life*, 1937, email sent to CL 28-6-17
16   Lees Milne, James, *Melford Hall, Suffolk, A property of the National Trust* p. 3
17   Hyde Parker, Ulla, *Cousin Beatie: A memory of Beatrix Potter* p. 29
18   Hyde Parker, Ulla, *Cousin Beatie: A memory of Beatrix Potter* p. 29
19   Hyde Parker, Ulla, *Cousin Beatie: A memory of Beatrix Potter* p. 29
20   Hyde Parker, Ulla, *Cousin Beatie: A memory of Beatrix Potter* pp. 29-30
21   Hyde Parker, Ulla, *Cousin Beatie: A memory of Beatrix Potter* p. 31
22   Hyde Parker, Ulla, *Cousin Beatie: A memory of Beatrix Potter* p. 31
23   BBC People's War David Ford
24   Beth Hyde-Parker now Lady Camoys to JS 9 August 2016
25   *East Anglian Daily Times* 26 February 1942
26   Mary King speaking to Sir Richard Hyde Parker 2 December 2007

Conclusion: Restoration and Reintegration

1   Longmate, Norman, *How We Lived Then* p. 499
2   Cartland, Barbara, *The Years of Opportunity 1939–1945* p. 265
3   Calder, Angus, *The People's War* p. 586
4   Robinson, John Martin, *The Country House at War* p. 2
5   Robinson, John Martin, *The Country House at War* p. 163
6   Roscoe, Barley, *Katharine Pleydell-Bouverie: A Potter's Life 1895–1985* p. 19
7   *Evening Advertiser*, 24 September 1952
·8   Lees-Milne, James, *Diaries 1942–1954* 14 June 1946
9   Robinson, John Martin, *The Country House at War* p. 172
10   Robinson, John Martin, *Requisitioned* p. 54
11   Martin Robinson, John Martin, *Requisitioned* p. 54
12   Blumenau, Ralph, *A History of Malvern College 1865–1965* p. 133
13   Rothschild, Mrs James de, *The Rothschilds at Waddesdon Manor* p. 126
14   Rothschild, Mrs James de, *The Rothschilds at Waddesdon Manor*, p. 126
15   Lees-Milne, James, *Diaries 1942–1954* 16 May 1946
16   Rothschild, Mrs James de, *The Rothschilds at Waddesdon Manor* p. 132
17   Rothschild, Mrs James de, *The Rothschilds at Waddesdon Manor* p. 122
18   *New York Times* 28 July 1983
19   *New York Times* 28 July 1983
20   Agnes R. Hartman to Dorothy and James de Rothschild 9 August 1946. © Waddesdon Manor Archive
21   Draft of Dorothy de Rothschild's speech to the Cedar Boys, 1983 © Waddesdon Manor Archive
22   Peter Gortatowsky to James and Dorothy de Rothschild 22 March 1946

© Waddesdon Manor Archive

23 Peter Gortatowsky to Dorothy de Rothschild 6 July 1983 © Waddesdon
    Manor Archive

24 Lees-Milne, James, *Diaries 1942-1954* 1 March 1946

25 http://www.brocket-hall.co.uk

26 *The Assumption Chronicle*, October 1944

27 Evelyn Waugh to Ann Fleming, 1958

28 Waugh, Evelyn, *The Life of Right Reverend Ronald Knox,* p. 298

29 Waugh, Evelyn, *The Life of Right Reverend Ronald Knox,* p. 301

30 Meakin, Avril, *Howick's Seven Tales of the Unexpected* p. 50

31 Meakin, Avril, *Howick's Seven Tales of the Unexpected* p. 56

32 Valentine, Ian, *Station 43* p.177

33 Mackenzie, Compton, *Dr Beneš* p. 340

34 Beith, Richard, *The Postal History of the Free Czechoslovak Forces in Great
    Britain 1940–1945* p. iii

35 Franz Kaplan, *Czechoslovak Forces – Cholmondeley Park* 25 May 2000

36 Linderman, A. R. B., *Rediscovering Irregular Warfare: Colin Gubbins and
    the Origins of Britain's Special Operations Executive* p. 127

37 Wilkinson, Peter and Bright Astley, Joan, *Gubbins & SOE* (introduction)

38 Wilkinson, Peter and Bright Astley, Joan, *Gubbins & SOE* p. 217

39 Clement Attlee to Lord Selborne 21 June 1946

40 Linderman, A. R. B., *Rediscovering Irregular Warfare: Colin Gubbins and
    the Origins of Britain's Special Operations Executive* pp 178-9

41 Wilkinson, Peter and Bright Astley, Joan, *Gubbins & SOE* p. 239

42 Wilkinson, Peter and Bright Astley, Joan, *Gubbins & SOE* p. 242

43 Wilkinson, Peter and Bright Astley, Joan, *Gubbins & SOE*89%

INDEX

Achnacarry Castle 229
Ackroyd, Joan 86, 97
Acrobat Network 316
Acton, Cardinal Charles 66
Acton, Charlotte 67–8
Acton, Lady Daphne 67–8, 73–4, 75, 78, 84, 91, 93, 96, 97, 390–1
Acton, John, 3rd Baron 66–7, 68, 74–5, 77, 82, 94, 389, 390, 391–2
Acton, Pelline (later Marffy) 11, 67, 76, 78, 84, 86, 87, 91, 94–5, 96, 99
Acton, Sir Whitmore 66
Adam, Robert 19–20
Adams, Reg 265
Addington Manor, Buckinghamshire 255, 278, 280
Adler, Barney 165, 167, 172, 182
Air Raid Precautions (ARP) 287
Albertella, Sister 27, 28, 29
Aldenham Guide Company 91–2
Aldenham Park, Shropshire 11, 65–8, 74–99, 389–90, 392
   chapel 82
   convent school occupancy 74–99
   hauntings 81–2
   history of 66
Alethea, Sister 76, 78, 83
Allan, Stuart 226, 237
Allied Breweries 16
Alnwick 151, 153
American GIs 362–6, 367, 370
   black soldiers 363–4
Anderson, Sir John 124
Anglo-German Fellowship 17
Anglo–German Club 17
animal husbandry 92–3, 276, 291
ANTHROPOID 280–3, 285, 396, 397
anti-invasion preparations 44, 194–8

arms dumps 178, 195, 214
Auxiliary Units 178, 180, 183–5, 187, 195–210, 212–13, 214–17
   'Black List' 177
   Home Defence Service (HDS) 178
   observers 196, 214–15
   Operational Bases 207–8, 216
   signal control stations 212–13
   Special Duties Section (SDS) 178, 196–7, 212, 213, 214
Anton, Jane 83
Apostles group 241
appeasement policy 259–61
Ardennes offensive 363, 364
Arisaig House, Lochaber 220–53, 397
   history of 220
   interior plan 231–2
   SOE training facility 220–1, 229, 231–48, 251–3, 280
Armia Krajowa see Poland, resistance fighters
Army
   Melford Hall training centre 366–7, 369–74, 380
   requisitioning 358, 359–60
   vandalism 360–1
Arnhem, Battle of 172
Ashridge Park, Hertfordshire 277
Asquith, Katharine 391
Astley, F.D.P. 220
Astley, Joan Bright 191, 222, 397
Astley-Nicholson, Charlotte 229, 232
Aston Abbotts Abbey, Buckinghamshire 255, 273–6, 394, 396
   Czech president-in-exile 273–6, 285
   interior plan 274
Atkin, Malcolm 177, 195

Atom Smasher 134
Attlee, Clement 124, 222
Audley End, Essex 247, 326–55, 393–4
  evacuees 327
  FANY personnel 337–8
  house plan 338–9
  Station 43 326–55, 393–4
  transfer to English Heritage 354–5,
    393
  valuable artefacts, protection of 328
Auxiliary Territorial Service (ATS)
    165, 210–12, 213, 332
Auxiliary Units 178, 180, 183–5, 187,
    195–210, 212–13, 214–17
Aylesbury 43, 44, 287

Baden-Powell, Lady 91–2
Bader, Sir Douglas 172
Baissac, Lise de 250
Baker, Audrey 47–8, 50, 52, 57
Baker, Sir Herbert 142
Baker Street see Special Operations
    Executive (SOE)
Bannockburn 220
Baring, Anne Cecilia 97
Baring, Evelyn (later, Lord Howick)
    392
Bartlett, Grace 49–50
Bartlett, Pat 92
Bath Assembly Rooms 379
Battle of Britain 121, 123, 173, 256,
    271, 272–3
Bazley (gardener at Aldenham) 77, 78,
    79, 94
Bearsted, Lady Dorothea 161, 164,
    165, 180–1
Bearsted, Marcus, 1st Viscount
    160–1, 166
Bearsted, Walter, 2nd Viscount
    159–62, 166, 168–9, 171–4, 176,
    388–9
  in charge of Home Defence Service
    (HDS) 178
  MI6 activities 176–9, 180
  philanthropy 180–1
  seconded to Special Operations
    Executive 178
Beasley, Dorothy 19

Beaton, Cecil 163
Beaulieu, Hampshire 247
Beeston Castle, Cheshire 363
Beith, Richard 272
Bell, G.K.A., Bishop of Chichester 37
Bell, Private R.H. 369
Bělský, František 272, 395
Beneš, Bohuš 261, 262
Beneš, Edvard 255, 257, 258–60,
    261–2, 265, 266, 267, 272, 273–4,
    277, 278, 279, 281, 285, 394–5
Benrad, Adam 346–7, 349–50, 352–3
Benson, Captain Ian 206, 208, 209,
    210
Bentley-Hunt, Anthony 183, 184, 197
Berkeley Castle, Gloucestershire 126
Berry, Colin 35
Bertram, Major Anthony 289, 290,
    291–3, 296, 300, 318, 396
Bertram, Barbara 287, 289–91, 293,
    295, 296–7, 300–7, 311–16,
    317–21, 396
Bertram, Jerome 396
Bertram, Nicky 291, 297, 396
Bertram, Tim 291, 297
Bessborough, Lord and Lady 46
Bevin, Ernest 124
Beyts, Major Geoffrey 205–6, 207,
    223
Beyts, Ruby 205
Bickerton, Florence 151
Bidwell, Dafne 83
Bignor Manor, Sussex 396
  evacuees 291, 293
  safe house 287–8, 289–90, 293–7,
    300–7, 311–15, 318–21
Bilderberg Group 400
Bilewicz, Private Kazimierz 343
Bingham, Phyllis 334, 336
Bismarck, Otto von 255
Blaber, Steve 298, 311
Black, Henry 44, 388
black propaganda 177
blackout 112
Blenheim Palace 105–22, 382–3
  British Council occupancy 121
  Canadian Armoured Division
    119–20

history of 109
MI5 occupancy 121
restoration 382–3
school occupancy 105–21
valuable artefacts, protection of 10
Bletchley Park 10, 174, 193
Blitz 18, 121, 162–3, 173, 239, 256
Blitzkrieg 117, 194
Bloch, Denise 250
Bloomfield, Julie 32
Bluglass, Harry 172
Blunt, Anthony 241
Bodenheimer, Hans and Georg 387
Bohemia 256, 257, 258, 279
Boissier, A.P. 126–7, 128–9
Bolitho, Michael 246
Booker, Bill 298, 311
Botting, Douglas 239, 241, 252
Bottomley, Air Vice-Marshal N.H.
    124
Bourne, Cardinal 70, 72
Bowdon House, Berkshire 277
boy scouts 196, 215
Bramshill Park, Hampshire 17
Brassey, Maria 61
Braybrooke, Lady Dorothy 327–9
Braybrooke, Henry Neville, 7th
    Baron 327
Braybrooke, Henry Seymour Neville,
    9th Baron 329, 354
Braybrooke, Richard, 8th Baron 329
Braybrooke, Robin, 10th Baron
    343–4, 354
Brickendonbury House,
    Hertfordshire 235
Bride, Christine 52, 53–4
Bridgnorth 65, 80, 86, 91, 96–7
Briggens (Station XIV) 330, 337, 343,
    352
Brisland, Marjorie 25
British Council 121
British Expeditionary Force 6–7, 117,
    185–6
British Resistance Archive 380
British Secret Service 174
    destruction of records relating to
        179–80
    see also MI5; MI6

Brocket, Arthur Ronald, 2nd Baron
    17, 232–3
Brocket, Charles, 3rd Baron 389
Brocket Hall, Hertfordshire 13–35,
    389
    bomb damage 23
    Brocket Babies 18, 34–5, 389
    Brownies (unmarried mothers)
        26–33
    history of 16–17, 19–22
    interior plan 20–1
    maternity home 13–15, 18–19, 21,
        22–35, 389
    Ribbentrop Bedroom 17, 22, 35
Broderick, Father 80
Brodsworth Hall, Yorkshire 359
Brooke, Lieutenant General Sir Alan
    223
Brown, Lancelot ('Capability') 29,
    119, 355
Brown, Peter 126
Brown, Stephen 118, 120, 126, 130–1
Bruce Lockhart, Robert 266–7, 275
Buckmaster, Maurice 230, 250
Bunbury 269, 270
Burgess, Guy 17, 241
Burrow, Walter 104
Butler, R.A. 'Rab' 124–5, 131–2
Butzbach, Bertha 43

Cain, Frances 172
Cain, Major Robert 172
Călinescu, Armand 193
Callaly Castle, Northumberland 149
Cameron, Sir Donald 1, 229
Cameron-Head, Frances 1–2, 226, 252
Camp X, Canada 331
Camusdarach 233
Canadian Armoured Division 119–20
1 Carlton Gardens, London 162
Caroline (goat) 311–12, 319
Carr, Norman 62
Cartland, Dame Barbara 376
Carton de Wiart, General 193
Cedar Boys 43–4, 63, 386–8
The Cedars, Buckinghamshire 42, 43,
    386–7
chaff 134

Chamberlain, Neville 17, 47, 260
Chang (dog) 154–5
Channon, Sir Henry 'Chips' 45
Chapman, Andy 34
Cheltenham College 103
Chesterton, G.K. 71
child evacuees
   German Jews 43–4
   homesickness 57
   new experiences 56–7
   parental visits 55–6
   see also school evacuees
children's homes 46
   see also Waddesdon Manor
Chippendale, Thomas 19
Cholmondeley Castle, Cheshire 270,
   395
   Czech emigres 270, 272
   Royal Navy hospital 270
Christie, Agatha 71
Christmas celebrations 25, 57–9, 63,
   155
Church of England Children's Home,
   Muswell Hill 31, 32
Church of St Mary Magdalene,
   Woodstock 114
Churchill, Clementine 55
Churchill, Winston 7–8, 55, 118, 122,
   123, 131, 163, 173, 185, 193, 221,
   260–1, 272, 277, 288, 325, 333,
   353, 398
Churchill's Toyshop see Ministry of
   Defence weapons research and
   development (MD1)
Cichociemni 343
Cipriani, Giovanni Battista 20
City of London Maternity Hospital
   14, 18, 35
City of London School 103, 126
Clare, Sister 76–7
Claridges 8, 163
Clarke, Kenneth 173, 174
Clarkson, Jeremy 172
class system 124
Cobham, Lord 384
code-breaking 176, 186, 192, 325
Colchester 366
Cold War 180

Coldstream Guards 127, 128, 144
Cole, Harold 244
Cole Pottery 202
Coleshill House, Wiltshire
   Auxiliary Units base 183–4, 185,
      200–1, 202–10, 215, 217, 380
   evacuees 202
   fire 379–80
   history of 200
   interior plan 200–1
   post-war 378–9
   sale of 379
Columbia Market Nursery 59
Colville, John 46, 323, 324
Commandos 7, 187, 190, 194, 229,
   233, 235, 236, 314
Committee of Imperial Defence 5
Communism 17, 222, 241, 268, 271
Compensation (Defence) Act, 1939
   252
Confrière de Notre Dame 314
conscription 6
convalescent homes 37, 138, 140
   see also Howick Hall
convent schools 65–6, 74–99
convoys 169, 171
Cook, Ernest 217, 379, 380
Cook, Les 33–4
Cook, Margaret 137, 143–4, 146–7,
   148, 149, 150, 151, 152, 153, 154,
   155, 156, 157
Cottiss, Corporal 339, 343
country houses
   post-war losses of 378, 382
   requisitioning see requisitioning
Crace, Jim 35
Crawford, Lord 382, 386
Crelling, Caroline 57–8
Croft, Captain Andrew 198–9
Crosfield, Helen 53, 54
Croydon Aerodrome 170, 262
Croydon Education Committee 47, 52
Croydon Nursery 48
Croydon Queen's Road Nursery 48
Croydon Toddlers' Home 48
Čurda, Karel 283
Curran, Joan 134
Czech Jews 284

Czech Republic 396
Czechoslovak Independent Brigade 270, 272–3
Czechoslovak National Council 265
Czechoslovak Pioneer Companies 271
Czechoslovak Red Cross 275
Czechoslovakia 255–65
  German annexation of the Sudetenland 189, 261
  German occupation of 264, 265, 267, 277–8
  government-in-exile 8, 265–6, 272, 273–8, 285, 396
  independent republic 256–7
  intelligence service 256, 262–6, 267, 278–9
  resistance fighters 267–72, 278, 279–85
  returning servicemen, treatment of 395
  Soviet rule 394–5
  Spanieláci 268, 271
  UK-based servicemen 255–6
  Velvet Revolution 395

D-Day 150, 156, 170, 171, 363, 365, 367
Daladier, Edouard 265
Dalton, Hugh 221–2, 223–4, 232–3, 267, 354
Davies, Martin 173
Davis, Private George 364
Dawnay, Anne 144, 147, 152, 154–5
Dawnay, Lieutenant Colonel Ronald 144
de Wesselow, Roger 230
dead-letter drops 196–7
death duties 378, 379, 381
Decker, Otto 387
declaration of war 47, 107, 193
Defence (General) Regulations 1939 1
Delaye, Pierre 318–320
Denmark, invasion of 117
Department of Education 104, 127
Desborough, Lord and Lady 7–8
Destailleur, Gabriel-Hippolyte 39
Detection Club 71

Devereux, Geoffrey 217
Devonshire, Georgiana, Duchess of 142
Dill, General Sir John 223
Ditlef-Nielsen, Christian 367
divorce 33–4
Dockar-Drysdale, Barbara 11
Dodds-Parker, Douglas 192, 335
Dominic, Sister 75–6, 77, 81, 82, 84, 92, 94, 97
Dorchester Hotel 162–3
Dowling, Alannah 79, 81, 88, 91, 95
Dowling, Jane 91, 93
Duff (dog) 289, 311
Duff, Sir Patrick 102, 104, 105
Duncannon, Eric 46
Dunkirk evacuation 7, 92, 185, 194
Dutch Resistance 8
Dutton, Ralph (later, Lord Sherborne) 6

Earl Grey tea 142
economy, post-war 376–7
Eden, Anthony 267, 285
Edward VIII 17
Eisenhower, General 163
Elkington, Dr 116
Elliot, Walter 37
Elliott, Major 104, 105, 106, 107, 109, 127
Emergency Powers (Defence) Act 1939 1
English Heritage 354–5, 393
Enigma code 176, 192, 193
episcopes 146
Esher, Lord 386
Essex Board 110, 112, 328
Essex, Mary, Countess of 273, 276
evacuation
  waves of 3
  see also child evacuees; school evacuees
Evelina Hospital for Sick Children 38
Exton Hall, Rutland 99

F-S (Fairbairn–Sykes) fighting knife 235, 236, 344
Fairbairn, William (Dan) 233–5, 236–7, 280

Farley, Flight Lieutenant 300
Fawley Court, Buckinghamshire 336
Fensome, Sergeant Alfred 330, 331, 343
Fenwick, Hettie 83, 392
Fiocca, Henri 249, 250
fires, house 10, 140–1, 362, 372–4, 378, 379–80
First Aid Nursing Yeomanry (FANY) 327, 331–7, 398
  communications work 335–6
  Free-FANYs 332, 334, 335
  SOE affiliation 332–5, 336–7
First World War 5, 41, 70, 119, 138, 160, 161, 187, 189, 291, 332
Fishguard, battle of (War of the First Coalition) 185
Fleming, Ian 176
Fleming, Peter 207, 216, 217
Flersheim-Sichel Institute 42
food 51, 60, 95, 165, 271, 301, 312–13
  celebrations 58, 172
  rationing 94–5, 313
Foot, M.R.D. 174, 187, 195, 231, 251, 336
Ford Castle, Northumberland 149
foreign and Commonwealth services personnel 3, 120–1, 186, 255–6, 270–1, 272–3, 333, 358
  see also American GIs
foreign governments-in-exile 8, 288
  Czech 8, 265–6, 272, 273–8, 285, 396
  Dutch 8, 277
  Norwegian 8, 277
  Polish 8, 277, 325, 394
Foreign Legion 267–8
Foreign Weapons School 245
Forster, E.M. 397
Fourcade, Marie-Madeleine 319–20
Fowey 363
Fox Hill Home 48
Frampton, Alan 50
France
  fall of 3, 91, 268, 288
  French Resistance 216, 248–50, 249, 251, 288, 289, 292, 293
Franklyn, General Sir Harold 215–16

František, Sergeant Josef 273
Fraser, Simon, 15th Lord Lovat 225, 228–9
Free French 122, 277, 288–9, 292, 384
Freilich, Irwin 387
Fuller, Major General John 17

Gabčík, Jozef 280–4, 285, 396
Gaitskell, Hugh 400
Gamwell, Marian and Hope 332, 334
Gano, Stanislav 192
Garramor House 245, 340, 349
Garrow, Captain Ian 249
Gaulle, Charles de 8, 277, 288, 289
Gaunt, Revd Canon H.C.A. 101, 104, 105, 106–8, 109–10, 113, 114, 117, 118, 120, 122, 125–7, 128–30, 132, 133, 135, 383
George IV, King 20, 21
George VI, King 374
German invasion threat see anti-invasion preparations
German Jews 41–5, 169, 181
  Kindertransports 181
German–Soviet Non-Aggression Pact 1, 192, 222, 271
Gibson, Major Harold 262–3, 264, 266
Giles, Sir Harold 368
Glanusk, Lord 210
Glasnacardoch Lodge 233, 241, 245
Glenshian House 226
Glover, Doreen 24–5
Godby, June 25, 26
Godby, Stella 25
Gortatowsky, Peter 388
Government Code and Cipher School 174, 176
government departments, relocation 102–3, 104
Grand, Major Lawrence 175, 177, 178, 187, 190, 195
Granlund, Lorna 152, 153
Great Depression 181
Great Malvern 102, 103, 119, 125
Great Reform Bill, 1832 142
Greek government-in-exile 8

Green, Mrs (Waddesdon Manor housekeeper) 45, 50–1, 58
Grendon Underwood 336
Grenfell, Billy 68, 70
Grenfell, Julian 68, 70
Grey family 142–3
Grey, Charles, 5th Earl 140–1, 145–6, 155, 392
Grey, Corporal Eric 203, 206
Grey, Lady Elizabeth 144
Grey, Lady Mabel 140, 141, 143–4, 148–9, 150, 153, 156, 392
Grey, Lady Sybil (later, Lady Middleton) 137–8, 140, 141, 155, 156
Griffiths, Violet 61
Gruenebaum, Guenter 44
Gubbins, Colonel Colin McVean 398–401
  character and qualities 188–9, 191, 224
  death of 400
  decorations 398–9
  First World War service 189
  forms Auxiliary Units 195, 199, 204–5, 209
  post-war life 398–400
  recruited to MI(R) 190–3
  with the SOE 210, 222, 223–4, 231, 232, 266, 279–80, 325, 334, 335–6, 397, 398
  writes pamphlets on guerrilla warfare 190–1, 224
Gubbins, Michael 398
guerrilla warfare 186–7, 189, 190–1
  distaste for 191, 236–7
  see also specific combat groups
Gurney, Ivor 62

H2S radar system 134
Haakon VII, King 277
Haigh Hall 382
Hale, Miss 147
Halifax, Lord 17, 265
Hall, Major R.F. 227
Hankey, Flight Lt Stephen 317–18
Hannant, Joan 137, 144, 150
Hannington Hall, Wiltshire 211, 212

Harrow School
  Malvern College evacuated to 126–32
  Officer Training Corps 131
Harston, Major Bill 207
Hartwell 379
Havel, Václav 396
Haw-Haw, Lord 102
Hawker, Janice 24
Hazlerigg, Diana 165
Heelis, William 368–9
Heligan House, Cornwall 363
Henderson, Oonagh 205
Henlein, Konrad 259
Hern, Norah 14, 31
Hesketh-Prichard, Captain Alfgar 240
Heuman, Gert 387
Heydrich, Reinhard 247, 278, 279, 280, 281–3, 284
Hill, Mabel 51–2, 53
Hill Top, Cumbria 368–9
Hinton Ampner, Hampshire 6
Hiroshima 376
Hitler, Adolf 17, 134, 198, 211, 222, 258–60, 282
Hodgart, Matthew 245, 246
Hodgson, Vere 8
Holdsworth, Gerald 177
Holford, Robert Stayner 143
Holland, Lieutenant-Colonel J.F.C. 187–8, 189–90, 193, 194, 195
Home Defence Service (HDS) 178
Home Guard 197, 214, 215, 227, 342, 345, 367–8
Hook, Glenys 56–7
Hope-Falkner, Robert 165
Horner, Edward 68, 391
hospitals
  civilian–military shared use 138, 139
  maternity 13–15, 18–19, 21, 22–35
  suspension of patient admission 18
  see also military hospitals
Howarth, Stephen 167–8
Howe, Corporal Peter 330, 331, 342
Howick, Charles, 2nd Baron 392–3
Howick Hall Convalescent Home 140

Howick Hall, Northumberland
137–57, 392–3
fire 140–1
interior plan 146–7
military hospital 137–57
Hunt, Squadron Leader John 298,
311
Hussey, Christopher 109, 114
Hyde Parker, Beth 367, 368, 370
Hyde Parker, Sir Richard 367, 368,
370–1, 382
Hyde Parker, Lady Ulla 367, 368, 369,
371, 373, 380, 381
Hyde Parker, Sir William 367–8, 369,
371, 372, 374, 380, 381

Ilfracombe 271
illegitimate children 26, 28–33
adoption 29–30, 31
tracing relations 32, 33
incendiary bombs 130
Independent Companies 194, 229
see also Commandos
Ingram, Douglas 196
International Brigades 268
International Committee of the
Movement for European Unity
399–400
internment 44, 271–2
Interservices Research Bureau see
Special Operations Executive
Inverailort Castle, Highlands 1,
226–8, 229, 252, 357
Ipswich 366
IRA 187
Iranek-Osmecki, George 347–8
Ironside, General 189
irregular warfare see guerrilla
warfare
Isle of Man 44
Iver 277

Jacobitism 220
Jebb, Gladwyn 222
Jefferies, Ted 215
Jefferis, Lieutenant-Colonel Millis
190, 206, 224
Joint War Organisation (JWO) 153

Jones, Inigo 200

Kaplan, Franz 268–70, 271, 395
Katýn massacre 326
Kay, Corporal 359–60
Kemp, Arthur 371
Kemp, Peter 221, 228–9, 239, 244
Kennedy, Constance 32–3
Kennedy, Major-General John 223
Kennkarte documents 351–2
Kentwell Hall, Suffolk 366
Kérillis, Henri de 258
Keynes, J. Maynard 376–7
Khan, Noor Inayat 250, 316–17
Kilmington Manor, Wiltshire 379
Kindertransports 181
Kindred, Herman 198
Kingsclere 364
Kingsdown House, Kent 361–2
Kirkpatrick, Roger 329
Kitchen, Sibyl May 368
Knox, Monsignor Ronald 9, 65,
68–74, 390, 391
at Aldenham Park 74, 75, 78–9,
84–6, 87–90, 93, 96, 97–8
Bible translation 73–4, 78, 86, 97–8,
392
Catholic convert 69, 70
crime author 71, 74
death of 392
friendship with Lady Acton 68,
73–4, 86, 93
The Mass in Slow Motion 89
radio hoax 71–2
sermons 88–90, 94
wit and intellect 68, 69, 84–5
Knoydart 245
Kolossal raid 18
Kristallnacht 42
Kubiš, Jan 280–4, 285, 396

Labour government 377, 378
Lainé, Elie 39
Lamb, Lady Elizabeth 20
Lamb, Sir Matthew 19
Lamb, Sir Peniston (later, Lord
Melbourne) 20
Lambourn 61

Langelaan, George 237–8, 247–8
Large Hadron Collider 134
Largo House, Fife 340
Lavenham 370
Lawlor, Monica 92
Lawrence, Guy 70–1
Lawrence, T.E. 187
Layton, Lieutenant Colonel Julian 42, 43, 388
Lea & Perrins of Worcester 104
Leach, Bernard 201
Leach, Pamela (later, Lady Niven) 336–7
Leamington Spa 271, 272, 276
Lees-Milne, James 354, 367, 375, 382, 386, 388–9
Lefort, Cecily 316
Leigh, Mike 35
Lemme, Captain J. 342
Lemsford House, Hertfordshire 31
Lend-Lease 376
Lestanges (French agent) 315–16
Levick, Murray 228
Ležáky 284
Lidice 284, 285
lime trees 255, 285, 396
Lindsay, Norman 370
Lipinski, Major Jan 342, 345
Lloyd Jones, Kitty 164
Local Defence Volunteers 117–18
Loch Morar 225, 233
Lochailort 226–8, 246
Lockhart, Squadron Leader Guy 307, 319
Locock, Malcolm 131
London County Council 46
Long Melford 366, 369, 374
Longford Castle, Wiltshire 201
Longmate, Norman 13, 103, 375
Lovat Scouts 220, 225
Lowe, Alan Brocket 16
Lowe, Leslie 14, 15
Lowe, Lily 13, 15, 16
Lowther Castle, Cumbria 361
Lulworth Ranges 360
Lysander aircraft 298–300, 307–9, 310, 318
Lyttleton, Oliver 124

M. Samuel & Co. 159, 163, 166, 181, 182
    at Upton House 163, 164–7, 172–3
    government projects 167
Macaskie, Claudia 85, 86, 95–6, 391
Macaskie, Nicola 83, 85–6, 89, 95, 96, 391
McCairns, James Atterby 298, 300, 307, 309–10
McCarthy, Albert 165–6, 182
MacDougall, Dr James 242
Mackenzie, Compton 259–60, 274–5, 277
Mackenzie, William 219
Maćkowiak, Captain Alfons (Alan Mack) 341, 342, 343, 349, 355
MacRae, Uilleamena 246
Maginot line 117
Majestic Hotel, Harrogate 2–3
Major, Colonel C.R. 210, 214, 223
Malvern College 101–35, 383–4
    at Blenheim Palace 105–21
    at Harrow School 126–32
    Free French members 122, 384
    history of 103–4
    requisitioning of 101–2, 104, 107–8, 127
    return to Malvern 122, 134, 135
    Telecommunciations Research Establishment at 123, 125, 127, 133–4, 314
Malvern College Harvest Camp 120
Malvern Hills 103
Manod Quarry 173–4
Marks, Sir Simon 181
Marlborough, Alexandra, Duchess of 108
Marlborough, John, Duke of 105, 106, 108–9, 112, 115–16, 121
Marlborough College 103, 124, 126
Mary, Princess Royal and Countess of Harewood 60, 155–6
Masaryk, Jan 272, 273, 276, 285, 395
Masaryk, Tomáš 257, 273
Mason, D.W. 171
maternity homes 13–15, 18–19, 21, 22–35
Matouš, Leopold 276

Maxwell, Gavin 9, 238–45, 246, 252
Mayday Nursery 48, 52
Meakin, Arthur 145, 157
Meakin, Billy 141, 145–6, 152, 156–7
Meakin, Charlie 145
Mechanised Transport Corps 295–6
Melbourne, William, 2nd Viscount
   21–2
Melford Hall, Suffolk 357, 366–74,
   380–2
  army training centre 366–7,
    369–74, 380
  fire 372–4
  history of 367
  restoration 374, 380–1
  transfer to the National Trust 381
Mells, Somerset 391
Menzies, Stewart 176, 179
Meoble Lodge 233
Meynell, Faine 88, 91
MI5 121, 174
MI6 174, 266, 279, 292
military hospitals
  convalescent hospitals 137–57
  estimate of beds required 139
  First World War 37, 116, 138, 140,
   160, 166
  foreign patients 149
  royal visitors 155–6
Military Intelligence (Intelligence)
  see MI6
Military Intelligence (Research) see
  MI(R)
Military Intelligence (Security) see
  MI5
Military Operations (Special Projects)
  see Special Operations Executive
Military Training Directorate 189
Millard, Bob 183–5, 197, 203–4
Milleret, Anne Eugenie 74
Minchin, Peggy 334
Minimax Fire Extinguisher Company
  180
Ministry of Aircraft Production
  (MAP) 127
Ministry of Aircraft Production
  Research Establishment 125
Ministry of Defence 360

weapons research and development
  (MD1) 190, 206
Ministry of Education 132–3
Ministry of Food 287
Ministry of Health 45–6, 47, 128, 138
Ministry of Information 23
Ministry of Supply 45, 167, 170
Ministry of Works (Office of Works
  until 1943) 101, 354, 382, 384
MI(R) 187–8, 190–3, 221, 222
missing in action (MIA) 150
Molotov, Vyacheslav 192
Molotov cocktails 118
Montacute House, Somerset 379, 382
Montessori schools 74
Morar Lodge 252
Moravec, Ata 283
Moravec, Lieutenant-Colonel Fratišek
  257, 262, 263–5, 266, 278, 279,
  280, 281, 394–5
Morrell, Jeffrey 359–60
Morrison, Herbert 124, 132
Morton, Colonel Harold 273, 274
Morville 83
The Mote, Kent 160, 166
Mulberry Bush School 11
Munich Agreement 256, 260, 285
Murray, Ingram 222, 224

Nagasaki 376
Nall-Cain, Sir Charles (later, Lord
  Brocket) 16–17
Nation, Captain William 365–6
National Gallery 173
National Gallery of Ottawa 49
National Library of Wales 173
National Organisation for
  Counselling Adoptees and
  Parents (NORCAP) 33
National Trust 379, 380, 381, 382,
  385–6, 389
Nazism 17, 42
  brutality 216, 249, 261, 278, 284–5
Nearne, Jacqueline and Eileen 250
Neate, Mo 32–3
Neurath, Konstantin von 277
New Zealand aircrews 62
Nicholl, Bob 141

Nickel operations 62
Northcote, Catherine (Sister John-
    Mary) 78, 79, 81, 83
Northumberland, Helen, Duchess of
    156
Norway
    Commando raids 190, 193–4, 229,
        251
    government-in-exile 8, 277
    invasion of 117, 199
Nosek, Major Antoni 349, 350–2, 355
nursery school *see* Waddesdon Manor

Oboe bombing targeting system 134
Office of Strategic Services (OSS)
    [USA] 178, 250
Officer Training Corps 12, 117, 118,
    131
Office of Works (Ministry of Works
    from 1943) 5, 102, 103, 105, 109,
    110, 112, 115, 122, 124, 126, 146,
    328
oil supplies 168–9
Old Manor House, Wingrave 276
Old Palace, Oxford 72
Old Rectory, Heydon 328–9
Olson, Lynne 8, 325
Operation Anthropoid 280–5, 396, 397
Operation Biting 123
Operation Caroline 312
Operation Gunnerside 251
Operation Market Garden 365
Operation Sea Lion 198
    see also anti-invasion preparations
Operational Bases 207–9, 216
Operational Training Units (OTUs)
    62
orphanages 46, 48
    see also Waddesdon Manor
Oswestry 271
Our Lady of the Assumption Convent
    School 66, 74–99
Oxford University 69–70, 240
Oxtalls Farm, Evesham 120

Paget, Lady Muriel 140
Paine, James 19
Pallinsburn, Northumberland 149

Panshanger, Hertfordshire 7
paradox of war 5
Paris Peace Conference 41
Patton, General 7, 362
Pelham Burn, Hamish 242, 243
Penecillin 116
Penrhyn Castle 173
Peover Hall, Cheshire 7, 362
Percy, Lady Mary 239
Perry, Barbara 25
Petherick, Major 212
petrol rationing 61, 148, 168
Petroleum Board ('Pool') 168, 169
pets, destruction of 15–16
Philby, Kim 17
Phoney War 117, 291, 327
Pickles, Revd 114
pig-husbandry 93, 276
Pleydell-Bouverie, Katharine 201–2,
    203, 217, 378, 379
Pleydell-Bouverie, Mary 201, 203,
    378, 379
Poland
    government-in-exile 8, 277, 325,
        394
    intelligence service 192, 325
    invasion of 192, 324
    Katýn massacre 326
    partitioning of 323
    resistance fighters 223, 324, 330–54
    returning servicemen, treatment of
        393–4
    Soviet occupation 324, 393
    UK-based servicemen 255–6
    war casualties 323, 393
    Warsaw Uprising 324, 353
Polar Medal 199, 228
Polish Jews 352
Polish Parachute Brigade 340
Political Warfare Executive (PWE)
    267
Ponsonby, Moyra 46
Popham, Hugh 332, 334–5
Portsmouth Day School for Girls 6
post-war Britain 376–8
Potiphar (bulldog) 75–6, 77, 84
Potter, Beatrix 368–9, 382
Pratt, Sir George 200

Pratt, Sir Roger 200
prefabricated housing 377–8
Prince of Wales Hotel, Harrogate 3
Prudential Insurance Company 181
psychopathic personality 242

Quinn, Helen 121

radar 123, 133, 134, 186
Railton, Matron 145, 152, 153
rationing
    food 94–5, 313
    petrol 61, 148, 168
    post-war 377
    sweets 55, 95
Reading, Lady 60
Red Army 394
Red Cross 18, 19, 138, 139, 140, 143,
    144, 148, 149, 150, 154, 156, 202,
    290
Red Cross nurses 144
Rees, Neil 276, 396
Reid, Matron 145, 148
Reith, John 72
Renault-Roulier, Gilbert (Colonel
    Rémy) 313–14, 321
requisitioning
    bids by services and departments
        357–8
    damage and compensation 6, 62,
        252, 357, 357–8, 383–5
    legislation governing 1
    pre-war survey and assessment 5
    resistance to 7–8
    small properties 287
    villages 360
    voluntary offers of homes 5
resistance networks 177, 223, 251
    agents' kits 304–7
    conducting officers 292, 295, 303,
        314
    couriers 244, 249, 288, 292, 293,
        295–6, 316, 348
    delivery of agents into occupied
        Europe 295–6, 297–300,
        307–11, 317–18, 320, 348–9,
        350–1, 352
    female agents 248–50, 316–17,

        319–20, 332–3
    Nazi infiltration 279, 294
    new identities 345–6, 349–50
    safe houses 287–8, 289–90, 293–7,
        300–7, 311–15, 318–21, 351
    skills and training 341–4
    see also under Czechoslovakia;
        France; Poland
Retinger, Josef 399
Reynolds, Sir Joshua 114
Rhubana Lodge 233
Ribbentrop, Joachim von 10, 17, 192
Richardson, Sir Albert 380–1
Ringway 247, 340
Ritchie, Charles 163
Robinson, John Martin 357, 360, 378,
    382, 383
Rønneberg, Lieutenant Joachim 251
Roper-Caldbeck, Lieutenant Colonel
    Arthur 331, 344
Rose, Charlie 235, 236
Rospigliosi, Princess 390
Rothschild, Alice de 40, 43
Rothschild, Anthony 181, 273
Rothschild, Dorothy de 37, 38, 40–1,
    43–4, 45, 47, 48, 50–2, 52, 53,
    55–6, 57, 58, 60–1, 61, 63–4, 385,
    386–7, 388
Rothschild, Ferdinand de 38–40
Rothschild, James de 37, 40–2, 44–5,
    48, 49, 52, 59, 63, 384, 385, 386
Rowden, Diana 316
Rowe, A.P. 132–5
Roy, James 110–11, 114, 115, 116, 117,
    118, 119, 120
Royal Air Force (RAF)
    138 (Special Duties) Squadron 349
    161 Squadron 298–300, 307–11
    310 and 312 (Czechoslovak)
        Squadrons 272–3
    delivery of agents into occupied
        Europe 297–300, 307–11,
        317–18, 320, 348–9, 350–1, 352
    requisitioning 357–8
Royal Air Force Service Police 298
Royal Army Service Corps 61, 203,
    330
Royal Dutch Shell 160, 161

Royal Engineers 208
Royal Observer Corps 209
Royal Signals 213
Rubens Hotel, London 325
Ryder, Sue (later Baroness Warsaw)
    337–8

sabotage 197, 229, 246, 248, 279, 346,
    354
safe houses 287–90, 351
Saffron Walden 331, 342, 344
St John auxiliary nurses 144
St John's Wood 287
St Paul's Church, Knightsbridge 334
Samuel, Gerald 161
Samuel, Marcus see Bearsted, 1st
    Viscount
Samuel, Peter 159, 160, 163, 164, 182
Samuel, Sir Herbert 181
Samuel, Tony 160, 182
Samuel, Walter see Bearsted, 2nd
    Viscount
Sandys, Duncan 400
Saxe-Coburg and Gotha, Duke of 17
Scandinavian resistance networks 177
Schneidau, Philip 300
school evacuees 6, 46
    convent schools 65–6, 74–99
    curriculum 83–4, 90–1
    games and sports facilities 79–80,
        91, 112
    illnesses 95–6, 116
    opposition to school evacuation
        124–5
    parental visits 83
    shared facilities 103, 126–32
    see also Malvern College
Schweiger, Barbara 59–60
SCISSORFORCE 194
Scott, Captain Robert Falcon 228
Secret Intelligence Service (SIS)
    174–5, 224, 262, 266–7, 397
    Section D 175, 177, 178, 179–80,
        188, 195, 222
    see also MI6
Seebohm, Caroline 361
Selborne, Lord 280, 398, 399
Selm, Major 263

Shell Aircraft 172
Shell Film Unit 169–70
Shell Transport and Trading
    Company 160, 167–72, 176, 180
Shell-Mex House, Bishopsgate 168
shooting parties 80–1
Shrewsbury School 70, 103
Shropshire Yeomanry 67
signal control stations 212–13
Signals Training Establishment 125
Sikorski, General Władysław 277,
    325–6, 333
Sinclair, Admiral 'Quex' 174, 175
Singapore, fall of 26, 215
Skepper, Charles 316
Skinner, Kate 51
Smiley, Jane 11
Smith, George 164, 165
Smith, William 66
Smutný, Dr Jaromír 276
SOE see Special Operations Executive
Soviet Union
    German invasion of 222, 272
    and Katyń massacre 326
    occupation of Poland 324, 393
Španiel, General Oldřich 276
Spanieláci 268, 271
Spanish Civil War 268
Speaight, Robert 83–4
Special Air Service (SAS) 228, 397
Special Duties Section (SDS) 178,
    196–7, 212, 213, 214
Special Forces Club 399
Special Operations Executive (SOE)
    7, 11–12, 178, 187, 188, 191, 199,
    210, 219–53, 278, 279–80
    agent characteristics 229–30, 231
    Baker Street headquarters 224–5
    conducting officers 292
    cover titles 225
    FANY-affiliated members 332–5,
        336–7
    female operatives 248–50, 332–3,
        348
    foreign recruits 229, 233, 256, 272
    forgery section 238, 247, 330,
        346
    formation 188, 222

Special Operations Executive
(SOE) – *continued*
French Section 230, 250
Polish Section 326, 330–53
post-war 397–8
survival techniques 238, 241–2
training 220–1, 224, 227–9, 230–48,
326, 341–4, 396–7
weaponry and devices 193, 235, 236,
241, 281
wound up 188
Spencer-Chapman, Lieutenant
Colonel Freddie 228, 233
Spencer-Churchill, Lady Sarah 107
Stalin, Joseph 323, 326
Stansted Park, Devon 46
stay-behind fighters *see* Auxiliary
Units; Special Duties Section
Steinhardt, Hugo and Lily 42, 43, 387
Stepney Jewish Lads Club 161
stillborn babies 34
Stirling, Colonel Sir David 228
Stobiecka, Ulrich 387–8
Stock, Miss E.F. 23
Stranks, Mabel 203
Strømsheim, Birger 251
Strutt, Ronald 390
Stuart, Charles Edward (Bonnie
Prince Charlie) 220
Sudbury 261, 370
Sudetenland 257, 258, 259, 262, 285
suicide capsules 315
Summers, Harry 2–3
Sutton Park 271
sweet rations 55, 95
Swithinbank, Audrey 336
Swordland 233, 245–6
Sykes, Eric (Bill) 233, 234–5, 236,
248
Szabo, Violette 250

The Tablet 72, 73, 82
Táborský, Edvard 276
Tangmere 298, 299, 302, 307–9, 311,
317, 320
Tattenhall 363, 364
taxation, post-war 378
Taylor, Catherine 41, 59

Telecommuncations Research
Establishment (TRE) 123, 125,
133–4, 314
Temple, Beatrice 211–12, 213–14
Temple, William, Archbishop of
Canterbury 213
Terling Place, Essex 67, 94, 96
Terra Nova Expedition 228
Territorial Army (TA) 176, 188
Thümmel, Colonel Paul (Agent A54)
263–4, 266, 278
Thurston, Sylvia 340
Tipu Sultan 316
Tissot, Mr (Waddesdon Manor chef)
51, 60
Titmuss, Richard 5, 46, 139, 358
torture 230, 243, 244, 314, 315, 316,
317, 320
total war 4, 194
Traigh House 233
Trojanek, Colonel Karel 395–6
Troubles (Ireland) 187, 189
Tyneham 360

U-boat warfare 134, 135
UKULELE 248
United States Naval Advanced
Amphibious Training Sub Base
363
University of Wales 173
unmarried mothers 26–33
Upton House, Warwickshire 10,
159–73, 181–2, 388–9
gardens 164, 166
merchant bank operation 163,
164–7, 172–3
safekeeping of valuables 173–4
transfer to the National Trust 389
see also Bearsted, Walter, 2nd
Viscount
US intelligence service 178–9

V1 flying bombs 134, 308
V2 rockets 3, 94, 371
Valentine, Ian 324, 350
Vanbrugh, Sir John 109, 119
VE Day 98–9, 375–6, 393
Velvet Revolution 395

Verity, Group Captain Hugh 299–
  300, 308, 310, 316, 317, 318, 320
Victoria, Queen 21–2, 40
VJ Day 376
Voluntary Aid Detachment (VAD)
  140, 147, 152

Waddell, Pat 333
Waddesdon Manor, Buckinghamshire
  10, 37–64, 384–6
  army petrol depot 55, 61
  damage and compensation 384–5
  estate income and running costs 63
  history of 38–9
  nursery school and orphanage
    45–64
  restoration 385
  transfer to the National Trust
    385–6
  valuable artefacts, protection of 49
  Westcott airfield 57, 62
  WVS stores 60–1
Wake, Nancy 248–50
Wallington, Northumberland 149
Wanborough Manor, Surrey 230
War Damages Act 384
war service badge (for children) 91
Warnford Park, Hampshire 361
Warren, Suzanne 244–5
Warsaw Uprising 324, 353
Warwicker, John 178, 183, 198,
  209–10, 212
Watts, Sergeant Alan 330, 331
Waugh, Evelyn 70, 73, 239, 361–2,
  390–1
Wawrzkowicz, Bronisław 346
Webb, Philip 220
Webber, Constance 89
Welborn, Corporal Joan 210
Welles, Orson 72
Wellington, Duke of 142
Westcott 57, 61, 62
Westcott Hill Wood 62
Westonbirt Arboretum 143
Whaddon Chase hunt 273
Whitburn, Iolanthe 32
Whitehouse, Beatrice 59

Wilhelmina, Queen 8, 277
Wilkinson, Ellen 133
Wilkinson, Peter 216, 266, 400
Wilkinson Sword 235–6
Wilkinson-Latham, Jack 235
Williams, Bill and Audrey 277
Williams, Rowan, Archbishop of
  Canterbury 98
Williamson, Maude 149
Willis Organ 383
Wills, Mike 240
Window radar countermeasure 134
Wingrave Manor, Buckinghamshire
  255
winter of 1939–40 95, 96–7, 116–17
Woldingham 278
Wollaton Hall, Nottinghamshire
  364–5, 366
Women's Auxiliary Air Force
  (WAAF) 329
Women's Land Army 148
Women's Royal Naval Service
  (WRNS) 152
Women's Voluntary Services (WVS)
  60, 63, 293
Wood, Susan 93
Woodruff, Douglas 73
Woodstock 120, 121
  see also Blenheim Palace
Woolf, Philip 62
Woolf, Virginia 96
Woolton Pie 60
Worbarrow 360
Wormwood Scrubs 121
Wycombe Abbey School 124
Wyld, Jack 171, 184, 197

Yalta Conference 393
YMCA 180
York 271
Young, Harold 374
Young, Colonel Jimmy 243
Young, Mary 374

Zając, Warrant Officer Gabriel 343
Zarine, Marie-Anne 92
Zawacka, Elżbieta 348